Education: Mirror and Agent of Change

Education:
Mirror and Agent
of Change
A Foundations Text

Gail M. Inlow
Northwestern University

HOLT, RINEHART AND WINSTON, INC.

New York Chicago San Francisco Atlanta
Dallas Montreal Toronto London Sydney

*Dedicated to
leaders everywhere, who,
cognizant of the dangers of power,
employ it not to fulfill themselves,
but to serve others.*

PHOTO CREDITS

Preface

Formal education mirrors the existent while readying learners for the emergent. As a mirror, it reveals a world in the throes of change: a world in which the indigent are restive, minority groups are in protest, open and closed systems are in ideational or physical conflict, and technology threatens man's humanness. Indeed, an old way is giving way to a new one in a world order surcharged and explosive.

All major institutions of the society—formal education, government, the church, and the family—are reacting to, and at times actually reeling under, the impact of impinging social forces. In education, the impact is dramatic, as evidenced explicitly in the areas of curriculum, instructional method, teachers, and students.

In curriculum, the keyword is relevance—a shibboleth in today's academic world. Actually, the goal in curriculum has always been relevance, but each new generation must first determine what it believes man should be and what he should become, and then ask education to provide curriculums that contribute to those outcomes. It is an awesome task, but definitely an essential one. As education contributes to these outcomes, it needs to assume a balanced posture between old and emerging values, between time-tested and evolving curriculum content. That education is experiencing difficulty in arriving at a proper balance both reflects, and is a precipitator of, the unrest that characterizes the American society. In the past few years, curriculum scales have tipped significantly in the direction of provincial and immediate concerns, as witnessed by the demands of student-protest groups throughout the country for increased emphasis on the here and now. If these demands become too strident, and their curriculum implementation becomes too excessive, a

countering return to more cosmic and universal concerns will likely characterize curriculum change in the future.

In instruction, as well as curriculum, the impact of change is also pronounced. The world of electronics is making increasing inroads into classrooms. In fact, television, computers, language laboratories, and teaching machines are commonplace in today's schools. Surprisingly, the world of psychology and psychiatry, as influencers of instruction, lag, if at all, but a few paces behind electronics. I refer here to the mounting influence on instructional method of guidance philosophy and practices.

Teachers themselves are similarly undergoing dramatic change—a reaction, once more, to the crescendo of social change in the American and greater world order. No longer obsequious and docile, teachers are increasingly independent and assertive. Their goal, which may soon become reality, is for a decisive voice in policy decisions that vitally affect them. The rapid growth of unionism in their ranks is symptomatic of their mounting aggressiveness.

And students, not to be outdone, are in the vanguard of change. Militant first in colleges and universities, they are becoming increasingly so in high schools throughout the country.

If student protesters are black, their struggle, in all likelihood, is for an increase in black populations in colleges and universities, an increase of their numbers in school or college faculties, more black history, and a more decisive voice in other matters of crucial personal and social concern to them —matters, often, that lie outside the direct purview of formal education. *If student protesters are members of Students for a Democratic Society,* their efforts are often nihilistic, directed against the power-wielding establishment. Significantly, student anarchists are notoriously inarticulate or mute about what should replace the institutions they seek to destroy. *If student protesters are activists but not members of the two previously-named groups,* they generally are young people disillusioned over the inability or refusal of the culture to convert humanistic ideals into practice. Most student activists are more knowledgeable about the tactics of protest than about the changes that should follow in the wake of protest.

We make no extensive coverage in this book of the student-protest movement. It needs, in my opinion, to jell for a few

more years before it can be assessed with the breadth and accuracy necessary to do it justice. Chapter 13, however, deals with it, although briefly, in the discussion of higher education.

The bright hope for the world of the future is a culture dedicated, or at least more dedicated, to those values that make man human. Standing highest in the taxonomy is man's need to believe in himself: this imposes a psychological commitment. A comparable need is for man to believe in, and respect, others: this imposes a social-ethical commitment. A third need is for man to become more knowledgeable: this imposes an intellectual commitment. A fourth need is for man to become more physically and emotionally whole: this imposes a health commitment. Collectively, these constitute the following charge to formal education: take into the nation's schools as many of the young as are capable of being educated, reach them with a thoughtfully designed and sensitively implemented program, and help them to become their potentials.

I have organized the book around the themes of a culture in ferment; formal education as both a public and private enterprise; formal education as a many-faceted, dynamic operational process; learners, both normal and exceptional, as deserving of programs tailored to their uniqueness; and teachers as pivotal in all phases of education at work. The focus throughout is on elementary, secondary, and higher education framed in a cultural setting—in a setting that looks to the past for explanation, to the present for implementation, and to the future for refinement or substantial change. The book espouses the view that American education is an individual right and a social obligation.

Its intended audience is teacher candidates enrolled in courses such as Orientation to Education, Foundations of Education, Principles of Education, American Education, Introduction to Education, Social Foundations of Education, Introduction to Teaching, and History of Education.

My sincere thanks go to the following personal and professional associates who helped the evolving manuscript become reality: R. Freeman Butts, whose suggestions and criticisms were insightful; Helen Beloungy, whose editorial assistance was invaluable; George A. Beauchamp, who matched wits with me over many educational issues; Robert Baumgartner, Wilfred Danielson, Deva Howard, and Anne Hub-

bard, Deering Library friends, who tracked down valuable reference sources for me; Joanne Smutny who was consistently encouraging; my several typists who kept pace with all production efforts; and Muriel Olson, my sister, and Ray Olson, my brother-in-law and professor at Ball State University, who were always supportive, interested, and contributive, and who sharpened my thinking in ways too numerous to mention.

I am grateful also to other close members of my family; Joanne, Ron, Rick, Bev, Meg, Deb, and Robbie.

G. M. I.

Evanston, Illinois
November 1969

Contents

Education: Mirror and Agent of Change

Part One
A Culture in Ferment

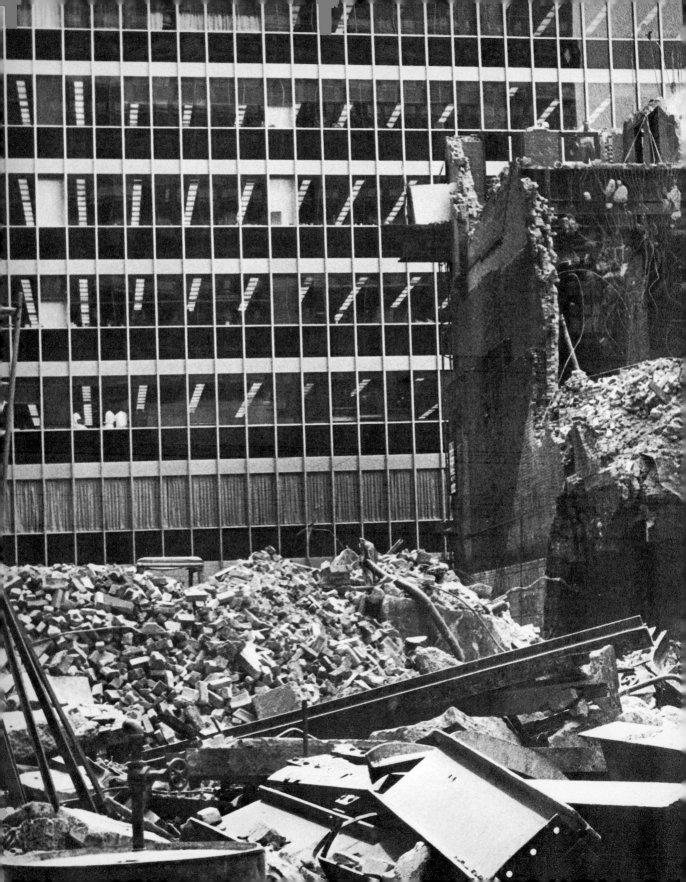

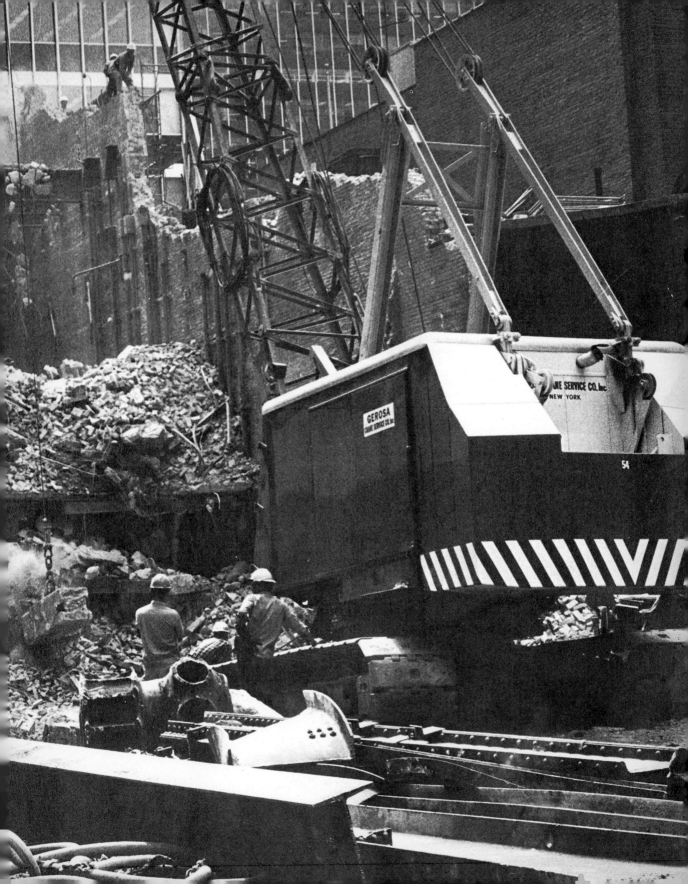

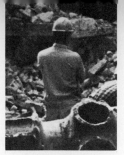

Chapter

1

Change
in the
Social Order

Life is a process of continual change. People are born and pass progressively through various stages of growth. An object may have one shape today and a different one tomorrow. Ideas undergo constant mutation, and values are refined from generation to generation. According to legend, the phenomenon of change even cast its shadow over the Garden of Eden. In the legend, Adam said to Eve: "Uncertainty is our lot; change is our destiny." Whether Adam did or did not thus philosophize to Eve is whimsically conjectural; if he did, he would have been the first of a countless number to react in one way or another to the phenomenon of change.

Many people react negatively toward change. A few, the emotionally disturbed, defend themselves against it through the psychological process of denial. Others, in the same category, who are more normal but no less negative, view it as an unhappy departure from the "good old days," and go through life trying to turn back the clock. Many in a second category are more fatalistic than negative toward change. Their position is: "Since you cannot avoid it, go along with it." A third category includes individuals who see change as not only inevitable but basically positive. Their position is: "Because it is basically good, incorporate it into your pattern of life."

This last position constitutes the philosophical frame of this book. It is a teleological position that presumes man to be intrinsically positive and the universe to be basically orderly. Not blind to such negative forces as pain, hunger, bigotry, disease, and physical holocausts, it conceives them more as issues that challenge the best in man than as forces of evil over which he has no control. The position commits man to pursue his destiny in a world that refuses to stand still.

PHENOMENA THAT ATTEST TO CHANGE

The proposition that change characterizes all life finds substantiation in the world both of the theoretical and the practical, of the inanimate and the animate, in fact, along almost every known continuum of existence. Four convincing supports of the proposition's validity are the life of any individual, biological science, physical science, and philosophy.

Patterns of Human Life

The life pattern of any individual is a study in change. A male sperm fertilizes a female egg. This act sets in motion an evolving progression that leads the growing organism from fetal existence to birth, to infancy, to childhood, to latency, to adolescence, and finally to adulthood. The direction of progression is from dependence to independence: from a lesser to a greater ability to cope with himself and his environment. The infant is incapable of sustaining life without the aid of a mother or mother surrogate. The growing child becomes increasingly independent of the mother and the family for the material and affective necessities of life. The adolescent strives for autonomy. And the adult, if normal, demands it.

Forces that give impetus to growth are both inborn and environmental. As inborn, they compel human organisms to behave in a manner characteristic of the species: for example, to seek food, warmth, psychological security, and social gratification. As environmental, they lead human organisms to adapt to and assess both themselves and their social orders. Man's genetic attributes, so viewed, atrophy or develop in response to environmental forces. The human psyche, indeed, is a dynamic product that responds both to genetic and environmental forces. Collectively, these serve notice on all human organisms that change is their destiny. The status quo thus is an abstract concept but lacks absolute identity in the real world. In the real world, change is *a* dominant, if not *the most* dominant, controlling characteristic.

Theories of Evolution

The thesis that change characterizes life received strong support from the thinking and writing of Charles Darwin (1809–1882). His *On the Origin of Species*, 1859, portrayed the human race as ever evolving. This portrayal, until recently, fanned to white heat the emotions of many, particularly those of religious fundamentalists. The fundamentalist version of creation is that man is conceived and created in God's image— already evolved, not evolving. Darwin saw man as progressively evolving from a less to a more adequate and complete state. The first version depicts man as endowed with changeless essence; the second depicts him as an ever emerging phenomenon.

8

According to the Darwinian postulate, living species of all kinds perpetuate themselves from age to age, but not without change. Rather, they undergo variation in response to the subtle process of mutation. These are the processes that enable life to adapt in an increasingly effective way to an environment. Through adaptive selection, organisms increase in vigor and dominance. Through maladaptive selection, organisms become increasingly vulnerable to extinction. In any event, Darwin conceived life in its many forms not as constant but as changing; not as the same forevermore but as evolving.

Darwin's work has had ramifications that are as much philosophical as scientific. Philosophically it implies conclusions regarding human value and the nature of being. Apropos of the human-value issue, some Darwinians have implied that the fittest will, and should, inherit the earth. This implication runs counter completely, or at least in part, to the Judeo-Christian ethic. Apropos of the issue of being, Darwin concludes that nature will determine which of any species are worthy of survival and which others are destined for extinction.

In contrast to natural selection, contemporary research and scholarship in biochemistry and sociology show that man can directly effect changes in trait selection, trait transmission, and selective survival of any species. To the extent that biochemistry is successful in predetermining and also controlling genetic traits, it will have pre-empted part of the role assigned by Darwin to the methodical processes of nature. And, comparably, to the extent that sociology, abetted by education and government, proves successful in changing intrinsically the life patterns of the socially downtrodden, it too will have pre-empted part of the role assigned by Darwin to nature.

Although admitting that Darwin undoubtedly raised more philosophical issues than he resolved scientifically, he deserves great respect for the new light he cast on the phenomenon of change. He took from the absolutists some of their complacency and propelled the borderline skeptics into more careful thought. Unquestionably, he dealt a body blow to the concept of the changelessness of man and his world.

Evidence from the Physical Sciences

The thesis that life is a process of continuous change finds still further support in the functional world of physical science. In fact, the basic

message of the physical scientist today is that the physical world is not static but perpetually evolving, that it may have one shape today and a different one tomorrow, that its elements are never independent but relational.

This open-ended view of the universe derives support from such evidence as the following: that hydrogen atoms are in a continuous process of creation and change; that matter, time, space, and energy are not fixed but always interrelated; and that even the so-called "known" is usually too tentative and approximate to warrant any finality in regard to it.

In this connection, any methodical study of the history of physical science reveals a pattern characterized as much by error as by truth. Such a study, if nothing else, testifies to the evolutionary nature of scientific knowledge and insight. For instance, Benjamin Franklin (1706–1790) two centuries ago contributed significantly to the world's knowledge about electricity. Yet, today, most of his ideas about positive and negative electric charges are either passé or in process of being rejected. Until recently, most physical scientists believed matter, in its totality, to be constant; their modern counterparts reject this view. They espouse Einstein's theory that matter and energy are interchangeable. Two millenia ago, Greek scientist-philosophers conceived atoms as incapable of division, and John Dalton (1766–1844) gave support to this conception. But a century later the concept was revealed to be fallacious and thus was rejected.

Philosophy as Witness

Philosophy, too, depicts life as a process of continuous change. Literally, philosophy is the love of wisdom. Historically, the philosopher was the wise man of his culture, the profound human oracle. He was the one viewed as having deeper insight into reality and truth than the common man. A more contemporary view is that everyone needs to be, and in fact is, a philosopher.

The nature of philosophy bears out this latter point of view. Traditionally, philosophy has included the three areas of *ontology* (the nature of being), *epistemology* (the nature of knowledge), and *axiology* (the nature of values). To the extent that these three areas challenge all men with issues of common interest and concern, all men are philosophers.

10

Philosophical questions have perplexed man through the ages. Is there a God? If there is, what is "He" like? What is man? Is he temporal or eternal? Is he intrinsically good or bad? What is the relation of the soul or psyche to the body? Does man have control over his actions, or are the latter genetically or environmentally predetermined and externally controlled? By what standards should man judge right and wrong, beauty and ugliness? What within the world of knowledge is authentic and what spurious? And what factors determine both?

Thinking individuals have divided along many lines in their search for answers to these and other profound questions about man and the universe. In respect to the issue of reality, two opposing views have emerged: one is that ultimate reality is of supernatural origin; the other is that it is of natural origin. Those espousing the first deductively assume the existence of a God figure. Those espousing the second either totally reject the possibility of a God figure, as do the materialists; or, for lack of proof, they take an agnostic position, as do the logical positivists. In respect to the issue of knowing, some regard divine revelation, others regard the power of reason, and still others regard sense empiricism to be the primary sources of knowledge. In respect to the issue of values, individuals differ over the significance of selected values, over what the sanctioning sources should be (external or internal authority), and over the changelessness of values.

Irrespective of differences, most philosophical systems depict man as dynamic—faithful to his destiny only when progressing from where he is toward where he should be. Obviously, the various systems assess outcomes in widely different ways. Generally speaking, they divide into closed and open systems. The closed systems operate deductively from principles and concepts sanctioned in advance by some form of constituted authority: God or universal truth, for example. Perennialism, with its base the great ideas of the ages drawn from the great minds of the ages, is illustrative of the universal-truth sanction. Closed systems, in effect, having announced a priori what ends are laudable for man, assess change in terms of his rate of progression toward them.

Open systems, in contrast, start with few or no a priori values, holding man, individually or collectively, responsible to work them out for himself. Existentialism, one of these open systems, posits that man exists first, and, in the process of existing, creates and takes on qualities of human essence. Man lives, and by living he becomes. An individual is not just a single cut from the common cloth of humanity.

Rather, he is unique because he lives his life in a unique way. He works through to his own values, makes his own decisions, and takes responsibility for his own actions.

Pragmatism, too, starts with few or no a priori values. It depicts nothing in nature as necessarily fixed or permanent, nothing as intrinsically right or wrong. Rather, practices and ideas are right or wrong only when people, after trying them out in daily living, prove them to be right or wrong. And what is deemed good or bad by one social group at one point in time may be viewed in a different or contrasting way by another social group at another point in time.

Whether philosophical systems are closed or open, however, they support the thesis that life and change go hand in hand. Closed systems pre-establish the directions of change. Open systems lead to their establishment a posteriori.

CULTURE IN TRANSITION

Across almost the entire spectrum of life, the old order is indeed changing, giving way to the new. In the social domain, two revolutions are taking place simultaneously. One is a revolution of the "have-nots" against the "haves." The poor of the world, with their goal the better things of life, are marching toward that goal with mounting force. A second is a revolution of race in which nonwhites are engaged in an inexorable struggle for first-class status. In the political domain, closed ideological systems are locked in mortal combat with open systems. And in the realm of the natural sciences, technology is literally shaking the world. Caught up in the maelstrom of change, most of us share

Bertrand Russell's sentiment that "Very little remains of institutions and ways of life that when I was a child appeared as indestructible as granite."[1]

The Indigent

Of the almost 3 billion people in the world, only a minority live without want. The majority "still go barefoot; the majority still do not have enough to eat; the majority are still wretchedly housed; the majority are still exposed to unnecessary accidents and disease; the majority are still living in ignorance and superstition."[2]

To Commager, the covering term *majority* embraces "two thirds of the people of the globe." To Hoffman, it embraces 1.25 billion people, exclusive of the 650 million Mainland Chinese.[3] To Ferman and associates, it embraces 33 to 35 million Americans who live on incomes of under $3,000 yearly for a family of two or more, and $1,500 for a single person.[4] To Soule, it embraces "two thirds, if not more, of the Latin-American population who are physically undernourished, to the point of actual starvation in some regions. . . ."[5]

To the middle and upper classes throughout the world, poverty is more textbook topic than living fact. Individuals from these economically privileged classes have little firsthand experience with poverty. The tourist who takes a 60-mile-an-hour look at the shanties of the "poor white trash" in Louisiana, the amateur adventurer who slums for a single evening in the Black Belt of Chicago, the world traveler who looks the other way in New Delhi, or the American industrialist who lives a prophylactic existence in Mexico City—all these may see poverty superficially, but they cannot know its corroding and searing effects. Tens of millions subsist on marginal existences. Starvation stalks their ranks. The raw earth of rural areas or the cobblestones of

[1] Robert E. Egner, *The Basic Writings of Bertrand Russell, 1903–1959* (New York: Simon and Schuster, Inc., 1961), p. 51.

[2] Henry Steele Commager, "The United States in the World Community," in Edwin Fenton, *32 Problems in World History* (Glenview, Ill.: Scott Foresman and Company, 1964), p. 232.

[3] Paul G. Hoffman, *One Hundred Countries: One and One Quarter Billion People* (Washington, D.C.: Albert D. and Mary Lasker Foundation, 1960), p. 9.

[4] Louis A. Ferman, Joyce L. Kornbluh, and Alan Haber (eds.), *Poverty in America* (Ann Arbor: University of Michigan Press, 1965), p. 2.

[5] George Soule, "An Underdeveloped Society" in Leften S. Stavrianos et al. (eds.), *Readings in World History* (Boston: Allyn and Bacon, Inc., 1962), p. 469.

dimly lighted city streets are often their beds. And infant mortality, chronic illness, and illiteracy are poverty's constant companions.

The causes of economic inequities consist chiefly of the following: (1) greed on the part of the haves, (2) ignorance and resulting impotency on the part of the have-nots, (3) the dogged persistency of living patterns, and (4) the awesome complexities of the problems of poverty elimination.

Greed, one of the seven deadly sins, unquestionably lies at the root of much of the poverty in the world. From time immemorial, individuals of almost every social group (a few utopian secular and religious groups to the contrary) have made material possessions a supreme, if not actually *the* supreme, concern of their lives. Obviously, when certain individuals acquire a greater share of the world's goods, other individuals, of necessity, have to settle for less. When the pattern of distribution becomes excessively one-sided, unjustifiable affluence manifests itself at one end of the continuum, with intolerable hardship standing out at the other end. Such extremes bring on an accompanying subordination of the humanistic values that civilized man claims to live by. If poverty is a social evil, and if cupidity is its root, then the social order in general, and formal education in particular, have a mandate to act. Specifics of the action plan will undergo development in subsequent chapters.

Ignorance in the ranks of the poor is a second cause of poverty. But unlike cupidity, ignorance is both cause and result. Ignorance, unquestionably, is an open road to poverty; but poverty, just as unquestionably, is an open road to ignorance. Thus, these two social parasites combine to make common capital of misery.

14

The relationship between ignorance and poverty has a correlate in the comparison of years of formal education with annual income. The data in Table 1.1, pertaining to males in the United States in the year 1966, are illustrative:

TABLE 1.1

Years of Formal Education	Annual Median Income 1966, of Males, 25 Years and Older
less than 8 years	$2,576
elementary-school graduate	4,210
9–11 years	5,534
high school graduate	6,458
13–15 years	7,222
college graduate	8,748
17 years or more	9,613

Source: Kenneth A. Simon and W. Vance Grant, *Digest of Educational Statistics,* OE-10024-68 (Washington, D.C.: U.S. Department of Health, Education, and Welfare, 1968), p. 15.

The analogous data in Table 1.2, pertaining to years of formal education and life income, are additionally illustrative.

TABLE 1.2

Years of Formal Education	Lifetime Income of Males, Age 25 to 64
less than 8 years	$154,332
elementary-school graduate	203,248
9–11 years	240,184
high school graduate	282,456
13–15 years	333,141
college graduate or more	450,868

Source: Simon and Grant, *Digest of Educational Statistics,* p. 15.

Data pertaining to the unemployed serve as yet a third illustration. At the mid-1960s, in the ranks of the unemployed, one person in ten had not completed elementary school; only one in 50 of these had completed college.[6] Among college graduates, the period of unemployment was also of shorter duration.

[6] Harry Kursh, *The United States Office of Education* (Philadelphia: Chilton Company—Book Division, 1965), p. 36.

The persistence of living patterns and routines constitutes a third reason why poverty tends to perpetuate itself. Styles of living, like people, change slowly indeed, with the familiar, old ways always resisting the unfamiliar news ways. Desiring change, yet fearful of it, the indigent of the inner city, the dweller of the Southern bayou, the farmhand of the back country, or the wetback of the California fruit orchard fights only half-heartedly for a new life. Traditional patterns have an insidious way of sealing in defeatism.

The complexities that characterize the task of poverty alleviation are yet a fourth reason for its tenacity. Factors that are economic, political-social, and personal mitigate against any simple solution. Economically, for instance, direct handouts from governmental or private agencies, although unavoidable under emergency conditions, can rarely be more than short-term expediencies. When these handouts become excessive, they tend to upset the delicate supply-and-demand balance so essential to a free-enterprise economy. Rather, the greatest need is for the materially disadvantaged to be incorporated naturally into the economic order. Implementation of this goal, however, encounters difficulties, some of which are often nearly insurmountable.

At the political-social and personal levels, problems are no less complex. For instance, slums in the inner city stubbornly resist attempts at elimination. And when social forces are successful in razing them, the dispossessed do not necessarily adjust comfortably to high-rise apartment living. Nor do families transplanted from impoverished farms adjust any better to new town or city environments. Problems associated with poverty alleviation are as complex as human nature, inbred social institutions, and tradition itself. And the problems are as difficult to solve as suspicion is difficult to overcome, as illiteracy is difficult to eliminate, and as altruism is difficult to attain.

Yet, despite obstacles, poverty is responding to social pressures. The highly developed countries of the West, and the many developing countries of Africa, South America, and Asia are attacking with mounting vigor their age-old enemy. Most of the developing countries, unwilling to await the slow processes of evolution, increasingly solicit and receive from their more highly developed neighbors advanced scientific and social know-how, as well as direct economic aid.

Beyond question, the poor, collectively and individually, are in revolt against squalor and misery. They are increasingly resolved to stamp out deprivation as a way of life.

16

The Struggle for Racial Equality

The strivings of the indigent for the good life find a parallel in the strivings of racial groups for social equality. Both turn on the issue of poverty. The struggle of the races, however, extends well beyond the material into the psychological and the social. In effect, all racial and ethnic groups are engaged in a struggle for self- and social acceptance. Every world citizen, irrespective of race, desires a self-image of which he can be proud and needs social acceptance as a means to that end.

The world contains nearly 3 billion individuals of many races and cultures,[7] who converse in approximately 2800 languages.[8] They derive "from a common ancestry, and all belong to the same single species, Homo sapiens."[9] Belonging to the same species, they are more alike than different. They have analogous biological organs, systems, and

[7] W. S. Woytinsky and E. S. Woytinsky, *World Population and Production* (New York: The Twentieth Century Fund, Inc., 1953), p. 49.

[8] Woytinsky and Woytinsky, p. 51.

[9] Ashley Montague, *Man in Process* (New York: New American Library of World Literature, Inc., 1962), p. 34.

functions. They have common physical, psychological, and social needs, interests, and desires. They have mental capacities that differ little, if at all, from race to race. And no one race is favored with a higher quality of humanness than any other.

Along with their fundamental likenesses, racial groups differ in a number of ways. First, they differ externally in regard to such characteristics as skin color, hair texture, facial features, and body size. Second, they differ culturally. Within this dimension, they differ to the extent that any one group has had significantly different experiences with its environment than a contrasting group. Climate, soil, topography, proximity to other cultures, demographic (population) influences, and social inheritances are some of the many factors that make for cultural differences. All these factors, among others, have combined to make America and Americans what they are today. Early settlers brought from the mother country a cultural heritage that embraced attitudes and beliefs about government, religion, education, and individualism. These, however, underwent modification as the settlers adapted to the conditions and influences of the New World. From the interplay of these forces, a new culture emerged.

The central emphasis of the topic under discussion, however, is not the differences but the likenesses among people and groups. And because of these likenesses, *all* racial groups are entitled to respect from all other groups, and to a place of dignity in the world social order.

Interestingly, this concept of the basic rights of all people has been slow in developing. To Plato (B.C. 427–347) slavery was a social issue, not a moral one. It was right, he thought, for a lesser slave group to serve the needs of a favored philosopher-ruler group. Four hundred years later, writers of the *New Testament* stigmatized all Jews "forevermore" by holding them responsible for Christ's crucifixion. It was not until 1965 that the Pope officially removed the stigma. For two millenia, "bad" theology had made a mockery of brotherhood. Serfs in the Middle Ages, colonials until recently, and "common" laborers in any age exemplify the slow development of this concept.

Today the concept is taking firm hold among the Negroid and Mongoloid races. Members of these races are currently crusading for their social, psychological, and economic rights—rights which are theirs by reason of their membership in the human race. The struggle for racial equality is just one more instance of the world in transition, one more instance of the phenomenon of change in operation. At a practical level, it is a fact of life that teacher candidates cannot afford to ignore.

18

Open and Closed Political Systems

Political, like racial and economic, ideologies and systems, today as always, are vying with one another for positions of eminence and dominance in world affairs. The competition, basically, is between the open system of democracy and the closed system of totalitarianism.

Each evolving culture, in effect, has to answer to its satisfaction these three fundamental political questions. Who will govern whom? What role or roles will the governed play? And what power group will provide answers to either of these questions? Cultures throughout history have differed widely in their responses. To the first question, cultures have responded with priestly rulers, secular kings, triumvirates, emperors, feudal lords, dictators, elected heads of state, communist secretariats, and others. The role of the governed has extended from one of passivity to one of active participation in the governing process. To the question of what force should operate as the ultimate source of authority, the range has extended from a single monolithic leader to all the adults in a given culture.

Generally speaking, from the time of the Roman Empire to the present, the trend in government has been away from authority exercised by the few toward authority exercised by the many. The Anglo-Saxon nations have been largely responsible for this directional shift. Yet the trend is not, by any stretch of the imagination, inexorable or irreversible. After all, the ghosts of Hitler and Mussolini are not yet at rest. Imperialism, both in the communist and in the free world, is slow to breathe its last. Franco may be less powerful, but he is still in power. And, in South America, liberalism is still foreign to most political and social practices. These and other similar instances, too many to be detailed here, are reason enough for only moderate optimism in any assessment of democratic gains.

The greatest contemporary political encounter is the one between the communist and the noncommunist world. This confrontation pits: (1) the Soviet Union, Mainland China, and their satellites against the democratic nations of the western world; (2) government by a chosen few against government by the many; (3) closed political thinking, deductively oriented, against open political thinking, inductively oriented; (4) statism against individualism; and (5) dialectical materialism as the supreme source of values against the Judeo-Christian ethical system as the supreme source of values.

19

With the passage of time, the nature of the encounter has changed. From the early twentieth century until the 1930s, communism was more an incipient or latent threat to the free world than an actual menace. However, on the eve of World War II, when Russia and Germany signed a nonaggression pact, the threat took on immediacy. Then, when Germany attacked its erstwhile ally, Russia changed loyalties, becoming a Western ally for reason of mutual expediency.

For two decades after the close of World War II, the communist and the noncommunist worlds were open and avowed antagonists. They vied militarily, most notably in Korea; they vied politically throughout the world for national loyalties; and they vied ideationally everywhere for the minds of men. By the late 1960s, the two worlds had reached a point of near rapprochement. With Czechoslovakia admittedly excepted, conflict is conceding to conciliation. Russia, for instance, is becoming increasingly attracted to the economic incentive system; the United States, at the same time, is modifying the incentive system in order to protect against social abuses. As another instance of emerging synthesis, individual rights are slowly increasing in communist countries; state controls to protect individual rights are on the ascendancy in most democratic countries.

Hopefully, the most important result of the encounter between East and West will be an awakening in both to a keener sensitivity to humanistic values. The Western world, on its part, needs to convert into meaningful action what it has long professed to believe about human rights and freedoms. If this is even an approximate outcome, the phenomenon of change will once more have served the cause of humanity.

Technology and Social Change

 The technological revolution, in great part, has been responsible for the social and political upheavals taking place throughout the world. Some of the scientists who made the revolution inevitable are Roger Bacon (1214–1294), Johann Gutenberg (1398–1468), Galileo (1564–1642), and Sir Isaac Newton (1642–1727). The Industrial Revolution, which began in England two centuries ago, spreading throughout the world, served as a necessary preliminary to the technological revolution of the present day.

Technology, in effect, is applied science. It has to do with the world

of automation. It embraces, for instance, machines on the production lines of all industrial economies—machines that now perform tasks previously performed by men and women. It embraces jet-propelled airplanes, electronic computers or "brains" and electronic systems designed for the brains. It embraces such trade terms, and the processes associated therewith, as data input, data manipulation, and data output. It embraces television—commercial, educational, and closed circuit; electronic programming; tape recorders and related processes; Hollerith Punch Cards; and microfilming.

The machine age, unquestionably, has wrought wonders. Its hardware is dramatic, and the extent and quality of its products are staggering to the imagination. However, the negative impact of technology on man, as man, dims much of its luster.

Fundamentally, automation's domain is the world of things—most of them material things. As viewed by many, its criteria of efficiency are greater output, increased speed and precision of production, man-hours saved, decreased travel time, or precision of computation. And under the proper circumstances, these criteria cannot be faulted. Few, for instance, object to more and better automobiles moving along a production line in less time. Few object when a commercial passenger flies coast to coast in greater safety and comfort as well as in less time. Few fault a military establishment for feeding data into an electronic computer and, in seconds, receiving better answers than the best human statisticians could formulate in hundreds or thousands, maybe even millions, of hours.

Yet these related outcomes made possible by technology are legitimate only when they serve the cause of man, not just as a consumer of material things but as a human being. In this connection, I am convinced that the following tenets of humanism should have inviolability, irrespective of the status of technology at any time.

1. Man's individuality is the supreme value of life.
2. Man is emergent, not static.
3. Man's fulfillment along lines of the rational, the affective, and the physical should be a lifelong goal.
4. Man's human worth increases in proportion to the magnitude of the progression toward this goal.
5. Man's personality fulfillment, relatively speaking, is a result of man's commitment to others. The ultimate of this commitment is altruism.
6. The best social order is one that serves the cause of individualism best.

To the extent that these tenets are valid, technology is an unadulterated blessing only when it enhances the basic dignity of individuals. This it does, for instance, when it makes the otherwise arduous life of the laborer more tolerable, when it increases the amount of leisure time for creative things, when it leads to a more equitable distribution of the essentials of living—in general, when a social order employs technology as a means to defensible social ends.

The key issue, thus, is whether the American social order is slave to, or master of, technology. It is slave to the extent that mechanical things and processes relegate man to a place of secondary importance. It is slave, for instance, when workers are depersonalized cogs, when they have no voice in decision-making, or when they are casually expendable. It is slave in a social setting when man gravitates too much toward amusement gadgets and too little toward human companionship. It is slave in an emotional setting when man, lost in the bigness and detachment of a highly industrialized economy, becomes alienated from himself and from other important humanistic values. It is slave in an educational setting when mechanical instruments and methods crowd out the human touch.

A social order that enslaves itself to technology, however, cannot justifiably blame the latter for its enslavement. If honest, it has to blame itself for allowing its values to become distorted. The American social order, having, for too long, sold too much of itself to materialism, needs

22

at the moment a soul-searching value inventory. It needs such an inventory, among other reasons, for having allowed science to become monolithic. As recently as 1968, the federal government, in the area of basic and applied research (exclusive of defense), allocated to industry and education combined $4,381,500,000 for the physical sciences, $1,584,400,000 for the life sciences (medicine, biology, and agriculture), $209,300,000 for the social sciences, $124,400,000 for the psychological sciences, and nothing for the humanities per se.[10] On a comparative basis, the results appear as 69.6, 25.2, 3.3, 1.9, and 0 percents.[11]

Are the combined sciences 20 times as important as the combined areas of the social sciences, the psychological sciences, and the humanities? Are the physical sciences almost three times as important as the life sciences, or 20 times as important as the social sciences? Or 35 times as important as the psychological sciences? Scarcely! Then why the extreme one-sidedness of the ratios? An honest answer, I think, has to be that our life values are more distorted than most of us will admit. The technological revolution, in general, and Sputnik, in particular, are mirrors, not creators, of this distortion.

Somewhere along the line, those humanistic values that are etched into our verbal traditions, those values that millions claim as their birthrights, need to gain operational ascendancy. We cannot continue to allow foreign nations to formulate our values. Neither can we allow our values to wither for want of practical implementation. Instead, the fundamental values that America claims to live by need to be implemented in a consciously patterned positive way of life.

A CLOSING THOUGHT

As the process unfolds, change—that common denominator of all existence—once more will be manifesting itself. Undeniably, the spirit of revolution is loose in the world. The poor are increasingly bestirring themselves. The dark-skinned races are in active resurgence. Conflicting political ideologies are locked in combat. And man is exchanging technology's power to ameliorate for its sinister power to harm.

[10] Simon and Grant, *Digest of Educational Statistics,* p. 111.

[11] Apart from research and development, the federal government has given at least limited support to the humanities. For instance, the National Foundation on the Arts and Humanities Act of 1965 allocated $20 million to the humanities, broadly conceived, for each of the years 1966 through 1969.

Confronted on all sides by change, the American social order faces two choices. One embraces such evasive tactics as rationalizing the problem, postponing action on it, and continuing to hold on to outdated patterns. The second choice is realism wherein the American culture, recognizing change as a ferment built into nature, identifies with it, and, in the words of one commentator, "becomes its headquarters."[12]

Regarding this second choice as the only one for rational people to make, I have woven it into the texture of this book. Because change characterizes all of life—people, social institutions, political patterns, and the physical world—education cannot avoid involvement with it. Education, rather, needs to become its ally.

To
Stimulate
Thought

1. Erich Fromm, a well-known psychoanalyst-philosopher, holds that the brotherhood-of-man concept is difficult, if not downright impossible, to implement in a free-enterprise economic system. Take a stand on this issue and elaborate it.

[12] Van Cleve Morris et al. *Becoming an Educator* (Boston: Houghton Mifflin Company, 1963), p. 144.

A CULTURE IN FERMENT

2. Many concede that phenomena such as physical growth, social customs, and human knowledge yield to change. However, they are less willing to concede that moral and spiritual values comparably yield to change. In this connection, list the more basic of these values that, in your opinion, are the same today as "they always have been."

3. What hopes do you think technology holds out for the human welfare of people?

4. Should the more affluent in the world make sacrifices, even great ones if necessary, to guarantee a decent standard of living for the deprived? Give reasons for your answer.

5. Assuming identical environments, past and present, do you believe that the behavior of all racial groups would be comparable? Would they all measure up to essentially the same intellectual and social levels? Defend your position.

6. To what extent do you think people are affluent or needy, slow or gifted, indolent or energetic, as a result of willing themselves to be one or more of these? What factors in addition to volition may also be operative?

REFERENCES

Fenton, Edwin, *32 Problems in World History* (Glenview, Ill.: Scott Foresman and Company, 1964).

Ferman, Louis A., Joyce L. Kornbluh, and Alan Haber (eds.), *Poverty in America* (Ann Arbor: University of Michigan Press, 1965).

Frost, Joe L., and Glenn R. Hawkes (eds.), *The Disadvantaged Child: Issues and Innovations* (Boston: Houghton Mifflin Company, 1966).

Harrington, Michael, *The Other America* (New York: Crowell-Collier and Macmillan, Inc., 1962).

Hoffman, Paul G., *World Without Want* (New York: Harper & Row, Publishers, 1962).

Linton, Thomas E., and Jack L. Nelson, *Patterns of Power: Social Foundations of Education* (New York: Pittman Publishing Company, 1968).

Maury, Marion, *The Good War* (New York: Macfadden-Bartell Corp., 1965).

Montague, Ashley, *Man in Process* (New York: New American Library of World Literature, Inc., 1962).

Morris, Van Cleve, *et al.*, *Becoming an Educator* (Boston: Houghton Mifflin Company, 1963).

Pettigrew, Thomas F., *A Profile of Negro Education* (Princeton, N.J.: D. Van Nostrand Company, Inc., 1964).

Smith, Brewster, *Social Psychology and Human Values* (Chicago: Aldine Publishing Company, 1969).

Thelan, Herbert A., *Education and the Human Quest* (New York: Harper & Row, Publishers, 1960).

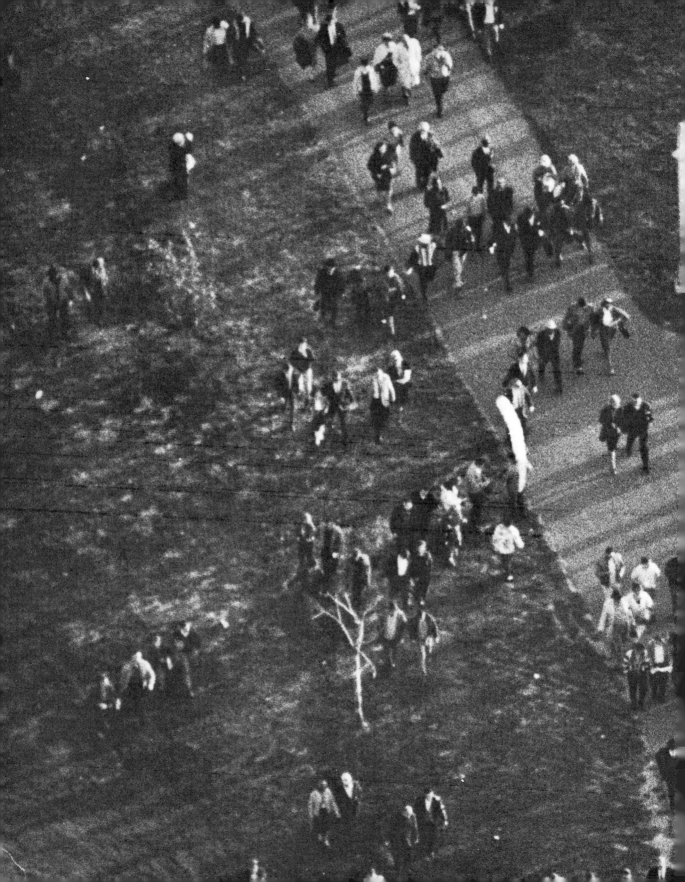

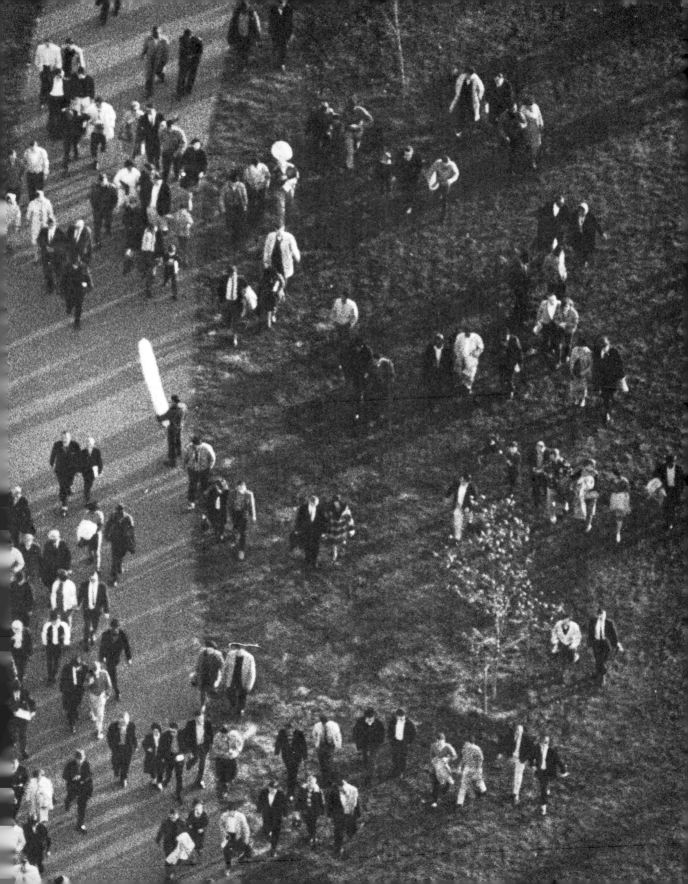

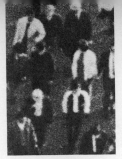

Chapter

2

Education
Determines
Its Course

A social order committed to a given style of living logically expects its social institutions to reflect and blend into whatever that style might be. For instance, the institutions of a communist social order live under a mandate to espouse the dogma and practices of communism. Conversely, the institutions of a democratic social order live under a mandate to espouse the dogma and practices befitting an open system of thinking and living.

EDUCATION AND HUMANISM

Formal education, as one of the most significant of all social institutions, has a built-in mandate to operate within the frame of reference of the social group it serves. In the Western world, this frame, as indicated earlier, is a humanistic one, encompassing the following values.

First and foremost, individual man is of supreme worth. Furthermore, he is an emerging essence, with total personality fulfillment constituting both his birthright and his commitment. He progresses toward this fulfillment through, but never at the expense of, others. Rather, humanism commits him to assume responsibility not only for his own fulfillment but for that of others—to be his brother's, as well as his own, keeper. Or, as stated by the existentialist, the model man acts at all times as if he were acting for the entire human race.

The rights of humanism, which at the philosophical level appear to be fixed and stable, at the practical level are elusive and mutable. Earned, rather than given, they must be fought for, nurtured and defended. And individuals earn them by combating successfully the threats imposed by psychological alienation, the lure of power, and one-sided personality development.

Threats to Humanism

Psychological alienation   Within a cultural frame that is basically humanistic, education nonetheless has to protect children and youth against the ever-present threat of alienation. Education's allies in the process, however, are potent ones. This country's basic documents hold up individualism as a value second to none. Most forthrightly the Dec-

laration of Independence holds "these truths to be self-evident, that all men are created equal, that they are endowed by their Creator with certain unalienable Rights, that among these are Life, Liberty, and the Pursuit of Happiness . . ." The Preamble to the Constitution embraces human welfare as one of its most vital concerns. The First Amendment relates sensitively to man's freedoms; and the Fourteenth, just as sensitively, to his rights. Common law, statutory law, and court decisions combine with the country's more basic documents to establish the individual man as a creature of great worth, entitled to respect, protection, and self-realization. A second powerful ally is modern secularism, which holds that man can, and should, find fulfillment in this life, without reference to the hereafter.

Yet despite the strength of these precedents, education has to fight relentlessly against forces that alienate individuals from themselves and from their cultures. One of the most insidious of these is ignorance, mortal enemy not only of education but of freedom and truth. A basic truism is that man, if uninformed, cannot be free. For one reason, he cannot know freedom for what it truly is. For another, he falls easy prey to those who would take freedom away. In either event, ignorance makes autonomy unattainable, breeding dependence instead. Dependent, helpless, resentful, and frustrated at his impotence, the ignorant man withdraws from others and becomes increasingly alienated from society. The culmination is self-abasement and self-alienation.

As another agent of alienation, poverty, as stated in Chapter 1, unites with ignorance as a partner. Together, they flourish in provincialism, misery, apathy, aggressiveness, and defeatism. The child of the city slums, of the barren farm, of the blighted river front, or of the run-down trailer camp comes to school chronically undernourished, poorly clothed, and psychologically starved, often for reason of parental neglect. He soon develops a sense of worthlessness. This alienated child needs, more than anything else, to feel that he can contribute to society. An educational system, grounded in humanism, cannot, without culpability, ignore this need. Many welfare programs are facing up to it somewhat. But much more needs to be done both by government and by other agencies. When searing poverty comes to school, alienation accompanies it. Both set back the cause of learning.

A third cause of alienation is bigotry, which also was discussed in Chapter 1. Since racism divides man from man by identifying some individuals and groups as more worthwhile than others, alienation is the inevitable result.

A fourth cause is poor mental health which, by definition, separates any afflicted individual both from himself and from his environment. It does this in many ways: by distorting his view of reality; by making him excessively retiring or aggressive; by lowering his tolerance to stress; by making him hyperemotional; by interfering with his human relationships. These symptoms block his ability to learn, inhibit his growth, and deny him independence and self-realization.

Emotional maladjustment ranges from the mildly debilitating to the seriously disruptive. In its most benign form in so-called normal individuals, it reveals itself in faulty human relationships, in unproductivity in work, and in frustrations created by the competition of conflicting values. Also, in so-called normal individuals, emotional maladjustment reveals itself in certain defense mechanisms. These, in effect, are ego-protecting devices that act as smoke screens to obscure personality inadequacies. Thus the student, shattered by an *F* in geometry, holds poor teaching to be the cause; he *rationalizes*. The wife, unable to grow up emotionally and feeling guilty about it, identifies her husband's immaturity as the cause; she *projects*. The threatened mother, fearful that her daughter will marry, pooh poohs her love relationship as puppy love; she *denies*. The father, threatened by the increasing masculinity of his teen-age son, yet shamed by his fears, shoves the emotion into his unconscious; he *represses*. The fourth-grader, unable to get the attention at age nine that he got at age six, reverts to temper tantrums; he *regresses*.

Every individual employs defenses to cushion himself from reality which is sometimes too much for him to bear. Overused, however, they create such a gap between him and the world in which he must live as to make reality elusive. Furthermore, he may ease into neurotic patterns or psychotic states. Neurotic patterns are characterized by anxieties, phobias, or compulsions. These, often without apparent organic cause, give rise to behavior that at best fails the test of normalcy and at times may even be bizarre. Psychotic states are pathological ones, with diseases such as schizophrenia, paranoia, or manic-depressive psychosis patently manifest.

Poor mental health, irrespective of its degree of severity, operates as a force that alienates people from themselves and others. As such, it is an enemy of humanism. No educational system with its roots in humanism can avoid a confrontation with it. This topic will undergo further development later.

A fifth cause of alienation is the increased size and complexity of **31**

our society which, by its very nature, poses a threat to individualism. As the nation's population grows, the relative importance of any single person in it seems to diminish. As industry becomes ever more gargantuan, employer-employee relations become ever more distant and impersonal. As the size of government increases, so too does the psychological distance between it and the individual. Fading is the social closeness that once characterized interdependent neighbors, receding are possibilities for private ownership of local business concerns, gone is the political individualism of the historically famous town meeting. Size has either diminished their importance or pre-empted them completely.

Our vast and depersonalized culture tends to alienate man more and more from life's deeper meanings. As a result, education has a greater commitment today than ever before not just to "train" children and youth but to humanize them. Although this is a shared responsibility, it is one that education cannot, and should not, ignore. Only the truly human person is able to retain his selfhood while living in a world of detached bigness.

Power If alienation is a threat to humanism, as indeed it is, power is just as much so. As commented on in Chapter 1, today's world is still seeking satisfactory answers to the age-old conundrums: Who should guide whom? What are the legitimate uses of power? These, individually and collectively, perplex families, school organizations, civic groups, and governmental agencies. Relating these questions to our American culture, I hold that power exercised legitimately should conform to the following tenets.

1. Most fundamentally, all determinations in regard to power should emanate from the country's humanistic traditions.
2. Thus, power exercised by any one individual over others should be power exercised for the welfare of others, not for the ego-uplift of the power wielder.
3. The governed should decide who will exercise this power and in what way.
4. The law of parsimony should apply to the exercise of power: the wielder, that is, should employ only the minimum amount required in any given situation.
5. Power through others rather than power over others should constitute the ultimate goal.

When any society, even a democratic one, fails to keep watch over the manner in which its leaders employ the power invested in them, it courts disaster. The reason resides in the closeness of the relationship between mental health and the exercise of power. The maladjusted person is a dangerous power risk: because unfulfilled, he tends to build up his ego at the expense of others. The healthier the person emotionally, the safer he is as a power risk: because fulfilled, he does not sacrifice others to his ego needs.

Power unquestionably is a heady intoxicant. In the recent past, it imbued Hitler with psychotic visions of grandeur and Sukarno with political illusions of glory. In our own country today, it is luring leaders in government, in industry, in education, and even in religion to give higher priority to the causes of self than to those of humanity. Throughout the centuries, only three antidotes have proved effective. Two of them—counter power and power allowed to die by the weight of its own intensity—are negative antidotes. The only positive one is altruism, a product of mental-health fulfillment. In a world as vulnerable to destruction as ours, do cultures and their educational systems have any choice left but the last one? The answer may be obvious, but how slow most are in arriving at it.

One-sided intellectualism   Individuals and cultures that worship the idol of intellect are guilty of yet another serious affront to humanism. Their preoccupations, almost unilaterally, are with mind, knowledge, understandings, and the rational man. The greatest strength of their position emanates from the undeniable importance of the values to which they ascribe. In fact, only the irrational, the provincial, or the religiously narrow would regard cognitive values as other than eminently important. Their position also draws strength from tradition. Plato and Aristotle, particularly the former, early gave it support by setting the philosopher-ruler on a throne of unassailability. Catholicism in the Middle Ages continued the tradition. And today such individuals as Robert M. Hutchins (*b.* 1899), Jacques Barzun (*b.* 1907), and James B. Conant (*b.* 1893) are not about to let the tradition die.

Yet the position, in my opinion, is highly vulnerable. *First,* most who adopt it assume, or at least imply, that the mind is a discrete entity; that it has, at best, only an incidental relationship to the affective and physical components. Biologists and psychologists, for a half century or more, have laid bare the falsity of this assumption. So too, from time immemorial, have the surgical convalescent, the grief-stricken person,

33

the anxiety-ridden neurotic, or the social outcast. All of these could testify eloquently to the close relationship between the emotional and the social, on one hand, and the intellectual, on the other. *Second,* these same intellectualists imply, or state, that the mind is capable of being trained as an independent entity. This possibility lost out when psychologists laid formal discipline to rest. And into the grave with it went the assumption that the mind is a single unitary component. Its replacement is the concept of mind as totally organismic, an entity that is coextensive with all systems of the human organism. *Third,* proponents of the intellectualist position usually become so enamored with the intellects of the more talented that they tend to deprecate the equally important intellects of the less talented. In so doing, they bring into being a class society which accords respect to individuals not on the basis of a composite of personality intangibles, but of the mental component only. This approach leads to a *House of Intellect* (Barzun style), wherein an intellectual in-group has exalted status. Should intellectual values be thus measured in absolute terms of how much or in relative terms of how well? Is not the issue more what any individual does with the intellectual attributes he possesses than with how extensive the attributes are?

FUNCTIONS OF FORMAL EDUCATION

Within this established frame of humanism, formal education performs three significant functions. First, it serves as an agent of transmission, communicating selectively to each new generation the cumulative knowledge and traditions of the past. Second, it acts as an agent of adaptation. In this role, it helps the young to adjust to their world. Third, it acts as a catalyst of personality development. In this role, it readies individuals to desert their provincial worlds for the evolving world of the "not yet." This third is a developmental function. The three functions, thus, are the *transmissive,* the *adaptive,* and the *developmental.*

The Transmissive Function

It is the transmissive function that enables any culture to survive. In primitive cultures, parents or selected tribal representatives assumed it.

34

In civilized cultures, formal education, for reasons of efficiency and economy, customarily assume the lion's share of it. A social group first decides what in a culture is important and then has formal education transmit it to the young. Most fundamentally, education transmits the values that the social order lives by. In the Western world, these are the humanistic ones discussed previously. Education relatedly transmits language and computational skills, selected knowledge, fundamental understandings, opinions, attitudes, appreciations, and social mores.

35

Simply stated, culture is the composite experiences of a social group. Formal education identifies and transmits the most important of these experiences to each new generation.

The process of transmission, however, is not as simple as it sounds. For one reason, cultures differ over what is or is not important, over what is or is not worthy of transmission. For instance, the American nation today is divided over the relative importance in the schools of science education, of sex education, of teaching about communism, of linguistics, of certain of the literary classics, and of creative writing—just to name only a few. Another issue that complicates the process has to do with differential institutional responsibilities for learning. The home, the church or synagogue, and the school often operate at cross purposes in this regard. A third complicating factor has to do with the phenomenon of learning readiness. Students differ widely in their abilities to respond to the stimuli of transmission. Yet, despite these and other attendant complexities, education in any civilized society stands out as probably the most important agent of cultural transmission.

The Adaptive Function

To the extent that formal education succeeds in executing its transmissive function, it succeeds correspondingly well in executing its adaptive function: that is, in helping the young to fit into and relate to their environments. In effect, education transmits, so that learners on their way to fulfillment can better adapt to their worlds.

Unfortunately, education's interest in the cause of adaptation is often a misunderstood one. The so-called life adjustment curriculum, popular in the thirties and forties, may well be the primary reason. Many feel that the proponents of this curriculum, in attempting to correct the inappropriateness of the traditional classical curriculum for the slow and average, have overemphasized the cause of the practical. Certain extremists have, for instance, oversold the curriculum values of vocational education, of dating and marriage as curriculum components, of home-and-family-living education, and of uplift projects conducted by students in local communities. In general, many advocates of the life adjustment curriculum have erred in assuming that the school should deal directly with all the major problems young people will have to face in their daily living. Life adjustment education, carried to an extreme, tends to neglect abstract learning, and to play down the fact that much

educational endeavor has ultimate, not immediate, benefits. Education does not have to, nor should it, relate only to the present. Neither should the schools be exact replicas of life outside the schools. To the contrary, schools need to be future- as well as present-oriented; abstract- as well as sense-experience-oriented.

The constructive compromise rests somewhere between the excessively present-centered practical and the equally excessively future-centered theoretical. Schools that most nearly effect this compromise are those with a curriculum that, as far as possible, starts with the immediate before plunging into the cosmic, that is sensitive to the developmental needs of children and youth, that attends to the emotional problems of students as well as to their academic growth, that allows certain speech colloquialisms in given locales rather than insisting on overstandardization, and that regards extracurriclum activities as educationally important. All of these, and a host of others, fall within the purview of the adaptive function.

An illustration is in order. A typical fifteen-year-old male student is enrolled in high school as a tenth-grader. Important among his needs, as would be expected, are an adequate self-image, satisfying peer relationships (with both boys and girls), satisfying parental relationships, achievement that meets at least minimum school standards, and a value system that meets both his own standards and those of the group of which he is part. These represent immediate growth needs as well as long-term life needs. How might the high school help him to meet these needs and thus adapt more appropriately to his environment?

To enhance his self-image, the school, while accepting him warmly, would challenge him with tasks that he could complete successfully. To help him improve the quality of his peer relationships, the school would give him social opportunities, both in and out of the classroom, to relate to others. The extracurriculum would prove invaluable in this regard. Additionally, the school would take a frontal curriculum approach to such topics as the behavior of social groups, sex education, and personality dynamics. To help him improve the quality of his relationships with his parents, the school would lean heavily on indirection (psychological transfer, that is, from other school experiences), only incidentally on didactic methods. To help him know academic success, the school, as previously indicated, would attempt to tailor a curriculum to his needs and interests. To help him refine his value system, the school would rely on this same tailored curriculum, on occasional didactic teaching, and on school authority figures, who would exemplify

37

the values that they desired to inculcate in students. All these approaches would serve, directly or indirectly, the cause of adaptation.

The Developmental Function

While serving the cause of adaptation, these methods would also serve the all-important cause of personality fulfillment—the cherished goal not only of formal education but of life itself. And the fact that progress toward it is measured in relative rather than absolute terms constitutes no indictment of its fundamental importance.

The fulfilled person is the whole person, the autonomous person, the self-actualized person. By whatever label, he has claim—greater claim, at least, than most to the following attributes. His greatest asset is that when he looks at himself, he basically is able to accept what he sees—his personal limitations as well as his personal assets. In brief, his self-image is satisfactory. He accepts what he cannot change and alters what he can. Then, as he looks at life outside himself, he sees reality authentically. This acceptance of self and of external reality enables him to relate more empathically to others. Thus he meets the social test; and he meets the rational test by becoming a knowledgeable individual possessed of a rich store of facts and understanding. These serve him well as he thinks openly and reflectively about all of life. Through his many confrontations with life, he develops a value system by which he lives—a value system that undergoes change even as he himself changes.

The developmental function of education unquestionably is the most complex and laudable of the three. And despite the many problems posed, it shines as education's lodestar. Education, in effect, transmits in order to enable learners to adapt, and thus to increase the possibility of their becoming their potentials.

OVERVIEW OF EDUCATIONAL GOAL PRONOUNCEMENTS

Educators today, while generally accepting these three functions as bona fide, differ as to their relative importance and as to the curriculum approaches that will best implement them. These differences, however, tend to be more procedural than substantive. This has not always been **38**   so, as the following historical overview will reveal.

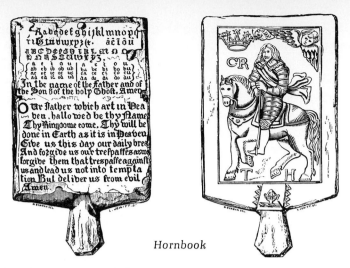

Hornbook

Reprinted with permission of the Macmillan Company from *Story and Verse for Children* by Miriam Blanton Huber and Lynd Ward. Copyright 1940, 1955 by Miriam Blanton Huber.

The Committee of Ten

Early settlers brought to the Colonies a body of classical and puritanical values inherited from the mother country. The classical influence, deriving from the Greeks, demanded reverence of the rational components of mind and intellect. The puritanical influence, of then current vintage, demanded loyalty to dogma as well as a reverence of the products of education. The resulting ideal was a hard-driving, productive man of intellect, faithful to his God and his religion.

With the passage of time, the religious but not the rational aspect dimmed. The latter, in fact, is still in evidence today. It was very much in evidence in the early 1890s when the historically famous Committee of Ten, under the leadership of President Charles Eliot of Harvard, deliberated on the purposes of education. The committee's deliberations took place in a transitional culture, one that was moving from agrarianism to urbanization, from hand production to machine production, from close community relationships to detached ones, and from a society controlled by the affluent to one increasingly controlled by a rapidly expanding middle class.

The National Education Association, sensitive to the possible educational implications of the cultural revolution, brought the Committee of Ten into being, commissioning it to redefine or reaffirm the purposes

39

of secondary education. Its membership, a clue to the dominant educational power structure, consisted of five college presidents, one professor, the Commissioner of Education, and three school principals.

The committee's 1893 *Report* revealed a conservative stand on almost all educational issues. Like Marquand's George Apley of literary renown, members of the committee were too much a product of tradition to be able to perceive the present realistically and to relate to it. Throughout the *Report*, the committee, despite its claims regarding the comprehensive nature of the high school, conceived it primarily as a college-preparatory institution responsible almost exclusively for disciplining the minds of student learners. All subjects of the curriculum, in the words of the *Report*, were to "be used for training the powers of observation, memory, expression, and reasoning; and they would all be good to that end, although differing among themselves in quality and substance."[1] Furthermore, the committee proposed that most high school courses be started a year or two earlier than was the then current vogue.

Unquestionably, the Committee of Ten was out of step with the times. Surefooted and articulate when treating of secondary education for the intellectual elite, it was uncertain and confused when prescribing for the educational needs of the average and slow. The committee seemed oblivious to the fact that secondary education was soon to serve not the upper 5 to 10 percent of the nation's youth, but almost all of it, that immigrants needed to be oriented educationally as well as economically into the culture, that the industrial revolution was not to be turned back, and that the nation's rapidly expanding middle class was no longer to be denied. The Committee of Ten fought a rearguard action against change, but like other such actions, it stemmed the tide of progress only temporarily.

Some Other Committees

Educational reform was too much in the air to remain suppressed for long. Once aroused, it precipitated a rash of national committees that came into being in the last decade of the nineteenth and the first two

[1] U.S. Department of the Interior, Bureau of Education, *Report of the Committee on Secondary School Studies, Appointed at the Meeting of the National Educational Association, July 9, 1892* (Washington, D.C.: Superintendent of Documents, Government Printing Office, 1893), p. 52.

A CULTURE IN FERMENT

decades of the twentieth century. Selected from among these committees, the following five are listed with brief comments made about them.

Committee on the Correlation of Studies (1893–1895). This group continued the work of the Committee of Ten, applying the recommendations, as feasible, to the field of elementary education.

Committee on College Entrance Requirements (1895–1899). This group addressed itself to the formulation of "a uniform system of accounting for courses, by time and preparation."[2] However, the Carnegie unit of credit per se did not come into being until a decade later. This topic will be elaborated in Chapter 8.

[2] Harold Spears, *The High School for Today* (New York: American Book Company, 1950), p. 313. Much of the content of the present section also comes from the same source, pp. 304, 312–314.

Committee on Six-Year Courses (1905–1909). The focus of this committee was the 6–6 plan of educational organization, which divided the conventional 12 years of schooling into six years of elementary and six years of secondary education.

Committee on the Economy of Time (1903–1913). This committee studied the feasibility of eliminating selected "nonessential" subjects from the elementary curriculum to make room for replacements pushed down from the secondary curriculum.

Committee on the Articulation of High Schools and Colleges (1910–1913). As the title suggests, the central concern of this committee was to coordinate the curriculums of high schools and colleges.

Commission on the Reorganization of Secondary Education

If the Committee of Ten was the retiring champion of a waning educational point of view, the Commission on the Reorganization of Secondary Education was the emerging champion of an ascendant one. The membership of this second professional group, unlike that of the earlier one, consisted primarily of public school personnel. Its concern was for the development of youth along many lines, not just along cognitive ones, for education of the less-talented many as well as the more talented few.

The commission's most memorable product was the Seven Cardinal Principles of Education, promulgated in 1918. They quickly attained a position of eminence as statements of educational goals. Though they were called principles, they were actually topical headings for areas in which secondary education, as viewed by the commission, should foster growth. The seven consist of the following:[3]

1. Health
2. Command of fundamental processes
3. Worthy home membership
4. Vocation
5. Citizenship
6. Worthy use of leisure
7. Ethical character

[3] Commission on Reorganization of Secondary Education, *Cardinal Principles of Secondary Education,* U.S. Office of Education Bulletin, No. 35, 1918 (Washington, D.C.: Government Printing Office, 1918), pp. 10–11.

A CULTURE IN FERMENT

These goals were viewed as applicable to elementary as well as secondary education. That they moved education off the dead center of intellectualism is obvious; whether they moved education too far off that center is debatable. From a 1918 point of view, many could argue that the commission, in order to effect badly needed change in the educational system, was compelled to counter intellectual overemphasis with social overemphasis. From today's perspective, many logically conclude that the commission, though implying intellectual aims, was remiss in not detailing them boldly. Their argument posits that the cognitive, the affective, and the psychomotor domains are never discrete, but always interactive and reinforcing.

The Educational Policies Commission

For two decades the Seven Cardinal Principles gave direction to educational theory. Because broadly general, however, they gave less functional direction to educational practice. In 1938 they were superseded by a more detailed statement of objectives, appearing in *The Purposes of Education in American Democracy,* a publication of the Educational Policies Commission, which was a subsidiary of the National Education Association.

This commission grouped a total of 43 aims under the four major headings of objectives of self-realization, objectives of human relationship, objectives of economic efficiency, and objectives of civic responsibility.[4] Under the first (self-realization), the educated person, for instance, was depicted as having an appetite for learning, as being a "participant and spectator in many sports and pastimes" and "skilled in listening and observing." Ten other conditions were specified. Under the second (human relationship), the educated person was identified as needing to "enjoy a rich, sincere, and varied social life," and to appreciate "the family as a social institution"—these were two of the eight considerations. The third category (economic efficiency) embraced ten objectives, and the fourth category (civic responsibility) embraced 12. The emphasis throughout was on children and youth first as members of society and only second as learners.

[4] Educational Policies Commission, *The Purposes of Education in American Democracy* (Washington, D.C.: National Education Association, 1938), pp. 50, 72, 90, 108.

Imperative Educational Needs of Youth

In 1944 the Policies Commission came forth with yet another goal pronouncement, this time under the caption, "Imperative Needs of Youth." The commission conceived the schools as responsible for ten growth tasks: namely, to help learners develop marketable skills, maintain good health, understand the rights and duties of citizenship, understand the significance and obligations of family living, know how to be good consumers, understand the methods of science, develop esthetic appreciations, know how to use leisure time wisely, develop and live by a sound value system, and grow in the powers of rational thinking.[5] In effect, these were the Seven Cardinal Principles dusted off and elaborated a bit.

The Harvard Report

A year later, in 1945, the so-called *Harvard Report* appeared, committing educators to "prepare an individual to become an expert both in some particular vocation or art and in the general art of the free man and the citizen."[6] That Harvard espoused the cause of vocationalism was a surprise to the educational world. The report stopped short of proceduralizing the recommendation.

Two Recent Statements

In 1956, the White House Conference on Education, not to be outdone by previous committees and commissions, also came out with a statement of educational goals. For the most part, this was a rehash of previous pronouncements. However, it gave formal sanction to a formerly implied goal, namely, the "ability to think and evaluate constructively and creatively."[7]

Then, in 1961, the Educational Policies Commission, this time in collaboration with the American Association of School Administrators,

[5] Educational Policies Commission, *Education for All American Youth,* (Washington, D.C.: National Education Association, 1944), pp. 225–226.

[6] The Committee on the Objectives of a General Education in a Free Society, *General Education in a Free Society* (Cambridge, Mass.: Harvard University Press, 1945), p. 54.

[7] The Committee for the White House Conference on Education, *A Report to the President* (Washington, D.C.: U.S. Government Printing Office, 1956), p. 90.

A CULTURE IN FERMENT

accorded abstract thinking a position of high priority among educational outcomes. This act in itself raised no educational eyebrows. What did was the concession among the conference participants that the esthetic and the industrial-arts subjects, as well as the academic ones, could contribute to this outcome. In the words of the conference report, the abilities of learners to analyze, to deduce, and to infer "may be developed in the course of mathematical study, but they may be developed as well through experiences in esthetic, humanistic, and practical fields, which also involve perception of form and design. Music, for example, challenges the listener to perceive elements of form within the abstract."[8]

A POSITION STATEMENT

In the context of known reality, man is of the highest value. The position avoids religion because education has to avoid it. Thus the position is not irreligious but nonreligious. Within this secular frame, man's highest purpose is to develop and refine his innate humanity. He most nearly attains this outcome when he most nearly becomes his potential. Man's humanity encompasses many values—intellectual, affective, and physical. In Western cultures, intellectual values are rarely questioned, for to question them would be to question the long-cherished ideal of the rational man, the man of reason. Thus, the many components of cognition—knowledge, comprehension, application, and reflective thinking—have uncontested respectability.

But not comparably so the values in areas of the emotional, the social, the esthetic, the ethical, and the physical. Most who view rationality per se as a monistic (single important) essence logically regard these other values as only contingently important. But should emotional adjustment, social relating, esthetic appreciation and performance, ethical values, and physical wholeness have only contingent status? I think not. Many see these outcomes as spontaneous products of cognition. But has not experience proved this assumption to be not only invalid but naive? Nietzsche's brilliance did not make him an emotionally whole person, nor did Kierkegaard's make him a social person. Musical and artistic geniuses are not necessarily intellectual geniuses also. Neither does knowledge necessarily convert one to ethical behavior. And none of these has more than an incidental relationship with physical health.

I postulate the goals of civilized man and, commensurately, the goals

[8] Educational Policies Commission and American Association of School Administrators, *The Central Purpose of American Education* (Washington, D.C.: National Education Association, 1961), pp. 17–18.

of formal education in an enlightened society to lie broadly along many dimensions. Conceived in this context, education not only has to transmit in order to help learners to adapt to their environments, it has to function in a social frame wherein personality growth, broadly viewed, can and will take place.

Education restricted to the domain of the cognitive and regarded as the property of the intellectual elite has frightening possibilities. It constitutes a gamble that the world, under the present circumstances, can ill afford. One reason resides in the awesome power of science to destroy. This power in the hands of the emotionally unstable has Frankenstein-like possibilities. And the more intellectual a maladjusted individual might be, the greater his potential for evil. A second reason resides in the ability of the mass communications media to be utilized, when the occasion warrants, as eloquently for the wrong as for the right.

It is an accepted truism that man's scientific know-how today has far outdistanced his humanistic and social understanding. If this is a valid truism—and I believe it is—education's ultimate goal can be none other than the self-actualized individual: the man of reason, to be sure, but also the man of feeling, the man of emotional stability, the man capable of altruistic action. Admittedly, this goal imposes heavy burdens on education and teaching personnel. But with the stakes so high, I question if education has a choice.

To Stimulate Thought

1. Do you believe that individualism is in greater jeopardy today than it was, for instance, two or three decades ago? Explain.

2. Develop the statement that the uninformed cannot be truly free.

3. Develop the statement that "only the truly human person is able to retain his selfhood while living in a world of detached bigness."

4. In our American culture, the concept of line and staff provides a frame for the exercise of power. To what extent does it tend to alienate individuals inside or outside the ranks of education? What antidotes can you propose, if any?

5. Develop the theme that the intellect cannot be trained as a single unitary component.

6. Elaborate the definition: "Culture is the composite experiences of any social group."

7. Develop the theme that probably the most important single psychological need is a satisfactory self-image.

8. Identify any one of the goal pronouncements included in the chapter; then evaluate it as to its strengths and weaknesses.

9. Take the author's "Position Statement," and evaluate it.

REFERENCES

Bloom, Benjamin S. (ed.), *Taxonomy of Educational Objectives. Handbook I: Cognitive Domain* (New York: David McKay Company, Inc., 1956).

Commission on Education and Labor, House of Representatives, *Education Goals for 1965* (Washington, D.C.: U.S. Government Printing Office, 1965).

Commission on Reorganization of Secondary Education, *Cardinal Principles of Education*, U.S. Office of Education Bulletin No. 35, 1918 (Washington, D.C.: U.S. Government Printing Office, 1918).

Educational Policies Commission and American Association of School Administrators, *The Central Purpose of American Education* (Washington, D.C.: NEA, 1961).

Educational Policies Commission, *The Purposes of Education in American Democracy* (Washington, D.C.: NEA, 1938).

Inlow, Gail M., *The Emergent in Curriculum* (New York: John Wiley & Sons Inc., 1966), Chap. 1.

Krathwohl, David R., Benjamin S. Bloom, and Bertrand B. Masia, *Taxonomy of Educational Objectives. Handbook II: Affective Domain* (New York: David McKay Company, Inc., 1964).

Morphet, Edgar L., and Daniel L. Jesser, *Designing Education for the Future* (New York: Citation Press, 1968).

Phi Delta Kappa, *Values in American Education* (Bloomington, Ind.: Phi Delta Kappa, Inc., 1964).

Platt, John R., et al., *Dialog on Education* (New York: The Bobbs-Merrill Company, Inc., 1967).

Rubin, Louis J. (ed.), *Life Skills in School and Society* (Washington, D.C.: Association for Supervision and Curriculum Development, 1969).

Shoben, Edward Joseph Jr. (ed.), *Problems and Issues in Contemporary Education* (Glenview, Ill.: Scott Foresman and Company, 1966).

The Committee for the White House Conference on Education, *A Report to the President* (Washington, D.C.: U.S. Government Printing Office, 1956).

The President's Commission on National Goals, *Goals for Americans* (New York: The American Assembly, Columbia University, 1960).

U.S. Department of the Interior, Bureau of Education, *Report of the Committee on Secondary School Studies, Appointed at the Meeting of the National Education Association, July 9, 1892* (Washington, D.C.: Superintendent of Documents, U.S. Government Printing Office, 1893).

Part Two
Public Control
of
Education

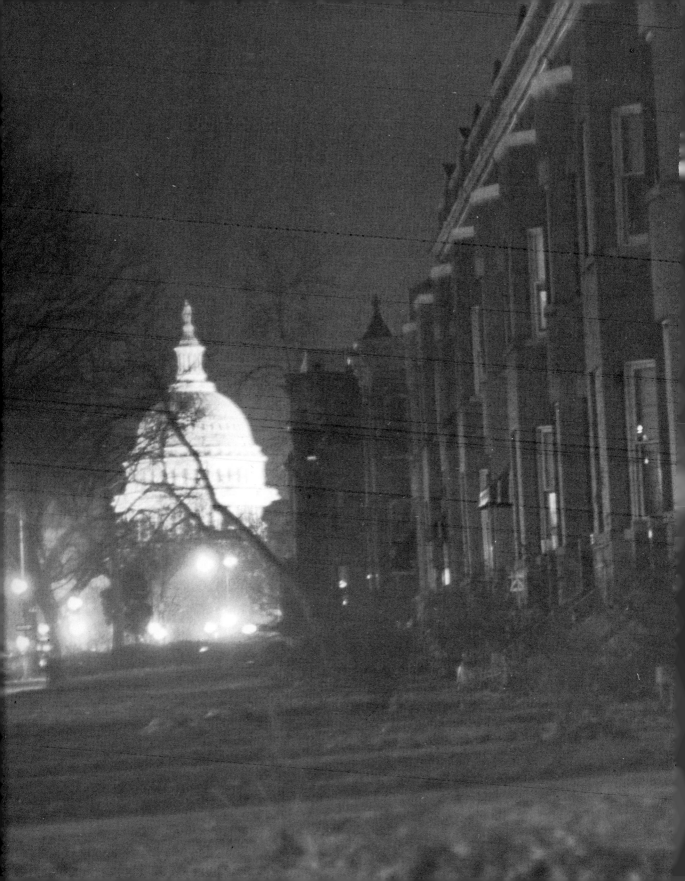

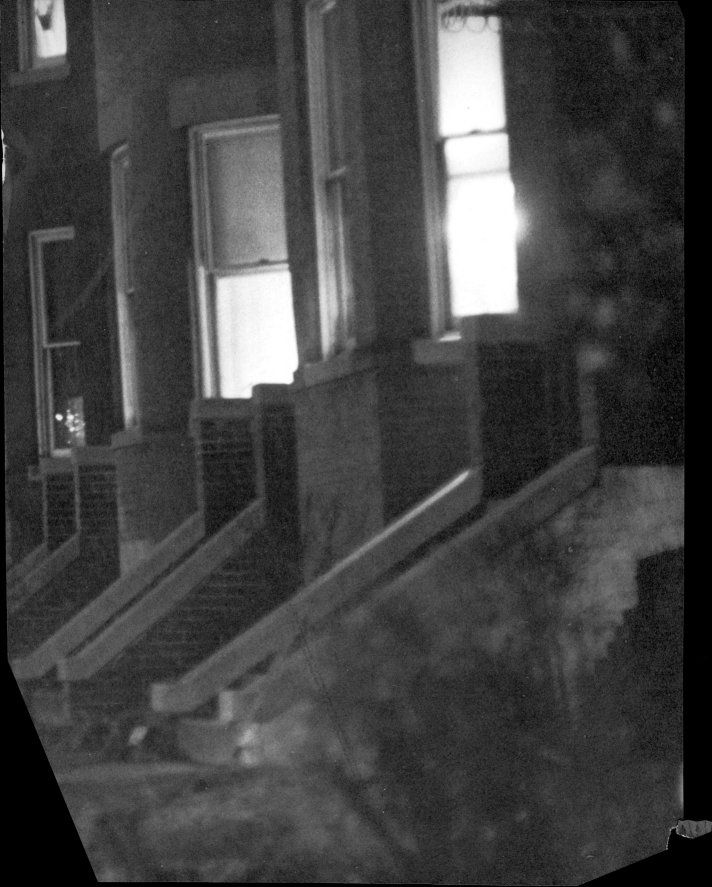

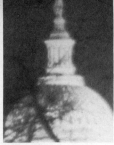

Chapter

3

Federal
Responsibility
for
Education

Formal education casts its influence across the face of the entire nation. It is a vital part of the lives of all communities whether rural or urban, inner city or suburban, industrial or residential. It is no respecter of race, religion, sex, politics, or economic status. It reaches into trailers and tenements as well as into mainline hotels and penthouses. Formal education is definitely big business, as the following statistics will attest.

In the fall of 1968, an estimated 36.7 million public and nonpublic school pupils were enrolled in the nation's elementary schools, 14.2 million in secondary schools, and 6.7 million in colleges and universities. These collectively make a total of 57.6 million.[1] In the same year, elementary school teachers totaled 1,227,000; secondary school teachers, 909,000; and teachers in higher education, 504,000.[2] In the fall of 1967, public school districts totaled 21,990.[3] In 1967, the nation spent approximately 33.0 billion to operate its elementary and secondary schools: public (29.2 billion), nonpublic ($3.8 billion).[4] This amount represented 6.9 percent of the gross national product. It also represented an operational expenditure of $623 for each student enrolled in public school.[5]

AN HISTORICAL OVERVIEW

This vast enterprise of formal education in the United States finds social sanction in a long tradition of favorable attitudes. The Anglo-Saxon tradition, for centuries now, has been as much an educational tradition as a political one. The ways of democracy truly are the ways of education. And freedom unquestionably thrives on a rich diet of education, whereas it withers on a diet of ignorance.

In the Colonial period, however, education was an agency less of the social-political world than of Christian orthodoxy. The Calvinist position, which then prevailed, went something like this. A personal

[1] Kenneth A. Simon and W. Vance Grant, *Digest of Educational Statistics,* OE-10024-68 (Washington, D.C.: U.S. Department of Health, Education, and Welfare, 1968), p. 2.

[2] Simon and Grant, p. 5.

[3] Simon and Grant, p. 44.

[4] Simon and Grant, p. 17.

[5] Simon and Grant, p. 61.

God created the universe, including all living things, in the literal manner described in *Genesis*. Adam, by sinning in the Garden of Eden, transmitted his depraved nature to all who followed. Man, because depraved, needs a savior to expiate his sins. As a mere sojourner on earth, his one and only important function is to ready himself for the afterlife. This he does through approved liturgy and personal meditation, with biblical knowledge basic to both. Thus, education's role, according to the Calvinist position, was first and foremost a religious one—to groom man for the hereafter—and only secondarily to prepare him for the practical demands of life here on earth.

Education's curriculum in early Colonial days revolved around the *New Testament* and the *Psalms*, around prayers, religious stories, moralistic maxims, and aphorisms. The secular features of the curriculum were regarded, at least theoretically, as little more than necessary means to a fundamentally religious end. Children intoned "In Adam's fall, We sinnèd all." In 1641 (ca.) John Cotton, the famous Puritan minister, wrote a short catechism, whose pious platitudes were to reach many generations of school children. It bore the ponderous title *Spiritual Milk for American Babes Drawn Out of the Breasts of Both Testaments for their Soul's Nourishment*. In 1662, Michael Wigglesworth's *Day of Doom* came into print. This publication graphically depicted Hell fire and damnation as the fate of those who rejected salvation through Christ. These are only two of the many religious curriculum materials that characterized education in early Colonial days.

Generally speaking, religion was either a central or supporting theme in every facet of formal education. It was obviously central when recitation of prayers and verses from the *Holy Scriptures* was a basic part of academic drill and when denominational publications were used as textbooks; it was little less so in hornbooks[6] and primers.[7] Schoolmasters, furthermore, exacted obedience, punished, and held up high standards of learning—all in the name of religion. In effect, religion with its many faces and trappings was almost as evident from Monday to Saturday in schoolhouses as on Sunday in churches. Benign or austere, it was very much present.

[6] The hornbook was a paddle-shaped piece of wood with parchment or horn covering it. The latter contained learning material pertaining to the alphabet, spelling, and other aspects of academic drill. (See illustrations on p. 39.)

[7] *The New England Primer*, published around 1700, is the best known of these. It is said to have sold three million copies during its academic lifetime. For further details, see Paul L. Ford (ed.), *The New England Primer* (New York: Dodd, Mead & Company, Inc.), 1899.

By the end of the seventeenth century, Calvinism was gradually mellowing, other milder faiths—the Quaker and Anglican in particular —were becoming increasingly influential, and rational secularism was gaining in influence. In addition, pulsations of nationalism were beginning to mount—first slowly, then rapidly—becoming intense around the middle of the eighteenth century. Political and economic considerations began to compete ever more actively and successfully with concern for the life hereafter.

These influences, in the composite, led to changes in educational views and patterns: to the concept that children are basically good, not basically depraved; to an increase in nonreligious curriculum materials; to motivation conceived more as an intrinsic than an extrinsic set of forces; to learning that emphasized understanding more than memory; to the need for man to question the status quo before accepting it.

A number of individuals, indirectly or directly, contributed to these changes. Rousseau, with his view that man is inherently noble and his emphasis on the values of sense empiricism and individual discovery, made a significant contribution. William Penn, in his *Reflections and Maxims,* made a similar contribution. Another Quaker, the revered Anthony Benezet, argued eloquently that education should be for all— Negro, Indian, and white man—and should be characterized by humanity and warmth on the part of educational leaders. Samuel Johnson and Benjamin Franklin, at midcentury, gave sanction to education's growing concern for the practical and the utilitarian.

By the end of the Colonial period, education was resting fairly comfortably on a social and political base. The religious base remained, but it was no longer dominant. The social-political-economic needs of a practical society were gaining ascendancy over unitary religious ones. Government, industry, and community affairs had to be attended to. Mounting differences with the mother country had to be resolved. The scholarly professions had to be served. Life in general was moving from the primitive simple to the sophisticated complex. As a result, the secular purposes of education became increasingly controlling.

The Colonies, confident of independence from England, bent to the task of formulating an official base for their anticipated new existence. This base, when finally developed, consisted of a composite of constitutional, statutory, and judicial pronouncements.

An aphorism often heard today is that education is a federal concern, a state responsibility, and a local function. It is a federal concern for the logical reason that no nation can perpetuate itself, much less grow, **55**

without the life-giving strength of formal education. Thus the most central and powerful of our cultural establishments, the federal government, has a role in education that is intrinsic, vital, and inescapable.

THE CONSTITUTION OF THE UNITED STATES AND EDUCATION

The Constitution of the United States depicts the role of education inferentially rather than specifically. The word education, in fact, does not appear a single time in the Constitution; yet the Government's posture toward education is a positive one. The Preamble and Article 1, Section 8, for instance, entrust the federal government with the "general welfare" of all the people. The Fourteenth Amendment makes the government a custodian and protector of the privileges and immunities of all the people. And even though the Tenth Amendment, through its so-called general clause, establishes the several states as operationally responsible for education, it does not for that reason consign the federal government to the role of a mere observer. Unquestionably, the federal government has a significant stake in education. How could the situation, in fact, be otherwise?

FEDERAL STATUTES AND EDUCATION

Congressional legislation has intermittently strengthened the national base of education, committing education to serve national as well as state and local purposes. The following selection of enactments, dating from 1785 to the present, provide an overview of the federal government's involvement in education.

Land Ordinance, 1785. Western expansion was one of the major problems confronting the nation in post-Revolutionary war days. But so was education. In the Land Ordinance of 1785, the Continental Congress, having decided to sell land in the Northwest Territory, conceived the following plan: to divide the land into townships, six miles long and six miles wide; to divide each township into 36 sections of 640 acres each; and to reserve one of these sections, the sixteenth in each township, "for the maintenance of public schools within the said township."

Under the provisions of this act, and its sequel of two years later, the federal government allocated 80 million acres of land to be used

for public school purposes. One writer refers to this as an "empire . . . one-third larger than the New England States combined."[8] Another says: "The area provided was approximately the size of Texas."[9]

Northwest Ordinance, 1787. This ordinance, adding to the provisions of the earlier one, is best known for its ringing declaration of faith in education: "Religion, morality, and knowledge being necessary to good government and the happiness of mankind, schools and the means of education shall forever be encouraged." Thus, several years prior to the ratification of the Constitution of the United States, the federal government was already making educational plans for the future of the fledgling nation.

Statehood Enabling Acts, 1802 for Ohio to 1959 for Hawaii. The federal government granted land as a bonus for statehood. Most states received two sections; Utah and Arizona, four.

Morrill Act, 1862. The government donated yet more land to the various states, this time 30,000 acres per congressman, for the founding of colleges. According to Tiedt: "The colleges and universities established under the Morrill Act now include sixty-eight institutions whose combined enrollment represents 20 percent of all undergraduates, while they constitute only 4 percent of the total number of colleges and universities in the country."[10] Land-grant institutions today include, among

[8] Paul Monroe, *Founding of the American Public School System* (New York: Crowell-Collier and Macmillan, Inc., 1940), p. 196.

[9] Sidney W. Tiedt, *The Role of the Federal Government in Education* (New York: Oxford University Press, 1966), p. 16.

[10] Tiedt, p. 18.

others, the Universities of California and Illinois, Massachusetts Institute of Technology, Michigan State University, Ohio State University, and University of Texas.

Hatch Act, 1887. This act allocated funds to the states for the establishment of agricultural experimental stations in land-grant colleges.

Smith-Hughes Act, 1917. This now famous piece of legislation allocated monies to the states for support of vocational and home-economics education in the schools. The original allocation of less than $2 million in 1917 rose to a total of approximately $7 million in 1960. The act set forth specific criteria, administrative and program, that the states had to meet in order to qualify for appropriations. Thus, controversially, it established the federal government as a controlling as well as a funding agency of education. The George Dean Act of 1936 and the George Barden Act of 1946 broadened the base of the original Smith-Hughes Act.

Lanham Act, 1941. The purpose of this act was to cushion the impact made on local school systems by newly erected military establishments. The schools in such places, for instance, as Norfolk, Virginia; San Diego, California; and Fort Leonard Wood, Missouri; were in dire straits as a result of the mass influx of the children of the federally employed.

The Serviceman's Readjustment Act, 1944. This so-called GI bill guaranteed to returning servicemen educational opportunities scarcely even dreamed of before—and all liberally subsidized by the federal government. Veterans were entitled to approximately one month of education at the institution of their choice for every month's military service. Furthermore, living expenses for themselves and their families were financed by federal funds. Unquestionably, the Serviceman's Readjustment Act gave a lift to the nation's entire economy.

National School Lunch Act, 1946. This act constituted one of the federal government's earlier involvements with poverty in the schools. It provided free or low-cost lunches to the indigent, depending on need. A school milk program was added in 1954. The appropriation for 1947 was $75 million, and for 1949, $92 million. Funds were made available both to public and to nonprofit private schools. The program has to provide meals on a nonprofit basis. Lunches, in the words of the law, have to "meet minimum nutrition requirements prescribed by the Secretary of Agriculture on the basis of tested nutrition research."

National Science Foundation Act, 1950. This important piece of legislation brought the National Science Foundation into being, establish-

ing it as an independent instrument of the Executive branch. Its functions are to: (1) promote scientific research, (2) provide fellowships and institutes for the training of scientists and teachers of science, (3) prepare and disseminate information, and (4) improve course content. It is controlled by a director and a board of 24 members, all appointed by the President of the United States. It serves both education and industry. Of the $125 million it spent in 1965, 40 percent went into education and 60 percent into industry.

Federal Impact Laws (PL 815 and 874), 1950. These extended the Lanham Act to cushion the effects of the Korean War on local school systems.

National Defense Education Act, 1958. This federal law, 85–864, was America's counter to Sputnik of the preceding year. Its primary concern was to update mathematics and the natural sciences in the public school curriculum. The methods consisted of stepping up the research performed by multidiscipline representatives and granting fellowships to teachers for attendance at regional institutions. Two other important concerns were the updating of modern languages and the improvement of educational guidance services for the gifted. The law authorized the expenditure of over one billion dollars for the period 1958–1962.

As originally conceived, the NDEA bypassed the humanities, the social sciences, and the applied arts. From 1964 on, it appropriated limited sums for the updating of English, the social sciences, education of librarians, and education of disadvantaged youth. Yet the emphasis is still one-sidedly in support of the natural sciences, mathematics, the modern languages, and educational guidance for the gifted.

Manpower Development and Training Act, 1962. This appropriated monies for the training of those generally regarded as unemployable because of physical, mental or emotional handicaps.

Vocational Education Act, 1963. The stated purpose was to "improve existing programs of vocational education, to develop part-time employment for youth who need the earnings from such employment to continue their vocational training on a full-time basis." The act authorized appropriations of $60 million for 1964, $118 million for 1965, and $177 million for 1966 to be spent for the vocational purposes covered by the act.

Economic Opportunity Act, 1964. This so-called war-on-poverty act is the one under which the Head Start Program for economically underprivileged prekindergarten children and the Neighborhood Centers

59

for adolescents are programmed. The thesis underlying the Head Start Program is that the culturally disadvantaged will be better prepared for kindergarten and first grade if they have an enriched preliminary experience first. Medical, dental, and counseling services are a vital part of the program.

Civil Rights Act, 1964. This act withholds federal monies from school systems that fail to meet governmentally established standards of racial desegregation.

Elementary and Secondary Education Act, 1965. This act was passed initially for the period 1965–1968, but was subsequently extended. It appropriated just under one and one-half billion dollars for the following purposes: (1) education of children from low-income families, (2) upgrading of school-library resources, (3) the establishment of regional educational centers (on a multiagency basis) to provide otherwise unavailable services to nearby schools and other public agencies, (4) educational research and training, and (5) the strengthening of state departments of education. Almost one billion dollars was appropriated for purpose (1) alone.

Higher Education Act, 1965. This act was passed for the benefit of professional individuals who needed additional education, for college students from low-income families, and for the upgrading of institutions of higher learning that were having financial difficulties.

National Foundation on the Arts and the Humanities Act, 1965. Long in coming, this act was a departure from the decade-long preoccupation of the federal government with the natural sciences. It conceded that "a high civilization must not limit its efforts to science and technology alone but must give full value and support to the other great branches of man's scholarly and cultural activities." For the three-year period 1966–1969, it made a modest annual allocation of approximately $20 million for projects, productions, and workshops in the various areas of the arts and humanities.

The term *arts* as used in the act embraces

music (instructional and vocal), dance, drama, folk art, creative writing, architecture and allied fields, painting, sculpture, photography, graphic and craft arts, industrial design, costume and fashion design, motion pictures, television, radio, tape and sound recording, and the arts related to the presentation, perfection, execution, and extension of such major art forms.

The term *humanities* embraces

language, both modern and classic; linguistics; literature; history; jurisprudence; philosophy; archeology; the history, criticism, theory, and prac-

tice of the arts; and those aspects of the social sciences which have humanistic content and employ humanistic methods.

The International Education Act of 1966. The implemented outcomes of this act are undergraduate and graduate centers, located primarily in colleges and universities, designed to advance the cause of international understanding. The methods of implementation consist of classroom instruction, training institutes, research, and cultural exchanges of personnel.

The opening words of the act capsule its purposes:

> The Congress hereby finds and declares that a knowledge of other countries is of the utmost importance in promoting mutual understanding and cooperation between nations; that strong educational resources are a necessary base for strengthening our relations with other countries; that this and future generations of Americans should be assured ample opportunity to develop to the fullest extent possible their intellectual capacities in all areas of knowledge pertaining to other countries, peoples, and cultures; and that it is therefore both necessary and appropriate for the Federal Government to assist in the development of resources and trained personnel in academic and professional fields, and to coordinate the existing and future programs of the Federal Government in international education, to meet the requirements of world leadership.

Education Professions Development Act, 1967. This act, PL 90-35, revises the Higher Education Act of 1965. It extends the Teachers Corps through the academic year 1969–1970. More important, it suggests and underwrites means of attracting added qualified personnel into formal education. The personnel sources it taps consist, among others, of capable high school youth; former teachers who are interested in returning to teaching; and artists, craftsmen, artisans, scientists, and persons from other professions and vocations, including homemaking, who are interested in taking on part-time or temporary teaching responsibilities. The act allocated approximately $340 million, beginning July 1, 1968, to state educational agencies, colleges and universities, and interested teacher candidates.

All these statutory acts reveal the federal government as dynamically involved in educational affairs. Since 1958 the extent of its involvement has increased dramatically. Whether this has been accompanied by a comparable increase in federal control is a heated question. It is my considered opinion that although federal control of education is definitely on the upswing, it is still within tolerable bounds. And it must remain within these bounds if education is to continue as a state responsibility and a local function.

61

In this regard, a distinction should be made between aid designed to serve the welfare of individuals, singly or collectively, and aid designed to exploit individuals in the national interest. The various land-grant acts of the past, and the current programs for the disadvantaged fall definitely into the service or welfare category. So did the NDEA Act of 1958, so long as it remained true to its announced emergency function. To the extent, however, that it continues to subsidize the natural sciences beyond the point of emergency need and to sell short the humanities and the social sciences, the federal government will be at least on the fringes of exploitation of the individual. Federal interests, like state and local interests, need to be served in a balanced way within the frame of the nation's humanistic traditions. Ideally, federal interests should be compatible with state and local, as well as individual, concerns. When the interests are at wide variance with one another, the welfare of the individual should be the deciding factor.

THE FEDERAL JUDICIARY AND EDUCATION

The Constitution of the United States and federal legislation make up two sides of an equilateral triangle of authority in education. The federal judiciary through its network of courts constitutes the third. The latter comes straight from the traditions of English common law, in which judicial rulings rest on the precedent of previous decisions. Common law operates within the frame of the principle of *stare decisis*—"let the decision stand." For example, private schools today are uncontestedly legal because in 1925 the Oregon case of *Pierce v. Society of the Sisters of the Holy Name of Jesus and Mary* established their legality. As another example, foreign language instruction is legal in the nation's schools today because in 1881 the Supreme Court of Illinois, in the case of *Powell v. Board of Education,* ruled that foreign language instruction was legal so long as the basic medium of communication was the English language. This decision was confirmed a number of times thereafter in other states.

However, precedent does not operate as an absolute and immutable force. If it did, it would constitute a formidable enemy of social change. Precedent governs so long as the climate of social opinion remains essentially the same. It gives ground when the climate reflects significant change. Illustrative, in this regard, is the Supreme Court case of *Brown v. Board of Education,* 1954. As far back as 1896, the Supreme Court of the land, in the case of *Plessy v. Ferguson,* had legitimatized the practice of racial segregation on trains, and, by inference, in schools. This came to be known as the separate-but-equal doctrine. In 1954, however, the Supreme Court, sensitive to the change that had taken place in public opinion, ruled that discrimination based on race, color, creed, or national origin was illegal in the schools.

Organization of the Federal Judiciary

It is important at this point for the reader to have an overview of the judicial system of the United States. The federal judiciary embraces courts at three levels. Alone and eminent at the top is the Supreme Court of the United States, the only court sanctioned as a specific entity by the Constitution. Article III gave it birth: "The judicial power of the United States shall be vested in one supreme court, and in such inferior courts as the Congress may from time to time ordain and

63

establish." The Supreme Court has jurisdiction over cases in which treaties and maritime disputes are substantive issues, and in which the following parties are disputants: The United States, two or more states, one state and a foreign power, one state and a foreign citizen, one state and a citizen of another state, citizens of two different states, and members of the diplomatic-consular service. The Supreme Court is a trial court (a court of primary jurisdiction) in cases involving ambassadors, public ministers, and consuls. In all other cases, it is an appellate court (a court of judicial review).

In its appellate role, the Supreme Court concerns itself with the legality of state constitutional provisions, state laws, and federal laws. In this role, it has had many confrontations with education. The sensitive pressure points have been the First Amendment, in connection with religion in the schools; the Fifth Amendment, in connection with loyalty oath cases and other cases pertaining to individual rights; and the Fourteenth Amendment, in connection with the Negro's right to "equal protection of the laws." Yet it should be remembered that the Supreme Court, in its appellate capacity, acts only on cases that have moved spirally through the proper lower courts, and only then on cases it elects to consider.

Regional (or circuit) courts, 11 in number, have status second only to that of the Supreme Court itself. They are appellate in function, reviewing, for the most part, cases tried in the lower district courts. There are 88 of the latter, which are the trial courts within the federal judiciary, at least one in existence in every state.

In addition to these federal courts, each state has its court system. The state supreme court (which is never a federal court) stands at the pinnacle. Eleven states additionally have intermediate appellate courts. And all have trial courts of varying importance, with the justice-of-the-peace court usually lowest in order.

Within this organizational frame, the book's focus now shifts to some court cases that reveal the nature and extent of the federal government's involvement, past and present, in education. We note at the beginning that the vast majority of cases pertaining to education start and stop at the state level. Even those that through appellate channels get to a state supreme court usually stop short of federal involvement. Thus, the ensuing statement, though general, is a valid one, namely, that individual states adjudicate almost all cases that fall into the following educational categories: the school as a corporate entity under **64** state control, school organization, school finance, attendance policies,

rights of pupils, rights and responsibilities of school authority figures, instructional materials, teaching methods, and most curriculum matters.

However, the federal government and certain state or local educational authorities have been court antagonists many times over two controversial social issues: (1) the status of religion in the schools, and (2) the status of minority racial groups, particularly Negroes, in the schools. The most noteworthy cases in each of these two areas have reached the Supreme Court of the United States; most have not gone beyond the 11 federal circuit courts. The following cases, irrespective of the level at which ultimately adjudicated, stand as fundamental landmarks in education.

The Federal Judiciary and Religion

Apropos of religion, the federal government and education, from Colonial times to the present, have had differences in regard to these four issues: the status of private schools, released time for religious instruction, the status of religious rituals in the schools, and the right of schools to enforce adherence to patriotic symbols.

The status of private schools Any history of American education reveals the existence of two categories of schools, public and private, **65**

with both generally regarded as legitimate. Challenging this legitimacy, the State of Oregon, in 1922, passed a statute requiring all children to attend public schools. Three years later, in the now famous case of *Pierce v. Society of the Sisters of the Holy Names of Jesus and Mary,* 268 U.S. 510, 45 S. Ct. 571 (1925), the Supreme Court ruled the statute to be unconstitutional. While recognizing the right of the state to set standards for and to regulate all schools within its borders, the Court ruled that:

> The fundamental theory of liberty upon which all governments in this Union repose excludes any general power of the State to standardize its children by forcing them to accept instruction from public teachers only. The child is not the mere creature of the State; those who nurture him and direct his destiny have the right, coupled with the high duty, to recognize and prepare him for additional obligations.

The Supreme Court of the United States thus established the legality of all private schools that met acceptable state standards. What it did not establish, however, was the right of states to finance private schools, in part or in full. It came to grips with this issue later. One instance was in the case of *Cochran et al. v. Louisiana State Board of Education et al.,* 281 U.S. 370 S.C. 335 (1930). The State of Louisiana had passed a statute authorizing schools to furnish free textbooks to students in attendance at both parochial and public schools. Did this law make the state an ally of denominational religion? The Supreme Court ruled that it did not, holding that textbooks exist for the benefit of children, not of a school or of a religion. "The school children and the state alone are the beneficiaries." The Court held, however, that "Among these books, . . . none is to be . . . adapted to religious instruction."

The Cochran case gave birth to the so-called *child-benefit* principle in regard to nonpublic education. A second case, *Everson v. Board of Education of Ewing Tp.,* 330 U.S. 167 S. Ct. 504 (1947), enlarged the child-benefit base to include the transportation of children to private schools. The legality of the transportation issue depended on an interpretation of the statement in the First Amendment: "Congress shall make no law respecting an establishment of religion." The court's interpretation was this: "The Amendment requires the state to be a neutral in its relations with groups of religious believers and nonbelievers; it does not require the state to be their adversary."

Still to be ascertained and drawn, however, are the outward limits of the child-benefit principle. Do these limits embrace teacher salaries,

capital expenditures, and school maintenance costs? At present, they certainly do not. In the future, they might.

Yet as long as the First Amendment continues as the standard, governmental aid will have to stop short of the point where denominational religion begins. The courts will continue to search for and mark off this theoretical point. But it will always be an elusive one; and it will change from time to time.

Released time for religious instruction   According to at least one of the more valid sources, the "practice of schools to release children during the school day in order that they may receive religious instruction had its beginning in Gary, Indiana, in 1914."[11] This controversial practice "came to court" in the mid-1940s. It was ultimately adjudicated by the Supreme Court in the case of *People of State of Illinois ex rel v. Board of Education of School District No. 21, Champaign County, Illinois,* 333 U.S. 203, 68 S. Ct. 461 (1948).

The Champaign school system had incorporated into its curriculum, for grades 4–9, a unit on religion, taught cooperatively by clergymen from Catholic, Jewish, and selected Protestant faiths. Classes met 30 minutes per week, with attendance voluntary. Students who elected not to attend the religious classes engaged in substitute activities elsewhere in the school building. Mrs. Vashti McCollum, a parent and school patron, initiated action for mandamus (a court order to demand law enforcement) against the Board of Education. Her contention was that the practice violated the First Amendment in respect to the establishment of religion, and the Fourteenth Amendment in respect to the privileges and immunities of citizens. The Supreme Court agreed, by a 5–4 vote. Justice Black concluded the majority opinion with this:

> Here not only are the State's tax-supported public school buildings used for the dissemination of religious doctrines. The State also affords sectarian groups an invaluable aid in that it helps to provide pupils for their religious classes through use of the State's compulsory public school machinery. This is not separation of church and state.

The McCollum case thus made it illegal for education to utilize school property for the purpose of instruction in formal-religion.

Four years later, the Supreme Court ruled on the legality of religious instruction, on a released-time basis, outside the limits of school property. The case in point was *Zorach v. Clausen,* 343 U.S. 306, 72 S. Ct.

---

[11] Robert R. Hamilton and Paul R. Mort, *The Law and Public Education,* Second Edition (New York: The Foundation Press, Inc., 1959), p. 29.

679 (1952). Justice Douglas, spokesman for the majority in an 8–1 vote, summed up the issue as follows:

New York City has a program which permits its public schools to release students during the school day so that they may leave the school buildings and school grounds and go to religious centers for religious instruction or devotional exercises. A student is released on written request of his parents. Those not released stay in the classrooms. The churches make weekly reports to the schools, sending a list of children who have been released from public school but who have not reported for religious instruction.

The Court held that religious instruction off school grounds on an incidental basis was not in violation of the First Amendment. By "incidental," the Court had in mind a Catholic attending mass on a "Holy Day of Obligation," or a Jew being "excused for Yom Kippur," or a Protestant taking an afternoon off "for a family baptismal ceremony." The Court, however, avoided the issue of how much released time would be considered reasonable.

The status of religious rituals in public schools   For years, state courts have ruled in a surprising variety of ways on the legitimacy of such public school practices as *Bible* reading, prayer, and hymn singing. The following questions have been axial. Do rituals that are optional in the schools have different legal status from those that are required? What *Bible* is the "true" *Bible:* the King James, the Standard Revised, the Douay, or some other? Is occasional *Bible* reading or prayer, in a public school, religious in a denominational sense or social sense? Do religious rituals in schools have a different status from those in a courtroom, at a patriotic gathering, or at an opening session of Congress?

In 1962 and 1963, respectively, the Supreme Court brought these and related questions to judicial review in three significant cases. The first was the case of *Engel v. Vitale,* 370 U.S. 421, 82 S. Ct. 1261 (1962). The New York State Board of Regents had composed and recommended that schools adopt the following prayer: "Almighty God, we acknowledge our dependence upon Thee, and we beg Thy blessings upon us, our parents, our teachers, and our country." The Board of Education of Union Free School District No. 9 in Long Island officially ordered that the prayer be recited daily following the salute to the flag. Parents of ten pupils from various religious faiths "took the case to court."

In a 6–1 decision (Justices Frankfurter and White abstaining), the Supreme Court held the prayer to be unconstitutional. Justice Black, as spokesman for the majority, wrote:

It is neither sacrilegious nor antireligious to say that each separate government in this country should stay out of the business of writing or sanctioning official prayers and leave that purely religious function to the people themselves and to those the people choose to look to for religious guidance.

Religious rituals in the schools underwent yet further analysis in the cases of *Schempp v. School District of Abington Township,* 201 F. Supp. 815 (Pa., 1962); and in *Murray v. Curlett,* 228 Md. 239, F. Supp. 179 (1962). In the first case, a Pennsylvania statute required pupils and teachers to read ten verses from the Holy Bible, without comment, at the opening of school each day. In the second, the City of Baltimore required the reading of the Bible along with recitation of "The Lord's Prayer," although schools, upon receipt of written requests from parents or guardians, excused pupils from attendance at these religious exercises. The Supreme Court reviewed the two as companion cases. At the trial-court level, Maryland had alleged the *Bible*-reading rituals to be secular in nature, with "promotion of moral values" their intent. The Supreme Court ruled otherwise. Furthermore, the Court held the optional-attendance feature of the Murray case to be immaterial and irrelevant. In both cases, the Supreme Court ruled the exercises to be in violation of the First Amendment.

Justice Clark, in his opinion for the majority, concluded with this statement:

> The place of religion in our society is an exalted one, achieved through a long tradition of reliance on the home, the church, and the inviolable citadel of the individual heart and mind. We have come to recognize through bitter experience that it is not within the power of government to invade that citadel, whether its purpose or effect be to aid or oppose, to advance or retard. In the relationship between man and religion, the State is firmly committed to a position of neutrality. Though the application of that rule requires interpretation of a delicate sort, the rule itself is clearly and concisely stated in the words of the First Amendment. . . .

The Vitale, the Schempp, and the Murray decisions eased out a religious tradition that for decades had held on tenaciously. Yet its demise had to come. In the last analysis, organized religion is more than a body of beliefs about man and God—it commits man to the act of worship, which is untenable in public schools.

Despite the aforementioned rulings, however, religious instruction in public schools is legitimate in the following circumstances: when integral to courses such as world or ancient history, when an essential part of a literary work such as *The Scarlet Letter* or *Arrowsmith,* and when central in an elective course in comparative religions. But even **69**

in these instances, a clear line between "instruction about" and "indoctrination in" (including worship) needs to be drawn.

The right, if any, of public schools to enforce adherence to patriotic rituals The priority in public schools of religious belief over the observance of patriotic rituals, or vice versa, constituted the themes of two important court cases in 1940 and 1943. The first was the case of *Minersville School District v. Gobitis,* 310 U.S. 568, 60 S. Ct. 1010 (1940). In this, the Supreme Court addressed itself to a regulation adopted in 1935 by the School Board of Minersville, Pennsylvania, requiring all pupils and teachers to salute the American flag as part of a daily patriotic ritual. The penalty to pupils for nonadherence was expulsion. By a 5–4 vote, the Court held the regulation to be legal. It stated that "The act of saluting the flag does not prevent a pupil, no matter what his religious belief may be, from acknowledging the spiritual sovereignty of Almighty God, by rendering to God the things that are God's. . . ."

Encouraged by the Gobitis case, the West Virginia Board of Education, in 1942, passed a resolution requiring all pupils and teachers, daily, to join in the "Pledge of Allegiance to the Flag." The resolution stipulated that "refusal to salute the flag [would] be regarded as an act of insubordination and . . . be dealt with accordingly."

Several members of the Jehovah's Witnesses faith refused to abide by the resolution, taking the case to court. The plaintiffs, found guilty by the trial court, appealed the case. As a final step, the Supreme Court, despite its previous decision in the Gobitis case, moved in to assess once again the issue of which should have priority when religious conviction conflicts with enforced participation in patriotic rituals. The case bears the label of *West Virginia State Board of Education v. Barnette,* 319 U.S. 624, 63 S. Ct. 1178 (1943). Interestingly, Chief Justice Hughes and Justice McReynolds had recently retired. Justices Jackson and Rutledge had replaced them, and Justice Stone had become the Chief Justice. By a 6–3 vote, the Court overruled its previous decision. Justice Jackson, writing the opinion for the majority, stated eloquently:

> If there is any fixed star in our constitutional constellation, it is that no official, high or petty, can prescribe what shall be orthodox in politics, nationalism, religion, or other matters of opinion, or force citizens to confess by word or act their faith therein . . .

> We think the action of the local authorities in compelling the flag salute and pledge transcends constitutional limitations on their power and invades the sphere of intellect and spirit which it is the purpose of the First Amendment to reserve from all official control.

The Federal Judiciary and Race

During the past several decades, race has taken over from religion as a major source of controversy between education and the law. Until the Civil War, the prevailing policy throughout most of the country was to keep Negroes ignorant, or, at best, to educate them only for menial responsibilities. For a 30-year period following the Civil War, education for Negroes was aimless and uneven. Then in 1896, as mentioned earlier, the Supreme Court left-handedly sanctioned for education the separate-but-equal doctrine. The case in point was *Plessy v. Ferguson,* 163 U.S. 537, 16 S. Ct. 1138 (1896), its central theme being the seating of Negroes on trains. This doctrine dominated educational organization for more than a half century, and might have dominated it even longer except for the country's lackadaisical adherence to the "equal" part of the doctrine. Far from equal, educational programs and facilities throughout most of the country notoriously favored Caucasian groups at the expense of Negroid groups.

On May 17, 1954, in the memorable case of *Brown v. Board of Education of Topeka,* 347 U.S. 483, 74 S. Ct. 686 (1954), the Supreme Court repudiated the separate-but-equal doctrine. The Brown case constituted a review of four lower-court cases, one each from Delaware, Kansas, South Carolina, and Virginia. In all of them, "minors of the Negro race . . . were seeking admission to the public schools of their community on a nonsegregated basis." All the plaintiffs contended "that segregated public schools are not 'equal' and cannot be made 'equal,' and that hence they are deprived of the equal protection of the laws." The Court's decision was forthright and unequivocal:

> We conclude that in the field of public education the doctrine of "separate but equal" has no place. Separate educational facilities are inherently unequal. Therefore we hold that the plaintiffs and others similarly situated for whom the actions have been brought are, by reason of the segregation complained of, deprived of the equal protection of the laws guaranteed by the Fourteenth Amendment.

Since 1954, the courts have been busy ruling on questions related to the Brown-case decree. The story goes something like this.

1. Desegregation can take place gradually, but school authorities have to show good faith in carrying out the decree: *Brown v. Board of Education of Topeka,* 349 U.S. 294, 75 S. Ct. 753 (1955).

2. But the pace of desegregation cannot be too gradual. Little Rock, for instance, employed a number of subterfuges, one being the danger

71

of white hostility, which were ruled against in the case of *Cooper v. Aaron,* 358 U.S. 1, 78 S. Ct. 1401 (1958). In the cases of *Goss v. Board of Education* [Tenn.] 301 F. Supp. (2d) 164 (1962), and of *Mapp v. Board of Education* [Tenn.] 203 F. Supp. 843 (1962), a ten- to twelve-year period of implementation was deemed excessive.

3. Gerrymandering school boundaries (drawing boundaries in favor of a particular group) with segregation the aim is illegal: *Evans v. Buchanan,* 207 F. Supp. 820 (1962). Yet the law has stopped short of demanding schools to redistrict with desegregation the sole goal.

The Supreme Court during the past two decades unquestionably has advanced the cause of racial equality. Its precedent has been the spirit of humanism expressed in our basic legal documents. What is needed now is for education to take over from law with a program so steeped in humanistic values that social change will follow the path of peace rather than violence.

A POSITION STATEMENT

The federal government—through the Constitution, through legislation, and through evolving law—is making its presence increasingly felt at all levels of formal education. And the federal government, it should be remembered, is an institution of the people and by the people. It is neither a vindictive monster nor a messianic entity. It is what people make it.

The federal government plays its best role when it champions the humanistic rights of all the people, the right of optimum development being one of these. In this role, it remains neutral before such value terms as white, black, Jew, Gentile, Catholic, Protestant. But it is not neutral before such other value terms as privileged or underprivileged, high or low per capita expenditures for education, and education or miseducation. Far from being neutral, as a government of *all* the people, it has a mandate to take action on such inequities as the following.

In 1967–1968, the average salary of teachers throughout the nation was $7,296. In Mississippi, however, it was $4,735; in Alaska, $9,658.[12]

In the same year, as indicated in Table 3.1, the current educational expenditure per pupil (in average daily attendance) in the lowest three and highest three states, respectively, were as follows: Mississippi, $346; South Carolina, $427; and Alabama, $403; New Jersey, $807;

72   [12] Simon and Grant, p. 43. See Chap. 17 for further details.

Alaska, $976; and New York, $982. This disparity far exceeds the cost-of-living differentials in the various regions.

TABLE 3.1 ESTIMATED OPERATIONAL EXPENDITURE PER PUPIL IN AVERAGE DAILY ATTENDANCE IN PUBLIC ELEMENTARY AND SECONDARY DAY SCHOOLS, BY STATE: 1967–1968

State	Current Expenditure	State	Current Expenditure
Alabama	$403	Montana	$674
Alaska	976	Nebraska	492
Arizona	640	Nevada	626
Arkansas	441	New Hampshire	571
California	639	New Jersey	807
Colorado	621	New Mexico	640
Connecticut	715	New York	982
Delaware	665	North Carolina	461
District of Columbia	693	North Dakota	554
Florida	554	Ohio	591
Georgia	506	Oklahoma	547
Hawaii	659	Oregon	664
Idaho	515	Pennsylvania	657
Illinois	621	Rhode Island	721
Indiana	612	South Carolina	427
Iowa	580	South Dakota	586
Kansas	582	Tennessee	461
Kentucky	475	Texas	493
Louisiana	618	Utah	512
Maine	490	Vermont	615
Maryland	702	Virginia	554
Massachusetts	728	Washington	613
Michigan	628	West Virginia	484
Minnesota	725	Wisconsin	691
Mississippi	346	Wyoming	690
Missouri	532		

Source: Simon and Grant, *Digest of Educational Statistics,* p. 62.

In the same year, Mississippi, with a per capita income of $1,751, spent 5.57 percent of it on education; and Arkansas, with a per capita income of $2,015, spent 5.12 percent of it on education. Comparable statistics for the District of Columbia were $3,969 and 3.73 percent; for Connecticut, $3,678 and 3.88 percent.[13]

[13] Simon and Grant, p. 61.

These statistics, as merely a sample of the many that might be presented, reveal unevenness of educational opportunity as a national characteristic. One reason for this unevenness lies in the federal government's notorious propensity for dealing with lesser educational problems while turning away from the greater need for equalization legislation across a broad national front. In special legislation, the record is reasonably good. For example, when the vocational problem began to smolder early in the century, the federal government countered with the Smith-Hughes Act. Again, when the national defense seemed threatened by Soviet technological advances, the federal government responded with the National Defense Education Act.

However, the country's educational establishment requires more than emergency attention from the federal government. Far more than that, it requires an equalization plan conceived by the best educational minds available. I propose that these educators establish criteria against which any local educational program could be adjudged adequate or inadequate. The federal government would then, on an ability-to-pay arrangement, underwrite the necessary costs of an adequate program in every one of the nation's school systems. Of necessity it would work procedurally through the states in implementing the plan.

The task of conceiving and implementing such a plan admittedly would challenge all concerned with its complexities. But what is the alternative? Impoverished communities perpetuating themselves for want of adequate educational opportunities for the young? Conceivably so, but the American ideal demands more.

A reasonably high educational floor everywhere in the country, although not a panacea, would accomplish the following ends. First, it would bring the nation more in line with the stated educational goals it has traditionally espoused. Second, it would eliminate the blackboard jungles. Third, and most important, it would substitute dignity for indignity, and hope for despair in the ranks of the have-nots. The thesis here is that the federal government, as an agency of last resort, needs to neutralize the extremes of social deprivation, including educational deprivation, when those agencies with primary responsibility are unable to accomplish that same outcome.

THE UNITED STATES OFFICE OF EDUCATION

When the country was young, the enterprise of education, at the federal level, developed more by trial and error than by purpose. However, as

the country matured and educational problems became increasingly more complex, the lack of formal organization and administration became apparent. Thus the Congress, in 1867, brought into being the Office of Education. The law decreed as follows:

> There shall be established, at the city of Washington, a department of education, for the purpose of collecting such statistics and facts as shall show the condition and progress of education in the several states and territories, and of diffusing such information respecting the organization and management of schools, and school systems, and methods of teaching, as shall aid the people of the United States in the establishment and maintenance of efficient school systems, and otherwise promote the cause of education through the country.

The law further stipulated that the Office of Education would be headed by a Commissioner of Education, to be appointed by the President. The salary was set at $4,000 per annum. His staff was to consist of three clerks, at salaries of $2,000, $1,800, and $1,600, respectively. Henry Bernard, Connecticut legislator, lawyer, and educator became the first Commissioner; John Eaton, a former Civil War general from Tennessee, the second.

From a humble beginning in 1867, the Office of Education has grown tremendously during the first century of its existence. The operating budget, which was $13,000 in 1867, was approximately 15 million dollars in 1964. In 1966, the office disbursed only slightly less than three and a half billion dollars.

The work force, which consisted of only three clerks in 1867, had risen to a total of 2623 employees by 1966.[14] A subsidiary of the Department of Health, Education, and Welfare, the U.S. Office of Education is organized into the following components.[15]

1. *A Commissioner of Education*
2. *Four Program Bureaus:* for elementary and secondary education, adult and vocational education, higher education, and research
3. *Seven Office Elements:* for international education, federal-states relations, administration, information, legislation, program planning and evaluation, and contracts and construction service
4. *Four Service Elements:* Office of Equal Educational Opportunity,

[14] Special Subcommittee on Education, *Study of the U.S. Office of Education* (Washington, D.C.: U.S. Government Printing Office, 1967), p. 2.
[15] Accurate as of 1966, the information comes from Office of the Federal Register, *United States Government Organization 1966-67* (Washington, D.C.: U.S. Government Printing Office, 1966), pp. 366–67.

Office of Disadvantaged and Handicapped, National Center for Educational Statistics, and Commission for Field Services

The U.S. Office of Education operates nine regional offices in Atlanta, Boston, Charlottesville, Chicago, Dallas, Denver, Kansas City, New York, and San Francisco. Functionally, it collects and disseminates educational information and data; enters into contractural arrangements with cooperating institutions and agencies; provides consultative services; administers grants; and, alone or with other agencies, operates selected educational programs. The 110 new titles that appeared in 1962 in its publication list attest to the size of this one function.

Some other agencies through which the federal government implements its growing educational program are the Departments of Defense, State, Agriculture, and Interior; the National Science Foundation; and the Veterans Administration. Whether the government should canopy these under the United States Office of Education, I leave for others to discuss.

To Stimulate Thought

1. React to the statement that education serves the cause of religion, liberally viewed, by developing the powers of reflective thinking.

2. It has been suggested that the federal government develop a national curriculum and impose it on all school systems in the country. Take a stand, pro or con, on this proposition, and justify your position.

3. Do you agree with the author that the federal government, from the late fifties to the middle sixties, went too far in building up the natural sciences at the expense of the humanities and the social sciences? Elaborate your view. If you can find time, read C. P. Snow's provocative treatment of this issue in *The Two Cultures and the Scientific Revolution.*

4. Do you approve of the recent or current antipoverty programs, which have been subsidized liberally by the federal government? Defend your stand.

5. Distinguish between legislative and judicial controls by the federal government over education.

6. Elaborate the statement that the Supreme Court has appellate powers primarily and thus spends most of its time in the process of judicial review.

7. Many feel that the Supreme Court erred in ruling as it did on *Bible* reading and prayer that are engaged in for "mood" purposes in schools. What is your position on this controversial issue?

8. Defend the statement that an elective course in comparative religion, offered at the high school level, probably falls within the frame of existing law.

9. Which should have priority, religion or patriotism, when the two are in conflict? Elaborate.

10. Define the term *gerrymandering* in respect to school boundaries.

11. Should the courts force school systems, irrespective of population makeup, to combine the races—when the several races are in proximity, that is?

12. Under what circumstances is it likely for the Supreme Court to go counter to a previously rendered decision?

REFERENCES

Association for Supervision and Curriculum Development, *Educational Leadership* 26 (December 1968)—apropos of court decisions.

Babbidge, Homer D., Jr., and Robert M. Rosenzweig, *The Federal Interest in Higher Education* (New York: McGraw Hill, Inc., 1962).

Clift, Virgil A., Archibald W. Anderson, and H. Gordon Hullfish, *Negro Education in America* (New York: Harper & Row, Publishers, 1962).

Duker, Sam, *The Public Schools and Religion* (New York: Harper & Row, Publishers, 1966).

Educational Policies Commission, *Public Education and the Future of America* (Washington, D.C.: National Education Association, 1964).

Fellman, David, *The Supreme Court and Education* (New York: Bureau of Publications, Teachers College, Columbia University, 1960).

Fulbright, Evelyn R., and Edward C. Bolmeier, *Courts and The Curriculum* (Cincinnati: The W. H. Anderson Company, 1964).

Inlow, Gail M., *The Emergent in Curriculum* (New York: John Wiley & Sons, Inc. 1966), Chap. 10.

Kursh, Harry, *The United States Office of Education* (Philadelphia: Chilton Company—Book Division, 1965).

Mayers, Lewis, *The American Legal System*, rev. ed. (New York: Harper & Row, Publishers, 1964).

Snow, C. P., *The Two Cultures and the Scientific Revolution* (London: Cambridge University Press, 1959).

Tiedt, Sidney W., *The Role of the Federal Government in Education* (New York: Oxford University Press, 1966).

U.S. Department of Health, Education and Welfare, *American Education,* 5 (December 1968–January 1969)—apropos of legislation.

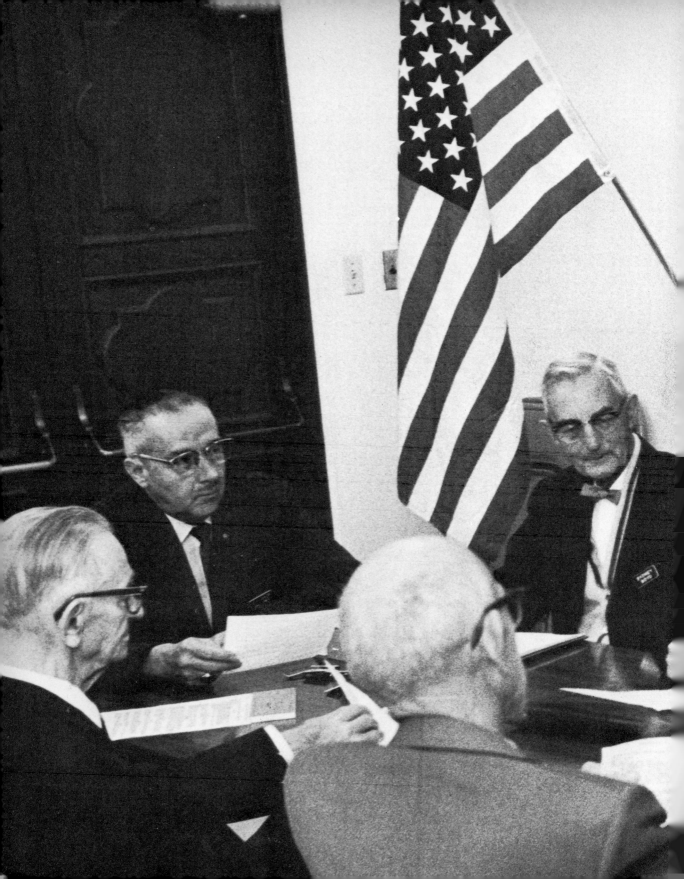

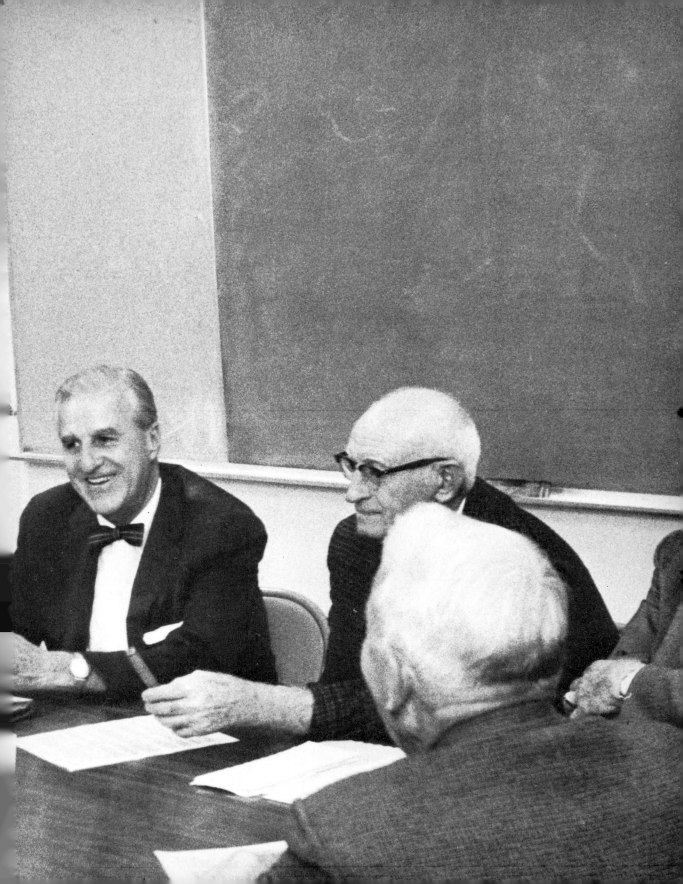

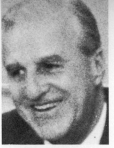

Chapter

4

State Governments and Local School Systems

As established in Chapter 3, the federal government is a guardian of human rights. One of the more basic of these is the universally acknowledged right of the young to an education. It is a right that transcends geography, economics, politics, race, and religion. The federal government plays its educational role both directly and indirectly: directly through legislation and court decisions pertaining to education; indirectly by ever impressing on state educational personnel its deep concern for the welfare of all the people.

STATE RESPONSIBILITY FOR EDUCATION

Within this frame of federal interest, each state has legal responsibility for making education an ongoing concern. States derive their educational powers from the Tenth Amendment: "The powers not delegated to the United States by the Constitution, nor prohibited by it to the States, are reserved to the States respectively, or to the people." Thus the thousands of school systems in the country that appear to be local in nature are in fact instrumentalities of the various states. The members of any local board of education relatedly are officials of the state in which the school system they serve is located. The teachers are agents of the state. The school property is owned by the state. And the school program is under control of the state. Despite the operational functions performed by any local group, final authority resides in the state, and only there.

Legal Sanctions for Education

School systems in any state derive their operational powers from three sovereign components: the state constitution, the legislature, and the courts. These are depicted relationally on p. 96 (A Typical State Organization for Education), along with the educational echelons which, in one way or another, the three bring into being.

The state constitution The constitution of every state contains provisions for education in that state. In Arkansas, for instance, the constitution declares that the "General Assembly shall provide for the establishment and maintenance of a general and efficient system of free public schools." In Minnesota, the constitution commits the "Legislature . . . [to] establish a general and uniform system of public schools." The Constitution of Hawaii contains more detailed provisions:

> The State shall provide for the establishment, support and control of a statewide system of public schools free from sectarian control, a state university, public libraries and such other educational institutions as may be deemed desirable, including physical facilities therefor. There shall be no segregation in public educational institutions because of race, religion or ancestry; nor shall public funds be appropriated for the support or benefit of any sectarian or private educational institution.

The constitutions of a number of states contain specifications that are often surprisingly detailed. Missouri, for example, stipulates that "a fourth of state revenues shall accrue to education." The constitution of California details the mode of election of state superintendents and county superintendents. The Utah constitution requires schools to teach the metric system. The constitutions of 11 states establish the length of the school term. Alabama's constitution commits the "Legislature . . . [to] establish, organize and maintain a liberal system of public schools for children between 7 and 21 years of age." Unquestionably, the 50 constitutions vary widely in their provisions for education; yet each is foundational to the enterprise of education within its borders.

The state legislature Being broadly descriptive only, each state constitution depends on state legislatures and state courts to make education operational. The state legislature is the primary agency of implementation; in effect, it legislates education into functional existence. The constitution contains the mandate; the legislature carries it out. In carrying it out, the legislature establishes the pattern of educational organization, effects a fiscal plan to provide support for the educational operation, establishes the scope of the operation, identifies and defines the duties of the functionaries involved in it, and proceduralizes other areas deemed essential to its success.

Through mandatory legislation, states establish minimum standards that all school systems must meet or exceed. Common to such legislation are provisions relating, for instance, to compulsory pupil attend-

82

ance, minimum number of days in the school year, minimum salaries of teachers, teacher tenure, standards of health and safety, required curriculum content—these and many others. Within the frame of mandatory legislation, however, local school systems have extensive discretionary powers. For example, they customarily have the right to go beyond minimum requirements in any named area, to carry out mandated requirements in specialized ways, and to supplement the state's requirements with local options of diverse kinds.

School law in most states, like the constitutions of selected states, is sometimes very specific. The following three excerpts from the school code of Wisconsin are illustrative. The first relates to the curriculum:

Reading, writing, spelling, English grammar and composition, geography, arithmetic, elements of agriculture and conservation of national resources, history and civil government of the United States and of Wisconsin, citizenship and such other branches as the board determines shall be taught in every elementary school. All instruction shall be in the English language except that the board may cause any foreign language to be taught to such pupils as desire it, not to exceed one hour each day.

A second relates to the indigent child:

Any principal or teacher in charge of any public school shall report to the authority administering poor relief for the municipal unit wherein such school is situated, the name and address of any child in such school whose parent, guardian, or other person having control, charge or custody of any such child, is without sufficient means to furnish any such child with food or clothing necessary for such child to attend school as required by law.

A third pertains to health:

All teachers, school authorities and health officers having jurisdiction shall not permit the attendance in any private, parochial or public school of any pupil afflicted with a severe cough, a severe cold, itch, scabies, lice or other vermin, ringworm, impetigo, epidemic jaundice, Vincent's angina (trench mouth), infectious conjunctivitis (pink eye), or any contagious skin disease, or who is filthy in body or clothing, or who has any communicable disease so designated by the state board of health unless specifically exempted in the Rules. The teachers in all schools shall, without delay, send home any pupil who is obviously sick even if the ailment is unknown, and said teacher shall inform the parents or guardians of said pupil and also the local health officer as speedily as possible, . . .

Parents, guardians, or other parents having control of any child who is sick in any way, or who is afflicted with any disease listed in Rule 17, shall not permit said child to attend any public, private or parochial school or to be present in any public place.

83

The state judiciary   Individual states, like the federal government, are dependent selectively on judicial bodies for sanction of their educational practices. In this connection, the reader should bear in mind that common-law decisions rendered in a given state are binding only in that state and that the courts move into the educational arena only when the legality of school legislation or of school practices is open to question. The courts and educational authorities are frequently juxtaposed in respect to issues such as the following: rights and duties of teachers, tort liability of teachers and board members, contracts, teacher tenure, retirement, loyalty oaths, pupil attendance, curriculum offerings, school districting, racial integration, and religion.

State Requirements in Specific Areas

Educational requirements in the 50 states, although similar in respect to program fundamentals, differ across a wide range of program specifics. Certain of these, arbitrarily selected, are incorporated into the present discussion.

Curriculum provisions   All states require the school systems under their control to make curriculum coverage of a designated hard core of subject-matter content. For the elementary school, the hard core customarily embraces the areas of language arts, arithmetic, American history, geography, science, health, physical education, art, and music. For the secondary school, requirements are not quite as uniform. American history is a requirement of 48 states; three to four years of English, of 44 states; physical education, of 40 states; mathematics, of 36 states; health, of 32 states; civics, of 28 states; and state history, of 22 states. Six states (California, Connecticut, Michigan, North Dakota, Oklahoma, and South Carolina) require driver education. Eight states, in 1964, required teaching about communism.[1] A few states have established sex education as a requirement. All in one way or another, require the teaching of humaneness, of morality, of patriotism (including proper care and display of the flag), and of the evils of narcotics.

Generally speaking, states are only broadly prescriptive in the area of curriculum. With the exception of Hawaii, they hold local systems responsible for making the curriculum operative.

[1] Roland F. Gray, "Teaching about Communism: A Survey of Objectives," *Social Education,* **28** (February 1964), p. 71.

PUBLIC CONTROL OF EDUCATION

Compulsory attendance   As of 1965, all but three states (Mississippi, South Carolina, and Virginia) had statewide compulsory attendance laws. The three named exceptions make attendance a local option. The respective compulsory-attendance laws were passed, by date, as indicated in Table 4.1.

TABLE 4.1   COMPULSORY ATTENDANCE LAWS, BY STATE

Massachusetts	1852	Illinois	1883	Arizona	1899
Vermont	1867	North Dakota	1883	Iowa	1902
New Hampshire	1871	South Dakota	1883	Maryland	1902
Michigan	1871	Montana	1883	Missouri	1905
Washington	1871	Minnesota	1885	Tennessee	1905
Connecticut	1872	Nebraska	1887	Delaware	1907
Nevada	1873	Idaho	1887	North Carolina	1907
New York	1874	Colorado	1889	Oklahoma	1907
Kansas	1874	Oregon	1889	Arkansas	1909
California	1874	Utah	1890	Louisiana	1910
Maine	1875	New Mexico	1891	Alabama	1915
New Jersey	1875	Pennsylvania	1895	Florida	1915
Wyoming	1876	Kentucky	1896	Texas	1915
Ohio	1877	Hawaii	1896	Georgia	1916
Wisconsin	1879	West Virginia	1897	Alaska	1929
Rhode Island	1883	Indiana	1897		

Source: August W. Steinhilber and Carl J. Sokolowski, *State Law on Compulsory Attendance,* Circular 793 (Washington, D.C.: U.S. Government Printing Office, 1966), p. 3.

Age requirements for school attendance   Among the 47 states with compulsory attendance laws, the maximum age for beginning enrollment in 7 states is six years; in 37, seven years; and in 3, eight years. In respect to the minimum age of required attendance, in 36 states it is sixteen years; in 6 (Maine, Nevada, New Mexico, Pennsylvania, Tennessee, and Wyoming) it is seventeen years; and in 4 (Ohio, Oklahoma, Oregon, and Utah) it is eighteen.[2]

Length of school year   For the year 1963–1964, the number of days that schools were in session, by state, ranged from 171 days in Alaska to 182.9 days in Missouri.[3] This range, it is to be noted, pertains to the time that schools were actually in session. State laws pertaining to

[2] Steinhilber and Sokolowski, p. 3.
[3] Research Division, National Education Association, *Ranking of the States, 1968* (Washington, D.C.: N.E.A., 1968), p. 16.

school attendance are often out of step with practice. Around 1960, the legal range was from a low of 120 days for Nevada to a high of 190 days (including legal holidays) for New York. The mode was 180 days. Tennessee and Virginia, interestingly, had lower requirements for elementary than for high schools: 160 versus 180 days for Tennessee; 170 versus 175 for Virginia.[4]

The trend in regard to length of the school year is upward. Kentucky, as a noteworthy example, ranked last in length of the school year in 1959–1960, but made 185 days a legal requirement in 1962. In the same year the requirement in Texas was raised from 120 to 165 days; and in 1963 in North Dakota, it was raised from 175 to 180 days.

Textbook selection   In 26 states, textbook selection is a local affair. In 22 states, school systems make selections from multiple lists prepared at the state level. In two states (California and North Carolina), school systems have little option in the selection of textbooks.

State Boards of Education

With education big business in every state, the administrative function necessarily is an important one. In all but four states (Illinois, Michigan, North Dakota, and Wisconsin),[5] the central administrative agency for education is the state board of education. This agency is of three functional types: regulatory, governing, and dual.

A *regulatory* state board is one that performs its educational mission in a decentralized way. It establishes policy and program in breadth, leaving to subordinate agencies the detailed task of operating the program. Its day-in and day-out function is supervision. A board of this type exercises supervisory control over other agencies: over the public school system, over colleges or universities, over a specialized educational agency, or over all of these.

A *governing* state board, in contrast, is one that exercises operational control over some phase of education, and in the case of Hawaii, over the entire educational enterprise. Boards of this type, in all states except Hawaii, exercise direct control over individual state colleges or universities, over entire state university systems, over vocational-

---

[4] Steinhilber and Sokolowski . . . , pp. 14–102 (lists requirements by individual states).

[5] Edgar L. Morphet, R. L. Johns, and Theodore L. Reller, *Educational Administration* (Englewood Cliffs, N.J.: Prentice-Hall, Inc., 1959), p. 194.

education programs, over education for the handicapped, or over some other specialized educational function.

The *dual* type is one that is both regulatory and governing. In practice, it customarily is regulatory over the public school system in the state and governing over one or more other individual educational agencies or functions within the state.

From this point on, the terms state board of education *or* state board, *unless otherwise indicated, will refer to a board that operates in a regulatory capacity over the school system of a given state.*

Now to the question: What are the major functions of a state board of education? One source identifies them as follows:

1. To administer certain service functions, such as the certification of teachers and the distribution of state aid
2. To serve in a judicial capacity in controversies in school districts
3. To serve as an enforcement agency for legislative regulations and mandates
4. To observe the operation of the school system and advise the legislature as to desirable changes in structure and regulation
5. To exercise leadership in the development of the educational system
6. To provide mandated and voluntary services to towns and cities[6]

[6] Robert R. Hamilton and Paul R. Mort, *The Law and Public Education*, second edition (New York: The Foundation Press, Inc., 1959), p. 84.

Additional functions include these: to engage in research, to disseminate information to school districts, to appoint (in states where organization dictates) a chief state school officer, to identify and systematize the functions of the state department of education, to integrate the educational function with such other important functions as health and social welfare, and to act as a unifying force in relations with the federal government and with local school systems.

State boards come into being in a number of ways. In the majority of states, the governor appoints them. In a sizable minority the people elect them. In four states the members serve *ex officio*. In New York the state legislature appoints them.[7]

In all states, including the four which have no board, the functional mission of education is performed by departments of education. These vary in membership size from 1900 in New York to 30 or fewer in Alaska and Wyoming. "The national average is one staff member for each approximately 10,000 public school students."[8]

In 1784 the state of New York brought into being the first board of education. Then, as now, it bore the title Board of Regents. Virginia, South Carolina, Vermont, and Missouri created state boards during the next half century. Massachusetts followed suit in 1837; Connecticut, in 1839.[9] By late mid-century, the state board had become an organizational fixture in the country.

The Chief State School Officer

All states have a chief school officer. The state of New York once again was first in this regard, appointing Gideon Hawley to the post in 1812. The exact duties of the superintendent vary from state to state. In all, however, he performs administrative and executive functions. A typical job description would read somewhat as follows:

> The chief state school officer is to work cooperatively with the state board of education (or comparable agency) to the end of maintaining the establishment of education at a high level of efficiency throughout the state; exercise leadership over the state department of education; formulate and

[7] Arthur W. Foshay (ed.), *The Rand McNally Handbook of Education* (Skokie, Ill.: Rand McNally & Company, 1963), pp. 32–33.

[8] Foshay, p. 35.

[9] R. Freeman Butts and Lawrence A. Cremin, *A History of Education in American Culture* (New York: Holt, Rinehart and Winston, Inc., 1953), pp. 256–257.

recommend necessary improvements in educational legislation, policies, and program; when these are sanctioned, interpret them to local school systems and supervise their implementation; act to resolve policy misinterpretations and misapplications in local school systems; make arrangements for the in-service growth of teachers and school administrators; engage in educational research; and submit reports, as required, to the governor, state board, or legislature.

The authority possessed by a chief state school officer and the functions he performs are, in great part, dependent on the manner in which he obtains office. In 22 states, the people elect him; in 23 states, the state board selects him; and in five states, the governor appoints him.[10] When he holds office by popular election or direct appointment, there is the ever-present danger of divided allegiance. A board with no voice in determining its leader might work at cross purposes with him. This is the reason for the following stand taken by the National Council of Chief State School Officers: "It is desirable that the board elect a chief state officer on a nonpartisan basis and determine his compensation and his term of office. He should serve as executive officer of the board and head of the state department of education."

EDUCATION AS A LOCAL FUNCTION

By Constitution and law, education is a federal concern and state responsibility. In practice, however, it is very much a local function. The phenomenon of decentralization in the United States, in fact, is probably education's most distinctive organizational feature.

As early as 1642, the Massachusetts Bay Colony decentralized education to the level of the town or township. In its historically famous law of that year, the colony commissioned officials of each local unit to get children ready "to read and understand the principles of religion and the capital laws of this country, and to impose fines upon such as shall refuse to render such accounts to them when they shall be required; . . ." Five years later, in the so-called "Old Deluder Satan Act," the Colony aligned the forces of education (and thus religion) against the forces of the Devil.

[10] Robert F. Will, et al. *State Education: Structure and Organization,* OE-23038, Misc. No. 46 (Washington, D.C.: U.S. Department of Health, Education and Welfare, 1964), p. 47.

It is therefore ordered that every township in this jurisdiction, after the Lord has increased them to the number of fifty householders, shall then forthwith appoint one within their town to teach all such children as shall resort to him to write and read, whose wages shall be paid either by the parents or masters of such children, or by the inhabitants in general, by way of supply, as the major part of those that order the prudentials of the town shall appoint; . . .

As frontiers receded and as colonists spread into newly created settlements, residents increasingly clamored for the right to have their own institutions. Townships, as a result, were often subdivided, with schools erected more to meet the needs and desires of local groups than those of larger political units. Thus, early in the history of the nation, the concept of education as a local function became an accepted cultural phenomenon. And Hawaii's departure from it in 1959 was not at all a reversal of the time-honored trend. Rather, it was a natural extension of the educational pattern that had characterized Hawaii when it was a territory.

Except for Hawaii, the centralist-localist issue is not one of an either-or choice. Instead, it is one of the relative amount of authority that a state and the local school systems within it should possess. States have resolved the issue in different ways. The Southern states, along with California, Delaware, Indiana, Maryland, New York, and Ohio, have leaned toward the centralist position, investing in state boards and departments a high degree of operational control over local educational practices. And these states definitely are on sound legal ground. In fact, assuming sanction by the electorate, they, like Hawaii, could shift completely to a centralist position. Most of the Midwestern, Far-western, and selected Eastern states have leaned more toward the localist than the centralist position.

The case for a high degree of state control over education goes something like this. The state, because of its wide range of authority can, by playing a strong hand, assure that all local school systems will meet reasonably high educational standards. When it plays a weak hand, the likelihood exists that some schools will sink to levels well below minimum acceptable standards. However, there is the risk that a state which plays a strong hand may be bureaucratic rather than efficient, may champion conformity rather than excellence.

Conversely, the case for a high degree of local control finds support in the thesis that increased local involvement leads to increased local support and thus to better education. The risk, however, is that local

interest, if not carefully controlled, may result in provincialism, narrowness, and cultural detachment.

The constructive compromise is for central control at the state level to be strong enough to neutralize narrow localism, but not so strong as to dull local interest and initiative. The customary result of this middle-of-the-road approach is a partnership of complementing opposites. The current trend, although only a modest one, is toward greater centralism. Local narrow-mindedness in regard to race and religion have been the moving forces behind this trend.

Local Boards of Education and School Districts

The local board of education is the agency officially responsible for schools at a community level. However, we reiterate here that school boards are state, not local, agencies. Local board members hold office through legislative sanction; thus they are officials of, and owe primary allegiance to, the states in which they serve. Their allegiance to a local community is purely a secondary matter. Yet, within this frame of state affiliation, most local boards of education are able to serve the legitimate purposes of the communities they represent.

School districts and boards have legal authority of three types: powers delegated to them directly by the state, powers implied by such delegation, and powers required by them to meet their legal obligations. Boards of education are corporate bodies of the several states. Thus board members, when performing official functions in a sane and reasonable way (sometimes when not), have the same immunity from legal liability as do the states themselves.

States differ, however, in respect to the liability of school boards, as corporate bodies, for the negligent acts of teachers and custodial employees. Some states operate under the principle of *respondeat superia*: the superior is responsible for his subordinates. These states, to a varying degree, hold school boards responsible as corporate bodies for the negligent acts of employees. New York, Connecticut, and New Jersey are selected instances.

Most other states, until recently, have operated under state immunity from the wrongful acts of employees. This assumption of automatic immunity, however, is undergoing increasing scrutiny in the courts.

An Illinois tort case (legal action taken for a wrongful civil act) in 1959 cast a shadow over its legality. The case was the one of *Molitor*

91

v. Kaneland Community District No. 302, 163 N.E. (2d) 89 (1959). It had to do with the injury of a pupil, allegedly caused by a school bus driver's negligence. The trial court dismissed the suit, holding that the state, and thus a school district, had absolute immunity from tort action. In 1962, however, the Supreme Court of Illinois overruled the trial court, declaring that, irrespective of precedent, a school district is liable for the negligent acts of its personnel. In a parallel case, namely *Holytz v. City of Milwaukee*, 115 N.Y. (2d) 618, (1962), the Supreme Court of Wisconsin abrogated the governmental immunity precedent, ruling "that a public body shall be liable for damages for the torts of its officers, agents, and employees occurring in the course of the business of such public body." Only the future can tell whether these decisions rendered in the two states of Illinois and Wisconsin will ultimately lead to a federal Supreme Court decision along the same line.

How board members attain office   Generally, board members hold office as the result of popular vote, with elections, for the most part, being nonpolitical in nature. In suburban areas, the prevailing method is for caucus groups to submit a slate of candidates. Accepted professional protocol is for the position to seek the candidate, not vice versa. Yet, admittedly, such protocol is ignored as often as it is observed. In large cities board members often hold office by appointment, with mayors frequently making selections from a list submitted by a nonpolitical professional committee. Of all school boards in the country, 85.9 percent are elected, and 14.1 percent are appointed in one way or another.[11] Board members universally hold office for overlapping terms in order to assure continuity of experience.

Size of boards of education   The membership size of boards of education is from three to 19, with rural districts tending to have fewer members; city districts, more members. The national distribution is as follows: three to four members, 3.5 percent; five members, 51.8 percent; six members, 8.7 percent; seven members, 23.9 percent; eight to nine members, 10.0 percent; and over ten members, 2.2 percent.[12]

Length of office of board members   Ninety-six percent of all local school board members hold office for three to six years.

[11] Alpheus L. White, *Local School Boards: Organization and Practices*, OE-23023, Bulletin No. 8 1962 (Washington, D.C.: U.S. Department of Health, Education, and Welfare, 1962), p. 8.

92   [12] White, p. 14.

Education of board members   Of all local school board members in the country, 48.3 percent are college graduates; 44 percent are high school graduates; and 7.7 percent, less than high school graduates.[13]

Composition of school boards   Board members, by percentages as indicated, belong to the following occupational categories, as listed: (1) business owners, officials, and managers, 34.5 percent; (2) professional and technical people, 27.4 percent; (3) farmers, 12.4 percent; (4) sales and clerical workers, 6.9 percent; (5) housewives, 7.2 percent; (6) skilled laborers and foremen, 6.7 percent; (7) retired, 2.0 percent; (8) others, 2.9 percent.[14] One or more women hold membership on 43.6 percent of all boards in the country. However, only 12.8 percent of the boards have two or more women members.[15]

[13] White, p. 18.
[14] White, p. 25.
[15] White, p. 22.

Duties of school boards   In one way or another, all boards perform the following functions:

1. Select, hire, and/or work with a chief school officer
2. Hire teachers and employees
3. Formulate broad operational policies and procedures
4. Approve district lines (in the larger systems)
5. Approve school budgets
6. Purchase school property and supplies
7. Endorse, or suggest modifications in, the academic program developed by the professional staff
8. Enter contracts
9. Levy taxes and borrow money (in systems that are independent of political units)

The Local School Superintendent

All school systems have a chief school officer of some kind. He generally bears the title of superintendent of schools, but in certain small school districts he may have some other title such as supervising principal or teaching principal. In Arkansas a board may not appoint a superintendent unless the community has a population of at least 2500. In Maine the requisite is 75 teachers. In Washington it is two school buildings. In Iowa the requisite is the existence of one high school in a township unit.[16] Irrespective of requisites, there are approximately 13,000 local school superintendents in the country.[17] Of these, 23 percent have a bachelor's degree, 54 percent have a master's degree, and 21 percent have a doctor of philosophy degree.[18]

The following include the more important responsibilities of a chief school officer.

1. Serves as chief executive officer of the board of education
2. Exercises leadership over all phases of the instructional program: planning, goal determination, curriculum development, and evaluation

[16] Foshay, p. 85.

[17] Foshay, p. 84.

[18] American Association of School Administrators, *Professional Administrators for American Schools,* 38th Yearbook (Washington, D.C.: National Education Association, 1960), p. 26.

3. Relates closely to key organizations and individuals in the community in order to secure their interest and cooperation and to maintain a sensitivity to prevailing community attitudes and opinions
4. Exercises leadership in the screening of prospective faculty members and other important school employees, recommending for hiring those finally approved
5. Has responsibility for the in-service growth and welfare of the school staff
6. Interprets the school program to key personnel of the various public relations media in the community
7. Prepares the budget, submits it to the board, and administers it when approved
8. Keeps abreast of growth needs of the school system, ascertaining that building and maintenance plans keep pace with those needs
9. Relates professionally with other chief school officers for purposes of professional growth and improvement in the school program

An Administrative Dilemma

Whatever the type or size of the school system, its administration is a many-sided and demanding function. The three major areas of responsibility are: (1) the educational process with its many faces; (2) personnel administration, which includes in its purview parents, teachers, pupils, and community representatives; and (3) business administration, which includes school finance as an always important, and sometimes volatile, ingredient.

No one denies the importance of these administrative functions; but there is disagreement over the relative importance of each of the three, and over which of them, if any, a busy school administrator might justifiably delegate to subordinates. Generally speaking, school administrators regard the educational and personnel functions as too vital to be delegated. Conversely, board members generally regard the business and finance function as too vital to be delegated. The result is an administrative dilemma.

The only way out of the dilemma is for superintendents, whenever possible, to sell business-oriented board members on the priority of educational and personnel administration in school programs. The task is rarely an easy one. Yet even when resistance is great, the effort needs

95

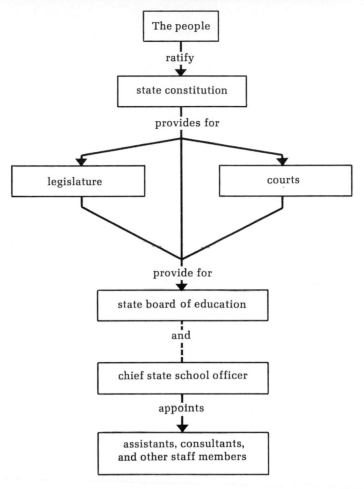

to be made. The argument should include the following: Let the super-intendent be an educator first, and if time and talent permit, also a business manager. But do not let the second function interfere unduly with the first. The basic thesis is that competency in curriculum, in learning, in personnel administration, and in professional affairs at community, state, and national levels is elusive or unattainable for the administrator who is consistently bogged down in budgetary and re-lated business affairs. Fundamentally, then, an essential responsibility of any superintendent is to help board members gain clear perspective of his professional role. Failure in this regard is harmful not only to the individuals directly involved, but even more to the educational pro-gram that ultimately bears the impact of his failure.

The Building Principal

The position of building principal, although different in title from that of the school superintendent, requires essentially the same qualifications and competencies. In the words of one source, "The research available shows no important differences between the characteristics of effective leadership in superintendents and principals."[19] The duties of the two positions, however, do differ, as illustrated in Table 4.2.

TABLE 4.2 CONTRASTING DUTIES OF SCHOOL SUPERINTENDENT AND BUILDING PRINCIPAL

Duties of the Superintendent	Duties of the Principal
1. Works directly with the board of education.	1. Works indirectly with the board of education.
2. Works only incidentally with teachers.	2. Works intimately, day in and day out, with teachers.
3. Is intimately involved in the finance and building program for the entire system.	3. Is involved in these matters primarily as related to the instructional needs of a single building.
4. Plans broadly for curriculum concerns, relying on others to develop and implement them.	4. Sometimes participates actively in curriculum development; always participates actively in curriculum implementation.
5. Cooperatively with the board, develops and promulgates policy for the entire system.	5. Translates systemwide policy into action; develops and promulgates building policy.
6. Relates to key community agencies and individuals.	6. Relates to parents and local neighborhood agencies.

The above distinctions are not valid for all school systems because boards, superintendents, and principals themselves differ too widely for one list of duties to apply universally. The trend in forward-looking systems, however, is for boards and superintendents to place increasing powers and responsibilities in the hands of building principals and building faculties. Such a pattern enhances the professionalism of those to whom authority is delegated; but it does add to their work loads and make heavier demands on their time.[20]

[19] Morphet, Johns, and Reller, p. 283.

[20] Because of the general nature of this book, I have not made coverage of the staff members customarily found in larger school systems. These consist primarily of business-management functionaries and curriculum specialists in the various learning areas. They have staff, not line, status. Thus, their roles are advisory in nature.

97

Categories of Districts

School districts throughout the country differ widely in type and size. In certain places, they are coterminous with town, county, or city boundaries; in other places, they cut across one or more of these. The majority are independent of local political units; a minority, particularly those in large cities, are dependent on such units. Most local school districts have governing powers; some, however, have only supervisory powers.

Functionally, districts divide, among other ways, into the following four categories: elementary school, secondary school, unit (or unitary), and intermediate.

Elementary school districts are most prevalent in rural areas where the population characteristically is sparse. They also are prevalent in certain communities of selected Midwestern states. Illinois is a noteworthy example. In many Illinois systems, elementary and secondary education are administratively separate.

Secondary school districts, as the name implies, serve grades 7–12, 9–12, or 10–12, depending on school organization and law. The secondary school district customarily embraces a number of "feeder" elementary school districts. The Niles-Township high school system of Skokie, Illinois, for instance, serves nine public elementary school districts and several parochial school districts.

Unit districts serve both elementary and secondary educational levels within a community. Of the three, the unit district is the most practical and the most defensible fiscally. It is the best guarantor of curriculum articulation and program continuity. It can more readily avoid duplication of staff and services. And it can keep in bounds the competition that tends to develop among contiguous school units.

Intermediate units, unlike the first three named, are supervisory or regulatory rather than governing in nature. They exist in 35 states, the exceptions being Alabama, Alaska, Delaware, Florida, Georgia, Kentucky, Louisiana, Maryland, Nevada, New Mexico, North Carolina, Tennessee, Utah, Virginia, and West Virginia.[21] Usually, they are coterminous with county lines. In New England, they embrace, in a less evenly patterned way, clusters of contiguous local school units. The intermediate unit, in composite, performs two important functions. First, as an agency interpolated between the state department of education and a local school unit, it helps local units both to keep abreast of state policy

[21] Foshay, p. 90.

and to implement it. Second, as a professional unit in its own right, it provides miscellaneous services to small school units, which are unable to provide these services for themselves. Personnel administration and business management are, as a rule, the major fortes of intermediate units.

Historically, the intermediate unit carved an important niche in education. With the passage of time, however, it has become less useful and thus less necessary. Three factors have contributed to its decline: (1) the growth in vitality of small school units throughout the country, (2) the increasing tendency of small school districts to combine into more efficient larger ones, and (3) the increased effectiveness of state departments of education.

Exactly what the future holds for intermediate units is a debatable question in educational circles today. There appears to be consensus at least on these three counts; (1) the number of intermediate units will continue to decrease; (2) the need for some kind of intermediate unit will continue to exist as long as weak local units continue to exist; and (3) intermediate units, slow in the past to upgrade themselves, definitely need to increase the pace of such upgrading in the future.

Number and Size of Districts

As indicated previously, an educational trend of the day is toward school-district consolidation. It is a trend that began to take shape around 1930 and that, as revealed in Table 4.3, has continued unabated since.

TABLE 4.3   TREND TOWARD SCHOOL-DISTRICT CONSOLIDATION

School Year	Number of School Districts
1931-1932	127,531
1941-1942	115,493
1951-1952	71,094
1961-1962	35,676
1964-1965	29,391
1966-1967	23,390
1967-1968	21,990

Source: The Table is a composite from Kenneth A. Simon and W. Vance Grant, *Digest of Educational Statistics*, OE-10024-68 (Washington, D.C.: U.S. Department of Health, Education, and Welfare, 1968), pp. 44–45; and Research Division—National Education Association, *Estimates of School Statistics, 1967–1968*, Research Report 1967-R 19 (Washington, D.C.: National Education Association, 1967), p. 6.

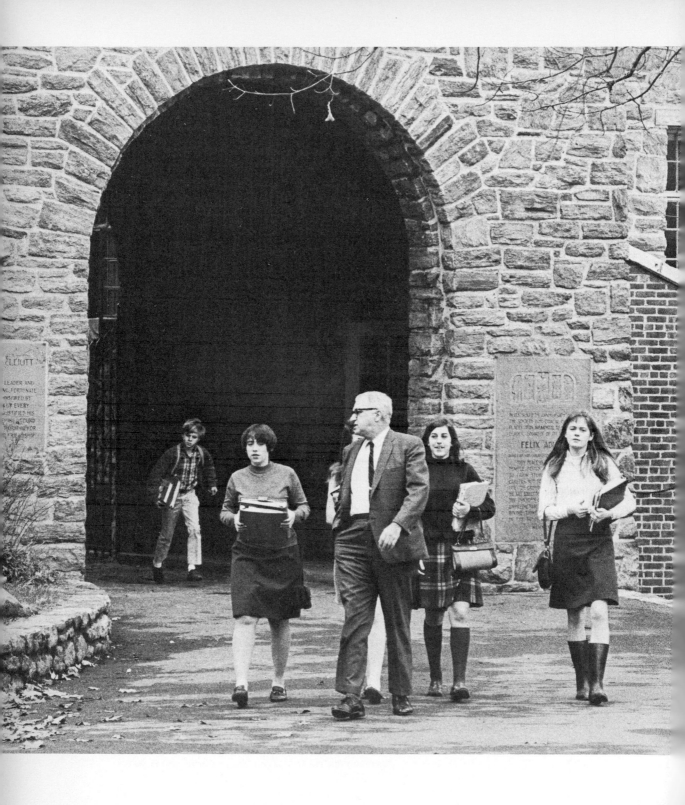

One important result of the consolidation movement has been a dramatic reduction in the number of one-teacher schools. There were 149,-282 of these in the year 1929–1930 and only 6491 in the year 1965–1966. Yet as late as 1966, 40 percent of the school districts in operation in the country had fewer than 300 pupils. A complete statistical picture of school districts by number and enrollment size, as of 1966–1967, appears in Table 4.4. The picture, beyond question, supports the conclusion that consolidation still has a long way to go.

TABLE 4.4   NUMBER OF PUBLIC SCHOOL SYSTEMS AND NUMBER OF PUPILS ENROLLED, BY SIZE OF SYSTEM: UNITED STATES, 1966–1967

Enrollment Size (Number of Pupils)	School Systems		Pupils Enrolled	
	Number	Percent	Number (in thousands)	Percent
1	2	3	4	5
All sizes	23,390	100.0	43,841	100.0
25,000 or more	170	0.7	12,590	28.7
12,000 to 24,999	350	1.5	5,730	13.1
6,000 to 11,999	880	3.8	7,293	16.6
3,000 to 5,999	1,726	7.4	7,178	16.4
1,800 to 2,999	1,819	7.8	4,251	9.7
1,200 to 1,799	1,636	7.0	2,416	5.5
600 to 1,199	2,838	12.1	2,437	5.6
300 to 599	2,723	11.6	1,185	2.7
1 to 299	9,380	40.0	761	1.8
None*	1,868	8.0		

* Systems not operating schools.
Source: Simon and Grant, *Digest of Educational Statistics,* p. 46.

To Stimulate Thought

1. Why do you think that states, for the most part, have refrained from controlling the enterprise of education at the central state level?

2. Assume that a state legislature passes a law requiring all high schools in the state to teach about communism. Debate the advisability of its taking

the next step, that of formulating state-sanctioned curriculum materials which it requires all schools by law to adhere to. Elaborate your answer.

3. Present the pros and cons of the chief state school officer's being (a) elected by the people, (b) appointed by the governor, (c) elected by the state board of education.

4. Argue for or against the thesis that compulsory attendance to the age of eighteen should be a requirement in all states.

5. Defend the statement that a local board of education should be independent of the local political power.

6. To what extent do you think local boards of education should be active in curriculum concerns?

7. In the hiring of faculty members in a small school system, what, in your estimation, should be the differential roles played by the superintendent and board?

8. Identify the greater merits of a unit system over an elementary school or a secondary school system.

REFERENCES

American Association of School Administrators, *Professional Administrators for American Schools*, 38th Yearbook (Washington, D.C.: National Education Association, 1960).

Beach, Fred F., and Robert F. Will, *The State and Education: The Structure and Control of Public Education at the State Level* (Washington, D.C.: U.S. Department of Health, Education, and Welfare, 1954).

Bean, John E., *Research in State Departments of Education*, OE-23040, Bulletin No. 26, 1965 (Washington, D.C.: U.S. Department of Health, Education, and Welfare, 1965).

Drury, Robert L., and Kenneth C. Ray, *Principles of School Law, with Cases* (New York: Appleton-Century-Crofts, 1965).

Fulbright, Evelyn R., and Edward C. Bolmeier, *Courts and the Curriculum* (Cincinnati: The W. H. Anderson Company, 1964).

Gardner, John W., *Self-Renewal* (New York: Harper & Row, Publishers, 1963).

Hamilton, Robert R., and Paul R. Mort, *The Law and Public Education* (New York: The Foundation Press, Inc., 1959).

Lynch, Patrick D., and Peggy L. Blackstone (eds.), *Institutional Roles for In-Service Education of School Administrators* (Albuquerque: University of New Mexico and The University Council for Educational Administration, 1966).

Remmlein, Madaline Kinter, *School Law* (Danville, Ill.: The Interstate Printers and Publishers, Inc., 1962).

Schloss, Samuel, and Alma M. Clarke, *Statistical Summary of State School Systems*, Circular 789 (Washington, D.C.: U.S. Department of Health, Education, and Welfare, 1965).

PUBLIC CONTROL OF EDUCATION

Simon, Kenneth A., and W. Vance Grant, *Digest of Educational Statistics*, OE-10024-65, Bulletin No. 4 (Washington, D.C.: U.S. Department of Health, Education, and Welfare, Office of Education, latest edition).

White, Alpheus L., *Local School Boards: Organization and Practices*, OE-23023, Bulletin No. 8 (Washington, D.C.: U.S. Department of Health, Education, and Welfare, 1962).

Part Three
Education as an Operational Process

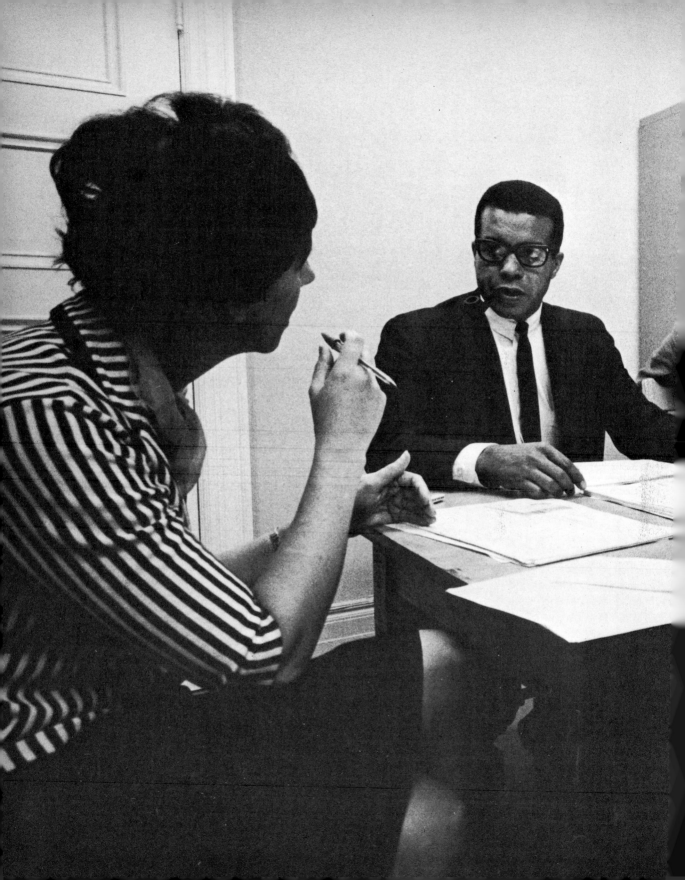

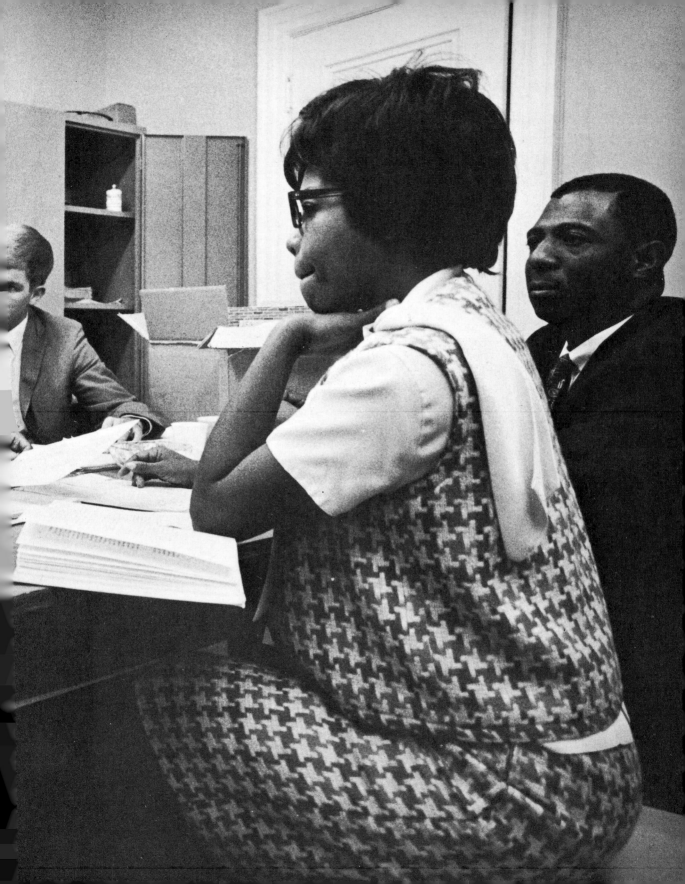

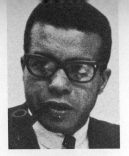

Chapter

5

Curriculum:
Theory
and
Development

Education as a federal concern and a state responsibility becomes operational in local communities. At this third level, legal sanctions, policy formulations, and broad procedural specifications find expression in some kind of systematic educational procedure. Such procedure inevitably embraces curriculum design in some form which, in turn, leads to learning activity. The theme of this chapter is curriculum—what it is, the theory that underlies it, and the steps involved in its development and implementation.

WHAT IS CURRICULUM?

First in priority is the fundamental question: What is curriculum? The question is easier to ask than to answer. Theorists differ too widely in respect to all curriculum considerations for any single response to be categorically correct. One writer comments that the term *curriculum* "covers school experiences like an umbrella. Name any facet of school activity you like, and it will be included in a modern concept of the term curriculum."[1] Despite differences in interpretation, most theorists agree that the curriculum of a school is a learning design of some kind, a master plan, an entity that endows learning with systematic orderliness. In its original Latin form, *curriculum* referred to a race or course to be run. Many schools attach the same meaning to the term today.

Among writers who offer definitions of curriculum, distinctiveness characterizes a few. Spears is quite descriptive in defining it:

> Unfortunately—or perhaps fortunately—*a curriculum is not described by its outward features*, but rather by the point of view of the thinking from which it springs. A curriculum is something *to be felt* rather than something to be seen . . . *An ounce of teacher enthusiasm and insight is worth a pound of curriculum masterminding.*[2]

[1] Donald F. Cay, *Curriculum: Design for Learning* (Indianapolis: The Bobbs-Merrill Company, Inc., 1966), p. 1.

[2] Harold Spears, *The High School for Today* (New York: American Book Company, 1950), p. 21.

Beauchamp defines curriculum as "the design of a social group for the educational experiences of their children in school."[3] Krug defines it as "the means of instruction used by the school to provide opportunities for student-learning experiences leading to desired learning outcomes."[4]

The author conceptionalizes *curriculum as the planned composite effort of any school to guide pupils toward predetermined learning outcomes.*[5] The definition embraces, among others, the following activities: determination of educational goals; translation of the goals into a learning design; instructional practices; and evaluation of pupil growth. Any curriculum, although primarily a product of advance planning by professional personnel, should lead to spontaneous learning on the part of pupils. Learning is then a product of well-conceived content and the dynamic properties of psychic energy.

CULTURAL VALUES AS THE CURRICULUM BASE

Although the process of curriculum-building is too complex to adhere to any prearranged pattern, it, like formal education in its totality, inevitably starts with the central values of its culture. In the Western world, as stated in Chapters 1 and 2, these highlight the individual as the supreme value in life. They portray him as a composite of rational, affective, and physical components, all important and all inseparably interrelated. They hold up altruism as the highest index of his maturity. Within the frame of these values, people obviously are of greater significance than material possessions. And every individual, by right of his humanness and irrespective of other factors, is entitled to those cultural essentials that make and keep him human. These include adequate food, shelter, clothing, medical care, occupational opportunity, and psychological acceptance. The quality and amount of these may differ from person to person, or community to community, but the level needs to be high enough for human worth not to lessen. Specifically, the minority-group member is no less entitled to a choice of residence, occupation, and public facility than his majority-group counterpart. The slow learner is no less entitled to grow toward his potential than

[3] George A. Beauchamp, *The Curriculum of the Elementary School* (Boston: Allyn and Bacon, Inc., 1964), p. 15.

[4] Edward A. Krug, *Curriculum Planning* (New York: Harper & Row, 1957), p. 3.

[5] For an elaboration of these outcomes, see Gail M. Inlow, *The Emergent in Curriculum* (New York: John Wiley & Sons, Inc., 1966), p. 7.

EDUCATION AS AN OPERATIONAL PROCESS

his more facile counterpart. And "power figures" in places of authority are no more entitled to special privileges than those over whom they exercise authority.

I do not agree with John Dewey that a school should be a miniature of the society of which it is a part. The processes of education are too specialized for this to be practical. However, I firmly believe that no school has the legal or moral right to operate outside the cultural values that frame it. These, in fact, constitute the only legitimate foundation for curriculum development.

Educational Objectives Deriving from Cultural Values

Within the broad frame of cultural values, education formulates its own goals. Some instances of such formulation have been included in Chapter 2. These embrace pronouncements by the Committee of Ten in 1893; the Seven Cardinal Principles enunciated by the Committee on the Reorganization of Secondary Education in 1918; two promulgations by the Educational Policies Commission of the National Education Association in 1938 and 1944, respectively; a statement by Harvard University in 1945; another by the White House Conference on Education in 1956; and one of the most recent by the Educational Policies Commission in 1961.

Generally speaking, American society, although not without extensive debate and much ambivalence, has given education a mandate to press toward the following outcomes:

1. Develop individual personality in areas of the
   a. emotional—to the end of self-acceptance and the attainment of other legitimate mental-health outcomes
   b. esthetic—to the end of appreciation and creation of the beautiful
   c. ethical—to the end of development of a sound value system
   d. intellectual—to the end of development of knowledge, understanding, and the ability to synthesize, and to think critically
   e. physical—to the end of maintenance of physical health and development of wholesome health habits.
2. Ready individuals to assume:
   a. an occupational role in the culture
   b. a consumer's role in the culture
   c. a home-and-family role in the culture.

111

3. Perpetuate the culture, including its:
   a. significant traditions
   b. significant events
   c. significant social institutions
   d. significant personalities.
4. Develop the social order by helping learners to think critically about:
   a. man's proper relationship to his fellow man
   b. man's proper relationship to his country, including his citizenship responsibilities
   c. man's proper relationship to the universe, the end being a feeling of cosmic belongingness.

Goals formulated by groups distantly removed from the classroom are often stated in general terms. A national or state organization, for instance, might go no further than to commit education to the goal of instilling and developing moral values in pupils. A school system, however, would tend to elaborate the goal. Illustrative is the following statement by the Evanston Community Consolidated School District No. 65, of Evanston, Illinois:[6]

> We believe that in our educational program we are dealing with matters of the mind and of the spirit and that we are building an appreciation of spiritual values into the lives of our pupils.
> Democracy is basically a religious idea about the unique dignity and worth of each individual. If we remember and teach the spiritual nature of this great ideal and not tend to think of democracy only in terms of physical power and possession, we can build inner strength in our young people that no alien philosophy can overcome.

A classroom teacher would be even more specific, detailing the goal into such hoped-for outcomes as: honesty in taking examinations, courteous treatment of fellow pupils, respect for those who hold differing opinions, accepting responsibility for actions, joining with others in formulating and living up to codes of action, respecting the property of others—these and many more.

For centuries, and especially during the past several decades, a central issue in curriculum—and one that has been elaborated previously—is whether schools should concern themselves with intellectual considerations exclusively, or with the total personalities of students also. The issue, however, is more academic than real. For one reason, teachers by law are surrogate parents in a broad sense, not just academic

112   [6] Evanston Community Consolidated School District No. 65, *School Outlook,* 1959.

parents. As such they are obligated to relate to the psychological and physical, as well as to the cognitive growth needs, of learners. Secondly, the emotional, the social, the ethical, and the physical components of learners are inseparable from the intellectual component. And last, the noncognitive areas of growth are too important for educators to ignore. Thus, the real issue is not *whether*, but *how much*, schools should be concerned with the total personality growth of students.

A CURRICULUM DESIGN

On the hard rock of cultural values translated into educational objectives, educational thinkers from early times have conceived and refined curriculum designs. Primordial man undoubtedly placed emphasis on the skills of physical survival. The colonizers of this country placed emphasis on religious values. Their eighteenth- and nineteenth-century counterparts decreasingly tapped the religious and drew increasingly on the secular for curriculum content. Irrespective of time or geographical location, formal education indoctrinates the young into important cultural traditions, helps them to adapt to their environments, and leads them toward personality fulfillment.

Sources of Curriculum

Although the sources of any school's curriculum are many and varied, the following are primary: (1) time-tested disciplines, which preserve the culture's store of knowledge; (2) emergent disciplines, which convey man's new and evolving insights; (3) the existing social order with its institutions, issues, and practices; (4) the unique needs and interests of individual learners; and (5) the contributions of those educators who interpret and teach the curriculum.

The time-tested disciplines At all educational levels the traditional disciplines hold a position of eminence. Brash indeed would be the academician who argued or acted otherwise. While educators confidently agree that the disciplines, in general, constitute a *sine qua non* of the educated mind, they are apt to be less confident when expected to identify the specific disciplines considered to be essential. In this connection, they face such questions as these. Is geology in the field of **113**

the natural sciences as much a prerequisite of the educated mind as biology, chemistry, or physics? Is social psychology in the field of the social sciences as much a prerequisite as history? Is a foreign language in the field of the humanities as much a prerequisite as the native language of an individual, or music as much as literature?

If these tangential questions are difficult for the reader to answer, how about the more fundamental question: Just what is a discipline? I have defined the term elsewhere as a body "of knowledge and concepts that emanate from and relate to a given life area; it consists of demonstrable and describable methods of discovering and validating knowledge and hypotheses within that life area; and it is ever evolving."[7] Like most definitions, however, this one is only the beginning of understanding. Concretions alone can give it true meaning.

[7] Inlow, p. 13.

The disciplines of greatest historical significance were the seven liberal arts of the Middle Ages—the *trivium*: grammar, logic and rhetoric; and the *quadrivium*: arithmetic, astronomy, geometry, and music. Of the seven, logic and rhetoric, as such, do not exist today as discrete subjects in the curricula of most schools. And music is not one of the so-called "hard-core" subjects. Whether or not this state of affairs weakens the case of such curriculum perennialists as Hutchins, Adler, and Van Doren is a moot question. Personally, I think that it does.[8]

The original disciplines, seven in number, have, through the ages, undergone both qualitative and quantitative change. The *natural sciences* today embrace the several disciplines of astronomy, biology, chemistry, geology, mathematics, physical geography, and physics. The *social sciences* embrace anthropology, economics, history, human geography, political science, sociology, and social psychology. The *humanities* embrace composition, the fine arts, the kinetic arts, language, literature, music, philosophy, psychology (other than social), and speech. With few exceptions, each of the nation's schools draws on all the above-named disciplines for curriculum content. But curriculum workers recurrently have to decide how much of each the curriculum of a given school should include, and in what form the content should appear: that is, whether it should appear as a discrete curriculum entity or as part of a fused curriculum entity. Fusion is characteristic in the elementary school curriculum; both fusion and discreteness are characteristic in the secondary school curriculum; and discreteness is characteristic in higher education.

One facet of the so-called "Great Debate" taking place in education today revolves around the question: Should the disciplines stand as the one and only source of any school's curriculum, or should they be considered as one, albeit a central one, of several sources? Jerome Bruner, a psychologist, in his widely quoted *Process of Education*, 1960, conceives the disciplines as the one and only legitimate source of curriculum. His answer to the knowledge explosion is for teachers (1) to lift from the disciplines their structure, that is, their major conceptualizations and methods of discovery; (2) to teach these conceptualizations, employing the methods of the discipline in the process, and (3) to let psychological transfer do the rest. Philip Phenix, an educational philosopher, expresses the same point of view when he states that "if

---

[8] These and others hold that education should be essentially the same for all individuals, irrespective of time or place.

learning time is to be economized, all material should come from the disciplines, and *none* from other sources."[9]

On this issue, I take issue with Bruner, Phenix, and others of like conviction, for the following fundamental reasons:

1. The term *discipline* is a subjective one, characterized by a wide variety of definitions and interpretations that should be clarified whenever the term is used.
2. Throughout the ages the disciplines have been evolving and emergent; thus any exclusive reliance on the disciplines as they were defined at any given time in history constitutes a status quo approach to knowledge and to life itself.
3. Scholars differ, from little to much, over what the seminal concepts are within any single discipline. This lack of agreement transmits uncertainty and instability to curriculum builders.
4. Bruner and Phenix regard the disciplines as comparably appropriate curriculum sources, irrespective of grade level: whether primary (K–3), intermediate (4–6), junior high (7–9), or senior high (10–12). This assumption of universal applicability needs validation in general, and extra-careful validation for school units below the high school level.
5. The disciplines in themselves are too unwieldly and cumbersome to relate directly to the specific problems of children and youth at any given moment; for instance: masturbation by a kindergartner; shyness in a first grader; a compulsive need to be first on the part of a fourth grader; faulty personal hygiene in a seventh grader; a faulty self-image in an uncomely ninth grader; or sexual precocity in a tenth or eleventh grader.

My position is far from antidiscipline; to the contrary, it is one of abiding respect for the liberating powers of most of the so-called disciplines. My own education at the collegiate level, undergraduate and graduate, was, for seven years, in a liberal arts college of a respectable university. However, anyone who holds that the disciplines, or any other single category of educational content, are the only avenue to the educated mind oversimplifies the issue. The disciplines unquestionably serve as learning models par excellence. They alone reveal a culture in perspective. But they are not the only curriculum avenue to insight.

[9] Philip H. Phenix, *Realms of Meaning* (New York: McGraw-Hill, Inc., 1964), p. 54.

The emergent disciplines The disciplines, like man and the universe, are dynamic. They change because life itself is a process of change. The disciplines are symbolic reflections of given life areas; thus they have authenticity only to the extent that they keep pace with emerging reality. The older disciplines undergo constant modification while fledgling disciplines are periodically struggling for recognition and status.

New disciplines come into being slowly, with assessment over long periods needed to decide whether they have or have not finally "arrived." Astrology, alchemy, and phrenology, understandably, lost the battle for acceptance. Yet, anthropology, geology, and political science won the same battle. Today, in the opinion of many, psychology (collectively or by branches) and demography are vying for status as disciplines. The future will pass judgment on the success of their effort.

The existing social order Yet a third legitimate source of curriculum content is the existing social order with its institutions, issues, and practices. Individual societies have governments, social establishments, commanding personalities, economic postures, human problems, and unfolding events. Societies collectively have these same components multiplied. Any curriculum that consistently operates outside the frame of these is one headed toward sterility. The issue is not one of the past pitted against the present, as Hutchins and other perennialists have been quick to suggest; neither is it one of education selling out to "presentism." Rather, the issue is whether education is to serve its legitimate function of communicating an evolving culture to the young. Courses in history that stop with 1950, in literature that ignore the prospective "greats" in the making, or in any area that fail to take note of current change point to a curriculum that progress has passed by.

The most cherished of education's many outcomes is rational individuals who think clearly and critically about themselves and the world around them. These are the individuals able to look beyond themselves to others, to channel change into positive directions, to become poised leaders in a social order badly in need of leadership. These individuals, I contend, mature best from exposure to a curriculum that draws substance from the functional present as well as from the recorded past.

The needs of learners To this point, it has been posited that the time-tested disciplines, the evolving disciplines, and the ongoing social order are three vital curriculum sources. Learners themselves constitute yet a fourth important source. No curriculum, irrespective of its anteced- **117**

ents, is functional unless it relates meaningfully to the differing interests, abilities, and needs of learners. But no curriculum is functional either unless it reaches into learners themselves for content. Thus learners, while serving as obvious focal centers of a curriculum conceived outside themselves, serve also as a valuable source of curriculum content.

With individualism a sacred value in the Western world, a curriculum best starts with the individual and works outward. This is the ideal. At the practical level, however, the complexities imposed by mass education make the ideal attainable only in part. As a compromise, curriculum designers customarily formulate a learning plan which, based on professional know-how and experience, they believe will meet the needs of most learners. Then they allow instructors latitude in applying the curriculum to, or altering it for, individual learners.

Specifically, for instance, individuals are sources of curriculum content when, as mentioned a few pages back, a teacher views shyness, ego deflation, and sexual precocity as invitations to action. Children and youth need to belong, to realize the pleasures of accomplishment, to have self-respect, to feel secure, to enjoy life, and to have confidence in the values they live by. Thus, whenever a teacher departs from a predetermined curriculum to address himself to a pupil's specific and immediate need, he reinforces the conviction that learners themselves are

sources of curriculum content. The school psychologist reinforces the same conviction when he counsels with a disturbed and unhappy youngster. So does the inner-city teacher when he discovers that acceptance of, and empathy for, the disadvantaged child is usually a necessary preliminary of academic learning.

The contributions of teachers   A fifth source of curriculum content is teachers themselves. They serve as primary sources when contributing new ideas and concepts to a school's curriculum. They serve most often, however, not as primary contributers, but as distillers of a content that emanates from other sources. In this second role, they contribute to curriculum by interpreting it, by highlighting certain aspects and making cursory coverage of others, by including certain curriculum materials and excluding others. They contribute to it through the impact of their personalities on their students.

Criteria of Significance and Priority in Curriculum

In its developmental stage, a curriculum is, or should be, an object of critical appraisal to its designers. When full blown and in operation, it becomes an object of critical appraisal not only to the designers themselves but also to diverse observers outside the profession. Parents understandably take an interest in it—but so do critics, informed and uninformed, of educational policy. Once in operation, a curriculum is public property. Critics zero in on it, and school personnel involved in it customarily have to justify and defend it.

When curriculum personnel are able to say "yes" to the following five basic questions, they have, in my opinion, the best grounds for defense of any given curriculum.[10]

Does the curriculum relate demonstrably to the purposes the school is committed to achieve?   As stated previously: a curriculum should rest on a foundation of cultural values. This is uncontested in the abstract, but it often becomes controversial when translated into action. In the translation national values occasionally are pitted against the state's or state values against a local community's. This is not surprising in view of the subjective nature of people and values.

[10] I have revised these somewhat since 1964 when I articulated them for later inclusion in Inlow, *The Emergent in Curriculum*, pp. 23–27.

Still education's frame has to be a humanistic one—a frame that commits education to advance the welfare of all pupils, irrespective of their differences. This position is no longer contestable. A school staff, then, that can defend its curriculum as congruent with the traditions of humanism passes the first test of curriculum appropriateness.

A school's staff passes the second test when its members can demonstrate that the curriculum is anchored in carefully thought-out educational goals. Consistent with my orientation, these need to lie along the several dimensions of the cognitive, emotional, social, ethical and physical. Or, in the wording employed earlier in the chapter, a school needs to develop individual personality; to ready individuals to assume occupational roles, consumers' roles, and home-and-family roles in the culture; to perpetuate the culture; and to develop the social order. A curriculum oriented exclusively to intellectual concerns, (if this is possible) fails the criterion of breadth. But, by the same logic, a curriculum oriented one-sidedly to home-and-family concerns fails the criterion of intellectuality. Neither pattern is defensible.

Does the curriculum draw in a balanced way from the several sources that feed into it? Curriculum sources, it will be recalled, are: the time-tested disciplines, the evolving disciplines, the existing social order, the needs of learners, and the contributions of instructional personnel. By the term balanced, however, we do not mean that all five should contribute equally at every educational level. Not at all! In the lower grades, for instance, the disciplines inevitably play a lesser role than they do in the higher grades. Stated in another way, they are modified for the lower grades and taught more straightforwardly in the higher grades. Because the young need an extensive exposure to concrete reality before they can maturely grasp abstract concepts, elementary school teachers rely heavily for curriculum content on the immediate world of the learners.

Teachers rely less heavily on concrete learning, however, as pupils advance through the grades. By the time pupils have reached the upper-middle grades, and certainly by the time they have reached the high school grades, most of them are ready for a balanced diet of abstract and concrete learning. The disciplines serve as vehicles for the abstract; the ongoing world and the individual learner himself constitute vehicles for the empirical concrete.

The disciplines serve the following important functions. First and foremost, they stand as tightly condensed pictures of life through the ages. And because condensed, they transmit man's cumulative store of

120

knowledge in an efficient and economical way. Second, the disciplines are unequaled as avenues to life's universals—man's emotions, his dilemmas, his failures, his successes. They also portray cultures both individually and comparatively: governmental structures, social institutions, problems, and antidotes. With little doubt, the disciplines are man's best single source of values. But they should not stand alone in a curriculum. When they do, they easily become detached from the mainstream of current living. They play their best curriculum role when integrated with everyday problems and when related to the uniqueness of individual learners.

Does the curriculum meet the test of learner readiness? Though a curriculum points toward clear-cut educational goals and strikes a proper balance among its several feeder sources, it is inadequate unless it meets the criterion of learner readiness. This criterion relates to the abilities, needs—both long- and short-term—and interests of learners. The implication is that curriculum workers should not formulate learning designs and then superimpose them arbitrarily on pupils. Such an approach might be functional if students were statistics, but it is never more than accidentally functional for most flesh-and-blood pupils.

Ideally, individual teachers should study individual learners first and only then tailor a curriculum for each. However, mass education, lack of time, and teacher limitations combine to make this approach impractical. Historically, the compromise has been a curriculum designed and indiscriminately applied at all grade or subject matter levels of a school system. Such an approach presupposes, for instance, that first graders in a given school in the Battery area of Manhattan Island are similar in makeup and background to first graders in a favored school in Queens—a presupposition too naïve to deserve comment. In any of the nation's large cities, a mean-average difference of from 20 to 25 IQ points between two schools, one in an upper-middle class and one in a slum area, would not be surprising. Dick and Jane, or Ivanhoe and Rowena, or Darwin and Mendel, might get by with flying colors in the one while falling academically flat in the other.

My point here is not to deprecate curriculum formulations designed as teacher guides. It is to criticize them when they are unduly prescriptive and when they arbitrarily restrict and constrict. In the last analysis, competent classroom teachers, inasmuch as they alone can determine a pupil's readiness for learning, are the best judges of which predesigned curriculum materials are appropriate and which are not.

121

Does the curriculum have a justifiable vertical and horizontal relationship among the various parts? This fourth criterion of significance has to do with integration and articulation: that is, the degree to which the various curriculum components interrelate. This criterion has both vertical and horizontal dimensions. A curriculum defensible vertically is one in which any single curriculum component has meaningful sequence from kindergarten through the high school grades. In the field of the social studies, for instance, a curriculum should progress more or less as follows: from the circumscribed environment of the individual to the ever-expanding environment of the human race; from the few to the many; from simple facts to concepts of increasing complexity; from the correlated overview to the intensive penetration of the single discipline; and, throughout, from knowledge and understanding to critical thinking. Not only social studies, but applied arts, fine arts, language, literature, mathematics, and natural sciences should evolve logically and psychologically in a vertically meaningful way.

A curriculum defensible horizontally is one in which the content of any segment integrates meaningfully with the content of all other related segments. Reading in grade 1, for instance, should integrate with all other components of the curriculum for any given child in that grade. Thus, rather than being "taught" only at 9 a.m. and 1 p.m. daily, reading would be foundational to most of the other learning activities taking place throughout the school day. By the same logic, United States history and American literature should not exist as unrelated subjects in grade 11 of a high school. Instead, either the respective teachers should relate them, or a single teacher should correlate them in a combined-subjects approach. The less mature the learner, the greater the likelihood of his needing help from teachers to achieve curriculum integration. The more mature the learner, the greater the likelihood of his being able to integrate the curriculum independently.

Does the curriculum lead to subsequent worthwhile learning? This fifth criterion—namely, education that leads to further education—is fundamental, but difficult to ascertain. Unquestionably, education that terminates with formal schooling fails in its basic purpose. Conversely, education that moves inexorably throughout life from one learning experience to another is education that fulfils its basic purpose.

A curriculum faithful to this criterion is one that relates functionally to the abilities, needs, and interests of students; and one that produces critical thinkers, not factual memorizers. The factual content of, for

instance, the decimal system, set theory, a tax law, a code of ethics, or Shakespeare's *Julius Caesar* is only the beginning of knowledge. Critical thinking about any one of these, however, represents education in the act of becoming a continuing process. It represents education moving toward its best. Facts learned in school may or may not transfer to life outside school; if the truth were known, most do not. But critical thinking, habitually encouraged and frequently employed in school, bodes well to become an established life pattern.

Participants in Curriculum Development

Participants in curriculum development range widely from lawmakers in the nation's capital to individuals of various orientations in local communities. The continuum includes the following: (1) individuals who, at the national level, influence social and educational policy in a general way; (2) statewide professional and political leadership groups, (3) local community pressure groups, (4) scholars from the various academic disciplines, (5) school administrators, (6) classroom teachers, (7) parents and students. Generally speaking, the greater the psychological distance from the classroom, the less the curriculum impact; conversely, the less the psychological distance, the greater the curriculum impact. This is merely another way of identifying education fundamentally as a local concern. National influences on curriculum generally are pervasive; state influences, though binding, are customarily general; only local influences control in a prescriptively detailed way.

Yet, despite the accuracy of the foregoing generalization, pressure groups removed from the classroom are mounting an increasingly vigorous campaign to influence curriculum in the nation's schools. The National Defense Education Act of 1958, re-enacted yearly since, has served to spearhead this campaign. The lion's share of NDEA funds, as stated in Chapter 3, has underwritten the updating of the natural sciences, mathematics, and modern languages in the schools. Specialists from universities and industry have joined hands with selected instructional leaders to prepare copious and lavishly supported curriculum materials. Some of these individuals, such as those who constitute the Physical Science Study Committee, the Biological Science Curriculum Study Committee, the Chemical Bond Approach Project, the Chemical Education Materials Study Committee, the School Mathematics Study Group, and the Modern Foreign Language Association meet together as curriculum groups.[11]

So constituted, they formulate for publication textbooks and extensive supplementary curriculum materials. A number of schools have adopted them as published. Yet it should be emphasized, in this connection, that the publications are intrinsically *curriculum resources*, not *curriculum mandates*. A given state or a given school has the right to adopt or not to adopt them. When they are adopted, classroom

---

[11] See Inlow, *The Emergent in Curriculum*, Chap. 7, for an elaboration of these large-scale curriculum projects.

teachers should have extensive latitude in converting the materials to instructional patterns.

Many individuals—scholars, professional educators, school administrators, teachers, parents, and others—often join together in curriculum planning. When knowledgeable and interested, they create a better curriculum than any one group alone could produce. In the last analysis, however, classroom teachers should be the final arbiters of curriculum designs. They alone are close enough to learners to ascertain the latter's unique abilities, needs, and interests. They alone should be the final judges of what curriculum materials are germane for the learners in their charge.

Curriculum Organization Schemes

From school system to school system, curricula differ as much in organizational design as they do in other respects. As stated early in the chapter, curriculum constitutes the planned composite effort of any school to guide pupils toward predetermined learning outcomes. As schools assume this guidance function, they weave curriculum into a variety of configurations, such as: (1) the single-subject curriculum, (2) the combined-subjects curriculum, (3) the broad-fields curriculum, (4) the life-function curriculum, and (5) the activity curriculum.

The *single-subject* approach is categorically exclusive in most high schools, parallels other approaches in many junior high schools, but is only auxiliary in most elementary schools. Illustrative of single subjects at the three levels are United States history, world geography, and spelling, respectively. The rationale behind the single-subject approach is identical to the one behind the single-discipline approach. It has two facets: that knowledge divides logically into distinct life areas, each of which has its own methods and rules; the second is that learners who have been exposed to knowledge thus atomized will be able to integrate it into a meaningful whole. This rationale, although never airtight, is more defensible for older than for younger pupils, for the more experienced than for the uninitiated, for the brighter than for the slower, and for the more mature than for the less mature. Thus the status of the single subject is more secure in the higher than in the lower grades of any school system.

Even under ideal conditions, teachers should never assume that psychological transfer from one subject to another will automatically **125**

take place. Instead they should instruct for transfer by relating ideas and concepts taught in one subject to ideas and concepts taught in another. A plural subject used with a singular verb is no more grammatical in a class in home economics than in a class in English. A favorable balance of trade extolled in a history class should not escape the arithmetical implications germane to a class in mathematics; nor should the phenomenon of increased life expectancy germane to a biology class avoid the social implications of that scientific phenomenon in a problems-of-democracy class. And malnutrition is not just a chemical consideration but a social and ethical one as well. The single subject unquestionably has made, and will continue to make, a significant contribution to learning. Its value always enhances, however, when teachers employ it as a springboard for psychological transfer.

In the late 1930s, education started to inch away from single subjects toward combined ones. *The Story of the Eight-Year Study*[12] by Wilford Aiken and his associates gave impetus to this move. The most significant conclusion of the study was that college performance does not suffer (in fact, generally improves) as a result of high school preparation in combined-studies curriculum arrangements that concentrate on learning content of immediate relevance to the lives of the learners.

In a *combined-studies* schema, two or more single subjects join to form a more or less composite subject. Such a pattern has for decades characterized the curricula of the more advanced elementary schools throughout the country. Since the time of the Aiken study, the schema has increasingly become the vogue in junior high schools, particularly in suburban systems. For a few years, it made a sizeable dent in the organizational patterns of high schools, but its influence there has waned since the early 1950s.

When subjects are loosely combined, retaining their essential discreteness, they generally bear the label of combined studies or unified studies. When definitely integrated, however, they generally bear the label of correlated or core studies. English and social studies are the subjects most commonly joined. Science and mathematics; English, art, and music; and English and a foreign language constitute less commonplace fusions or combinations. Within the single field of science, fusions of biology, chemistry, and physics are beginning to be essential.

When curriculum appears in a *broad-fields* pattern, it generally employs such labels as the language arts, the natural sciences, social

[12] Wilford M. Aiken, *The Story of the Eight-Year Study* (New York: Harper & Row, Publishers, 1942).

EDUCATION AS AN OPERATIONAL PROCESS

studies, or the fine and applied arts. The obvious purpose of the broad-fields arrangement is increased curriculum integration of related learning components. In actuality, the broad-fields pattern is merely an extension of the combined-studies pattern. Operationally, its impact has been primarily on the elementary and junior high school curricula.

A number of schools, mostly elementary, have organized the curriculum around so-called *life functions* or processes. Advocates of this plan seek a closer relationship between the academic experiences of pupils in a school and their actual experiences in life outside the school, with improved psychological transfer resulting. The curriculum components generally bear such labels as health, communication, citizenship, personal relationships, science in our lives, esthetics, the use of numbers, and others. The plan's critics tend to view it as a change more of labels than of actual curriculum content, pointing out that the plan draws substantially on traditional subjects for content. The critics also argue that the life-function curriculum either forces teachers into excessive preparation, even to the point of mastering sizable bodies of new content, or exposes learners to inadequate instruction.

I touch but lightly on the so-called *activity-curriculum* plan, which is a throwback to the thirties when child-centered enthusiasts were waging jugular warfare against their more stolid subject-centered counterparts. The characteristic features of an activity curriculum, at least in theory, are these: content that relates closely to the developmental needs and interests of learners, problem-solving activity by learners, a strong emphasis on the present, and an equally strong emphasis on social outcomes. To my way of thinking, these features are not the exclusive property of any single curriculum arrangement but are intrinsic to every arrangement worthy of the name curriculum.

ORGANIZATIONAL IMPLEMENTATION

As established earlier in the chapter, a curriculum design takes shape slowly. Curriculum builders first identify the values that control a culture. From these, they formulate educational objectives. Next, they draw up a curriculum design that appears to hold the greatest promise of achieving the formulated objectives.

The tasks that still lie ahead are those of curriculum implementation. The most complex of these grow out of the problems that confront teachers in converting a broad curriculum design to a functional instruc- **127**

tional medium. A curriculum plan can be broad at a school system or building level, but it inevitably has to become operationally specific at a classroom level. It is at this latter level that teachers interpret it, select from it, elaborate it, supplement it, integrate instructional method with it, and evaluate it. Some teachers organize it into learning units; all teachers, in one way or another, organize it into daily lessons. Because of the general nature of this book, however, I pass lightly over these topics.

At the administrative level, curriculum implementation is inseparable from these two problems: how a school should utilize teachers for best results, and how it should group pupils for instructional purposes. The first of these, teacher utilization, is many faceted. At the elementary level, it involves the issue of whether the primary grades should be self-contained, with a single teacher responsible for each classroom, or whether specialists in such subjects as art, music, and physical education should complement the efforts of the classroom teacher. At the junior and senior high school levels, it involves the issue of whether teachers should instruct in single subjects or in combined ones. At all levels, it involves the issues of team teaching versus the single teacher, of class size, teaching load, and supervision.

The second of these administrative problems, pupil grouping, is also many faceted. It involves the issues of homogeneous grouping versus heterogeneous grouping, large-class grouping in a team-teaching arrangement versus small-class grouping in a more conventional arrangement, and pupil effort under direct teacher supervision versus pupil effort in an independent-study arrangement. These topics too, in view of their specialized nature, receive only passing comment here. The one on pupil grouping, however, will undergo more detailed development in subsequent parts of the book.

A POINT OF VIEW

In the last analysis, a curriculum of any school is no more or no less than a learning design to help children grow. It joins forces with the more informal curricula of the home, the community, and the church or synagogue, to guide children and youth toward maturity. A school's curriculum, in the natural order of things, starts out behind the scenes as a creation of professional educators. It mirrors their professional insights about, and their past experiences with, groups of learners. A **128** curriculum constitutes an efficient approach to student learning.

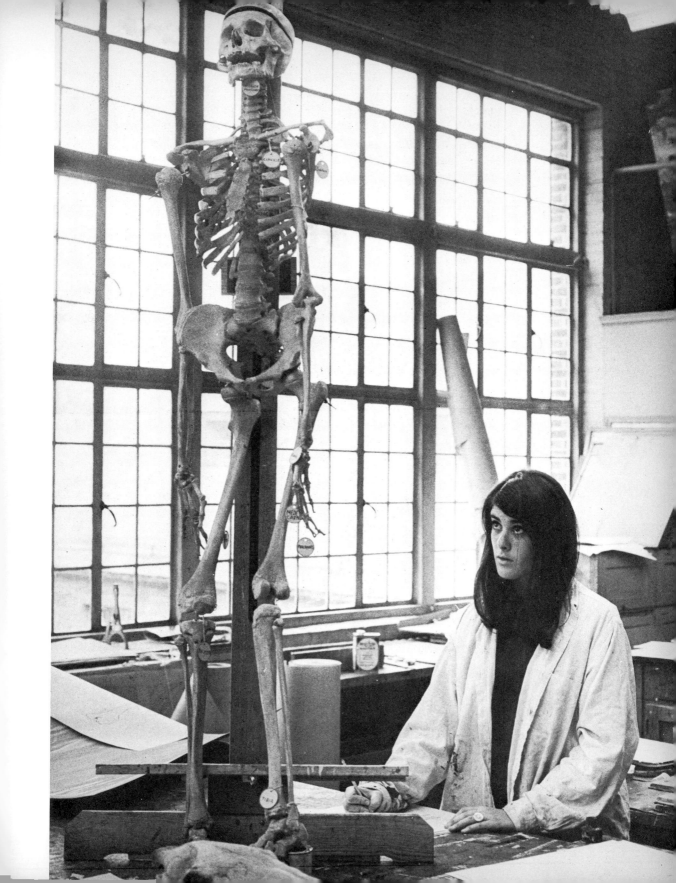

Schools invite criticism, however, when they assume that a preconceived curriculum will automatically meet the needs of all intended learners or of an individual learner. Schools invite criticism when they ignore the fact that a curriculum can never be more than an estimate—an educated guess about the activities that learners should engage in. Flexibility, then, is the needed ingredient of curriculum quality. I say with conviction that a curriculum can be effective only when teachers have the right and the insight to adapt it meaningfully to the abilities and needs of their pupils.

To Stimulate Thought

1. Review the several definitions of curriculum presented at the beginning of the chapter and identify the one you like best. Then defend your choice.

2. John Dewey consistently held that a school should be a miniature society. React to his stand and defend your point of view.

3. React critically to the contention of Bruner and Phenix, among others, that the disciplines per se should make up a school's curriculum. Defend your response in terms not only of your own intended teaching field but of other fields as well.

4. Following Bruner's and Phenix's line of reasoning, what disciplines, if any, should constitute the curriculum of grade 1, for instance?

5. What disciplines can you name that have achieved accepted status in the past hundred years?

6. Debate the assertion that single subjects are more defensible for older, more mature learners than for younger, less mature learners. Weave in the concept of psychological transfer in your response.

7. React to the author's point of view that a knowledgeable teacher should be the final arbiter of a curriculum's appropriateness.

8. Debate the pros and cons of a national curriculum for all schools in the United States.

9. Evaluate the author's contention that a curriculum plan conceived outside the frame of a known learning situation should be a *curriculum resource* only.

10. What role do you think liberal-arts scholars should play in curriculum development? If you conceive their role to be a significant one, should they first know the abilities and needs of the pupils to be affected by their curriculum efforts? Elaborate your stand.

EDUCATION AS AN OPERATIONAL PROCESS

REFERENCES

Association for Supervision and Curriculum Development, *Perceiving, Behaving, Becoming: A New Focus for Education* (Washington, D.C.: ASCD, 1962).

Association for Supervision and Curriculum Development, *What Are the Sources of Curriculum?* (Washington, D.C.: ASCD, 1962).

Beauchamp, George A., *Curriculum Theory,* 2nd Ed. (Wilmette, Ill.: Kagg Press, 1968).

Bloom, Benjamin S. (ed.), *Taxonomy of Educational Objectives: Cognitive Domain* (New York: David McKay Company, Inc., 1956).

Bruner, Jerome S., *The Process of Education* (Cambridge, Mass.: Harvard University Press, 1960).

Cay, Donald F., *Curriculum: Design for Learning* (Indianapolis: The Bobbs-Merrill Company, Inc., 1966).

Fraser, Dorothy M., *Deciding What to Teach* (Washington, D.C.: NEA, 1963).

Goodlad, John I., *Planning and Organizing for Teaching* (Washington, D.C.: NEA, 1963).

Goodlad, John, *School Curriculum Reform* (New York: The Fund for the Advancement of Education, 1964).

Hanna, Lavone, "Meeting the Challenge," *What Are the Sources of Curriculum?* (Washington, D.C.: Association for Supervision and Curriculum Development, 1962).

Keith, Lowell, Paul Blake, and Sidney Tiedt, *Contemporary Curriculum in the Elementary School* (New York: Harper & Row, Publishers, 1968).

King, Arthur R., Jr., and John A. Brownell, *The Curriculum and the Disciplines of Knowledge* (New York: John Wiley & Sons, Inc., 1966).

Miller, Richard I., *Education in a Changing Society* (Washington, D.C.: NEA, 1963).

Oliver, Albert I., *Curriculum Improvement: A Guide to Problems, Principles, and Procedures* (New York: Dodd, Mead & Company, Inc., 1965).

Phenix, Philip H., *Realms of Meaning* (New York: McGraw-Hill, Inc., 1964).

Taba, Hilda, *Curriculum Development: Theory and Practice* (New York: Harcourt, Brace & World, Inc., 1962).

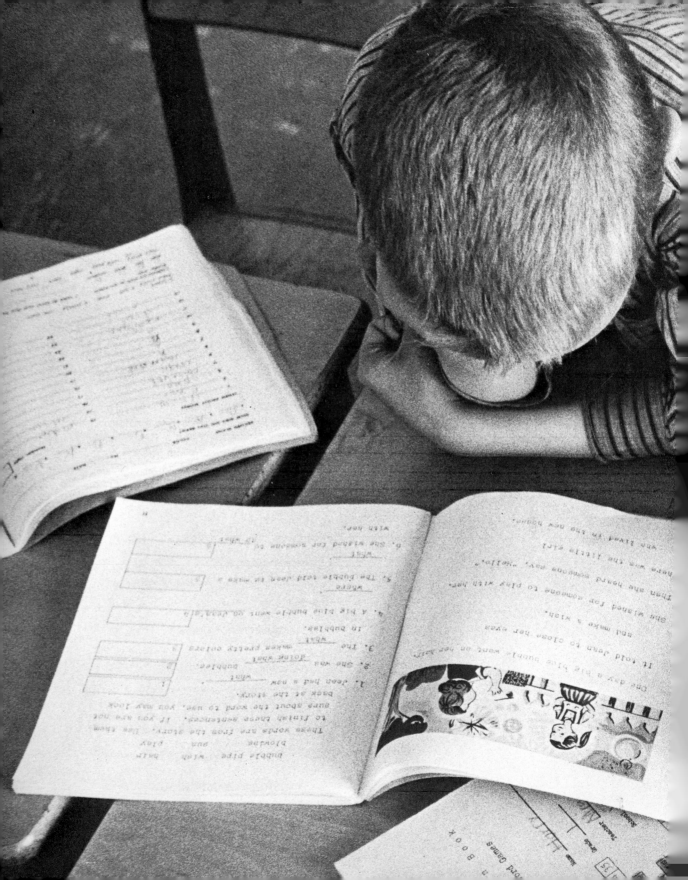

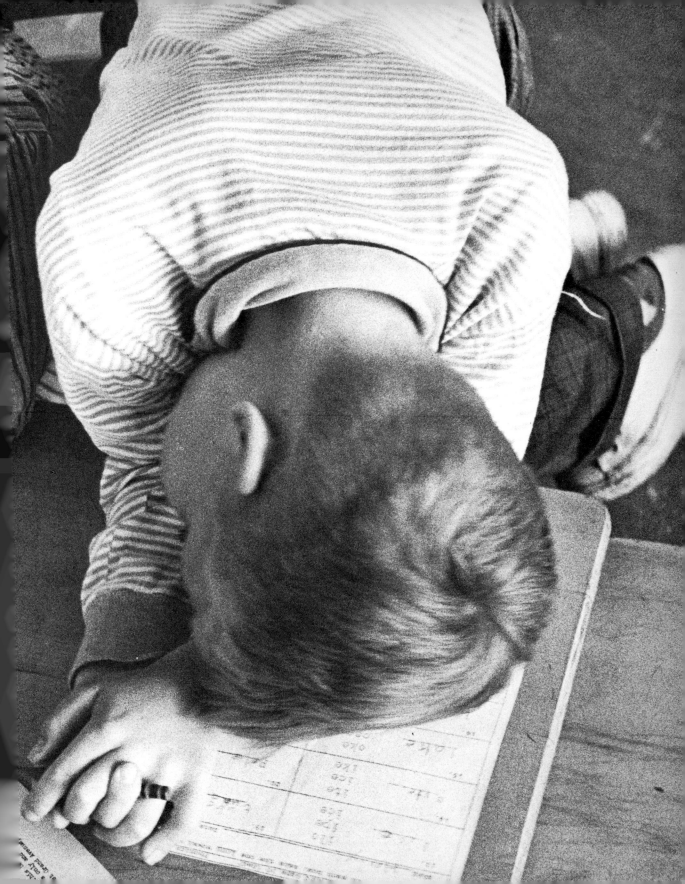

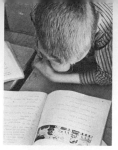

Chapter
6

The
Elementary
School

The right of the young to formal education goes unquestioned through-out the civilized world. Civilized societies have the obligation to honor this right. The reason for the universality of elementary education is that civilized cultures, desirous of remaining civilized, realize the necessity of educating each new generation in the ways of the controlling social group.

From this country's earliest beginnings, elementary education thus has been as much a part of the culture as religion, government, and the economic system. Today it is definitely big business, as the enrollment totals presented earlier in Chapter 3 and repeated selectively here at-test. Presented in Table 6.1 are the student enrollment figures for the nation's elementary and secondary schools in 1968.

At the opening of school in 1968, approximately 29 million children were enrolled in grades K–6 and 8 million additional in grades 7–8, the two adding to an impressive total of almost 37 million.

TABLE 6.1   PUPIL ENROLLMENTS, K-GRADE 12, UNITED STATES, FALL, 1968

School Level	Totals	Public	Nonpublic
K-grade 8	36,700,000	32,100,000	4,600,000
grades 9-12	14,200,000	12,600,000	1,400,000
totals	50,900,000	44,900,000	6,000,000

Source: Kenneth A. Simon and W. Vance Grant, *Digest of Educational Statistics 1968*, OE-10024-68 (Washington, D.C.: U.S. Department of Health, Education, and Welfare, 1968), p. 2.

Until the past century, the elementary school bore the label of common school. The school was "common," however, not in the sense of being ordinary or lacking in refinement but rather in being more or less open to all. The elementary school, by whatever label, constitutes a tacit admission on the part of any culture that the home is an inappropriate agency of formal education. It may be inadequate for one or more of the following reasons: education on an individual basis is excessively costly of time and effort; parents may not have the time to devote to the many tasks involved; they may lack the qualifications required; and, of particular significance, emotional and social growth are difficult, if not impossible, for a child to attain in social isolation

from peers. In contrast, formal education reaps the benefits of parsimony, discriminates in the selection of instructional figures, and provides a climate in which children are helped to grow affectively as well as intellectually.

SELECTED HISTORICAL ANTECEDENTS

Elementary education assumed a semblance of form soon after the landing of the founding fathers at Jamestown in 1607 and at Plymouth Rock in 1620. Formal education, in fact, lagged only a step or two behind efforts aimed at physical survival—the building of log shelters, the clearing of land, the planting of crops, and the fending against hostile natives. For a brief time only, these essential activities shunted education to the background. In this period, children received occasional didactic instruction from their parents. More often, though, they learned by living. Observation, exploration, and involvement were their learning methods.

Formal education as early as the 1630s began to emerge from the background. And, because it was a mirror of social and political differences among the colonies, it took on diverse organizational shapes and forms.

In the New England Colonies, formal education almost from the start took the form of a public function. Colony-wide laws, passed from time to time, established the broad legal frame; local control customarily wrote in the operational details. The town meeting usually constituted the major decision-making agency.

Puritans, in the New England Colonies, were the dominant religious group; thus church and state, in effect, were one and the same. And, because Puritanism was a potpourri of religious fundamentalism and classical humanism, the *Bible* and the classics, along with the basic educational essentials, made up the curriculum—at least for the gifted and culturally advantaged.

In these early Colonies, the so-called public schools differed in a number of ways from their modern counterparts. They were public in the sense of being controlled by established authority and of being open to most of the public, but not in the sense of being free to all of the public. Public schools received financial support from both governmental and private sources. Those parents able to pay tuition had to do so; parents unable to pay sent their children to school at public expense. Generally, however, the children of the poor received a more abbreviated education than did the children of the affluent—one that customarily stopped with educational and religious fundamentals.

In the Middle Colonies, diversity of religious belief was a dominant characteristic. Schools generally were church controlled: by Quakers, Dunkards, Moravians, Lutherans, or Mennonites, as several examples. Sectarian control of education was a compromise growing out of religious diversity. The quality of education suffered somewhat as a result.

In the Southern Colonies, with social stratification a controlling characteristic, education operated essentially as a private function. The landed gentry, who controlled the culture, actually pre-empted England's educational system and implanted it, with little change, into the Southern Colonies. It embraced such features as private "prep" schools, tutors, and other evidences of social exclusiveness. For the poor, it embraced such counter features as pauper or charity schools and apprenticeships. The various Southern Colonial governments became actively involved only as required to satisfy the minimum educational needs of paupers, orphans, and apprentices.

In the Colonial period, the curriculum of elementary education, although unified by religious bonds, generally divided along lines of classical and nonclassical content. Latin grammar schools, the first of which appeared in Boston in 1635, placed a heavy stress on classical learning. Eligibility requirements included, among other requisites, a solid grounding in reading, writing, and syntax. Enrollees typically were children from the favored socioeconomic classes. They enrolled at the age of seven or eight and maintained their student status for a period

137

of approximately seven years. The controlling purpose of most of the Latin grammar schools was to ready pupils for college and the professions; the classically oriented curriculum was tailored to that central purpose. Significantly, Harvard in the middle of the seventeenth century required entering freshmen to read Cicero by sight and to employ correct syntax in the translation of Greek.

The Latin grammar school has no counterpart in education today. In effect, it was an upper elementary school and a high school combined into a single organizational unit. Its goals were clear-cut, its student body was highly select, its curriculum was rigid, and its standards were exacting. The best covering statement about it is that it served well the social in-group of its day. Members of this group required the schools, on the one hand, to indoctrinate students with religious dogma, and, on the other hand, to inundate them in classical learning. The basic skills of communication were obviously fundamental to both.

Elementary education for the masses, only secondarily implanted in classical traditions, had as its central themes religion and the basic skills. For approximately a century, classes were conducted in the native language of the controlling ethnic group in any locale. Once the Anglican culture attained dominance, however, the English language took over as the accepted medium of communication. The three R's, framed in a religious setting, constituted the curriculum of the early Colonial schools. Yet as early as 1642, the first education law passed in Massachusetts introduced citizenship into the curriculum. It dictated that children be taught "to read and understand the principles of religion" and "the capital laws of this country" as well. The cause of the practical advanced yet another pace in 1685 when the Quaker Thomas Budd successfully argued that the schools, in addition to their other curriculum functions, should teach bookkeeping and a useful trade such as "woodworking, clockmaking, weaving, or shoemaking."[1] Budd was elementary education's forerunner of secondary education's Benjamin Franklin, steered the academy down utilitarian paths.

The New England Primer, written around 1700, was the most widely used teaching resource in the eighteenth century. Designed for the Puritans, it supplied teachers and pupils with alphabet drills and reading selections of a religious nature. The latter included Bible stories, moralistic preachments, the Ten Commandments, the Beatitudes, the Lord's Prayer, and the Apostles' Creed.

[1] R. Freeman Butts and Lawrence A. Cremin, *A History of Education in American Culture* (New York: Holt, Rinehart, and Winston, Inc., 1953), p. 77.

EDUCATION AS AN OPERATIONAL PROCESS

Elementary education in the colonies assumed many organizational faces. In New England, it often took the form of the *reading school,* which included reading and religion as its only curriculum components. In such a school, the hornbook habitually served both causes. It was a paddle-shaped board enclosed in parchment, on which were embossed various language symbols and religious selections. Another elementary organizational form was the *writing school,* generally more advanced than the reading school. Still a third was the so-called *dame* school, usually under the care of a neighborhood matron who instructed a small group in the skills of communication, in religion, and, at times, in the household arts. Yet again, elementary education often took the form of a master instructing an apprentice, of a parent instructing a child, or of an itinerant school master moving throughout a community instructing first one group, then another.

139

THE ELEMENTARY SCHOOL

In the eighteenth and nineteenth centuries, significant trends and events in elementary education include the following. Religion increasingly conceded to the secular. Greek and Latin lost ground to the vernacular. The curriculum broadened down many lines toward the practical. The quality and quantity of curriculum materials, particularly textbooks, improved dramatically. Teacher competency rose noticeably. Children attended school in increasing numbers. State rights over education, including the right to tax and to control, became firmly established. Pauper schools became passé.

These specific events are noteworthy:

1776 Pennsylvania became the first state to assert its authority over education.

1779 Massachusetts became the first state to grant to local school districts the authority to operate schools under their respective jurisdiction.

1806 The Lancastrian-Bell School, a transplant from England, opened its door in New York. Its features were formal lessons taught to precocious students, who then helped the instructor teach a class of 100 or more learners. Joseph Lancaster and Andrew Bell were responsible for its earlier inception in England.

1820 A Massachusetts law made geography a part of the curriculum.

1839 The first state normal school opened (in Massachusetts).

1850 The right of states to levy and collect taxes for the support of elementary education was settled by this midcentury date.

By this same date, except for the agrarian element in the South and submiddle-class groups elsewhere, elementary education had become the rule rather than the exception.[2]

1855 The first kindergarten (conducted in German) opened in Wisconsin.

1860 The first kindergarten (conducted in English) opened in Boston.

By the end of the nineteenth century, elementary education was a thriving institution woven into the social fabric of local communities throughout the nation. Its curriculum, less exclusively centered than formerly in the basic skills, consisted additionally of content from the social studies, natural sciences, health, and art. Faced with instructional

[2] Butts and Cremin, p. 237.

inadequacies, many of them glaring, elementary education had begun a campaign to upgrade standards of teacher preparation. Needless to say, the campaign is still in progress.

An important next step was for elementary education to absorb and apply the newer concepts that were evolving in the areas of child development and learning. The following are illustrative: that children pass through various growth stages, each with curriculum implications; that they pass through these stages at uneven rates; that children differ widely in abilities, interests, and needs; and that readiness is an essential of learning. At the end of the nineteenth century, elementary education was firmly on the threshold of modernity.

OBJECTIVES OF ELEMENTARY EDUCATION

With the coming of the twentieth century, the need for elementary education to identify, articulate, and be able to justify its purposes loomed as a major task. For over 200 years it had pursued a course that was more imitative than creative, that was more comfortable with the Western world's cognitive traditions than with the same world's developing psychological traditions. The thesis that knowledge alone was the answer to practically all problems except religious ones had become an established cultural truism.

Past patterns began to meet increasing resistance, however, from a number of advanced thinkers who, in the late nineteenth and twentieth centuries, challenged the society, including education, with their revolutionary ideas. One of these advanced thinkers was Sigmund Freud (1856–1939), the father of psychoanalysis. He disturbed the status quo greatly with his postulates about the unconscious mind, about environmental determinism, and about the possibility of individuals undergoing significant personality change. According to Freud, learners are as much products of their emotional selves as they are of their rational selves. They are composites of their total environments, past and present: composites of home, school, church, and community influences. Because they are products of powerful influences that lie outside as well as within themselves, they have only limited control over their behavior. The function of instructional personnel is to understand learners as complete individuals and administer to their psyches (psychological selves including the emotions) as well as to their rational minds.

George Herbert Mead (1863–1931) was another of these innovators. His central theme was that individuals are not born with identity but must work through to identity by social living. Human essence develops, and people become individuals, said Mead, only when they themselves work for such outcomes. To Mead, education was important because it constituted the surest approach to social communication and human relationships. In effect, Mead injected into education the social ingredient to complement the rational ingredient that had long been dominant. Mead's affect on education, however, was indirect; his primary influence was through others who shared his ideas.

One of these was John Dewey (1859–1952), whose impact on education has been nothing short of stupendous. He and other philosophical pragmatists, such as Charles S. Peirce and William James, espoused the following tenets: (1) truth is ever evolving, never fixed; (2) social workability and utility constitute its sanctions; (3) the social group is the sanctioning agent; and (4) experience in general, and the methods of science, in particular, supersede all *a priori* suppositions.

Another forward thinker, the psychologist-educator Edward L. Thorndike (1874–1949), made contributions to education almost too numerous to mention, much less describe. Significant among them were the following postulates: (1) that learning is a function both of the readiness of the learner and of the effect of learning on him; (2) that the classical subjects are not the panaceas that academically oriented scholars had long made them out to be; (3) that learning transfers from one situation to another only to the extent that any two learning situations share common components; and (4) that learning, to be good, does not necessarily have to be learning that is difficult or unpleasant.

Freud, Mead, Dewey, Thorndike and other forward thinkers at the turn of the century steered elementary education into new directions. Among other contributions, they established the fact of individual differences among learners; they disclosed behavior as an inwardly caused as well as an outwardly manifested phenomenon; they injected relativity into value theory, uprooting the latter from the dead center of absolute rightness and wrongness; they highlighted the social and emotional aspects of education, long concealed by the cognitive; and while steering education into new directions, they did so without deprecating the cause of the rational. Rather, they projected the rational into its proper role as one of several value components.

With philosophical thought changing the nature of education, formal goal pronouncements to mirror the many changes soon followed. The

EDUCATION AS AN OPERATIONAL PROCESS

Seven Cardinal Principles constituted one of these pronouncements. Although designed for secondary education, six of the seven principles —all but the vocational one—had equal applicability to elementary education. The six applicable ones were health, command of the fundamental processes, worthy home membership, citizenship, worthy use of leisure time, and ethical character.[3] Twenty years later, as indicated previously in Chapter 2, the Educational Policies Commission of the National Education Association identified 43 objectives as lying within the purview of elementary and secondary education. The Commission grouped these 43 under the four major headings of self-realization, human relationships, economic efficiency, and civic responsibility.[4]

In 1953, elementary education was responsible for yet a third pronouncement of objectives, with Nolan C. Kearney the guiding force. Kearney's investigative procedure embraced the following steps: (1) identifying the many goal formulations promulgated for elementary education in the United States; (2) assembling these into a master list; (3) submitting the list to a representative sample of elementary school theorists and practitioners, with the request that they indicate goal priorities; and (4) compiling the results into yet another statement of elementary school objectives. The statement in its completed form embraces the following nine categories:[5]

1. Physical development, health, and body care
2. Individual social and emotional development
3. Ethical behavior, standards, values
4. Social relations
5. The social world
6. The physical world (the natural environment)
7. Esthetic development
8. Communication
9. Quantitative relationships

Kearney elaborated each of the nine, annotating category 2, for instance, with the statement: "This category includes material that is

[3] Commission on Reorganization of Secondary Education, *Cardinal Principles of Education,* U.S. Office of Education Bulletin No. 35, 1918 (Washington, D.C.: U.S. Government Printing Office, 1918), pp. 10–11.

[4] Educational Policies Commission, *The Purposes of Education in American Democracy* (Washington, D.C.: NEA, 1938), pp. 50, 72, 90, 108.

[5] Nolan C. Kearney, *Elementary School Objectives* (New York: Russell Sage Foundation, 1953), pp. 52–113.

commonly associated with mental health, emotional stability, and the growth of personality. . . ." Its emphasis is "on such goals as understanding oneself and evaluating oneself."

Three years later, in 1956, the following ten objectives highlighted the Yale-Fairfield Study of Elementary Teaching: (1) physical health, (2) mental and emotional health, (3) communication, (4) quantitative understanding, (5) social relationships, (6) understanding the social environment, (7) moral and spiritual values, (8) understanding the physical world, (9) critical thinking, and (10) esthetic and creative development.[6]

From the foregoing, elementary education emerges as a many-dimensioned phenomenon. Faithful to the traditions of all civilized cultures, it accords the communications skills and selected important cultural antecedents a central place. But with each succeeding generation, it gives an increasingly significant place to the physical- and mental-health needs of pupils, to their social-growth needs, and to their ethical-value needs.

Freud, Mead, Dewey, and Thorndike did not dream their dreams in vain. Far from it, their dreams have come to fruition in the many elementary school classrooms of the country. Even the reactionary efforts in the 1950s and 1960s by an assertive coterie of intellectually oriented theorists failed to turn back the tide of liberal progress. The intellectualist crusade, while converting a few educational theorists to its cause, made little more than a dent in the thinking and behavior of the practitioners who were working day in and day out with the nation's young.

ORGANIZATIONAL ARRANGEMENTS IN ELEMENTARY EDUCATION

Once elementary school leaders formulate satisfactory educational goals, their next task is to program for them. Such a step involves both curriculum and organizational determinations. In a school setting, the order of priority would be curriculum before organization. In this theoretical setting, however, I have reversed the order, on the assumption that the treatment of curriculum will be more meaningful to the reader if preceded by a discussion of certain organizational arrangements.

[6] C. M. Hill and others, *Yale-Fairfield Study of Elementary Teaching* (New Haven: Yale University Press, 1956), Chap. 6.

Length of Elementary Education

One of the more basic of these considerations has to do with the length of elementary education, which historically has been a variable of time and place. Until the late nineteenth century, patterns differed so widely that prediction was impossible. By the century's end, however, an eight-year program throughout most of the country, with the exception of a seven-year program in the South, had become fairly common practice. Children usually completed the eight-year program by the age of thirteen or fourteen. And even in the South, the seven-year program increasingly conceded to the longer one.

With the advent and rapid development of the junior high school in the twentieth century, variable patterns again emerged. One obvious reason for the variability was that some school systems had junior high schools, whereas others did not. Those that did tended to think of elementary education as terminating when pupils entered the junior high school. Yet another reason for the variability was that junior high schools themselves differed in length and in the grades they embraced. Some were three-year schools encompassing grades 7–9 customarily, or 6–8 in certain instances. Others were two-year schools encompassing grades 7–8. Systems with junior high schools tended to think of elementary education as embracing only grades 1–5 or 1–6; those without such schools continued to think of elementary education as embracing grades 1–8. As of the moment, many, if not most, of those schools with grades 1–8 in a single building or complex tend, for the most part, to combine the upper two or three grades (7–8 or 6–8) into a junior high kind of organizational arrangement. The latter customarily involves greater departmentalization of subject matter, greater choice of curriculum electives, more homogeneous grouping, and more school activities, to enumerate only four differences.

Informal Divisions within Elementary Education

An elementary education arrangement conceived as noninclusive of the junior high school grades generally divides, depending on point of view, in one of two ways: into two informal units—primary and intermediate—or into three informal units—preschool, primary, and intermediate. The primary unit is the controversial one. Consensus supports the inclusion of grades 1–3, but opinion differs regarding the inclusion

145

of kindergarten and nursery education. The intermediate unit most often embraces grades 4–6; occasionally, however, it embraces only grades 4–5 in instances where a junior high school has pre-empted grade 6. Because of the limited scope of nursery school education, we have omitted it from the chapter's treatment. Only 1 percent of all school districts, in fact, operate a public nursery school.[7]

The kindergarten   A relative newcomer to elementary education in the United States, the kindergarten was introduced around 1860 as a private operation. Its influence has increased significantly with each passing year. In 1873, in St. Louis, Missouri, it got its first start as part of a public school system. The superintendent of schools, William T. Harris, was the prime mover.[8]

Throughout its century-old history in the United States, the kindergarten movement has had to struggle for status against heavy odds. Until recently, even its legal position was in question. Also, until recently, the qualifications of many of its teachers were definitely substandard. And the curriculum of the kindergarten has been consistently controversial.

As of 1967, approximately 65 percent of all five-year-olds in the country were enrolled in kindergarten.[9] The number undoubtedly would have been greater had it not been for the fact that 48 percent of all school districts did not offer kindergarten programs. In the North Atlantic region, 72 percent offer them, whereas in the Southeast region only 4 percent do.[10] Seven states have no provisions whatsoever for kindergarten education.[11] Generally speaking, kindergartens are more likely to be found in large systems, particularly urban ones, than in small systems, particularly rural ones.

This lack of universality of kindergarten education is a shortcoming in the overall educational design. Contrary to the views of many, kindergartens are not play schools, though children do play in them. Neither are they baby-sitting centers, though teachers, in addition to their more

---

[7] Lillian L. Gore and Rose E. Koury, *A Survey of Early Elementary Education in Public Schools* (Washington, D.C.: U.S. Department of Health, Education, and Welfare, 1965), p. 46.

[8] William B. Ragan, *Modern Elementary Curriculum,* 3d ed. (New York: Holt, Rinehart and Winston, Inc., 1966), p. 17.

[9] Simon and Grant, p. 30.

[10] Gore and Koury, pp. 46–47.

[11] Gore and Koury, p. 2.

EDUCATION AS AN OPERATIONAL PROCESS

professional functions, serve as baby-sitters. More than either of these, kindergartens (and nursery schools as well) are important places of learning. They are places where planned growth experiences supplement the less formal growth experiences of the home and community, where children move increasingly from egocentric patterns to social ones, where ethnic differences may function as an asset rather than a liability, where children whose mothers work are not placed at a disadvantage, where children develop language proficiency.

Kindergartens, in effect, are responsible educational components concerned with the physical, emotional and social growth and the learning readiness of preschool children. The society needs to hasten the day when these pupils will be recognized and treated not as *preschool* but as *school* children.

The primary division, grades 1–3 A second educational experience for children who have attended kindergarten, and a first for those who have not, is grade 1 (or its equivalent in a nongraded school). Children customarily enter grade 1 at age six and remain in the so-called primary grades for an average of three years. During this period, as also will be developed in more detail later in the chapter, reading receives the greatest single curriculum emphasis.

The intermediate division, grades 4–6 For children who have made normal developmental progress in the lower elementary division(s), the intermediate unit constitutes the next educational rung. Not usually a discrete organizational unit, it relates to the growth needs of pupils who, on the average, are nine to eleven (or twelve) years of age. These children predictively are mostly prepubertal, their interests are mostly homosexual, their avocations are legion, and their tolerance for physical activity is at times unbelievable.

Grading versus Nongrading in Elementary Education

A controversial issue in elementary education is grading versus nongrading.[12] The issue should be viewed in historical perspective. In Greco-Roman days, a one-to-one teacher-pupil relationship was the accepted instructional pattern. In such an arrangement, a tutor brought to the

[12] I develop this topic in chapter-length treatment in *The Emergent in Curriculum* (New York: John W. Wiley & Sons, Inc., 1966), Chap. 15.

learning situation his preconceived ideas about what the pupil should learn; the pupil, in turn, communicated in various ways to the tutor how well he was responding; and the two made common property of their problems.

As education increasingly became the right of the many, not just the privilege of a favored few, tutorial instruction conceded correspondingly to group instruction. And, in the new scheme of things, the issue of how pupils should be grouped demanded resolution. When the issue became critical in the nineteenth century, Horace Mann proposed the graded plan as an answer. The latter was the creation of John Sturum who had tried it out in 1537, in Strassburg, Germany. In line with Mann's proposal, and Germany's three centuries of experience with the plan, John Philbrick, in 1848, gave it a trial run in the Quincy School of Boston. The organizational plan immediately took hold and soon became the established one throughout the country.[13]

Chronological age constitutes the basis of pupil grouping in the graded plan. The underlying assumption is that children of comparable ages have commensurately comparable abilities, interests, and needs. That they do not, however, has long ceased to be a topic of debate, assuming that it ever was. For instance, children in the first grade, almost routinely, have a mental-age range of four years. And by "the time children complete the fourth grade, the [mental-age] range in readiness to learn . . . in most areas of achievement is approximately the same as the number designating the grade level."[14] What greater proof of heterogeneity within the frame of assumed homogeneity need we offer?

Cognizant of the many shortcomings of grading by age as a basis of class grouping, a small but dedicated group of elementary education theoreticians and practitioners have recently turned to nongrading as an antidote. Western Springs, Illinois, adopted the plan in 1934, but dropped it soon thereafter. Milwaukee and Appleton, Wisconsin, however, have stayed with the plan since 1942 and 1947, respectively.[15]

Identifying characteristics of nongrading consist of the following: (1) pupils are organized into a three-year block (which becomes a four-

[13] Credit for much of this paragraph goes to B. Frank Brown, *The Nongraded High School* (Englewood Cliffs, N.J.: Prentice-Hall, Inc., 1963), pp. 27–28.

[14] John I. Goodlad and Robert H. Anderson, *The Nongraded Elementary School* (New York: Harcourt, Brace & World, Inc., 1963), p. 13.

[15] Lillian Gore, "The Nongraded Primary Unit," *School Life,* 44 (March 1962), pp. 6–9.

year block for some); nongrading operates more customarily at the primary level, at times additionally at the intermediate level; (3) conventional grade designations go by the board; (4) each pupil—in theory at least—progresses at his own rate up a graduated curriculum ladder; (5) at the end of a three-year period, pupils not deemed ready for the next academic rung remain a fourth year; (6) in respect to this latter point, advocates of nongrading aver that three years make a better basis for a decision on retardation than does one year.

Personally, I favor nongrading even though regarding the alleged advantages as more artifactual than factual. By this I mean that they may be products of a school's readying itself for nongrading rather than intrinsic outcomes of the plan itself. In this connection, vertical articulation in curriculum is as much a possibility in graded units as it is in nongraded ones. So, too, is curriculum differentiation for individuals and small groups. However, the feature of teachers having three years to decide about retardations is, without doubt, a unique and potentially worthwhile asset.

Pupil Grouping in Elementary Education

Whether a school is graded or nongraded, it ultimately has to assemble children into class-sized learning groups. One possible arrangement is children grouped "homogeneously" along lines of one or more of the following criteria: age, academic achievement, intelligence, reading ability, social maturity, emotional maturity, physical characteristics, or other factors. The practice of homogeneous grouping, however, despite its allure, misses the mark in this important respect: pupils grouped for homogeneity along lines of one criterion or of several criteria generally remain noticeably heterogeneous along lines of other criteria. For example, pupils grouped according to reading ability will not necessarily be homogeneous in their responses to arithmetic, the natural sciences, the esthetic subjects, and the practical arts. And pupils reasonably homogeneous in intelligence predictively will not be comparably homogeneous in many, if not most, of the subject matter areas of the curriculum.

Homogeneous grouping in the elementary school is also vulnerable in that research reveals no significant differences in the performance of children grouped or not grouped when intelligence or academic achievement, or both, constitute the criteria. Probably a more accurate

149

statement is that existing research on homogenous grouping is notoriously ambivalent in its findings.[16] The following paraphrase and quotation support the validity of such a generalization. The library researcher, Ruth Eckstrom, first points out that whereas one educator (Henry Otto) pronounced homogeneous grouping to be harmful to bright students, another (A. Harry Passow) pronounced it to be beneficial to them. She concludes "that controlled experimental studies comparing the effectiveness of homogeneous and heterogeneous grouping, as evaluated by student achievement, showed no consistent pattern of results."[17]

Elementary schools that view ability or achievement grouping with skepticism generally turn toward heterogeneous grouping. The common practice of age grading leads inevitably to the formulation of heterogeneous grouping, at other times on heterogeneous grouping practices. and controlling the selective base beyond the single factor of age, form class groups along lines of such other factors as sex, socioeconomic status, ethnic and racial diversity. The current war on poverty and the prevalence of racial tension in the culture have increased the extent of this practice. The motive that underlies it is an understandable concern for the social, civic, and emotional development of students as well as for their cognitive growth.

Flexible grouping, a third approach, draws sometimes on homogeneous grouping, at other times on heterogeneous grouping practices. Flexible grouping is an inseparable feature of team teaching, as will be developed in a later chapter. More significantly, it constitutes a built-in feature of every classroom arrangement known to education today. Through its good services, teachers, irrespective of other impinging influences, may group pupils in a number of ways throughout a school day. For instance, primary-grade teachers may employ achievement grouping in the teaching of reading, natural science, or music. Upper-grade teachers may employ sex grouping in the teaching of body hygiene and related topics. Teachers of any grade may employ planned heterogeneous grouping in the teaching of social studies, physical education, art, or listening.

[16] See Harold G. Shane and James Z. Polychrones, "Elementary Education—Organization and Administration," in *Encyclopedia of Educational Research,* ed. by Charles W. Harris, 3rd ed. (New York: Crowell-Collier and Macmillan, Inc., 1960), pp. 421–430.

[17] Ruth B. Eckstrom, "Experimental Studies of Homogeneous Grouping, A Critical Review," *School Review,* 69 (Summer 1961), pp. 216–226.

EDUCATION AS AN OPERATIONAL PROCESS

My personal viewpoint is that in elementary education, homogeneous grouping that undergoes no alteration throughout a school day is unrealistically conceived and unnecessarily rigid. My viewpoint also is that heterogeneous grouping, commensurately unvaried, glosses over the known differences among learners. I am strongly in support of flexible grouping, employed sensitively by mature, understanding teachers within the frame of any kind of classroom arrangement.

The Self-contained versus the Departmentalized Classroom

Whether a classroom should be self-contained, partially self-contained, or departmentalized constitutes yet another controversial issue in elementary education. A self-contained classroom is one in which a teacher has responsibility for the entire curriculum of a given grade: he teaches all subjects. A partially self-contained classroom is one in which a teacher has responsibility for almost all the subjects of a given grade, the exceptions usually being art, music, and physical education—one or any combination of the three. A departmentalized classroom is one in which a teacher is responsible for a single subject such as science

or mathematics, or for two combined subjects such as English and social studies. Traditionally, the self-contained classroom arrangement has constituted the pattern of the primary grades; the partially self-contained classroom arrangement, that of the intermediate grades. A practice gaining momentum by the year, however, is for schools (mostly suburban) to departmentalize as early as grade 6, a few even as early as grade 4.

The two basic justifications for the self-contained classroom are these: a child is more secure when relating throughout a school day to one teacher instead of several; and curriculum integration, very important to the young, is a more likely outcome when all learning activities during a school day are under the direction of a single teacher. An assumption built into the plan is that the teacher is able to be, and will be, competent in all phases of a school's curriculum: arithmetic, art, health, science, physical education, safety, social studies, and the language arts including reading. The assumptions built into the departmental plan are these: first, that as children near puberty, they lose the need for a close child-adult relationship in the school; second, that as the curriculum increases in complexity in the higher grades, only teachers who are specialized can do it justice.

Until recently the foregoing assumptions pertaining to the self-contained classroom went relatively unchallenged. Yet at the same time, most conceded that in the self-contained classroom arrangement teachers almost habitually "taught through" their curriculum strengths more than through their weaknesses. Science and mathematics, in particular, suffered as a result. Even today, biology is the only natural science that receives anything approximating adequate emphasis in the intermediate grades; physics and chemistry suffer badly in comparison. And in mathematics, the newer curriculum designs are making increasing demands on teachers for sophisticated insights that many do not possess, and on schools for long-term curriculum continuity that they have difficulty in providing. The overall result is that the self-contained plan at the present time is undergoing serious scrutiny.

I make the following proposal as an escape from the dilemma: that the self-contained classroom remain unchanged as the organizational pattern for grades 1–3; then, starting with grade 4, that departmentalization begin to operate up through grade 6 in the following way. Teachers, except for activity specialists, would have curriculum competency either (1) in the physical and biological sciences and mathematics, or (2) in the language arts and the social sciences. Any one of

152

these teachers, in their specialties, would handle two learning groups daily, one in the morning and a second in the afternoon.[18] For schools financially unable to hire specialist teachers in physical education, safety, music, and art, the science-mathematics teacher would assume responsibility for the first two; the language arts-social studies teacher would assume responsibility for the last two. Ideally, however, such subjects would remain separate.

The proposal, I realize, is vulnerable on the following counts. First, depending on the instructional pattern replaced by the plan, it might entail a modest increase in a school's budget. Second, the plan would separate the child earlier from the single teacher of the self-contained classroom. Conceivably, however, such early removal would result in as many gains as losses. Third, the plan would fractionate the curriculum earlier by dividing it into two main blocks and a number of lesser ones. Yet close co-ordination among teachers and careful teaching for psychological transfer would tend to offset this possible shortcoming.

The strength of the plan lies in the greater subject-matter competency that specialist teachers would bring to the curriculum. With the knowledge explosion confronting the world today, this one intrinsic asset might be decisive.

THE SUBJECT-MATTER AREAS

The central theme of this present section is the curriculum content of elementary education—that is, the subject matter of learning. Such content, we once again assert, is defensible to the extent it advances pupil growth effectively and economically toward the legitimate goals of elementary education. Conversely, it is indefensible when failing or falling too far short of these goals. Generally speaking, broad fields of knowledge rather than separate subjects serve as the curriculum catalyst in elementary education. For instance, natural science customarily appears as a fused composite of biology, chemistry, physics, astronomy, and the earth sciences. Social studies, relatedly, appears as a fused composite of history, political science, sociology, economics, and perhaps anthropology. The sought-after outcome is breadth of understanding in a given content category rather than specialized insight into any single component of that category.

[18] The gist, not the details, of this proposal I credit to my friend and colleague George Beauchamp. He articulated it a number of times in our many give-and-take exchanges on education, in general and on elementary education, in particular.

The following principles, although intrinsic to education at any level, are singularly germane to education in the elementary school. The five listed, I regard as having unique significance.

1. Pupil readiness is an essential of learning. The abstract term readiness translates operationally into maturational readiness and experiential readiness. A pupil is maturationally ready to learn when he is physically and psychologically able and predisposed to interact with the stimuli of learning. Maturational readiness embraces such characteristics as visual and auditory acuity, emotional and social ability to relate outwardly, and mental ability to respond to the demands of a given learning situation. A pupil is experientially ready to learn when he has gained sufficient familiarity with his environment to be able to learn. A first grader, for instance, relates only vaguely to the word *elephant* unless he has seen an elephant or a picture of one. A fifth grader is ready to divide numbers only after first having learned to add, subtract, and multiply them. Any human being is ready to love only after first having been loved. Maturational readiness is more a genetic characteristic; experimental readiness, an environmental one.

Readiness, an important concern at all learning levels, is especially important in kindergarten education. The central purpose of the kindergarten, in fact, is to ready pupils experientially for the learning that will take place in subsequent grades. Kindergarten teachers arouse the curiosity of children about objects and events and about the names of things. They help children to explore and thus to expand their environments and encourage them to talk about their expanding environments. And as the experiences of children increase in magnitude and significance, they become ever more ready to relate with understanding to the symbols of education and life.

2. School experiences should interrelate closely with the developmental growth needs and interests of learners. The five-year-old as an emerging social organism needs socializing experiences in the kindergarten. The middle-grade pupil needs to develop the fundamental communication skills, to learn his appropriate sex role, to develop a system of moral values, and to develop satisfactory attitudes about himself. The adolescent needs to react wholesomely to himself and to members of the other sex. He needs to become increasingly independent of adults. He needs security as he faces his social and vocational future. All these constitute important developmental growth needs; thus education is vulnerable when failing to capitalize on them for learning purposes.

154

3. Learning ideally should move from the immediate environment of the pupil to an ever expanding environment outside the pupil.

4. Relatedly, learning should gain meaning from the perceptual real before channeling too early into the abstract general. Things come before ideas and concrete experiences before meaning.

5. Knowledge at its best is knowledge that results in critical appraisal. Thus learning should be more than the acquisition of factual content. It should be acquisition to the end of rational assessment of life with its many confrontations.

Now we turn to those areas where the five principles converge.

The Language Arts

The field of the language arts, for reason of its pivotal position, stands first in priority of treatment. The four communication skills that it embraces—reading, listening, writing, and speaking—are indisputably essential in any verbal-learning situation, irrespective of its nature. Foreign languages also fall under the heading of the language arts.

Reading In the elementary school, the queen of the language arts is reading. This is not to imply that children read more than they speak or listen, for they do not. But it is to state that with formal education operating from a base of reading, and life outside of school almost as much so, individuals who learn efficiently and well need first to read efficiently and well.

Reading divides pedagogically into the readiness phase, the emerging-autonomy phase, and the application phase. A pupil is ready to read when he is able to see verbal symbols, to hear sounds pronounced, and to understand first simple, then increasingly complex, verbal components. He is ready to read when, as a result of interacting meaningfully with his environment, he is able to bring meaning to the printed word as well as to extract meaning from it. He is ready to read when the entire composite of readiness factors motivate him into a proper mind set for reading. Readiness, although, as indicated earlier, is a cornerstone of kindergarten education, is only proportionately less the concern of education at higher levels.

The home contributes to reading readiness when parents or older siblings patiently listen and talk to children, take them to places of cultural interest and enrichment, tell them stories, communicate read-

ing interest by demonstrating it, provide them with developmentally appropriate reading materials, avoid baby talk or other forms of talking down, and make constructive uses of television. The school contributes to readiness by stimulating children with an increasing number and variety of objects, events, and human contacts. Pets, pictures, show-and-tell activities, songs, classroom objects, field trips, and classroom visitors—these and others are illustrative. The learner reflects readiness when his sight and hearing, his mental faculties, and his emotional and social postures are within the broad range of normal.

The child who is ready to read next moves into the emerging autonomy phase. The goals of this phase are the development within learners of an adequate sight vocabulary; the development of the ability to attack syllables, words, and longer elements independently; and the development of the ability to find needed help in the dictionary. In effect, the composite goal is for children to read, if not independently in an absolute sense, at least with a minimum of outside assistance. So equipped, they move next into the final application phase.

Every teacher in the elementary school should be a teacher of reading, administering to the reading needs of pupils at any given development level. An instructional figure is a teacher of reading when he contributes to reading readiness at any level; when he reads with individuals, with a small group, or with an entire class; when he diagnoses a reading test and follows up on the results; when he instructs in the use of a dictionary or library; when he stirs up interest in a book, a periodical, or some other literary medium.

Listening   This primal language-arts skill begins at birth, or not long thereafter, and for the first year or more of an infant's life constitutes the primary verbal contact with his environment. As he grows and enrolls in school, he learns in direct ratio to his ability to listen.

Very much aware of this relationship, teachers have long asked themselves whether listening responds, and if so to what degree, to the processes of formal education. While considering it to be less responsive than reading, for instance, they tend to regard the following as their minimum obligations in regard to it: to (1) be alert to faulty hearing, making referrals, as required, to school or family medical authorities; (2) control distractions so that the classroom environment is conducive to listening; (3) devote discussion time to the importance of listening, highlighting it as a tool of learning as well as an integral component of social courtesy; (4) communicate orally to pupils at their

156

level of understanding; (5) hold pupils to high standards of response to the oral demands of the school's curriculum; and (6) initiate curriculum situations of diverse kinds that call for the employment of listening skills, following up later on the results.

Writing Yet a third communication skill is writing, which involves not only cognitive understanding but mechanical dexterity. Because it is almost as basic as reading, it appears early in the curriculum of the primary grades and continues as a component of all subsequent grades. Initially, most schools teach the manuscript form of writing, shifting in the second or third grade to cursive writing. As pupils advance, writing progressively becomes an applied function, embracing language expression in its many forms: exposition, personal or business letters, poetry, description, narration, or creative writing. Whatever the medium, the goal of writing is the clear expression of ideas. No matter how significant a message is, it becomes obscure when language does not convey it adequately. Writing is no more or no less than a process of conveying meaning through verbal symbols.

157

THE ELEMENTARY SCHOOL

Speaking Of all the language arts skills, speaking or oral communication is dominant in the world of practical living. Thus the child, fortunately in some instances, unfortunately in others, brings to the school a pattern of speech habits that of necessity constitutes the take-off point for instruction. As in the case of writing, the central purpose of speech is communication of ideas or mood within the frame of acceptable language expression.

Teachers in elementary education advance the cause of oral communication in general ways. They:

1. Establish a climate in which pupils are able to talk freely about topics of interest to them (In kindergarten, show-and-tell time is a case in point; in any grade, encouraging pupils to air their views is a comparable case in point.)
2. Teach vocabulary building and variety of expression
3. Teach language structure (Incidentally in the lower grades, more directly, but almost never formally, in the higher grades.)
4. Employ the methods of conversation, choral speaking, creative dramatics, songs, and tape recordings to improve the speech habits of pupils
5. Refer to speech pathologists pupils in need of remedial help

A second language A relative newcomer to the ranks of the language arts in elementary education is the so-called second language. The National Defense Education Act of 1958 advanced its cause tremendously by providing liberal support for school programs and research in what today has become a vast array of modern foreign languages. Spanish and French are still the primary ones, but Russian, Chinese, Japanese, and many others have contributed to the swelling list.[19]

From the welter of controversy over the place of a second language in elementary education, these conclusions are at least tentatively emerging. If a second language is to be taught (and a growing body of observers and practitioners think that it should be), instruction should start not earlier than the fourth or fifth grade. The teacher of the second language should be fluent in it, but also conversant enough with the entire program of elementary education to be able to integrate instruction in the second language with related parts of the curriculum. The aural-oral (listening-speaking) method of instruction should be the con-

[19] See Elizabeth Keesee's 49-page booklet: *References on Foreign Languages in the Elementary School* (Washington, D.C.: U.S. Dpartment of Health, Education and Welfare, 1963).

EDUCATION AS AN OPERATIONAL PROCESS

trolling one. Ideally, language-laboratory facilities should be available and utilized. The second language studied by pupils in the elementary school should be the one they also will study later in the secondary school, and, as applicable, in college.

Social Studies

Instructional time devoted in the elementary school to the social studies is second only to that devoted to the language arts. The combined purpose of the social studies is the development in pupils of social understanding, social skills, and social attitudes. Understanding relates broadly to geographical regions, persistent world problems, and prevailing social concepts. It relates more specifically to important historical and emergent movements, events, and personalities; to the ways nations govern themselves; to the differing economic systems of various countries; to the influence of geography on the lives of people; to the importance of the world's natural resources and the need for their conservation; to poverty and hunger; to the myths of racism and ethnic supremacy; and to the increasing interdependence of people and countries. Such concepts as citizenship, competition, culture, democracy, demography, distribution, freedom, immigration, profit, rights, social institutions, state, taxation, wages, and welfare receive special treatment.

Social skills engendered by the more adequate programs consist selectively of the following: skills of logical thinking including insight into the fallacies of propaganda techniques; skills of social intercourse involved in informal and formal group situations; skills connected with the locating, reading, and assessing of information relating to the social studies; and skills involved in the use of such social-studies media as maps, globes, charts, atlases, census reports, and graphs.

The more adequate social studies programs seek to engender such desirable attitudes as: respect (but not uncritical respect) for the nation's pattern of life, including its ideals, basic beliefs, institutions, and social mores; high regard for those eminent individuals who contributed significantly to the American heritage; realism undiluted by chauvinism in the making of social assessments; and tolerance for differences throughout the world in such areas as race, religion, and political systems.

I state in summary and conclusion that an adequate social-studies **159**

program must be more than a composite of dates, facts, events, and personalities. It is, in addition, an avenue to social living, an opportunity for children to practice citizenship, a source of values, and a catalyst for attitude change. It is a phenomenon not of any single discipline but a composite of many. It takes the word social at its humanistic best and goes on from there.

The Natural Sciences

No component in the elementary school curriculum is more in the cultural spotlight today than the natural sciences. Sputnik, in 1957, revealed science education in the schools, and applied science in business and industry, to be in critical need of revision and updating. Colleges and high schools along with industry were the first to go on the attack, with elementary education soon following. Selected results were the Elementary School Science Project of the University of California, a project by the same name at the University of Illinois, the Project on Science Instruction in Elementary and Junior High Schools of the Commission on Science Instruction in Elementary and Junior High Schools, and the Science Curriculum Program of the Science Manpower Project of Teachers College, Columbia University—these are just a few.

Science education at any level has—or should have—these three goals: (1) acquisition by learners of selected content (facts, principles, and concepts) of the natural sciences; (2) employment by learners of the methods of the natural sciences in their day-to-day confrontations with life sciences; and (3) development within learners of controlled objectivity toward life's phenomena, both scientific and social. Until recently, the first goal was invariably dominant. During the past few years, however, elementary schools in increasing numbers have achieved at least a semblance of balance among the three.

The natural sciences in elementary education take the form not of single disciplines taught discretely, but of a composite or broad field of the many disciplines taught interrelatedly. The topics generally include the following: *living things*—plants, animals, human beings; *matter and energy*—friction, machines, heat, fuels, fire, sound, light, and electricity; and the *earth and universe*—the solar system in relation to the earth, chemical properties, water, climate, space, and space travel.

A current trend in science education is away from topics as entities to basic principles and generalizations. The following are illustrative:

160

(1) Existence is relative, always a function of organismic properties and forces that impinge on them. (2) Because matter produces energy, the total magnitude of the one is always related to the total magnitude of the other. (3) The earth is only an infinitesimal part of the total universe. (4) The methods of science enable man to manipulate forces for his own betterment. The advocates of this basic-concepts approach hold that concepts which are fundamental should spiral throughout the grades, taking on increasing sophistication at each higher-level.[20] Personally, I regard factual and conceptual content as congenial, not as mutually exclusive.

One of the more heartening developments in science education at both the elementary and secondary school levels is the movement toward learning through discovery. In the past, science teachers too often dictated the specific conclusions students should draw from scientific data. In contrast, today's teachers encourage learners more and more to derive and defend their own conclusions, extrapolated from given bodies of data.

An offsetting shortcoming at the elementary school level is the almost habitual unpreparedness of teachers in one or more fields of the natural sciences. The typical teacher of the self-contained classroom, with no more than two years of science credit in college, customarily knows too little about science to make it meaningful, much less fascinating, to young learners. Thus I return to the proposal made earlier in the chapter: the elementary school should hire teachers of science and mathematics who, beginning with grade 4, instruct in those subjects only. Poorly prepared teachers of science in the elementary school may be a major reason why science often is a feared and unpopular subject in the high school and in college.

Mathematics

The natural sciences unquestionably dominate the national scene, but mathematics often dominates the local ones. It does so because of the many changes that have taken place in mathematics education during the past several decades. In this connection, a common complaint of parents today is their inability to help their offspring with homework

[20] One of the more articulate spokesmen for this point of view is Jerome S. Bruner. He develops it in *Process of Education* (Cambridge, Mass.: Harvard University Press, 1960).

assignments in arithmetic. A major reason for this parental futility is that mathematics education in recent years has changed emphasis from the *what* and the *how* to the *why*. Schools today in increasing numbers are probing more than ever before into the fundamental properties of mathematics, including rationales that underlie mathematical processes and relationships. Facts, important though they are, are conceding more and more to understanding. Relatedly, deductive methods are conceding more and more to inductive ones. Drill remains but schools balance it out effectively with reasoning. The formulas also remain but they rely for understanding on the principles that underlie them. A child of the last generation early learned to divide fractions by inverting the denominator and multiplying. His counterpart today learns why the scheme works.

The so-called new mathematics embraces such terms or processes as set theory, the binary (base of 2) number system, the quinary (base of 5) number system, inverse operations, and the use of frames. Although these may be new ingredients in the instructional program of elementary schools, most of them are hundreds of years old. Elementary education has adopted them because they fit in well with the newer emphases in mathematics education. They serve equally well the cause of the *why* of mathematical concepts, the cause of reasoning, and the cause of discovery learning, all of which are fundamental components of any modern mathematics curriculum.

Health and Safety

The academic areas of the language arts, social studies, natural sciences, and mathematics are integral to elementary education everywhere. But so too are the two curriculum areas of health and safety, and the fine arts. These latter constitute the respective themes of this and the next section.

In elementary education, a minimum program of health and safety should embrace the following constituents: (1) teachers sensitive to the physical- and mental-health problems and needs of pupils; (2) teachers who personally handle routine health problems and who refer the more complex ones to specialized personnel; (3) medical, nursing, and psychological services committed to the tasks of accident and disease prevention, to the handling of referral cases, and to the administration of needed tests in such areas as sight and hearing; (4) health education as

162

an important part of the science curriculum of the classroom; (5) a physical-education program that relates sensitively to the developmental needs of children and youth; (6) fire-prevention instruction and drills; (7) school personnel who, with their opposites in other community agencies, cooperate on common matters of health and safety; and (8) careful housekeeping practiced in the school building and on school grounds.

The curriculum of health and safety should encompass the topics, and associated activities in connection therewith, of body care and hygiene, diet, communicable diseases, rest and sleep, posture, importance of proper exercise, healthful attire, accident hazards and prevention, and community hygiene. The stress throughout should be on before-the-fact prevention as much as on after-the-fact care. Instruction should be a cooperative affair involving the teaching staff, the medical staff, and also selected community representatives from time to time. It should culminate in practical outcomes, not just emphasize conceptual theory. In general, the program should be a balanced one with the goal of healthful living the controlling guide.

The Fine Arts

The esthetic subjects of art and music are two further components of importance in elementary education. And they hold a central, not a peripheral, position. For a select few pupils, the goal is performance quality. For the many, the goals are appreciation, esthetic development, emotional fulfillment, and leisure-time enjoyment.

Almost any philosophical position on education that extends beyond the cognitive reaches out to embrace the esthetic. Music has a long history of respectability, constituting one of the original seven liberal arts. In the Renaissance, painting and sculpture had achieved comparable status. Today, both music and art approach the status of the academic subjects. Even in Russia, where materialism is a controlling value, the fine arts are highly regarded.

Any program of the fine arts in elementary education should be varied, flexible, and pupil-centered. Fixed requirements, rigid group standards, and limited curriculum media defeat the purposes of the program. In contrast, flexible requirements, adaptable individual standards, and extensive exploratory media crown the purposes with success. A program that contributes to esthetic growth and emotional fulfill-

163

ment must, of necessity, be one in which individual learners are central. Any other emphasis is self-defeating.[21]

To
Stimulate
Thought

1. Assume a child educated in the home by a well-qualified parent. What aspects of his education might be found wanting? Elaborate.

2. Develop the concept attributed to Freud that "schools need to relate to pupils as dynamic personalities: sensitive, complex, and multidimensional."

3. Evaluate the objectives of elementary education contained either in the Kearney or the Yale-Fairfield promulgations. In your opinion, are all the objectives appropriate? What others, if any, need to be added? Would implementation be difficult or relatively easy?

4. In what grade do you think departmentalization should begin? Defend your position.

5. Identify what you believe might be the educational deficiencies of a beginning first grader who had not attended kindergarten.

6. Take a stand on homogeneous grouping in the intermediate grades of elementary education. Develop your case and defend it. If you are in favor of grouping, be sure to identify what your grouping criteria would be.

7. The currently popular Head Start Program for culturally disadvantaged four- and five-year-olds is a "readiness" program. Describe what this means to you, and predict what the effectiveness of the program might be.

8. Do you agree with the author that such curriculum content areas as health, art, and music have as much legitimacy as the academic subjects in elementary education? Defend your answer.

9. Most professional observers believe that elementary education should teach the methods of science as well as its content. What are the more important of those methods and how should they be taught?

10. Build a case for or against a second language in the curriculum of elementary education.

REFERENCES

Beauchamp, George A., *The Curriculum of the Elementary School* (Boston: Allyn and Bacon, Inc., 1964).

Collins, George J., and J. Scott Hunter, *Physical Achievement and the Schools*, OE-28008, Bulletin 1965, No. 13 (Washington, D.C.: U.S. Department of Health, Education, and Welfare, 1965).

Cutts, Warren G., *Research in Reading for the Middle Grades*, OE-30009, Bulletin 1963, No. 31 (Washington, D.C.: U.S. Department of Health, Education, and Welfare, 1963).

[21] I have omitted the applied arts from the discussion because they are more often curriculum components of the junior high school grades than of the lower elementary school grades.

164

Cutts, Warren G., *Teaching Young Children to Read*, OE-30014, Bulletin 1964, No. 19 (Washington, D.C.: U.S. Department of Health, Education, and Welfare, 1964).

Goodlad, John I., and Robert H. Anderson, *The Nongraded Elementary School* (New York: Harcourt, Brace & World, Inc., 1963).

Gore, Lillian L., and Rose E. Koury, *A Survey of Early Elementary Education in Public Schools* (Washington, D.C.: U.S. Department of Health, Education, and Welfare, 1965).

Gunderson, Doris V., *Research in Reading Readiness*, OE-30013, Bulletin 1964, No. 8 (Washington, D.C.: U.S. Department of Health, Education, and Welfare, 1964).

Heddens, James W., *Todays Mathematics: A Guide to Concepts and Methods in Elementary School Mathematics* (Chicago: Science Research Associates, Inc., 1964).

Hess, Robert D., Lee Jacks, and Roberta M. Baer, *Early Education* (Chicago: Aldine Publishing Company, 1968).

Jarolimek, John, *Social Studies in Elementary Education* (New York: Crowell-Collier and Macmillan, Inc., 1963).

Keesee, Elizabeth, *References on Foreign Languages in the Elementary School* (Washington, D.C.: U.S. Department of Health, Education, and Welfare, 1963).

Kimbrough, Ralph B., *Administering Elementary Schools* (New York: Crowell-Collier and Macmillan, Inc., 1968).

Merritt, Helen, *Guiding Free Expression in Children's Art* (New York: Holt, Rinehart and Winston, Inc., 1964).

Phillips, Harry L., and Marguerite Kluttz, *Modern Mathematics and Your Child* (Washington, D.C.: U.S. Department of Health, Education, and Welfare, 1965).

Pronovost, Wilbert, *The Teaching of Speaking and Listening in the Elementary School* (New York: David McKay Co., Inc., 1959).

Ragan, William B., *Modern Elementary Curriculum*, third edition (New York: Holt, Rinehart and Winston, Inc., 1966).

Sharp, Evelyn, *A Parents' Guide to the New Mathematics* (New York: E. P. Dutton and Co., Inc., 1964).

Slipcevich, Elena M., *School Health Education Study* (New York: The Samuel Bronfman Foundation, 1964).

The National Elementary Principal, January, 1968 (the entire issue is devoted to the nongraded school).

Victor, Edward, *Science for the Elementary School* (New York: Crowell-Collier and Macmillan, Inc., 1965).

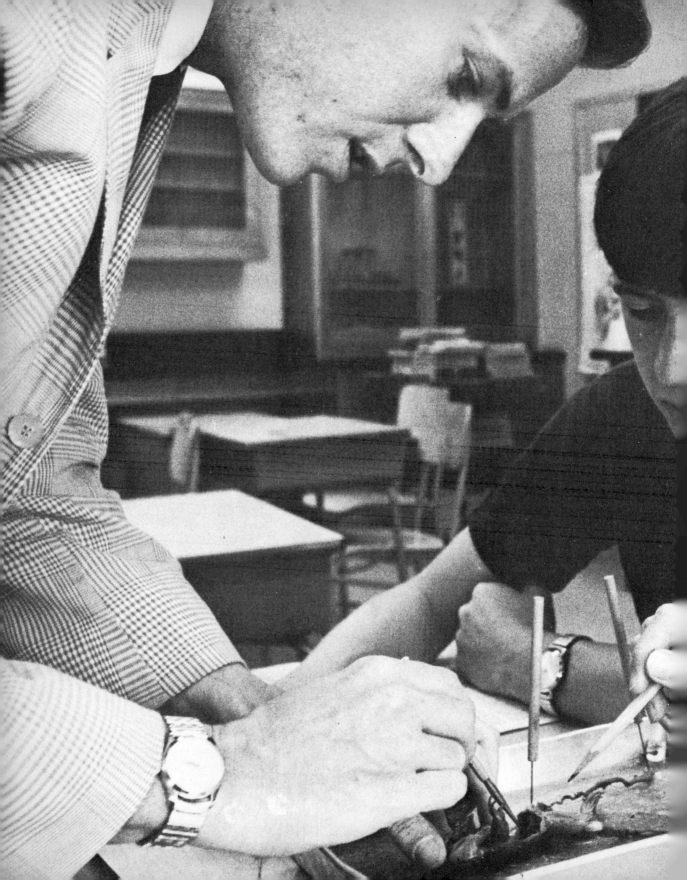

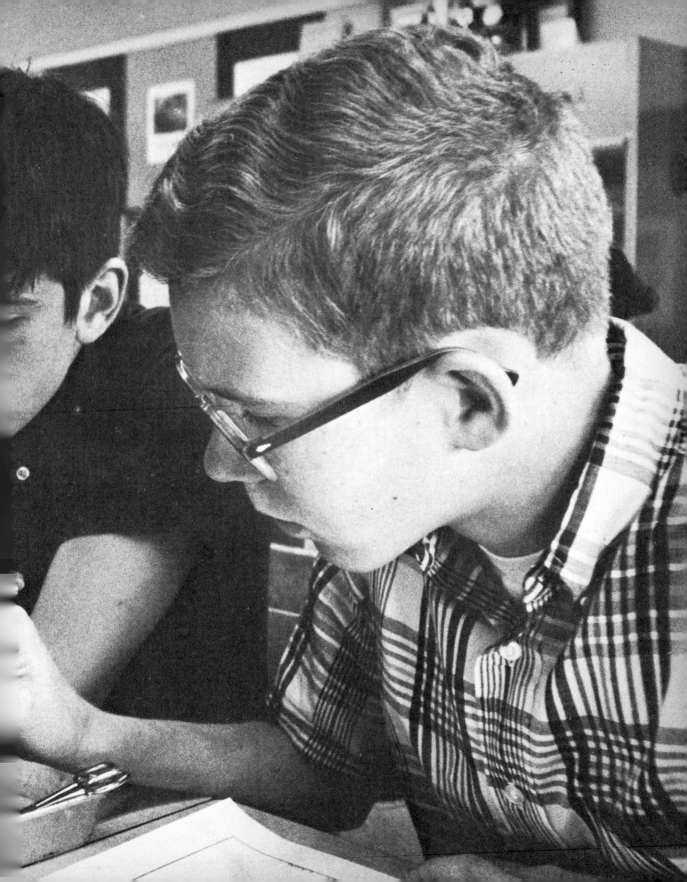

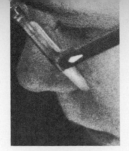

Chapter
7

The
Junior High
School

The junior high school is an organizational entity that builds on the developmental foundation of the elementary school and leads into the more advanced program of the high school. Discrete only in name, it varies widely both in organization and program throughout the country.

Organizationally, the junior high school is quite diverse. In respect to educational level, it incorporates grades 7 through 9 most often and frequently grades 7 and 8. In addition, grade 6, or grades 5 and 6 are incorporated occasionally. When it includes grades 5 and 6, it assumes the organizational shape of a *middle school*—the newest emerging entity on the educational scene. However, because the middle school is as yet in its infancy, thus only slowly feeling its way, we make no treatment of it per se in this book. Suffice it to say that it reaches from the middle elementary grades into the junior high school grades; also, that it tends to include such program features as curriculum diversification, modular scheduling, and modified departmental instruction.

The junior high school's plant sometimes has independent physical facilities, and sometimes it shares facilities with other educational levels. In respect to administration, it has its own principal and supervisory staff in certain settings, and shares these with a higher or lower educational echelon in others.

The junior high school had its inception in the wake of the Industrial Revolution, when only the socioeconomically favored attended high school and college, the nonfavored customarily dropping out of school after a few years of elementary education. At the turn of the century, of all pupils enrolled in grade 1, only 51.5 percent remained to start grade 7; 16 percent, to start grade 10; and less than 8 percent, to graduate from high school.[1]

As elaborated in Chapter 2, education at the turn of the century was in a crossfire from two opposing camps. In one, the scholarly elite took aim against education's allegedly growing anti-intellectualism. In the other camp, members of the expanding middle class struck out at the

[1] Edward L. Thorndike, *The Eliminiation of Pupils from School,* Bulletin No. 4 (Washington, D.C.: U.S. Bureau of Education, 1907), p. 15.

alleged exclusiveness of student body and program. Eliot, of Harvard, as will be recalled, was champion of the elitists. Grass-roots practitioners collectively championed the masses. The elitists argued that elementary education should be shortened, that a number of secondary school subjects should be pushed down into the elementary school, and that secondary education should take on increased academic vitality. Spokesmen for the common man argued that elementary and secondary schools as they then existed were too academic, too impractical, to serve the growing ranks of the nation's young.

Two well-known national groups sided with the scholarly elitists. One was the Committee of Ten under President Eliot's leadership. The other was the Committee of Fifteen. A third group, the Committee on College Entrance Requirements, sided with the critics of the elitists. Its major proposal was for a six-year high school.[2] In its report, the committee indicted both elementary and secondary education. Each, in the opinion of the committee, was oriented too much in the past and was failing the needs not only of the growing middle class but of the favored elite as well. In the midst of so much educational discontent and controversy, it is not surprising that a new organizational entity was about to emerge.

Historical studies of the junior high school differ somewhat over dates and places of its origin. Bunker, as one source, credits the school system of Richmond, Indiana, with housing, in 1896, the first seventh- and eighth-grade unit in a separate building.[3] Whether this was truly a junior high school, in the modern meaning of the term, is debatable. Two cities—Columbus, Ohio, and Berkeley, California—both take credit for bringing into being in 1910 the first separate three-year junior high school unit. Irrespective of place of origin, the junior high school, once having emerged as an organizational entity, developed with surprising rapidity. The number of separate three-year junior high schools increased from 55 in 1920 to 5040 in 1959. During the same period, the number of six-year high schools increased from 828 to 10,280,[4] resulting in a corresponding decrease in the number of four-year high schools. An even more recent portrayal reveals junior high schools, from 1952

2 National Education Association, "Report of the Committee on College Entrance Requirements," *Journal of Proceedings and Addresses* (Washington, D.C.: NEA, 1899), pp. 659–660.

3 Cited in Nelson L. Bossing and Roscoe V. Cramer, *The Junior High School* (Boston: Houghton Mifflin Company, 1965), p. 27.

4 Roland C. Faunce and Morrel J. Clute, *Teaching and Learning in the Junior High School* (San Francisco: Wadsworth Publishing Company, Inc., 1961), p. 8.

to 1963, to have increased in number by a half, and in total enrollments, by a fourth.[5] Suffice it to say that if numerical growth is the criterion, the junior high school is in a state of extremely good health today. Its growth along other lines will receive treatment in later sections of this chapter.

PURPOSES

In its early developmental period, the junior high school was running more away from, than toward, something. It was satisfied to leave behind such elementary school patterns and practices as the following: children, aged five to fourteen, housed in a single building and playing side by side on the same recreational field; a curriculum that was comfortable when dealing with basic skills but uncertain when dealing with the organized fields of subject matter; generalist teachers rather consistently beyond their depths in these same fields; learning activities decided exclusively by authority figures; paucity of exploratory activities in the curriculum; and, in general, a program geared more to the young child than to the emerging young adult.

What the junior high school needed, however, was not just to turn away from old directions, but to move assertively into new ones. In short, it needed to blueprint its purposes. As educators drafted a plan for the junior high school, they did so against a long-held conviction that broad educational purposes remain the same, irrespective of the learner's age. In other words, whether learners are enrolled in the elementary school, the junior high school, or the senior high school, they need to grow in the areas of the cognitive, the affective, and the psychomotor. A second controlling conviction was that education, irrespective of any learner's age, needs to conform to developmental growth characteristics. A third, and more obvious conviction, was that education, irrespective of any learner's age, has to operate from a base of accepted social norms and expectations.

Framed by these basic convictions, educators soon arrived at consensus in regard to the following specific purposes of the junior high school. They agreed that it should:

1. Effect a smooth transition of youth from childhood to adulthood

[5] Grace S. Wright and Edith S. Greer, *The Junior High School, A Survey of Grades 7-8-9 in Junior and Junior-Senior High Schools* (Washington, D.C.: U.S. Department of Health, Education, and Welfare, 1963), p. 3.

2. Relatedly, effect a smooth transition of youth from dependence to increasing independence
3. Effect a comfortable transition of pupils from elementary school to high school
4. Relatedly, effect a comfortable transition of pupils from the self-contained classroom to the departmental classroom
5. Project pupils into a curriculum characterized by increasing subject-matter emphasis
6. Introduce pupils to new exploratory activities in line with their developing needs, aptitudes, and interests
7. Orient the educational program specifically to the emerging emotional and social needs and interests of children about to become young adults
8. Permit learners to elect, under guidance, selected activities that relate to their uniqueness

ORGANIZATIONAL CHARACTERISTICS

Against this background of purposes, we turn now to selected organizational features that tend to characterize the junior high school. The reader should bear in mind throughout that the junior high school differs in varying degrees from system to system, and even, at times, from school to school within a given system. Thus the content of this and the several subsequent sections is more properly descriptive of the junior high school in the composite than of any single institution in actual operation.

The organizational characteristics of the junior high school are directly related to its student population and its program. The student population consists of preadolescents and early adolescents. The program thus logically evolves from the developmental growth needs of this age group.

Issues of External Organization

In administering to the educational needs of this group, communities take one of the two following organizational approaches. Either they establish units that are organizationally and/or physically separate from both feeder-elementary and receipt-secondary schools, or, within

172

the frame of existing school organization, they commit elementary and secondary schools to the program for junior high school youth. Curriculum divergence tends to characterize the first; convergence, the second.[6]

Educational theorists generally favor the junior high school as separate from, rather than as combined with, some other organizational unit. They justify their position on grounds of the uniqueness of the age group enrolled, and of the related uniqueness of the program needed to serve members of that age group. Their position is strongest when applied to youth who enter puberty some time during the so-called normal age period of eleven to fourteen; it is weakest when applied to youth who enter puberty belatedly. Yet even then they may argue, and quite convincingly, that educational organization is most defensible when a lower echelon relates to learners as children, when a higher one relates to them as young adults, and when a middle one relates to them as transitional individuals nearing or just having entered young adulthood.

The case for the separate junior high school, though not airtight, is, in my opinion, reasonably sound. Thus I align myself in support of it. Yet under a 6-6 plan, education can get the job done almost as adequately under the following conditions: when it separates younger and older youth both physically and administratively, when it administers a different curriculum for and employs different instructional methods in dealing with each of the two groups, and when it employs differing plans of classroom organization. Ideally, the junior high school should be a separate unit; practically, such separation is an economic impossibility for many communities that might otherwise prefer it.

Issues of Internal Organization

Junior high schools face problems not only of external organization but of internal organization as well. The block-time class, the length and number of class periods, and the problem of pupil grouping are central problems in respect to internal organization.

The block-time class   During the past several decades, the so-called block-time class has become an increasingly common characteristic of the junior high school. Simply stated, it is an organizational arrange-

[6] For enrollment details by organizational arrangement, see Bossing and Cramer, *The Junior High School*, p. 40.

173

ment in which a teacher and a learning group work together for a longer than average block of time. If the normal length of class period is 50 minutes, a block-time teacher meets with a single learning group for two or more of these 50-minute periods. While so engaged, he customarily instructs in two or more subjects; in addition, he may serve as homeroom adviser and guidance counselor as well. As of 1959, approximately 50 percent of all separate junior high schools with enrollments of 300 or more, and 30 percent of all junior-senior high schools with enrollments of 500 or more, reported some type of block-time scheduling for grades 7, 8, or 9.[7] In general, this scheduling pattern is more typical of large than of small schools, of suburban than of urban and small-town schools, and of grades 7 and 8 than of grade 9.

Many conceive the best feature of the block-time class to be its role of bridge between the self-contained classroom of the elementary school and the departmentalized classroom of the secondary school. It eases, rather than catapults, the young into a departmental arrangement. Furthermore, because of the prolonged period of daily contact between the block-time teacher and his students, the teacher is more likely to be pupil- than subject-centered in his instructional posture.

Others view the best feature of the block-time class as residing in

[7] Wright and Greer, *The Junior High School, A Survey* . . ., p. 20.

the outcome of curriculum integration. They contend that when a qualified teacher is responsible for two or more related subjects, integration is a more likely eventuality. The three subject-matter combinations most characteristic of block-time classes throughout the country are as indicated in Table 7.1. The data appear in percentages.

TABLE 7.1   SUBJECT-MATTER COMBINATIONS, BY PERCENTAGES, IN SCHOOLS THAT HAVE BLOCK-TIME CLASSES

	Language Arts–Social Studies	Science–Math.	Language Arts, Social Studies, Science, Math.
	Grade 7		
Junior high schools	80.8	16.3	12.3
Junior-senior high schools	55.5	23.3	9.6
	Grade 8		
Junior high schools	48.6	13.4	3.5
Junior-senior high schools	53.4	20.3	4.2
	Grade 9		
Junior high schools	16.4	2.3	1.3
Junior-senior high schools	8.3	4.4	1.0

Source: Adapted from Wright and Greer, p. 21.

The rationale behind the language arts–social studies and the science–mathematics combinations is that in each instance the two content areas are closely enough related to reinforce one another in a combined arrangement. Nor does the rationale lack for logical support. The rationale behind the more heterogeneous combination of language arts, social studies, science, and mathematics, however, has to find justification outside the factor of content relatedness. Some justify it on grounds of the importance of a school's keeping the hard-core academic subjects together under the leadership of a single teacher. Others justify it as the gentlest possible departure from the organizational scheme of the elementary school. The fact, however, that so few junior high schools employ the combination may well attest to its vulnerability.

Length and number of class periods   What most nearly approximates a model class period arrangement for the junior high school constitutes a second internal organization issue of importance. A school day of six academic class periods, each of 50- to 60-minutes duration, with a lunch period in addition, is the most common arrangement. A school

day of eight academic class periods, each of 40 minutes duration, with a lunch period in addition, is a less common arrangement.

The longer class period enables teachers to know pupils better because they are with them for a more extended time period; the longer period lends itself to such instructional schemes as supervised study, library research, and field trips; and because longer periods result in fewer periods, the curriculum is fractionated less. The primary advantage of the shorter period is that it enables learners to have experiences in a greater number of curriculum areas. Yet this gain in curriculum extensity is necessarily at the price of curriculum intensity.

The current innovative scheme of modular scheduling may well replace both of the aforementioned plans. Intrinsic in this scheme, the school day consists not of periods but of modules, each 15 to 20 minutes in length. A school administration combines these flexibly in a number of different ways to serve a fluid curriculum. This modular scheme may well be on the wave of the future. However, because of its newness and because of the general nature of this book, I leave to others the task of elaborating the topic.

Grouping for instruction   The question of the best pupil-grouping pattern is no less difficult for the junior high school than it is for the elementary school and high school. Irrespective of personal opinion on the issue, the reported facts of the case are these: 74 percent of all separate junior high schools, and 60 percent of all junior-senior high schools, employ some kind of homogeneous grouping as a basis for forming class sections. These figures rise to 81 percent and 74 percent, respectively, for larger schools and drop to 61 percent and 54 percent for smaller ones.

The larger junior high schools that employ homogeneous grouping do so in the subject-matter areas, by percents, as indicated in Table 7.2.

TABLE 7.2 HOMOGENEOUS-GROUPING PRACTICES, BY SUBJECT-MATTER AREA, IN SEPARATE JUNIOR HIGH SCHOOLS OF 300 OR MORE ENROLLMENT, AND JUNIOR-SENIOR HIGH SCHOOLS OF 500 OR MORE ENROLLMENT

	English	Mathematics	Social Studies	Science
Grade 7				
Junior high school	92.0	93.0	73.5	66.5
Junior-senior high school	96.1	93.5	82.4	86.4
Grade 8				
Junior high school	92.6	93.7	72.4	70.7
Junior-senior high school	94.7	93.9	79.7	81.0
Grade 9				
Junior high school	86.9	95.0	55.1	67.8
Junior-senior high school	91.7	88.1	59.5	68.2

Source: The data contained in this table and in the preceding paragraph have come from Wright and Greer, *The Junior High School, A Survey . . .*, pp. 14–18.

The major criteria employed by junior high schools in the formation of groups customarily include school achievement, intelligence, reading ability, and teacher estimates of personality characteristics. Less-frequently employed criteria are social maturity, physical maturity, and pupil interests.

In the last analysis, as will be developed in greater detail in Chapter 8, whether a school should or should not group homogeneously is more a function of subjective conviction than of research evidence.

Grouping in any area of curriculum content finds greater justification in cognitive than in social or emotional growth. Yet even in the single cognitive domain, the results of research are ambivalent. A personal point of view here is that homogeneous grouping can realize no more than nominal success unless the following conditions are present: a wholesome school climate in which slowness is not deprecated; a carefully conceived curriculum that varies qualitatively as well as quantitatively among groups; teachers selected and assigned to groups for reason of their special abilities and interests; and a marking system that does not take motivation away from the slow.

Assessing the evidence available on classroom grouping practices in the junior high school, I lean toward heterogeneous grouping in respect to the block-time offerings of language arts and social studies, and

177

toward homogeneous grouping in respect to the departmentalized offerings of science and mathematics. Heterogeneous grouping in the block-time class generally brings together youth who differ along the lines of race, economic background, social class, and ability. These differences tend to enhance social growth. Any handicap to language growth can usually be offset by small-group instruction under the leadership of the block-time teacher himself or by periodical remedial instruction under the leadership of, for instance, reading or remedial-speech specialists. Under this arrangement, slow learners escape the possible demoralizing effects of being in low-achievement groups for an entire academic day. At the same time, all children are able to progress more or less at their own rates in science and mathematics.

THE CURRICULUM

Turning now from the topic of school organization, we focus next on selected curriculum concerns. One of the more obvious is subject-matter content; a second, is school services; and a third, is pupil activities.

A basic introductory statement here is that, irrespective of age of learners or of other learning specifics, the primary sources of a curriculum remain unchanged. In all instances, they are the time-tested disciplines (individually or collectively), the emerging disciplines, the demands made by a controlling social order, the demands made by a learner's individualism, and the imprint made on a curriculum by an instructional figure. The kind, degree, and pattern of influence exerted by any one or any combination of these vary greatly, however, from one learning situation to another. And because of this variation, the respective curricula of the elementary school, the junior-high school, and the high school are characterized by significant differences.

The disciplines, for instance, appear with little structure in the elementary school, as parts of broad subject fields in the junior high school, and as both discrete and combined entities in the high school. The social order, as yet another curriculum source, impinges on the primary grades mostly in terms of the immediate environment, including the home, the classroom, and the school. In the upper elementary grades, it impinges in terms of an expanding local environment. In the junior high and senior high school grades, it extends the school curriculum beyond the immediate. The learner himself as still another

178

source makes curriculum demands in terms of his evolving needs and interests. And the teacher's imprint is left on curriculum as well.

The Subject-matter Curriculum

The more formal component of any school's curriculum consists of the subject-matter content that it embraces. In the junior high school, as previously indicated, this content appears in the form of broad fields of learning: for example, language arts, social science, or natural science. The nature and scope of the content are ever a function of at least the following two important controlling influences: educational outcomes and the needs of learners.

Included early in the chapter was a listing of educational purposes that, at least in the opinion of many, should give direction to the junior high school. They dealt with such specifics as these: the importance of pupils' moving with a minimum of confusion or upset, from one educational echelon to another; the importance of their meeting the problems of puberty with a minimum of trauma; and the necessity for the curriculum of the junior high school to meet, on one hand, the needs of the society, and, on the other hand, the needs of individual learners. In effect, the junior high school's mission is to relate to the mental, affective, and physical needs of the learners it serves. Included in this mission is the transmission of subject-matter content to learners. This unquestionably is an important responsibility and one that the junior high school needs to take seriously.

Three broad subject-matter categories   In the junior high school, subject-matter content customarily divides three ways: into *common learnings*, into *personal-interest offerings*, and into *health and physical education*. The common learnings, a bastion of general education, embrace the hard core of knowledge, skills, attitudes, and experiences that pupils need to share with others to ready themselves for a meaningful life. An irreducible minimum customarily consists of the basic skills; of a hard core of literature considered essential by the culture; and of basic conceptualizations in the areas of social living, mathematics, and the natural sciences. Health and physical education are categorized separately because they involve motor activity as well as verbal symbolism.

In addition to the common learnings included in junior high school   **179**

curricula to meet the needs of all, personal interest offerings are included to serve the preferences of individuals. Although these offerings are not unique to the junior high school, they are of greater significance in it than in either the elementary school or the high school. Pupil selection of courses, in fact, is woven into the very fabric of the junior high school. One reason for this is a broadly social one: a culture oriented in individualism logically expects its system of formal education to advance that same cause. A second reason is a maturational one: children and youth near the threshold of young adulthood need increasingly to make their own decisions, including certain curriculum decisions. A third reason is a motivational one: school is more attractive to learners when they make some of their own curriculum choices.

Personal-interest offerings in almost all junior high schools are fairly extensive. In suburban schools they tend to be exceptionally so. Collectively, they divide into the subject-matter categories listed in Table 7.3—and the list, although lengthy, is far from complete.

TABLE 7.3 PERSONAL-INTEREST CURRICULUM OFFERINGS IN JUNIOR HIGH SCHOOLS

Art	Foreign languages
appreciation	General business
ceramics	General shop
crafts	Graphic arts
design	Handicrafts
drawing	Home economics
metal and jewelry	Home mechanics
painting	Journalism
sculpturing	Metal work
Auto mechanics	Music
Cosmetology	instrumental
Creative writing	vocal
Current events	Photography
Debate	Printing
Drafting	Safety education
Dramatics	Science fair
Electronics	Typing
First aid	Woodworking

Admittedly, no single school offers all the curriculum choices listed in Table 7.3. If it did, community bankruptcy might well result. But the trend is for schools to increase the number and variety of such choices

EDUCATION AS AN OPERATIONAL PROCESS

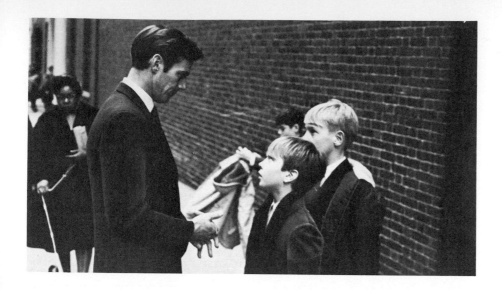

in deference to the social, maturational, and motivational rationales just mentioned. And these have all held up well in practice. Certainly few would deny that with the advent of puberty, young people desire increasingly to make their own choices and that young people desire increasingly to roll back the horizons of an expanding world. As education permits them to do both of these, their interest in school increases. Thus the personal-interest offerings in the junior high school stand out as having both intrinsic and contingent curriculum importance.

The third subject-matter category—health and physical education—we pass over lightly here in view of its coverage later in the chapter in connection with school services. Suffice it to say that any program of health and physical education needs to evolve from the developmental needs and interests of the age group served.

A proposed class schedule Drawing on the common learnings, personal-interest offerings, and health and physical education, I propose a daily class schedule with specifications essentially as presented on page 182. The schedule encompasses seven class periods for grades 7 and 8, and eight periods for grade 9—each period to be of approximately 45-minutes duration; the periods for the language arts–social studies combination in grades 7 and 8, however, to be of approximately 60-minutes duration. A lunch period of a half hour is additional. Each number in the figure designates *a* class period but not necessarily *the* period of the numerical designation.

181

Class Periods	Subjects		
	Grade 7	Grade 8	Grade 9
1 2	language arts–social studies combined		English social studies
3	←——————— mathematics ———————→		
4	science	science and personal-interest elective alternated daily	science, or personal-interest elective
	lunch		
5	←——————— health-physical education ———————→		
6	fine-arts survey	practical-arts survey	personal-interest elective
7	personal-interest elective other than one in the fine or applied arts		study
8			study

The features inherent or implied in this chart are as follows: The three subjects—language arts (or English), social studies, and mathematics—are included as requirements for each of the three years. The first two appear in a combined-studies arrangement in grades 7 and 8, and as separate subjects in grade 9. Science is a daily requirement in grade 7, an every-other-day requirement in grade 8, and a highly recommended option in grade 9. The fine and practical arts appear as survey courses in grades 7 and 8, respectively. In grade 7, for example, students might have experiences for four to six weeks each in such fine-arts subjects as vocal music, instrumental music, art appreciation, drawing, painting, ceramics, sculpture, and design. In grade 8, relatedly, they might have experiences in such practical-arts subjects as woods, metals, printing, electricity, mechanical drawing, foods, textiles, and home management. In grade 9, the personal-interest choices would take the form not of survey courses but of single subjects. The program of health and physical education would extend across the three-year range. The schedule is proposed as a guide, not as a blueprint for any school to follow verbatim.

School Services

The more formal curriculum of the classroom has a parallel in the less formal curriculum of the school services. The same educational goals—mental, social, emotional, and physical development—apply to each. The curriculum of the school services, although lacking the time-honored status of the formal curriculum, is, for that reason, no less important. It manifests itself most tangibly in the counseling services, the library services, and the health services.

Counseling services The counseling (or personnel or guidance) services find expression in face-to-face counseling, group counseling, and testing. Their purpose is self-actualization or personal fulfillment for the individual. In the junior high school, their scope includes both emotional and educational concerns as primary. The counseling services have both independent and contingent status: independent in the sense that emotional adjustment and clarity of psychological vision are their own reasons for being; contingent in the sense that pupils who are well adjusted emotionally are more capable of responding to the subject-matter curriculum of the school.

Programs of counseling in the various junior high schools of the country range from the almost nonexistent to the elaborate. One that veers toward neither of these extremes might possess the characteristics identified and described as follows:

Its operational center is the homeroom, which, in a minority of schools, is a distinct organizational entity. In the majority of schools, which are organized around the block-time class plan, the homeroom is an integral part of the common-learnings core. More often than not, it is a built-in feature of the English-social studies curriculum block. In such an arrangement, a teacher and class meet daily for approximately two hours. The focal concerns of the classroom are English, social studies, and pupil guidance. The teacher customarily meets with two class groups daily, one in the morning and one in the afternoon, for approximately two hours each. Because he knows the pupils better than anyone else, he is the logical choice for counselor.

In his role as counselor, he makes a continuing study of the approximately 50 students under his care. He acquaints himself with their personalities, their abilities, their interests, and their patterns of school performance. He counsels with them as a group and as individuals. His central concerns are mental health, social development, patterns of

183

behavior, school performance balanced against ability, class programs and schedules, and other problems of significance to them or the school. It is he who makes contact with other teachers in regard to problems and issues of mutual concern. It is he who, through interviews with parents, links the home with the school.

The homeroom teacher, whether a block-time teacher or not, usually fills the positon of central guidance functionary in any junior high school. Rarely is he a psychologist in the specialized sense of the term, nor does he act on problems that require specialized knowledge and insight. Since most problems of preadolescents and early adolescents, however, are nonpathological in nature, he constitutes the main line of defense in regard to them. He is the bridge between the self-contained classroom of elementary education and the departmental classroom of secondary education. His concern is for young people not just as students, but more significantly as people. Unquestionably his load is a heavy one, but if he did not carry it, someone else would have to.

A number of junior high schools employ specialized counselors to supplement the efforts of the homeroom or block-time teacher-counselor. In 1959, as reported by one source, approximately 65 percent of all separate junior high schools, and 55 percent of all junior-senior high schools, had the services of such counselors. Some of the smaller schools shared the services of a single counselor; some of the larger ones employed as many as four or five of them.[10]

In the composite, these specialized guidance personnel perform the following functions:

1. Promote, through in-service methods, the professional growth of teachers and administrators in the area of counseling and guidance
2. Counsel with pupils referred by classroom and homeroom teachers. These pupils generally have psychological problems serious enough to warrant at least some kind of psychiatric first aid
3. Administer and/or interpret standardized tests and inventories, including an occasional projective instrument (Rorschach or Thematic Apperception Test usually)
4. Counsel with parents on difficult cases
5. Coordinate the counseling program of the school with that of other community agencies involved in the same kinds of problems

[10] Wright and Greer, *The Junior High School, A Survey* . . ., p. 48.

Supplementing the counseling efforts of the homeroom teacher and guidance specialist, if any, are the four or five departmental classroom teachers with whom junior high school students associate during a typical school day. These individuals, because they are teachers, are *de facto* counselors. Among other functions, they observe and assess pupil behavior. They hold frequent face-to-face interviews with pupils and occasionally meet with parents. They record guidance information. They give tests on occasions and interpret test data regularly, relating the data to the learning process. They share personnel information with the homeroom teacher and personnel specialists, when the latter constitute part of the staffing pattern. In essence, they are the professional generalists of the guidance program, responsible not only for organized-learning content but for the learners themselves. They stand *in loco parentis*—in place of the well-informed, empathic parent. Thus, the legal as well as professional mandate is that they act at least as maturely

as the well-informed, empathic parent would act. This in itself constitutes a substantial counseling commitment.

Library services   Until a few decades ago, a school library was more a carefully guarded collection of books than an open invitation to students to engage in study and research. Its character was more reminiscent of a monastery than a center of learning. Today, however, the vogue is for libraries to be unforbidding places, with materials easily accessible. By their openness and availability, school libraries invite pupils to engage in discovery learning. Today the typical junior high school library is more a center for learning than a storehouse for learning materials. When facilities permit, entire classes go to it for group-learning purposes. Individual students go to it to consult preselected references, to discover new sources, to engage in free reading, and sometimes just to "free-wheel" for exploratory purposes. Teachers go to it for in-service updating; to arrange for specialized displays of books, book covers, periodicals, and pictorials; to use or schedule the use of audiovisual equipment; to view and listen to teletapes; and to arrange for library resources for their classroom or homeroom use. The classroom is still the primary learning center in all schools, but in many schools the library is a vital supplement.

In Wright and Greer's study, approximately 90 percent of the junior high schools of their sample had central libraries, and over 85 percent had libraries administered by specialized librarians. Only about 40 percent of the sample, however, had classroom libraries, more of these existing in grade 7 than in grades 8 and 9[11]

Health services   Administering to the physical and psychological health needs of youth constitutes a third service function of the junior high school. It is a function, obvious for us to state, shared with the elementary school and the high school. All three educational echelons provide first-aid nursing and medical care for pupils. All three incorporate in their curricula the topics of disease prevention and health. All three advance the cause of health through preplanned programs of physical education. Health programs in the junior high school are unique, however, because puberty is unique. In this growth period, young people have health problems associated with their transition from childhood to adulthood. These problems are dealt with later.

[11] Wright and Greer, p. 36.

Student Activities

The activities program has been integral to the junior high school from its very beginning. Around 1920, when the junior high school was burgeoning, the senior high school had already won its struggle for social as well as academic status. The moral asceticism of the Puritan and Victorian periods had faded, as had the intellectual asceticism of the "Eliot of Harvard" period. Thus, the stage was set for secondary education to activate its long dormant social function. In this regard, the junior high school seemed to come along just at the right time.

Any activities program, irrespective of grade level, rests on the following tenets:

1. Human beings are social animals.
2. They rise to greater heights mentally, emotionally, and physically when socially fulfilled.
3. Society, as well as individuals, reaps the collective benefits of such fulfillment.
4. Formal education, one of society's most potent agencies, occupies a central place in this scheme of socialization.
5. Thus formal education has a mandate to accept responsibility for, and to program for, its social purposes.

An important task of the junior high school, then, is to formulate and implement a social program designed to meet the developmental needs of the special age group served. The task is compounded, however, by the heterogeneity of the junior high school population, divided as the students are between preadolescence and early adolescence, and between less mature and more mature. Schools that overcome this problem usually do so by providing activities extensive enough to neutralize pupil differences.

Understandably, the dividing line between personal-interest offerings and student activities is not easily distinguishable. Thus some of the activities categorized here embrace a number already included in Table 7.3. Student activities appear in a variety of forms under such categories as band, orchestra, chorus, fine arts, intramural athletics, student government, clubs with an almost unbelievable range of titles, dance, dramatics, science fairs, and school publications.

A growing tendency is for junior high schools to absorb the program of student activities directly into the mainstream of the curriculum, requiring student participation in them just as they do in other subjects. **187**

Under such an arrangement, schools generally set aside one period a day, or sometimes three periods a week, for this phase of the school's program. The majority of junior high schools, however, believing that student activities should be supplemental to the regular curriculum, continue to provide them on an after-school basis. Educational theorists consistently espouse the first arrangement; school administrators, to judge from their practices, generally espouse the second. My preference is for a combination of both, with personal-interest offerings and student activities woven into a common pattern. The two certainly have enough in common to render their separation unnatural.

JUNIOR HIGH SCHOOL STUDENTS

The chapter's focus shifts now from the curriculum of the junior high school to its learners. This is not to imply that the latter have gone unheeded heretofore, for they have not. But it is my intention to establish them as objects of direct analysis in this section.

As I have stated before, junior high school pupils are a diverse lot. Admittedly, they have puberty in common, but to some of them it is no more than a phase to be lived through in the near future; to others, it is an ongoing biological and psychological experience of the here and now. And both groups are more heterogeneous than homogeneous. Any junior high school consequently is a potpourri of youthful humanity, but it is debatable whether individual differences among pupils are any greater at the junior high school than at the elementary or high school level.

Physical Characteristics

The most dramatic symptoms of differences are the physical ones. In a typical seventh grade class, one-half to two-thirds of the girls, by the end of the school year, will have experienced their first menstrual cycles. A number will have shot up in height, many will be obese—particularly in the hips and abdomen, and a few will look as much like women as girls. A smaller proportion of boys, a fourth or less in all, will have reached pubescence in the same year. They will look less mature than their female counterparts, but both groups will stand out

188

in sharp contrast to the prepubertal children of the same grade. By the end of the eighth grade, 85 to 90 percent of the girls, and 50 to 60 percent of the boys, will have entered puberty. These young people will tend to be awkward, overweight, and low in energy. Growth in their legs, arms, and noses will be especially noticeable. Acne and previously unmanifested allergies will be common.

Side by side with these fledgling adults will be prepubertals who are still children. Thus, in purely physical terms, these boys and girls will still be children. Consequently, in purely physical terms, men and women will be going to school with boys and girls. These differences, however, even when marked, will lose much of their significance when a curriculum has rich variety and when teachers relate to pupils as individuals rather than as arithmetical averages or as pitchers to be filled with premeasured learning content.

Emotional Characteristics

Puberty manifests itself no less observably in the emotions of junior high school students than it does in their bodies. In some learners, emotional change is covert and subtle; in others, it is obviously symptomatic and dramatic. Irrespective of manner and degree of manifestation, the following trails characterize seventh to ninth grade pupils—as individuals, sometimes; in the aggregate, always. They daydream a lot, and not just when they are alone and when the surroundings are quiet. They daydream even when they are with others and when their outer worlds are a crescendo of noise and activity. They are moody—at least more so than they were as nine or ten year olds. They worry about their changing bodies including real or imagined defects, and are acutely concerned about the opinions others have of them. Lacking confidence, they become easily embarrassed. Their interests are unstable, their attention spans short; thus they flit capriciously from activity to activity. Endowed with an excess of idealism, they readily develop crushes on "model" adult figures. They resist nonconformity like a passion. And they consistently chafe at, and sometimes rebel against, constituted authority. Emotionally, these young people are challenging in their complexity, stimulating in their unpredictability, amusing in their whimsicality, and inviting in their intensity.

189

Social Characteristics

The emotional patterns of junior high school students have correlates in their social interests and activities. Being nonconformist, they identify closely with their peer associates as individuals, and with the peer culture in the composite. Prone to intense loyalties, they tend to substitute emotionalism for rationality in assessing their friends and close acquaintances. With one foot still in childhood, they resist the heterosexual pressures that threaten to invade their comfortable homosexual province. But with one foot in adulthood, they find themselves irresistibly drawn to heterosexual interests and concerns.

As mentioned earlier, adolescents of either sex, almost by definition, are rebels—some more, some less—against adult authority, particularly parental authority. They desire independence almost as much as they desire one another. During their periods of rebellion, however, they do not necessarily grasp for moral codes that differ significantly from those of their respective homes. More important, they adopt codes that they themselves increasingly evaluate and ultimately internalize.

Mental Characteristics

In the cognitive domain, junior high students are once again in an in-between state. Throughout childhood, they have viewed the world as predetermined and controlled by others, in which new generations are expected to adapt to old patterns. In young adulthood they begin to view the world as evolving, as one that every individual and every new generation is expected to take responsibility for and change, hopefully, for the better. To the extent that the second view becomes controlling, transitional youth assume increasing responsibility for themselves and their environments. Correspondingly, they become increasingly interested in knowledge as a means to the end of personal and cultural improvement. As the world of the not yet beckons with its mysteries, young learners assume a more serious posture before knowledge. In the process, a school curriculum assumes more functional importance; it becomes a practical means to the end of narrowing the world of the unknown and of changing the world of the known for the better.

Junior high students, characterized by an increased seriousness of purpose, tend to be at least moderately well organized in their study habits. One reason is that their attention spans are longer than they

190

were. And possessed of a substantial body of knowledge and cognitive understanding acquired throughout six to eight years of schooling, they are better able to reason and generalize at increasingly mature levels. Teachers, blessed with such learning assets, wisely convert them to meaningful learning outcomes.

JUNIOR HIGH SCHOOL FACULTY

The instructional faculty of a typical junior high school consists of classroom and specialist teachers who must meet the following requirements: (1) to be competent in one or more academic or service areas; (2) to understand the abilities, interests, needs, and other characteristics of junior high youth; (3) to have a professional grasp of what the junior high school stands for, of its purposes and program; and (4) to be able to relate to youth and its problems. These call for a blending of scholarly and personal attributes.

As of 1960, 97 percent of all junior high school teachers had earned at least the bachelor's degree; 30 percent had completed additional work toward the master's degree; 10 percent had earned the master's degree; and slightly less than 1 percent had earned the doctor's degree.[12] Specialists were included in the faculties of some schools. Specifically, 83 percent of all separate junior high schools had the services of a school nurse; 48 percent, of a speech therapist; 44 percent, of one or more teachers of exceptional children; 43 percent, of an audiovisual specialist; 40 percent, of a reading specialist; and 40 percent of a school psychologist.[13]

A POINT OF VIEW

The junior high school is unquestionably a distinctive educational echelon. The learners challenge with their developmental unpredictability. The curriculum challenges with its diversity. And the extra-curriculum challenges with its essentiality. The junior high school is not just an upward extension of the elementary school. Neither is it a downward extension of the high school. Rather, it is a unit with its own

[12] Wright and Greer, *The Junior High School, A Survey . . .*, p. 70.
[13] Wright and Greer, pp. 65–66.

personality. Consequently, only those teachers who are able and willing to respond to its uniqueness should plan to teach in it. Those who are qualified for it will be stimulated by its demands and will receive significant personal and professional rewards from their involvement.

To Stimulate Thought

1. Build a case for or against the existence of junior high schools that are separate from elementary schools or senior high schools. Be specific.

2. Take a stand for or against the block-time class. Give reasons for your stand.

3. What subjects, in your opinion, are most logical for combination into a block-time class? Why?

4. Most junior high schools have science as a required offering in either grade 7 or 8, but not in both. Do you approve of this arrangement? Indicate your reasons.

5. Build a case for or against homogeneous grouping in the junior high school.

6. Define the term personal-interest offerings. Then indicate whether you agree or disagree with the emphasis (both in the curriculum and in the extra-curriculum) placed on them in most junior high schools.

7. Assume an unhappy, maladjusted child, experiencing acute anxiety over various conditions of puberty. Is it the function of the school, or the home, or both, to provide him with counseling help during this period? Defend and elaborate your choice.

8. As a departmental classroom teacher in a junior high school, describe what you think your role as counselor would be. Then detail a program of teacher education that would ready you, substantially, for that role.

REFERENCES

Alexander, William M., Emmett I. Williams, et al., *The Emergent Middle School* (New York: Holt, Rinehart and Winston, Inc., 1968).

Bossing, Nelson L., and Roscoe V. Cramer, *The Junior High School* (Boston: Houghton Mifflin Company, 1966).

Brimm, R. P., *The Junior High School* (Washington, D.C.: The Center for Applied Research in Education, Inc., 1963).

Bunker, Frank F., *The Junior High School Movement: Its Beginnings* (Washington, D.C.: W. F. Roberts Co., 1935).

EDUCATION AS AN OPERATIONAL PROCESS

Faunce, Roland C., and Morrel J. Clute, *Teaching and Learning in the Junior High School* (Belmont, Calif.: Wadsworth Publishing Company, Inc., 1961).

Fischler, Abraham S., *Modern Junior High School* (New York: Bureau of Publications, Teachers College, Columbia University, 1961).

Gesell, Arnold L., Frances C. Ilg, and Louise B. Ames, *Youth: The Years from Ten to Sixteen* (New York: Harper & Row, Publishers, 1956).

Illinois Curriculum Program, *The Junior High School Program in Illinois*, Bulletin No. A-1 (Springfield, Ill.: Office of the Superintendent of Public Instruction, 1961).

Koos, Leonard V., *Junior High School Trends* (New York: Harper & Row, Publishers, 1955).

Loomis, Mary Jane, *The Preadolescent: Three Major Concerns* (New York: Appleton-Century-Crofts, 1959).

National Association of Secondary School Principals, *News Letter*, Vol. 8, No. 5, May-June, 1961.

Noar, Gertrude, *The Junior High School, Today and Tomorrow* (Englewood Cliffs, N. J.: Prentice-Hall, Inc., 1961).

Popper, Samuel H., The American Middle School: *An Organizational Analysis* (Waltham, Mass.: Blaisdell Publishing Company, 1967).

Redl, Fritz, *Pre-Adolescents—What Makes Them Tick* (New York: Child Study Association of America, 1959).

Remmers, H. H., and D. H. Radler, *American Teenager* (Indianapolis: The Bobbs-Merrill Company, Inc., 1957).

Van Til, William, Gordon F. Vars, and John H. Lounsbury, *Modern Education for the Junior High School Years* (Indianapolis: The Bobbs-Merrill Company, Inc., 1961).

Wilson, William E., *The Junior High School: A Report Prepared by the Indiana Association of Junior and Senior High School Principals*, Bulletin No. 246 (Bloomington: Indiana Department of Public Instruction, 1961).

Wright, Grace S., *Block-Time Classes and the Core Program in the Junior High School* (Washington, D.C.: U.S. Office of Health, Education, and Welfare, 1958).

Wright, Grace S., and Edith S. Greer, *The Junior High School, A Survey of Grades 7–8–9 in Junior and Junior-Senior High Schools* (Washington, D.C.: U.S. Department of Health, Education, and Welfare, 1963).

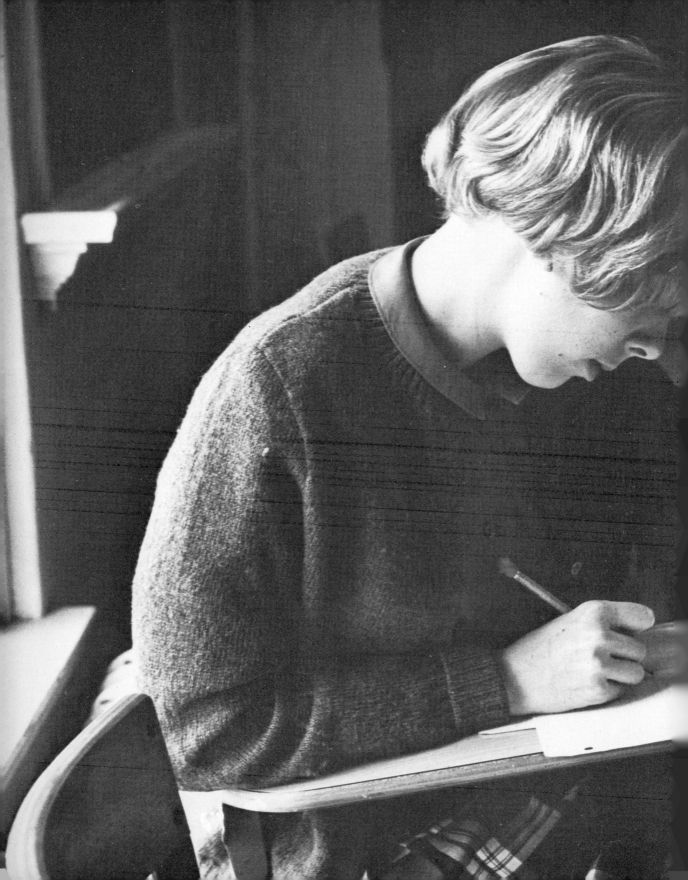

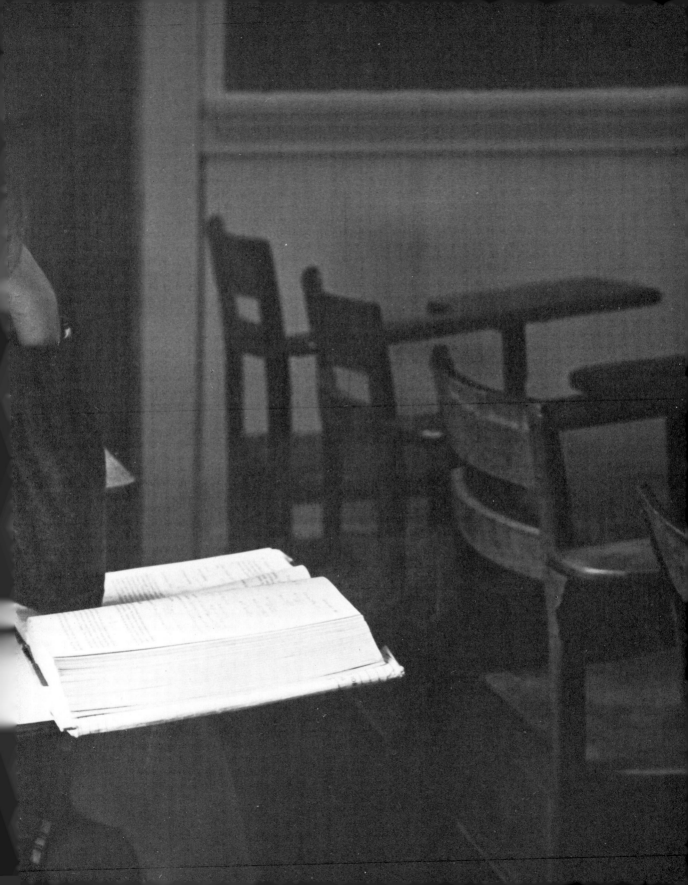

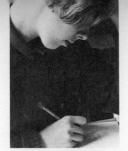

Chapter

8

*High
School
Organization*

The same Western traditions that shaped elementary education in the nation's infancy have been instrumental in shaping secondary education in the nation's developmental period. Secondary education rose in progressive stages on the groundwork of elementary education. Secondary education from its inception constituted a living testimonial to the thesis that if some education is good, more is that much better. The vision of all youth attending school until sixteen to seventeen years of age still stands as one of the noblest visions conceived by civilized man.

The essential question: Just what is a high school? is difficult to answer. To some, the terms high school and secondary school are interchangeable and embrace grades 7 through 12. To others, the high school is a sequel to the junior high school, beginning at grade 9 or 10 and ending with grade 12. Our use of the term falls into the latter category. It is arbitrarily condition by the grade dimensions that frame the past two chapters. The elementary school, the topic of Chapter 6, we depicted as a K–6 arrangement. The junior high school, the topic of Chapter 7, we depicted generally as a grade 7–8 or 7–9 arrangement.

In the present chapter, we logically depict the high school as a grade 9–12 or 10–12 arrangement. Yet we do refer back, on occasions, to grades 7 and 8. Irrespective of the grades embraced by any single high school, secondary education in the composite challenges with its many diversities and complexities. As stated by one writer: "The field is just now in a state of ferment. Change is the order of the day."[1]

SOME HISTORICAL ANTECEDENTS

Yet when was education *not* in a state of ferment? When was change in education *not* the order of the day? Rarely throughout the course of history, if the truth were known. For education cannot logically play its given role of agent of change without itself undergoing almost perpetual metamorphosis.

[1] Lawrence W. Downey, *The Secondary Phase of Education* (New York: Blaisdell Publishing Company, 1965), p. x.

The Latin Grammar School

The secondary school has a history that now is well into its fourth century. The secondary school appeared first as a hybrid transplant from England in the form of the Latin grammar school. Its birth date was 1635; the place was Boston. In the years that immediately followed, other such schools appeared in Roxbury, Dorchester, Cambridge, and Ipswich—all in the Bay Colony of Massachusetts.

The Massachusetts Bay Law of 1647 (the Old Deluder Satan Act) gave early legal sanction to secondary education, pronouncing forthrightly:

> that where any town shall increase to the number of one hundred families or householders, they shall set up a grammar school, the master thereof being able to instruct youth so far as they shall be fitted for the university, provided, that if any town neglect the performance hereof above one year, that every such town shall pay 5 pounds to the next school till they shall perform this order. . . .

Connecticut enacted a comparable law in 1650, after two Latin grammar schools had been established there—one at New Haven in 1641 and one at Hartford in 1642. However, these two laws, and similar ones passed in subsequent years, were too far ahead of their time to be strictly enforced.

Many, if not most, who write about the Latin grammar school depict it as a stereotype. They imply that all such schools were essentially the same. The Latin grammar school included in its enrollment, so they aver, children of ages seven to sixteen. It was a seven-year institution in the seventeenth and early eighteenth centuries, but became a four-year institution thereafter. Its curriculum consisted almost exclusively of Latin and Greek, with English a well-nigh neglected component.

Rejecting this stereotype, I hold that the Latin grammar school, throughout almost the entire Colonial period, was an institution of varying characteristics and patterns. Some of the schools were public—in the sense that the affluent paid tuition, whereas the poorer did not; others were exclusively private. In some, the average period of enrollment was longer than others. Some Latin grammar schools served the needs of college-bound students only; others served the needs of non-college-bound students as well. For the college preparatory student, Latin was primary, Greek secondary, and the "practical subjects" only tertiary, if that. For students not preparing for college, the "practical subjects" were primary, and the classical subjects were either secondary or nonexistent. As stated by Good:

198

The typical colonial grammar [Latin Grammar] school was a small day school in a middle class community; and it frequently taught the common branches to one group and Latin to another and smaller group who intended to go to college. To cite just one example: the school of Roxbury, Massachusetts, at the end of the colonial period had eighty-five pupils, and only nine of these were studying Latin. The rest were enrolled in the common branches.[2]

Along with their differences, however, Latin grammar schools had a number of more or less common features. Their daily programs were highly condensed and their schedules rigorous. Classes that extended from seven or eight in the morning until four or five in the afternoon were routine. Saturday classes were not unusual, though summer vacations were. Memorization was the chief method of learning. Small wonder that in Colonial days most children did not attend the Latin grammar school at all, and even fewer attended it to completion.

The Private School in the City, or the Private-Venture School

The Latin grammar school declined in importance because it was an aristocratic institution fighting a rear-guard action against mounting democratic forces. Its clientele consisted, at least in early Colonial days, primarily of the socioeconomic elite. Its emphasis on the classical languages served the few who were to go to college preparatory to entering law, the ministry, or some other learned profession. But this emphasis did not accommodate the needs of the many. And when, for the non-college bound, its emphasis shifted to the more utilitarian subjects, the result was a widening of the already existent social cleavage.

One answer to the socioeducational dilemma of the day was the so-called private school in the city, or the private-venture school. These institutions, located in such cities as Boston, Charleston, New York, and Philadelphia, offered practical subjects, on a cafeteria basis, to those in search of specific skills or knowledge. Some operated as day schools, others as evening schools. The single purpose of these schools was to meet the functional needs of a specifically oriented clientele. One such school had a curriculum that included "Writing, Arithmetick in whole numbers and fractions, Vulgar and Decimal, Merchants Ac-

[2] H. G. Good, *A History of Western Education* (New York: Crowell-Collier and Macmillan, Inc., 1960), p. 386.

counts, Algebra, Geometry, Surveying, Gauging, Trigonometry, plain and Spherical, Navigation in all kinds of sailing, Astronomy, and all other parts of the Mathematicks by Theophilus Grew." This pedagogue-entrepreneur advertised that he taught "Writing and Arithmetick at the usual rate of 10s per Quarter. Merchants Accounts, Navigation, for 30s per quarter."[3]

The Academy

The private-venture school was a noteworthy step in the direction of the practical, but it was not enough. Undoubtedly, it contributed in a direct way to the educational needs of its day; but its most significant contribution was an indirect one: it pointed the way to the academy.

The academy had its roots in England, but the resemblance between the academies of the New and Old World was more nominal than real. The academy that arose in the American Colonies differed from its English counterpart in the following respects: it was nonsectarian in leadership, secularly oriented in curriculum, and open to students from diverse socioeconomic levels. It differed from the private-venture schools in the following respects: responsibility for it was vested in a board of trustees; the profit motive was not a controlling one; its curriculum was not of the self-service variety but a carefully conceived design; and its staff met high professional standards for its day.

The moving force behind the academy in the Colonies was Benjamin Franklin, who in 1749 presented a theoretical plan for it in, *Proposals Relating to the Education of Youth in Pensilvania.*[4] His announced purpose for the academy was not necessarily to prepare youth for the professions but for "business, offices, marriages, or any other thing for their advantage . . ." In 1751 in Philadelphia, Franklin's theory became an institutional reality. This first American academy "had three departments: the English, the mathematical-scientific, and the classical. Later, in 1754, a philosophical department was added."[5]

Franklin's vision embraced a school that would accentuate the use-

[3] Quoted in Elwood P. Cubberley, *Readings in Public Education in the United States* (Boston: Houghton Mifflin Company, 1934), pp. 87–88.

[4] See Thomas Woody, *Educational Views of Benjamin Franklin* (New York: McGraw-Hill, Inc., 1931).

[5] E. Dale Davis, *Focus on Secondary Education* (Glenview, Ill.: Scott, Foresman and Company, 1966), p. 11.

EDUCATION AS AN OPERATIONAL PROCESS

ful: the social sciences, the natural sciences, and the English vernacular as well as the classical languages—the vocational and physical as well as the academic; that would draw no divisive religious lines; that would be well equipped and attractive. The vision embraced a school from which

"youth will come out . . . fitted for learning any business, calling or profession, except such wherein languages are required; and though unacquainted with any ancient or foreign tongue, they will be masters of their own, which is of more immediate and general use; and withal will have attained many other valuable accomplishments; . . ."[6]

Many of diverse orientations greeted Franklin's academy with enthusiasm. One of these was the literary Anglican, Samuel Johnson. Others were individuals from the ranks both of Tories and Whigs, of Puritans and non-Puritans, of rich and poor. Despite smooth sailing at the outset, the academy soon ran into troubled waters. The major causes were the still powerful influence of the classicists, the requirement of tuition payments, and private boards of control which were more supportive of the college-preparatory than of the utilitarian curriculum. In historical perspective, the academy stands out as an institution which, though born a bit prematurely, made a significant contribution to the progressive growth of secondary education.

The Early American High School

These important tasks remained to be accomplished: (1) to make secondary education accessible to all, irrespective of their socioeconomic status; (2) to provide a curriculum that would relate to the complex needs of the diverse population; (3) to make secondary education free in the literal sense of the word—free to both rich and poor; and (4) to establish the legality of this new configuration. Toward these ends a monumental step was taken when Boston, in 1821, opened the first high school in the country. This first school was for boys only. In 1826, Boston opened a comparable school for girls which, however, closed shortly thereafter.

Encouraged over the success of the new high school venture, Massachusetts decreed, in 1827, that every town of 500 or more families should establish a high school equipped to offer such subjects as

[6] Woody, pp. 129–130.

United States history, algebra, geometry, bookkeeping, astronomy, and surveying. The decree further stipulated that any town of 4000 inhabitants should also offer Latin, Greek, rhetoric, and logic. A subsequent law, passed in 1833, made the interesting observation that the purpose of the first English (Classical) High School of 1821 was to serve the educational needs of students not preparing for college:

> It was instituted in 1821, with a design of furnishing the young men of the city who are not intended for a collegiate course of study, and who have enjoyed the usual advantages of the other public schools, with the means of completing a good English education to fit them for active life and qualify them for eminence in private or public station.[7]

Despite the 1833 interpretation in respect to non–college-bound students, the 1827 Massachusetts law, by its requirement that Latin and Greek be included in the curriculum of larger schools, revealed a reluctance to break with the past. A fairer statement, probably, is that it revealed a desire to serve the needs of both the old and the new during a period of cultural transition.

This first high school was not long in making its presence felt elsewhere. Another appeared in Portland, Maine, in the same year. Others opened in Worcester, Massachusetts, in 1824; and in New Bedford, Salem, and Plymouth—all in Massachusets—in 1827.

The high school movement, conceived and nurtured in Massachusetts, grew steadily but not rapidly. Early in its growth period, it made inroads into the other five New England states and others along the Atlantic Seaboard. Ultimately it became a national institution, but not until after the academy had reached its growth pinnacle in the Civil War period. At the beginning of the Civil War, there were only 321 high schools in the entire country. By 1890 the number had increased to 2500; by 1965, to 24,000.

A very basic reason for the high school's slow progress toward national status was the absence in many states of legal support for it. Even in Colonial days, the laws universally recognized the so-called common school as a legitimate public institution, authorizing without equivocation financial and administrative support for it. The laws were much slower to recognize the high school as a comparably legitimate public institution. The right of a state to levy taxes for support of the high school was not firmly established until 1874. In 1872, the city (then

[7] Vernon E. Anderson and William T. Gruhn, *Principles and Practices of Secondary Education* (New York: The Ronald Press Company, 1962), p. 33.

EDUCATION AS AN OPERATIONAL PROCESS

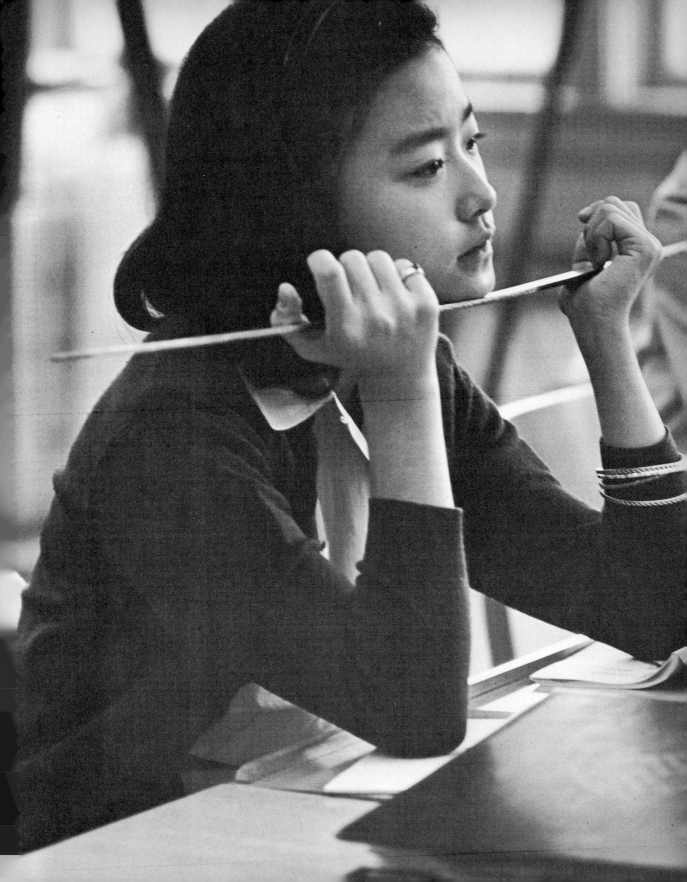

a village) of Kalamazoo, Michigan, had voted a high school into being, levying taxes for its construction and operation. A citizen named Stuart questioned the legality of this act in court. Through the appellate process, the case ultimately reached the state supreme court. Justice Cooley, who delivered the opinion of the court, called it a "naked question of law" as to whether the state of Michigan had authority "to make the high schools free by taxation levied on the people at large." He ruled that the state had that right, concluding his argument with this statement:

> . . . neither in our state policy, in our constitution, or in our laws, do we find the primary school districts restricted in the branches of knowledge which their officers may cause to be taught, or the grade of instruction that may be given, if their voters consent in regular form to bear the expense and raise the taxes for the purpose.

Some other states have ruled in a similar manner. As a result, the right of states to tax for high school purposes goes unquestioned today.

OBJECTIVES OF THE MODERN HIGH SCHOOL

By the end of the nineteenth century, the high school, having replaced the academy as the primary institution of secondary education, was an established educational fixture. However, it was searching then, as it has searched progressively since, for guiding aims and purposes. We shall now take up the history of that search. Some of the position statements and goal pronouncements have already been introduced in Chapters 2, 6, and 7.

The Committee of Ten

As the reader may recall, the Committee of Ten[8] was appointed in 1892 by the National Education Association to study and give direction to secondary education. Headed by President Charles W. Eliot of Harvard, it had a membership weighted heavily with college-oriented personnel. Its report of 1893 was a masterpiece of paradox. In recognition of the masses, it alleged the high school to be more terminal than college-

---

[8] National Education Association, *Report of the Committee of Ten on Secondary School Studies* (New York: American Book Company, 1893).

preparatory in purpose and scope. Yet details of the report were straight out of classical traditions. The report dealt almost exclusively with the academic subjects, and was anchored in the soon-to-be discounted theory of mental discipline. This theory held the mind to be a mental muscle that would strengthen when rigorously taxed by the hard-core disciplines. Thus curriculum content was evaluated in terms of its mind-training properties. In this same vein, the committee contended that the high school should make no differentiation in curriculum content for non-college-bound students; specifically, that the school should teach the same subjects, in the same way, and for the same length of time, irrespective of learner differences. Another recommendation was that high school courses, generally, should be started a grade or two earlier.

The Committee of Fifteen

This committee,[9] too, advocated that most high school subjects should begin earlier in the grades. It contended that German and French were appropriate subjects for grade 5; and Latin, Greek, and Roman history for grade 8. In the words of the committee, "Latin should be studied during the eighth year instead of English Grammar; and English Grammar should be studied during the sixth and seventh years."

The Commission on the Reorganization of Secondary Education

Passing over the Committee on College Entrance Requirements (which recommended a six-year high school), and the Committee on the Economy of Time (which recommended a shortening of the elementary school program), we turn now to one of the most important educational groups of all times: The Commission on the Reorganization of Secondary education.[10] This commission, as indicated previously, was the first educational body to make a clean break with the classical past, the first to take serious note of the changing nature of the high school population. The reason probably resided in the commission's membership: it

[9] National Education Association, *Report of the Committee of Fifteen on Elementary Education* (New York: American Book Company, 1895).

[10] Commission on Reorganization of Secondary Education, *Cardinal Principles of Education* (Washington, D.C.: U.S. Government Printing Office, 1918).

consisted not of college presidents or professors but of high school practitioners. The commission encompassed a general committee and 16 separate subcommittees, all active in one way or another in rethinking the problems of secondary education.

The commission made history in 1918 by committing secondary education to the pursuance of these seven cardinal principles of education.

1. Health
2. Command of fundamental process
3. Worthy home membership
4. Vocation
5. Civic education
6. Worthy use of leisure
7. Ethical character

These principles relate to the interests and needs of the many rather than the few and point to values that are broadly humanistic rather than strictly academic.

206

Purposes Stated by the Educational Policies Commission

Twenty years later, in 1938, the Educational Policies Commission[11] made an equally important goal pronouncement, which grouped some 50 objectives under the four headings of self-realization, human relationship, economic efficiency, and civic responsibility. And, for the first time in the history of this country, an educational organization made capital of the objectives of mental health.

Other Promulgations

Other goal pronouncements include one in 1945 which, under the auspices of Harvard University, appeared in *General Education in a Free Society*;[12] one in 1956 by the White House Conference on Education;[13] and another in 1961 made jointly by the Policies Commission and the American Association of School Administrators.[14] These more recent pronouncements have highlighted discovery learning and put new emphasis on reflective thinking.

Issues Raised by Goal Promulgations

Statements of educational objectives do not come about lightly. They are the result of serious consideration and soul searching. They tend to occur when society and education, dissatisfied with old directions and practices, wish to embark on new ones; or when society and education, convinced of the merit of existing directions and practices, desire to call special attention to them or refine them.

[11] Educational Policies Commission, *The Purposes of Education in American Democracy* (Washington, D.C.: National Education Association, 1938).

[12] The Committee on the Objectives of a General Education in a Free Society, *General Education in a Free Society* (Cambridge, Mass.: Harvard University Press, 1945), p. 54.

[13] The Committee for the White House Conference on Education, *A Report to the President* (Washington, D.C.: U.S. Government Printing Office, 1956), p. 90.

[14] Educational Policies Commission and American Association of School Administrators, *The Central Purpose of American Education* (Washington, D.C.: National Education Association, 1961), pp. 17–18.

Two goal issues have plagued secondary education since the Latin grammar school ceased being a single-purposed classical institution of learning. These two issues, which became acute around the turn of the present century, are the following. (1) Should the high school serve the needs primarily of the intellectual elite or the needs of all youth at intellectual levels down to low normal? (2) Relatedly, should the high school foster mental growth primarily or exclusively, or should it foster total personality growth conceived across a broad spectrum? We treat these in the order listed.

The issue of whether high school education exists for the elite or for all can be resolved only by looking beyond it to national purposes and to the American Dream itself. The message these convey is crystal clear: The American way is a democratic way, a humanistic way. The American way rises to lofty heights when the citizenry is well informed and enlightened; but it falls by its own weight, becomes a prey to demagoguery, when the citizenry is ill informed and unenlightened. Implementation of the American dream dictates that all individuals— gifted and slow, rich and poor, socially favored or out of favor—are completely deserving of the educational opportunities inherent in the high school.

The Committee of Ten blueprinted a high school that was tenable only for the elite—for the 5 to 10 percent of the eligible population in attendance in 1900. Despite its protestations to the contrary, the committee inadequately provided for the needs of the growing masses, a student body that in 1965 was to represent 90 percent of all eligible youth in the fourteen-to-seventeen age bracket.[15] However, in 1918 and 1938, respectively, the Commission on the Reorganization of Secondary Education and the Educational Policies Commission, recommended a program designed to meet the needs of the masses without neglecting the needs of the intellectually favored.

Interestingly, starting in the late 1950s, a highly verbal group, primarily from the ranks of the intellectual elite, led a crusade to return the high school to the gifted. Sputnik triggered this crusade. Leadership came from individuals as diverse as James B. Conant, scientist and former president of Harvard University; Admiral Hyman G. Rickover, USN; Arthur E. Bestor, professor of history at the University of Illinois; and Paul E. Woodring, staff officer of the Ford Foundation. All argued for a program that from most standards appeared to be too abstract

[15] E. Dale Davis, *Focus on Secondary Education*, p. 18.

and academic for the below-average student; or for a program that tended to relegate him to activities in the mechanical arts. These representatives of the so-called "New Establishment" were and still are outspoken champions of education geared to the elite. Many hold offices in national educational bodies. From these positions of influence, they have directed educational funds and exerted educational effort mostly in the interest of the academically talented. In my opinion, however, they have consistently oversimplified, and thus have neglected, the needs of students with average and below-average ability.[16]

The American way calls for an educational program sensitive to the needs of all learners. Ill-concealed elitism and impatience with the limitations of the common man go counter to this way. Grounded in intellectual snobbery, they veer dangerously toward aristocratic favoritism.

The second goal issue, restated, is this: Should the high school serve intellectual needs primarily or exclusively, or should it serve a broad range of personality needs as well? Theorists of the New Establishment, as might be expected, are prone to support the first alternative. On-the-job practitioners and theorists oriented in broad human values are just as prone to support the second.

The case for the intellectualist position goes something like this. Every major institution in a society exists because it can do something better than any other institution can. Thus, each should do what it does best. It follows, then, that the school should devote itself to intellectual development, the home to social and emotional development, and the church and synagogue to ethical and spiritual development. The case is vulnerable, I contend, because it overcompartmentalizes the agencies responsible for development of the young.

The case for the broader personality position, already elaborated in Chapter 2, goes in the following counter direction. Humanism constitutes the frame of American education. Within this frame, man, because he is organismic, learns as a totality—the mental, affective, and motor functions mutually reinforcing one another. Furthermore, the school is an extension of a stable home, and the teacher, as surrogate parent, stands in loco parentis. Within this frame, the high school is

---

[16] I give credit here to Professor Harry S. Broudy, professor of education at the University of Illinois. He has widely debated the issue of the New and the Old Establishments in Education. He views the New Establishment as being out of tune with American values, and the Old Establishment as in need of a theoretical base of support. Professor Broudy's address on this issue, in March, 1966, at the annual meeting of the Association for Supervision and Curriculum Development, was particularly noteworthy.

responsible for learner growth along a broad base—one broad enough to embrace the several components of the mental, emotional, social, ethical, and motor. This broad personality position is the one to which I subscribe. It is the one out of which I think, teach, and write.

HIGH SCHOOL STUDENTS

Teachers who adopt the broad personality position tend, more than their intellectualist counterparts, to internalize the money complex problems that accompany youth to the high school. The sheer size of the high school population itself contributes to the number and complexity of these problems. In 1966, for instance, approximately 13.2 million students were enrolled in grades 9–12, and 21.1 million in grades 7–12. The first statistic, as stated earlier in the chapter, represents 90 percent of all eligible youth in the fourteen-to-seventeen age bracket. It does not include atypical youth in schools for the handicapped or normal youth in federally administered schools.

Differences among High School Students

High school youth are indeed a diverse lot, coming as they do from a cross section of the total population. They range in intelligence from IQs of 70 to IQs of 160 or higher, in future educational plans from imminent dropouts to the college-bound, in future vocational plans from interests in menial labor to interests in professional-executive positions. They range economically from the indigent to the affluent, socially from the immature to the prematurely sophisticated, emotionally from the neurotic or even incipient psychotic to the well adjusted, behaviorally from the nonconformist to the conformist, and physically from the handicapped to the normal. Ethnically they range in ways far too numerous to bear inclusion here.

Similar Needs among High School Students

Despite these multifarious differences, however, high school youth share the characteristics enumerated and discussed below—characteristics not significantly different from those treated in Chapter 7 in con-

nection with junior high school students. In the composite, they constitute the developmental needs of adolescents and young adults, and they vary little from culture to culture. Specifically, high school students need:

1. *To develop adequate self-images by accepting themselves psychologically.* A prerequisite here is the acceptance of youth by close associates: parents, teachers, and peers. Another prerequisite is success of youth in school, without which self-acceptance becomes difficult or even impossible. The social and academic implications for the school, in this regard, are obvious.

2. *To develop adequate self-images by accepting, as normal and wholesome, physical changes in their bodies and body functions.* This need commits males to accept such secondary masculine phenomena as enlargement of the genitals, increase in body hair, and growth in facial features, bones and muscles. It commits females to accept such secondary feminine phenomena as growth of pubic hair, budding of the mammary glands, menstruation, and enlargement of the pelvic-hip region.

3. *To develop adequate self-images by accepting their primary sex roles.* This need reaches beyond body change into body chemistry and youthful psyches. It dictates that irrespective of sex identification, members of each sex need to be satisfied with the role that nature assigned them. The high school should be instrumental in helping to satisfy this need.

4. *To relate in socially acceptable ways to associates at all levels.* This constitutes the need for youth to develop social skills such as: conversational fluency, becoming acquainted with and observing the social amenities, and accepting others. The need, at a practical level, is for young people to know what to do and say, and to know how to do and say it, in an increasing variety of social situations. But beyond the level of veneer, the need is for youth to grow socially and emotionally toward the outcomes of sensitivity, empathy, and ultimately, altruism.

5. *To acquire fundamental skills, knowledge, concepts, attitudes, and the ability to generalize.* This is a need that, in the composite, constitutes the hard-core requisites of social, civic, and vocational success. This hard core goes by the name of general education.

6. *To gain a reasonable degree of economic independence or to adjust to the inevitability of its delay.* This need is realized in the following ways: part-time employment by students while in the high school,

211

dropping out of high school to secure full-time employement, receiving a family allowance, or adjusting to the reality of delayed economic benefits. Each family meets this need in a different way. Lower-class families tend to employ the first two methods in greater degree; middle-class families, the last two. Many high schools assist needy students by helping them secure part-time employment.

7. *To gain increasing independence from adults.* Half-child and half-adult, the adolescent craves independence from the adult world more, with the possible exception of sexual fulfillment, than he does any other growth outcome. He wants independence in the choice of friends, attire, hours, avocations, and habits. The adult world, on the other hand, which is responsible for his welfare, largely decides the amount and degree of independence he will have. In the case of the strong-willed, the emotionally maladjusted, or the spoiled, serious conflict frequently results. I feel, as many others have, that adolescents actually desire reasonable limits, not absolute freedom in respect to independence. Absolute freedom, in fact, is frightening in its possibilities. Thus the task of the high school is to satisfy, within limits, this need of adolescents for independence.

8. *To develop a system of values rationally thought out and internalized but not to flaunt them when they run counter to values of the home, school, or community.* In respect to value development, individuals characteristically are amoral as infants, expedient as younger children, conformist as older children and early adolescents, and rational assessors of values only as mature adults. The task of the high school in respect to value development is not an enviable one. It cannot blatantly go counter to family and community values. Neither should it stop short of teaching students to think reflectively about life in all its manifestations. The best solution actually resides in the process of reflective thinking itself. Etched into the process is the requirement that learners themselves think through life's issues to a justifiable conclusion. In this way, value conflict, if it eventuates, is more between the home and the learner than between the home and the school. Difficult though value conflict may be for learners, maturity is an unlikely outcome without it.

The most widely quoted list of the developmental needs and tasks of youth is one by Havighurst, published in 1952.[17] It embraces the following specifics:

[17] Robert J. Havighurst, *Developmental Tasks and Education* (New York: David McKay Company, Inc., 1952), pp. 33–71. By permission of David McKay Co., Inc.

1. Achieving more mature relations with age mates of both sexes
2. Achieving a masculine or feminine social role
3. Accepting one's physique and using the body effectively
4. Achieving emotional independence of parents and other adults
5. Achieving assurance of economic independence
6. Selecting and preparing for an occupation
7. Preparing for marriage and family life
8. Developing intellectual skills and concepts necessary for civic competence
9. Desiring and achieving socially responsible behavior
10. Acquiring a set of values and an ethical system as a guide to behavior

Some Facts about High School Students

On an average, boys earn lower grades and fail more often than girls. Boys do proportionately better work in science and mathematics; girls do better work in English and foreign languages. Seven of eight high school students live with both parents. Both sexes rate interest, security, self-expression, and social service as more important ingredients than the profit motive in an occupational choice. Male students customarily aim at vocational choices that, on the socioeconomic scale, rank higher than the vocations of their fathers.[18] And two-thirds of all students who enter high school remain to graduate.

ORGANIZATIONAL ISSUES

Having explored the three topics of antecedents, objectives, and student body of the high school, I turn now to some organizational issues, which, over a period of time, have elicited from mild to heated debate in educational circles. The issues are five in number: (1) the comprehensive versus the specialized high school; (2) departmentalization of subject matter; (3) the individual teacher versus the team; (4) homogeneous versus heterogeneous grouping, and (5) constant versus flexible length of class period.

[18] O. E. Thompson, "What is the High School Student of Today Like?" *Journal of Secondary Education,* 36 (April, 1961), pp. 210–219.

The Comprehensive versus the Specialized High School

Of the five, the issue with the broadest base is the first. It poses the question: Should the nation's high schools be comprehensive, specialized, or both? A high school that is comprehensive is one with a curriculum diverse enough to serve the needs of a highly heterogenous student population. Such a curriculum serves a given student body across the broad range of general, college-preparatory, vocational, and exploratory education. On the other hand, a high school that is specialized is one with a curriculum specifically designed to serve the needs of a relatively homogenous student body. Specialized schools generally are of two distinct types: vocational and college preparatory. The former, for the most part, is a direct product of the Smith-Hughes Vocational Act of 1917 and subsequent enabling legislation that has kept it in force. Its purpose is to prepare students directly for the world of work. The college-preparatory school, in contrast, is one that readies students for college. Its curriculum resultingly tends to be one-sidely academic.

For nearly a half century, the comprehensive high school has been the citadel of secondary education. During that time, it has been a social symbol as well as an institution of learning. In either guise—at least at the level of the ideal—it brings learners of diverse social and academic backgrounds and interests into its fold and stamps them all with the seal of respectability. While administering differentially to their

academic needs, it unites them in the areas of social and civic living. The specialized high school, on the other hand, is more socially divisive. Furthermore, it is prone to overemphasize its speciality and to de-emphasize interest areas that lie outside its speciality. Predictively, then, the academic programs of vocational high schools and the practical programs of strictly college-preparatory high schools are less adequate than their counterparts in comprehensive high schools.

My personal opinion on the issue at hand is that the comprehensive high school should not only retain its position of centrality in secondary education but should enlarge and solidify it. I grant, however, that for the comprehensive high school to serve a student population efficiently it should enroll more than the national median of 350 to 400 students. A population of 1000 is a realistic minimum.

Departmentalization of Subject Matter

The vast majority of high schools in the country, whether comprehensive or specialized, are organized along departmental lines. Under such an arrangement, students go from teacher to teacher, and usually from classroom to classroom, for subjects that in the elementary school are primarily the responsibility of a single teacher. In the high school, they generally are the composite responsibility of a number of specialized teachers, each performing in the curriculum area of his greatest strength. Under this scheme, a given instructor may teach only English or only history (perhaps only United States history), only vocal music, or only mechanical drawing. At times, however, particularly in small high schools with limited enrollments, he may teach two or even three subjects. But whether he teaches one, two, or three subjects, the student makeup of each class is different.

Justification for the departmental approach rests on the following assumption: that as learners become more mature, and as learning becomes more complex, the need for specialized competency in the teacher becomes increasingly essential. The recent knowledge explosion has contributed significantly to the logic and validity of this assumption. In fact, the teacher of today who does not keep abreast of current developments in his instructional specialty soon becomes dead wood on a high school faculty.

The approach furthermore rests on the assumption that high school learners are mature enough to transfer skills, knowledge, and under-

215

standings gained in one curriculum area to other areas. The validity of this assumption is tenuous enough to give learning theorists pause. Many students, for instance, "learn English" in an English class but leave their knowledge behind when entering an industrial-arts or typing class. Some who routinely employ the scientific method in the chemistry laboratory leap to finalized conclusions, without benefit of facts, in a civics class. And others are facile with formulas in a mathematics class but are unable to transfer them to a physics class.

Departmentalization unquestionably obligates teachers to instruct for psychological transfer. Each needs to relate specifics of his curriculum specialty to specifics of other curriculum specialties. Teachers of all subjects need to inquire of learners almost habitually: "What implications does the concept or approach we are grappling with here have in your classes in X, Y, or Z subjects, or in this or that life situation?" Failure of teachers to instruct for transfer, while not an indictment of departmentalization per se, definitely mitigates against its effectiveness.

The Individual Teacher versus the Team

Until recently, departmentalization automatically implied classrooms taught by individual teachers. The assumption built into this scheme, as already indicated, was that a single teacher, responsible for one, two, or three subject areas, would bring a high degree of scholarship and artistic competency to the instructional process. Events of the past two, or three decades, however, have generated skepticism regarding the validity of this assumption. One of these events has been the knowledge explosion precipitated by the electronics age; a second has been the upheaval in teaching methods that came in the wake of this revolution; and a third has been the guidance upsurge that has projected the needs of the individual students more and more into the learning spotlight.

These three influences have caused education—in elementary schools somewhat less, in secondary schools somewhat more—to experiment with team-teaching arrangements. The obvious hope is for improvement in the total instructional effort of any school. Experimenters make the assumption that when two or more knowledgeable, motivated, and cooperative teachers combine their talents, the quality of scholarship and learning is bound to improve. The assumption unquestionably has

216

logic on its side. However, I make only passing comment on the topic of team teaching here in view of the detailed coverage to be given it in Chapter 10.

Homogeneous versus Heterogeneous Grouping

The issue of the individual teacher versus the team has to do with the question of who will instruct learners once they have been grouped for instruction. The issue of homogeneous versus heterogeneous grouping has to do with an equally fundamental question of how learners will be grouped in the first place. With high schools departmentalized and graded in most instances, it follows that subject matter and grade placement constitute two grouping criteria. But beyond these, as will be developed later, high schools need to identify and employ other grouping criteria.

Procedural steps in the grouping process generally consist of the following:

The decision to group   Obviously the first step in grouping is the decision to do so. But for administrators and teachers, this decision is easier to make than to justify. In fact, any serious attempt at homogeneous grouping plunges them quickly into a morass of divided opinion. Teachers who have worked or are working with the plan (in the high school) generally testify to its merits. Professional educators who have made methical studies of the plan are likely to be more opposed to than in favor of it. And researchers who have conducted experiments with the plan are likely to be widely divided in regard to almost every aspect of the arrangement.

The following selected comments by researchers attest to their ambivalence.

1. . . . "The reporter's role is a sorry one. For he has to report that, by and large, the research evidence is disappointing."[19]

2. . . . "controlled experimental studies comparing the effectiveness of homogeneous and heterogeneous grouping as evaluated by student achievement, showed no consistent pattern of results."[20]

[19] Fred T. Wilhelms and D. W. Gibson "Grouping Research Offers Leads," *Educational Leadership*, 18 (April 1961), pp. 410–413.

[20] Ruth B. Eckstrom, "Experimental Studies of Homogeneous Grouping: A Critical Review," *School Review*, 60 (Summer 1959), pp. 216–226.

3. [Both bright and slow children] do better in high ability classes . . . [indicating that] ability grouping is harmful to most of the slow children.[21]

4. The evidence slightly favors ability grouping in regard to academic achievement, with dull children seeming to profit more than bright children.[22]

Unquestionably, the findings of research on homogeneous grouping constitute a pot pourri. The reason lies in the many variables of the learning process—curriculum, teacher characteristics, and learner dynamics—most of which research is unable to control. However, the unstable nature of research on grouping neither indicts nor vindicates the scheme. Rather, it forewarns schools to look not to objectivity but to subjectivity for justification of any grouping arrangement.

Criteria for grouping A school committed to homogeneous grouping sooner or later has to decide what criteria it will employ in the formulation of groups. Criteria, although differing in relative importance from subject to subject, generally consist of the following: intelligence, achievement in the content field in which grouping is to take place, reading ability, and certain intangibles of personality. Generally speaking, a multicriterion base leads to better grouping outcomes than does a single-criterion base.

Number of groups Another step of grouping is for a high school to decide how many groups it will have in any given subject field. The size of the student body is an important determinant in this. Extremely small schools are unable to group at all. Large ones tend to set up three to five groups, with junior high schools gravitating more toward three and high schools more toward five. Any fixed number, however, is admittedly arbitrary.

Assignment of teachers Yet another important task in homogeneous grouping is to assign teachers to class groups. In all instances, at least whenever practical, the controlling criteria should be the special abilities and individual preferences of teachers. Teachers assigned to classes of slow learners, for example, should court the assignment in the first place and should bring specialized talents to it. And classes for the gifted should not habitually be reserved for department heads or teach-

[21] John W. French, "Evidence from School Records on the Effectiveness of Ability Grouping," *Journal of Education Research,* 54 (November 1960), pp. 83–91.

[22] John I. Goodlad, "Classroom Organization," *The Encyclopedia of Educational Research* (New York: Crowell-Collier and Macmillan, Inc., 1960), pp. 221–225.

ers with more seniority than their colleagues. Such capriciousness is out of place in a profession.

A personal comment Irrespective of the many tasks and issues involved in homogeneous grouping, any school's major responsibility is to establish and maintain a climate in which grouping can operate in a healthy way. It should be a climate in which the school accepts all learners—slow, average, and fast—as equally deserving of education's best; in which the stigmatic terms *honors* and *remedial* are not employed; and in which teachers, parents, and students accept differences matter-of-factly, eschewing odious value judgments in the process. Only in such a climate can homogeneous grouping rise above the mental-health shortcomings that tend to characterize it at the present time.

Constant versus Flexible Length of Class Periods

Whether schools group students along homogeneous or heterogeneous lines, they need to follow some accepted pattern of class and course scheduling. Since as far back as 1909, the Carnegie unit has been axial in that pattern. In that year, the Carnegie Foundation for the Advancement of Teaching persuaded the accrediting associations to adopt a uniform standard for assessing the curriculum progress of pupils. The standard became known as the Carnegie unit. A student today earns one such unit of credit for successfully completing, during any given academic year, a course that meets 120 clock hours of time. The original minimum for graduation was 14 units. Today's minimum is 16 or more in all but two states, which require 15.

The Carnegie unit undoubtedly brought needed structure to the high school. But almost from the start, it developed "sclerosis of the flexibilities." Some of its shortcomings, past and present, are that it (1) overstructures curriculum content and class schedules, (2) assumes all courses to be comparably demanding and difficult, and (3) seldom takes qualitative outcomes into account.

As briefly commented on in the preceding chapter, a growing number of high schools today are countering scheduling and curriculum rigidities by employing the so-called *module* as a unit of measurement. These schools think not in terms of 40-, 50-, or 60-minute periods, but of 15- or 20-minute modules; not of classes that meet for periods of identical

length, but for ones that meet for periods of varying length, depending on the nature of the curriculum content, its level of difficulty, and the demands imposed by the learning process.

As a unit of class-length determination, the module unquestionably has *prima facie* superiority over the Carnegie unit. It has the shortcoming, however, of being extremely difficult to forge into an operational arrangement and, once forged, of being extremely difficult to administer. For these reasons, modular curriculum planning awaits an indefinite period of experimentation before high schools will be able to determine its workability.[23]

To Stimulate Thought

1. Do you believe that Latin and Greek have mind-training properties that make them valuable outside the frame of their subject-matter content? Defend your answer.

2. Start with the statement that any institution of public education must mirror the tenor and needs of its time. Then apply the statement either to the Latin grammar school or to the academy.

3. In your opinion, should a high school curriculum bend to meet the needs of very slow learners, or should slow learners rise to meet the demands of a prefixed curriculum? Develop your stand in some detail, validating it against the nation's basic values.

4. Build a case for either of the following two positions on goals: (1) Secondary education should be intellectually oriented primarily; or (2) secondary education should be total-personality oriented.

5. Develop the statement made in this chapter: "Adolescents actually desire reasonable limits, not absolute freedom. . . ."

6. Defend or take issue with the generalization that the mature should think openly and critically about all of life's major concerns. Inject the topic of religion into your answer.

7. Homogeneous grouping customarily relegates a disproportionate number of the lower socioeconomic classes to slow-learning groups. Relate this outcome to a school that professes to emphasize social-civic growth.

8. For your subject-matter major, take the so-called module, assign a time length to it, and then develop a week's program with it as the scheduling base.

[23] The topic of the module and modular planning is well developed in Robert N. Bush and Dwight W. Allen, *A New Design for High School Education* (New York: McGraw-Hill, Inc., 1964), Chap. 3.

REFERENCES

Anderson, Vernon E., and William T. Gruhn, *Principles and Practices of Secondary Education* (New York: The Ronald Press Company, 1962).

Bruner, Jerome S., *The Process of Education* (Cambridge, Mass.: Harvard University Press, 1960).

Bush, Robert N., and Dwight W. Allen, *A New Design for High School Education* (New York: McGraw-Hill, Inc., 1964).

Clark, Leonard H., Raymond L. Klein, and John B. Burks, *The American Secondary School Curriculum* (New York: Crowell-Collier and Macmillan, Inc., 1965).

Conant, James B., *The American High School Today* (New York: McGraw-Hill, Inc., 1959).

Cyphert, Frederick R., Earl W. Harmer, Jr., and Anthony C. Riccio, *Teaching in the American Secondary School* (New York: McGraw-Hill, Inc., 1964).

Davis, E. Dale, *Focus on Secondary Education* (Glenview, Ill.: Scott, Foresman and Company, 1966).

Downey, Lawrence W., *The Secondary Phase of Education* (Waltham, Mass.: Blaisdell Publishing Company, 1965).

Downey, Lawrence W., *The Task of Public Education* (Chicago: Midwest Administration Center, University of Chicago, 1960).

Franklin, Marian Pope, *School Organization: Theory and Practice* (Chicago: Rand McNally and Company, 1967).

Kandel, I. L., *History of Secondary Education* (Boston: Houghton Mifflin Company, 1930).

Smith, Mortimer, *The Diminished Mind* (Chicago: Henry Regnery Company, 1954).

Tompkins, Ellsworth, and Walter H. Gaumnitz, *The Carnegie Unit: Its Origin, Status, and Trends*, Bulletin 1954, No. 7 (Washington, D.C.: U.S. Department of Health, Education, and Welfare, 1954).

Wright, Grace, *Requirements for High School Graduation* (Washington, D.C.: U.S. Department of Health, Education, and Welfare, 1961).

Wright, Grace S., *Subject Offerings and Enrollments in Public Secondary Schools* (Washington, D.C.: U.S. Department of Health, Education, and Welfare, 1965).

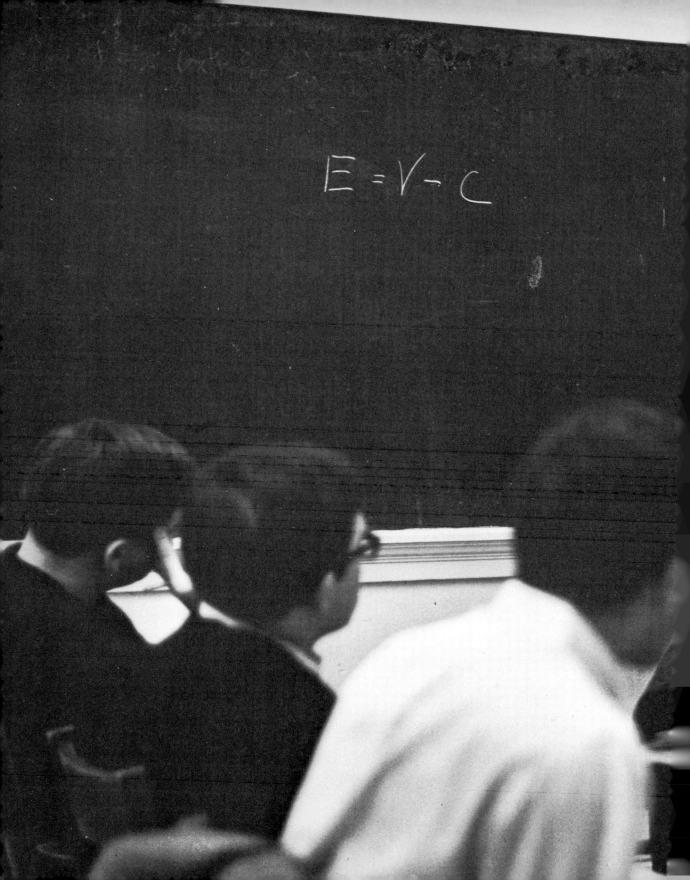

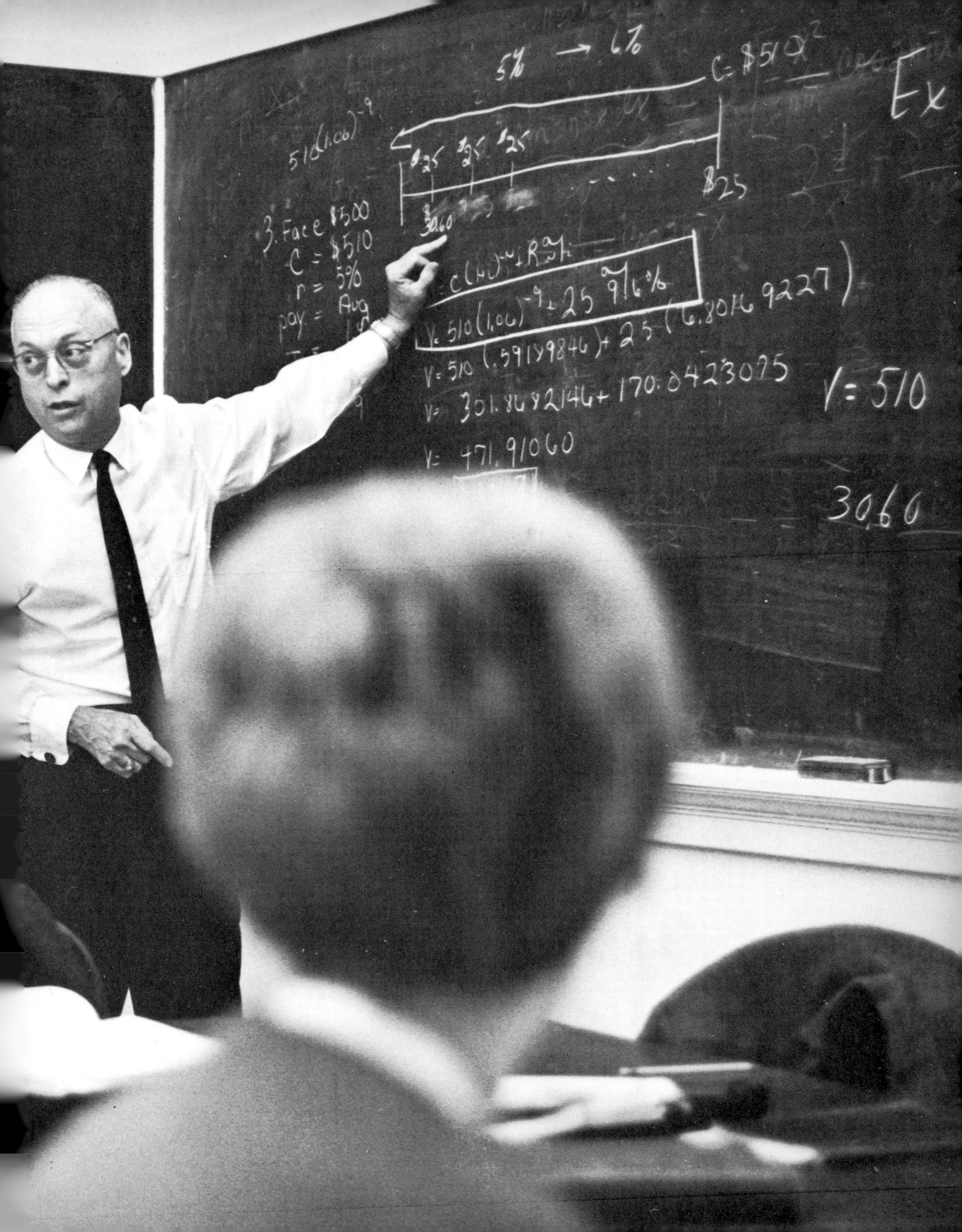
5% → 6%
3. Face $500
C = $510
r = 5%
V = 471.91060
V = 510
30,60

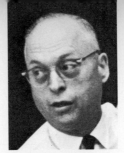

Chapter

9

*The
High School:
Its
Curriculum*

The preceding chapter's focus on the history, student body, and organizational issues of the high school leads appropriately into this chapter's focus on the high school curriculum. Curriculum, as I defined it earlier, is the planned composite effort exerted by a school to guide pupils toward predetermined learning outcomes. Thus curriculums differ from school to school in direct relation, more or less, to the degree to which their philosophies and goals differ. National values act to limit the range of differences; local values act to broaden it.

In this latter connection, curriculums of high schools in suburban communities customarily revolve around the five hard-core academic areas of English, social studies, natural sciences, mathematics, and foreign languages. These help students think abstractly and symbolically. They constitute a road that the more verbal are able to traverse with ease, but one that confronts the less verbal with serious, at times even insurmountable, obstacles. It is a road that leads unswervingly to college. At the other socioeconomic extreme, curriculums of inner-city schools customarily constitute a more even blend of the theoretical and the applied. They usually are comprehensive enough both to prepare the more verbal for college and to provide the less verbal with a broad choice of utilitarian electives.

THREE CURRICULUM CATEGORIES

Curriculum offerings of the American comprehensive high school customarily divide into the following three categories: (1) general education, (2) exploratory education, and (3) special education.

General Education

The first of these categories, general education, consists of those curriculum experiences needed by all to enable them to adapt to life and to find significant meaning in it. As stated elsewhere:[1]

[1] Gail M. Inlow, *The Emergent in Curriculum* (New York: John Wiley & Sons, Inc., 1966), p. 57.

General education is that part of a curriculum that opens the door to meaning in life. It opens the door by giving to all a shared core of knowledge, understandings, skills, appreciations and attitudes. Equipped with this core, individuals are better able to accomplish the goal of adaption while pressing toward the loftier goal of total development.

In the elementary school, the curriculum consists of both general and exploratory education. In the junior high school, it gives greater emphasis to exploratory education. In the high school, it continues to advance exploratory education while conceding in a more limited way to specialism. Yet while making such concessions, the high school curriculum accords general education a central position. Since verbal communication is basic both to group living and to critical thinking, the high school continues to emphasize the skills of reading, writing, speaking, and listening. Since computational skills are part of the fiber of life along many dimensions, the high school, at progressive levels of sophistication, continues to emphasize them. Since the social sciences, the natural sciences, and health play an important role in the lives of all, the high school continues to include some facets of each in its general-education offerings.

In any program of general education, the basic skills and a hard core of content in literature, the social sciences, the natural sciences, mathematics, and health usually go unquestioned. When the core additionally takes in content in the esthetic, motor, and manipulative fields, however, controversy almost invariably results. Yet who can deny that individuals realize fulfillment not exclusively from intellectual accomplishments but from esthetic and motor ones as well? Who can deny that the world is a happier one when the fine and kinetic arts brighten it? Or that a household runs more smoothly when its members are able to make routine mechanical repairs? Or that the population in general is less disease-prone when the people regard physical conditioning as important?

In the high school, general education or common learnings, so called, reside in the curriculum constants. The learnings are common, however, only in the sense that all students are required to earn the same number of credits in them. Within this quantitative frame, the curriculum content generally differs qualitatively because of differences among learners. In grade 9, for instance, slow learners customarily enroll in general mathematics; fast learners, in algebra.

Of the 16 to 17 Carnegie units required by most high schools for graduation, those in the curriculum constants divide nationally as follows:

226

Subjects	Carnegie Units of Credit
English	3 plus
Social studies	2
Mathematics	1 plus
Natural sciences	2 minus
Health and physical education	1 ($\frac{1}{4}$ unit each year)
Fine arts	0 plus
Industrial arts	0 plus
	9 units

The hope of the high school for the above offerings is that they will unite students with common bonds by including them in common (although not identical) learning experiences. The constants in any high school curriculum accomplish their intended purposes when they unite students with common bonds of skills, knowledge, understandings, attitudes, and appreciations. The resulting unity not only gives cohesion to the social order, but at the same time provides a needed base for individual growth.

Exploratory Education

The effect of general education is to make young people more alike; the contrasting effect of exploratory education is to make them less alike. The goal of the latter is to enlarge the interests of learners by opening new curriculum vistas to them. At times, exploratory education takes the form of a curriculum constant, a well-known instance being the survey course required of many ninth graders in the various fine and applied arts. In this course, many students are introduced, for instance, to oil painting, ceramics, metalwork, and mechanical drawing. Exploratory education most often takes the form of curriculum electives in previously unexplored curriculum areas.

Exploratory education makes it possible for learners to have new curriculum experiences without committing them to specialism. It enables them to explore the unknown and to broaden their horizons. In the process, they often uncover interests that may become permanent; they tend to take school obligations more seriously; and they derive satisfaction from seeing the world of the unknown narrowed.

THE CURRICULUM PROCESS AT WORK

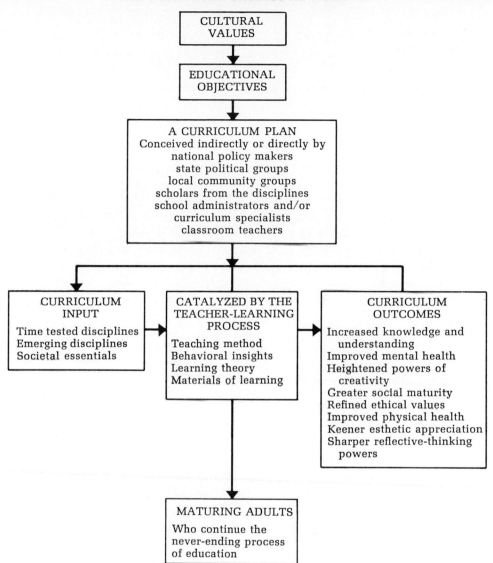

Special Education

Like exploratory education, special education is also oriented in individual interests and preferences. It differs from exploratory education, however, in that it allows learners to pursue their interests in greater depth in a given curriculum area.

EDUCATION AS AN OPERATIONAL PROCESS

The area might be vocational, for which the following curriculum patterns—in the field of the vocational specialties—would be typical.

Secretarial			Vocational		
Typing	2 units		Auto shop	2 units	
Shorthand	2 units		Woods	1 unit	
Office practice	2 units		Metals	1 unit	
Business letter writing	1 unit		Electricity	2 units	
	7 units		Graphic arts	1 unit	
				7 units	

The area might be in the category of the esthetic, with the following pattern typical.

Fine Arts

Basic art	1 unit
Drawing	2 units
Painting	2 units
General crafts	1 unit
Sculpture	1 unit
	7 units

Or, as a third possibility, the area might be an academic one, with the following pattern possible.

English

English 1, 2, 3	3 units
Drama	1 unit
School paper	1 unit
Creative writing	1 unit
Debate	1 unit
	7 units

Each of the above mirrors a curriculum pattern in which a specialized interest field has become dominant. And each in its own way poses the fundamental question of how much specialism high schools should allow. The question is particularly germane in the area of vocational education, which, at times, is an unquestionable antidote to the dropout problem in inner cities. In regard to vocationalism, the high school has four options.

1. One is a total rejection by the schools of any direct responsibility for vocational education. This rejection would constitute, at least in part, a reactionary return to outmoded classical traditions.

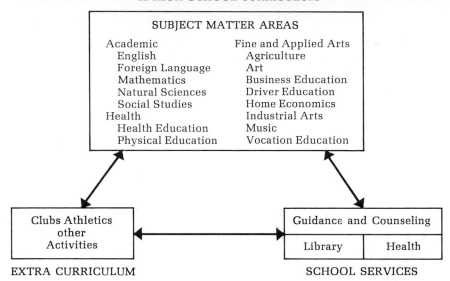

SUBJECT MATTER AREAS

Academic	Fine and Applied Arts
English	Agriculture
Foreign Language	Art
Mathematics	Business Education
Natural Sciences	Driver Education
Social Studies	Home Economics
Health	Industrial Arts
Health Education	Music
Physical Education	Vocation Education

Clubs Athletics other Activities

Guidance and Counseling

Library | Health

EXTRA CURRICULUM

SCHOOL SERVICES

2. A second option is a complete reliance by schools on the five hard-core academic areas as an indirect means of readying learners for future occupational demands. This option is vulnerable, however, on several grounds. For one thing, its base is exclusively verbal; thus it fails to exploit the vocational-learning possibilities inherent in nonverbal experiences. Furthermore, it assumes a one-to-one relationship to exist between the verbal world of formal education and the often nonverbal world of vocationalism.

3. A third option is for the high school to depart abruptly from past traditions and practices and make a direct assault on the practical. But this was the approach of the life-adjustment movement that achieved but limited success in the thirties and forties. It achieved only limited success because it was too "present" oriented, and because it operated too far outside the sphere of the academic disciplines.

4. A fourth option, and one I endorse, is for the high school to avoid both the classical and the practical extremes. In the process, it would play its comprehensive role seriously and discerningly. In such a role, the high school would not turn away from its three-way involvement in general, exploratory, and special education. Not at all. However, while maintaining the involvement, it would effect *one major change* in it and establish *one major control* over it. Some high schools are already taking these steps; yet they need to take them with greater assurance and

vigor. And not nearly enough high schools are taking them at all.

The *major change* I have in mind has to do with the academic subjects. These have had status from as far back as Greco-Roman days. They have changed with the passage of time, but societies have changed little in their abiding respect for them. Academic offerings in both high school and college either are synonymous with the time-tested disciplines or draw heavily on them for learning content. But in the process, the offerings tend to extrapolate content that, while appropriate for the capable, is less appropriate for the average, and usually not appropriate at all for the slow.

And in many, if not most, high schools, this state of affairs takes on dilemma proportions. The majority of high schools resolve it by "enduring" slow learners in the academic curriculum until they can channel them at the earliest possible time into the utilitarian subjects or into the status of dropouts. The primary reason for the dilemma resides in the Western world's basic conviction about the nature of the rational processes: it is that these are respectable only when operating at a high cognitive level; thus that they are the rightful possession of only the more talented, not of the run-of-the-mill learner. The concept of reasoning as a relative, not an absolute, mental process escapes this traditional view.

The result is a program in the academic subjects that predictively fails the needs of low-average and slow learners. It is a program that provides four units of English, but usually not more than two units in the social studies (civics and United States history), one to two in science (general science and biology or health), and one in mathematics (general mathematics). The program rarely entertains the possibility that slow learners might enroll in a foreign language. Yet the aural-oral (listening-speaking) methods of foreign language instruction offer as much promise for the slow as for the average and fast. The natural sciences and mathematics certainly embrace enough meaningful content for all learners, not just the upper half, to find profit in more than one or two curriculum offerings. And with the world notoriously retarded socially, anything less than a four-year program of social studies available to all challenges credulity.

Our intent here is not to seal the door to electives in the utilitarian subjects. Far from it. Rather, the goal is for high schools to open the door both to utilitarian and academic subjects for both slow and gifted students. More classical content alone would be defeating for the slow. But academic content measured and tailored to individual abilities and

231

needs might just resolve the high school's greatest dilemma, namely, how to ready the slow learner for post-school life.

In its attempts to ready both the slow learner and his more gifted counterpart, the high school is vulnerable when it sanctions overspecialization. This it does when it permits students of limited verbal ability to elect half of their four-year programs from business and applied-arts areas. This it also does when permitting students of high verbal ability to overspecialize in one academic area. The way for high schools to resolve the problem is for them to limit the amount of curriculum specialization permitted any student. This *major control* would permit up to, but not more than, a third of a student's total program to be spent on specialized subjects. Such a control would protect the domains of general and exploratory education, which should be eminent in any high school program. I concede, however, that in programming for exceptional learners (socioeconomically disadvantaged youth as one instance) high schools occasionally might need to waive the one-third limitation.

The issue, in part, is one of arithmetic: the more a student specializes in a shop program, a secretarial program, or an English-drama program, the less time he has for a broad general and exploratory education program. Furthermore, business and industry are increasingly interested in students who are not narrow "specialists" but who are balanced generalists in the communication skills, in computation, and in critical thinking. Business and industry say, in effect: "Give us the broadly educated person, and we shall train him in the specialized skills he needs."

In summary, I propose first that high schools formulate and implement academic programs geared to the needs of the less verbal as well as to those of the more verbal. So geared, they would constitute for the former a general preparation both for life itself and, in a supplementary way, for a vocation also. In the latter respect, such programs would ready students broadly for the countless demands of the world of work. Second, I propose that high schools place a ceiling on credit allowed in any one special content area, whether it be academic or vocational in nature.

I conclude here with suggested programs for five students whose goals differ widely. (See Table 9.1.) The following assumptions underlie the proposals: (1) the high school requires students to graduate with 17 Carnegie units of credit, but allows the talented to earn up to 20; (2) the high school generally limits units of credit in any single curriculum area to 5, but, for special cases, condones an increase to 7 or 8.

232

TABLE 9.1   PROGRAMS FOR FIVE STUDENTS WHOSE GOALS DIFFER

(1) A Future Engineer	Units	(2) A College-bound Male Student, Vocational Future Undecided	Units
English	4	English	4
Social studies	3	Social studies	3
Science	4	Science	3
Mathematics	4	Mathematics	2
Foreign language	2	Foreign language	2
Health and physical ed.	1	Health and physical ed.	1
Art and music	1	Art and music	1
Industrial arts	1	Exploratory electives	2
	20		18

(3) A Female Student, Post-high School Future Undecided	Units	(4) A Future Secretary	Units	(5) An Inner-city Disadvantaged Male Student, Probable Dropout	Units
English	3	English	3	English	3
Speech	1	Business letter writing	1	Social studies	2
Social studies	3	Social studies	2	Science	2
Science	2	Science	2	Mathematics	1
Mathematics	2	Mathematics (business arithmetic)	1	Health and physical ed.	1
Foreign language	2	Health and physical ed.	1	Art and music	1
Health and physical ed.	1	Art and music	1	Auto shop	2
Home economics	2	Typing	2	Wood shop	1
Art and music	1	Shorthand	1	Metal shop	1
	17	General office practice	1	Mechanical drawing	1
		Exploratory electives	2	Printing	1
			17	Electronics	1
					17

CURRICULUM OF THE ACADEMIC SUBJECTS

The curriculum of most high schools becomes operative through the following channels: the academic subjects, health and physical education, the applied arts subjects, the esthetic subjects, the extracurriculum, and counseling. We shall discuss the first five in the order listed, but briefly, in view of the general nature of the book. Counseling we shall treat in Chapter 11. The discussion will proceed generally along lines of objectives, offerings, issues, and innovations.

The curriculum of the academic subjects, as indicated several times previously, divides among the five areas of English, foreign languages, social studies, natural sciences, and mathematics. These are the areas that generally look to the academic disciplines for subject matter and, at times, for teaching method. These are the areas that have privileged status in colleges and universities. These are the areas which intellectuals accord greatest respect.

English

English in any high school curriculum includes language components as diverse as syntax, written expression, oral expression, listening, reading, and literature. Of the six, literature comes closest to being the exclusive responsibility of English departments. The other five are more or less shared responsibilities. Ideally, all high school teachers should be teachers of language expression. Practically, most who are not members of English departments take this responsibility rather lightly. Thus, the operational burden for English instruction in its many facets rests primarily on the shoulders of English teachers.

Objectives   The purposes of the language arts program of any high school are many and diverse. One source lists them as follows:[2]

1. Ease, accuracy, and fluency in speaking
2. Inclination and ability to listen attentively and critically
3. Growth in reading ability
4. Growth in interpreting and appreciating literature
5. Growth of the structure of the English language
6. Habit of using English appropriately
7. Ability to write clearly, concisely, and honestly
8. Ability and habit of writing legibly
9. Knowledge of reference sources and skill in using them effectively

Another source presents objectives in terms of learner outcomes which I present in abbreviated form here. The student needs to develop powers of expression, "have skill in intelligent reading and listening," be conversant with "the world today and appreciate contributions of the past," learn from literature "what men have thought and felt, and lived for in days gone by," "think logically," and develop language skills to the end of articulating ideas clearly and influencing others.[3]

Curriculum offerings   In all high schools in the country, English is a required subject for at least three years; in many, for four years. From grades 7 through 11, enrollment in English is at or near the 100 percent

[2] Ad Hoc Committee on English Language Arts in the Comprehensive Secondary School, *The Bulletin of the National Association of Secondary-School Principals*, **44** (October 1960), p. 49.

[3] The Commission on the English Curriculum of the National Council of Teachers of English, *The English Language Arts in the Secondary School* (New York: Appleton-Century-Crofts, Inc., 1956), p. 10.

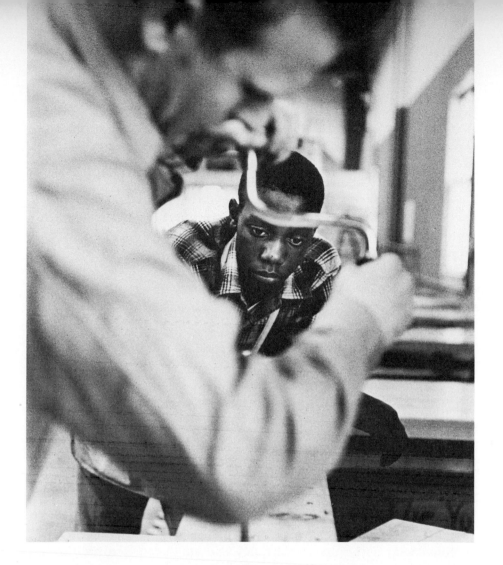

mark; in grade 12, it constitutes 84.2 percent of all seniors.[4] All high schools offer courses bearing such titles as English, English Regular, or English Grade 9, and so forth. Many also offer courses of a specialized nature. In the year 1960–1961, 44.8 percent of all public four-year high schools offered speech and public speaking; 27.1 percent, journalism; 17.7 percent, remedial or developmental reading; 13.8 percent, dramatics; and 3.4 percent, creative writing.[5]

[4] Kenneth A. Simon and W. Vance Grant, *Digest of Educational Statistics, 1968 Edition* (Washington, D.C.: U.S. Department of Health, Education, and Welfare, 1968), p. 34.

[5] Grace S. Wright, *Subject Offerings and Enrollments in Public Secondary Schools* (Washington, D.C.: U.S. Department of Health, Education, and Welfare, 1965), pp. 5–6.

EDUCATION AS AN OPERATIONAL PROCESS

Issues Some issues that teachers of English are debating today consist of the following.

1. What approach should high schools take in the teaching of grammar? The issue divides the traditionalists and the structural linguists. The traditionalists hold that language is a science supported by definitions and rules of grammar; furthermore, that students need to learn these definitiions and rules in order to become proficient in writing and speaking. The position is vulnerable on at least two counts: (1) first, many who do their memory work well are unable to transfer it functionally; (2) second, depicting rules of grammar as fixed implies that language is changeless, whereas it is dynamic and evolving.

Structural linguists, in contrast, conceive language as being in a continuing state of change. From this position, they view language as consisting of *vocabulary symbols* which do not depend on other words for meaning and of *grammatical symbols* which, as modifiers or function words, do depend on other words for meaning. The emphasis is on recurring patterns and positions of words. The approach is vulnerable because it is relatively new and has yet to undergo careful testing. Most of the 4 to 5 percent of the teachers who employ it today do so in conjunction with the traditional approach.

2. What is the proper place of composition in an English curriculum? The current answer of an outspoken few is that it should have a central, even a dominant, place. Conant, for instance, experting outside his own field of science, recommends that "The time devoted to English composition during the four years should occupy about half the total time devoted to the study of English."[6] Fraser views composition as being "part of each week's work, with exposition rather than creative writing stressed, and [with] subjects . . . derived for the most part from concurrent study of language and literature."[7] Unquestionably, the trend in most high schools is toward an increased emphasis on expository composition. Few, however, myself included, take Conant's extreme position. American, English, and world literature in its many forms, speech, and the science of language are too important to be overshadowed by composition.

3. What should high schools do about students with serious reading problems? Until the past half century, high schools labored under the

[6] James B. Conant, *The American High School Today* (New York: McGraw-Hill, Inc., 1959), p. 50.

[7] Dorothy M. Fraser, *Current Curriculum Studies in Academic Subjects* (Washington, D.C.: National Education Association, 1962), p. 49.

delusion that reading was solely the province of elementary education. However, when secondary education opened its doors to the masses, it soon came to recognize reading as a shared problem. The chronic reading problems of culturally deprived children have reinforced this point of view. Yet high schools have been slow to accept their share of the reading burden. In regard to this issue, I hold the view that future teachers of high school English will have to accept reading as an important responsibility and will have to prepare for it; if they do not, the better high schools will not hire them or will accord them second-class status in faculty ranks.

Innovations   A few innovations of importance characterize the high school English curriculum. (1) Structural linguistics, already discussed, is one. (2) Another is the employment of paper graders by some schools to assist teachers of English. Undoubtedly, teachers tend to assign more compositions when they have assistants to help in grading them. Yet teachers lose some of their personal touch as a result. For this reason, many hold that a reduction in class size is a better answer, albeit, an expensive one. (3) A third innovation is a design to increase the amount of free reading engaged in by students. The traditional approach, in this connection, was for students to read and then submit lengthy book reports on their reading. Today, teachers in increasing numbers are asking only for brief comments made on control cards instead of requiring book reports of substantial length. From some of the evidence available, this shift has achieved the desirable result of more reading by students and more enjoyment from their reading.

Foreign Languages

The language-arts program of secondary education encompasses not only English but foreign languages as well. As of midcentury, the foreign-language program was in a decline. In 1920, 27 percent of all high school students were enrolled in a modern foreign language; in 1955, the percentage had dropped to less than 15. The National Defense Education Act of 1958, however, not only stopped the downward trend but dramatically reversed it. It did so by underwriting research centers, teacher institutes, and expanded school facilities.

Objectives   Fifty years ago, the stock answer to the question, "Why teach foreign languages?" would have been, "To develop greater pro-

238

ficiency in English." The psychologist, E. L. Thorndike, however, exposed the fallacy of that answer. Specifically, he showed that a year's enrollment in a foreign language resulted in only 2 to 3 percentage points gain in English, a gain so small as to make the justification specious. Today, the answer to the same question is this: Foreign-language instruction has one, and only one, central purpose, namely, to help students learn a language to a point of being able to communicate satisfactorily in it. The communication outcomes sought are speaking, reading, and writing—essentially in that order. A secondary goal is to help students understand and appreciate cultures alien to their own. A tertiary one is to familiarize students with the literature of those cultures through the medium of the native language.

Curriculum offerings   As of 1964 the six languages with the highest enrollments in grades 9–12 were Spanish, French, Latin, German, Italian, and Russian, in the order named. These enrollments constituted the following percents, respectively, of the total high school population: 11.2, 10.4, 5.8, 2, 0.2, and 0.2.[8] Other languages taught in high schools throughout the country include Arabic, Chinese, Czech, modern Greek, Hawaiian, Hebrew, Japanese, Norwegian, Polish, Portuguese, Swahili, and Swedish.[9] The major gains in foreign-language programs have been made in the modern languages; Latin is barely holding its own; and Greek is infrequently offered.

Issues   Selected issues in foreign-language programs that are evoking dialogue today consist of the following.

1. What constitutes a model foreign-language program for the motivated, capable student? Most who debate this issue conclude that students should study one language to a point of reasonable proficiency rather than two or more to points of less proficiency. One controversial aspect of the issue resides in the question of when foreign-language instruction should begin. An emerging consensus, as indicated in Chapter 6, is that it should begin perhaps as early as grade 5 or 6, perhaps not until grade 7. Irrespective of the exact starting point, however, a growing number regard two years of language instruction up through grade

[8] Kenneth A. Simon and W. Vance Grant, *Digest of Educational Statistics*, 1968 Edition (Washington, D.C.: U.S. Department of Health, Education, and Welfare, 1968), p. 34. (1966 edition, p. 34.)

[9] International Bureau of Education and UNESCO, *Modern Languages at General Secondary Schools* (Geneva: UNESCO, 1964), p. 178.

8 as a goal toward which educators should press. A second controversial aspect lies in the question, for how many years of language instruction should a student enroll in grades 9–12. The answer of language-oriented specialists is four; some nonspecialists say four; others, three or two. Yet if the student is the "motivated, capable" one described earlier, the answer four is the most logical. Also, if the student is to continue the same language in college, as he should, a program with no gaps in it has unquestioned merit.

2. Should high schools offer foreign-language programs for slow learners? The traditional answer has been "no," the proffered reason being that an understanding of English syntax is a requisite to success in a foreign language. However, with the development in the fifties of the aural-oral (listening-speaking) method of instruction, this reason lost much of its validity. Yet most high schools still shy away from foreign-language instruction for the lower third or half of their student bodies. In my opinion, they should do an about-face on this practice. Children of below-average intelligence in every land learn their native tongues by listening to them and speaking them. Why, then, should not American youth of below-average intelligence have an opportunity to learn a second language in this same way?

3. How much subject-matter preparation constitutes a reasonable standard for teachers of foreign languages? This question asked in 1950, if nationwide practices had been the criterion, would have elicited the answer: either a teaching major or a minor. Today, however, schools in increasing numbers are regarding the minor as inadequate. Instead, they hold as essential a strong teaching major and speaking fluency in the language taught. And they regard travel in the country where the language is spoken as a valuable extra asset.

Innovations Several innovations of importance characterize the field of foreign-language teaching. Probably the most significant, as previously indicated, is the aural-oral (or listening-speaking, or audio-lingual) instructional approach. Its axial thesis is that students learn best when they first listen to and speak a second language for a lengthy period before grappling with its syntax. The language laboratory, as a second innovation, is a contributory but not an essential tool of the approach. Probably not more than 5 to 10 percent of high school foreign-language teachers employ the aural-oral approach in any consistent, methodical way. Thus it is only an experiment, at present. Logic supports it, but research evidence is not yet available to do likewise.

240

Another innovation has to do with the increase in the number of foreign languages that junior and senior high schools are offering. The fifteen listed a page or two back constitute only a fraction of the many that could have been listed.

Social Studies

A third component of the academic curriculum of secondary schools —social studies—is indeed an important one, beset as individuals and nations everywhere are with social problems too numerous and complex for them to solve.

Man himself is the most baffling problem of all. From whence did he come? What is he fundamentally? What are his highest values? And what is his destiny? These and related value questions have challenged and plagued civilized man through the ages. In regard to them, most conclude, as did Alexander Pope two and a half centuries ago, that "the proper study of mankind is man."

In formal education, the study of man is central not only in the social studies but in the humanities and most of the natural sciences, as well. In this connection, man is psychological, biological, and social. He is an inseparable composite of all of these. He is any single one only when external analysis artificially makes him so. The special province of the social studies in the study of man embraces the following categories: man as a psychological organism, the social-political institutions of cultural groups, economic systems, social relations, and the controlling reasons why cultural groups differ in their life styles.

Objectives The ensuing purposes are primary in the social-studies offerings of most high schools.

1. To impart significant knowledge and engender significant understanding about man individually and collectively. This general category customarily embraces the following specific topics:

   a. Individual man as a psychosocial human being
   b. The American way of life, including people, institutions, values, traditions, directions
   c. The ways of life of other cultural groups, including institutions, values, traditions, directions
   d. The general domains and specific methods of the several social-science disciplines, including anthropology, economics, geography, history, political science, psychology, and sociology

241

    e. Important major concepts of these disciplines

    f. Social reality in the world of the immediate

2. To develop in learners the skills of critical thinking. The goal in this connection is for students, as far as possible, to employ in their social-studies investigations the methods of the natural sciences and of linguistic analysis. It is to get them into the habit of coming to grips with key concepts in given situations, of generalizing authentically from those concepts, of forming hypotheses about needed future action, and of trying out those hypotheses empirically. Relatedly, the goal is to get them to hold the status quo suspect until it is validated, to eschew clichés, and to rise above unfounded biases that distort truth. All these are essentials of critical or reflective thinking, of problem-solving, of the scientific method. And all are almost as much at home in the behavioral as in the natural sciences.

3. To help learners formulate acceptable attitudes and values. And these do not necessarily need to conform to the standards of the status quo. Rather, they are end products of the reflective thought processes at work in each learner. The thesis is that teachers are responsible for communicating social expectation, but that learners are responsible for assessing it and acting on it in the light of the assessment.

Curriculum offerings   The social-studies subjects that in grades 9–12 attract the largest enrollments are the following, in the order named: (1) United States history, (2) world history, (3) beginning civics, (4) advanced civics, (5) problems of democracy, (6) economics, (7) sociology or social problems, and (8) psychology.[10] Since 1949, enrollments in world history have increased somewhat; in economics, they have declined; and in United States history and civics they have remained constant.

Issues   Of the many issues intrinsic in the social-studies area, the most knotty relates to social values and attitudes. But what are the approved values and attitudes, and how should schools cultivate them? The traditional approach has been for teachers, through the methods of verbal learning, to transmit factual knowledge about the social past and present, expecting such knowledge to result in social change in pupils. This is asking a lot. A second approach has been for teachers to indoctrinate with their own preconceived, and often narrow systems of social

242   [10] Simon and Grant, . . ., p. 34.

EDUCATION AS AN OPERATIONAL PROCESS

values. Obviously this is limiting, to say the least. A third approach, which was developed earlier, is for teachers to stimulate critical thinking about all social events and issues of the world's past and present. This approach places the burden on individual students to work through to their own value systems. It commits them not to accept the status quo but to assess it critically as a possible preliminary of change, or attempted change. Is there any other road to maturity than this?

A second issue has to do with curriculum content and continuity. It grows out of the question of what social-studies content is appropriate for what grades. For over a half century, the sequence for grades 7–12 has consisted, respectively, of world geography, American history, and civics; world history, American history, and problems of democracy. These six offerings divide into two consecutive cycles, each providing learners with an overview of world problems followed by an overview of the history and civic problems of their own country. The proffered justification for the first cycle is that it permits all learners, including high school dropouts, to leave education with a common background of social-studies experiences. The proffered justification for the second cycle is that it provides learners with content worthwhile in its own right and sophisticated enough to avoid needless duplication of content included in the first cycle.

These justifications, however, are more convincing at the level of the abstract than of the applied. In regard to the first cycle, only a relatively small number of students now drop out of school at the end of grade 9. Thus the need for the cycle to maintain a unity of its own has lost much of its validity. In regard to the second cycle, unnecessary repetition unquestionably characterizes it in many schools. Furthermore, the world history part of it exists as a curriculum elective in almost all schools. For this latter reason, it is possible for dropouts, and even graduates, to leave secondary education and remain unmoved, due to lack of awareness, by the urgency of major social problems in the world—an unfortunate state of affairs indeed.

Any future change in the social-studies curriculum of the secondary school should lead, in my opinion, to a revision of the currently popular cyclic arrangement. Exactly what should take its place, I leave for social-studies experts to detail. I am convinced, however, that one needed ingredient is a two-year course in world problems or world history, a course required of all students. Anglo-Saxon provincialism has dominated secondary education for too long. A needed antidote is an increased curriculum preoccupation with the non-Anglican world. **243**

Innovations We prematurely terminated the previous discussion of social-studies issues to avoid unnecessary duplication of the present discussion of social-studies innovations. The two actually go hand in hand. The following five innovations have been selected for brief coverage here. Their order of appearance is not necessarily their order of importance.

1. The recent upsurge of research in the field of the social studies in itself constitutes a very significant innovation. The research is taking place in colleges and universities, state departments of education, regional centers, and local school systems. Project Social Studies is illustrative in this connection. Initiated in 1962, the project underwrote for 1963 the establishment of social-studies research centers in the following eight institutions of higher learning: Carnegie Institute, Georgia, Harvard, Illinois, Minnesota, Northwestern, Ohio State, and Syracuse. Four additional ones—Amherst, Massachusetts Institute of Technology, San José State, and the University of California at Berkeley—were added in 1964. Some of their projects include, among others, the designing, at the University of Minnesota, of a social-studies curriculum for K-14, the preparation, at Ohio State, of economic curriculum materials for secondary schools, and the development at Syracuse of social-studies concepts.

A second catalyst of social-studies research is Title III of the NDEA Act, as revised in 1964. Through this act, funds were allocated for the first time to underwrite research and the purchase of instructional materials in the three areas of history, civics, and geography. Various state education departments, with California and New York probably the most noteworthy, have been a supportive third source. And local school systems, too numerous to mention here, have been the most supportive of all sources.

2. The search for a defensible value base constitutes a second important innovation. Research generally results in the identification of a hard core of cultural essentials from which individual learners are expected to think through to their own value conclusions.

3. A third innovation of note is the mounting emphasis being placed by theoreticians and teachers on the major concepts and generalizations of the several social-science disciplines. The thesis, which is a logical one, is that anyone who understands such concepts and generalizations will have gone a long way toward understanding the disciplines themselves. Thus learners grapple daily with such concepts of sociology as class, role, and status; of economics as deficit spending

and supply and demand; and of anthopology as enculturation and acculturation.

Relatedly, they grapple with generalizations growing out of those concepts. Three examples follow.

Social class is a correlate of family income, occupational status, place and quality of residence, and social inheritance.

In a period of economic recession or depression, federal spending should exceed federal income; in a period of economic prosperity, federal spending should be less than federal income. (Keynes)

Mental health is, in great part, a result of the ability of individuals to acculturate themselves, that is, to condition and adapt themselves to their environments.

4. Yet another innovation of significance in the field of the social studies is the increasing attention being given to inductive or discovery learning. In expository instruction, the teacher unilaterally gives answers to learners. In the method of directed discussion, the teacher, through the process of questioning, suggests answers without actually giving them. In inductive or discovery learning, students, with a minimum of structure, extrapolate their own answers. This method encourages students to generalize, to think critically, to become increasingly independent of authority figures.

5. The mounting interest of the several social-science disciplines in the high school program of the social studies constitutes a fifth innovation of importance. The learned societies of most of these disciplines are currently engaged in defining their social-studies roles and in preparing instructional materials for use in high school classrooms. The American Sociology Association, American Psychological Association, American Political Science Association, and American Economics Association are cases in point. These organizations are serving more and more as resource agencies for curriculum content and instructional method in the high school.

Natural Sciences

The natural sciences constitute a fourth component of the academic curriculum of the high school. Each of the several sciences stands as a systematized record of what man has learned through the ages about himself and the physical universe. Each employs its own methods of **245**

investigating man and the universe. Each is ever incomplete and ever evolving.

Objectives   The basic objectives of any natural science curriculum, at almost any level, consist of the following:

1. To communicate to learners the content of the natural sciences: certain content that is general education for all, other content that is technical education for the specialized few
2. To acquaint learners with the investigative methods of the respective sciences and to involve them in the investigative processes dictated by those methods
3. To engender in learners an interest in the unknown and to instill a desire in them to explore it
4. To imbue learners with the importance of generalizing only from ample data gathered and painstakingly analyzed
5. To convince learners, above all else, that the true scientist maintains a posture of openness to all life, of openness even to his own errors of procedure and judgment

Curriculum offerings   In public high schools in the year 1964–1965, the most common of the sciences offered, by grade and percent of pupil enrollment, were as follows:[11]

Subject	Grade	Percent of Enrollment
General science	9	63.5
Biology	10	79.6
Chemistry	11	37.0
Physics	12	22.1
Advanced general and physical science	12	15.9

These data support the conclusion that more students enroll in biology than in any other science course. The figure of 79.6 percent increases even more when physiology, botany, and zoology are added. The data likewise support the conclusion that the majority of students who enroll in biology in grade 10 do not continue with science after that. Relatedly, only 25 to 30 percent of all high school students complete four

[11] Kenneth A. Simon and W. Vance Grant, *Digest of Educational Statistics*, OE-10024-68, Bulletin No. 4 (Washington, D.C.: U.S. Department of Health, Education, and Welfare, 1968), p. 34.

EDUCATION AS AN OPERATIONAL PROCESS

years of science. The grade 12 percentages of 22.1 and 15.9 in physics and advanced general science, respectively, cited above, include some students enrolled in only one of these subjects, others in both. Other science courses, offered by some schools but not listed specifically above, include botany, zoology, physiology, aeronautics, astronomy, conservation, advanced biology, advanced chemistry, and earth science.

Issues   With the world of science so extensive and complex, and with curriculum possibilities so numerous, a recurring question in secondary education is how many units of science should high schools require? Before Sputnik, the answer generally was one. Since Sputnik, the answer, with which I agree, has been two. However, it is essential that curriculum designers plan this second year not primarily as an investment in future scientists; but rather as a step toward broadening the science horizons of all learners. The reverse has too often been the vogue.

Beyond this two-year requirement, science in many high schools runs into two obstacles. One is the obstacle of the small school which, because of limited enrollment, is unable to offer a four-year science program. Physics, for instance, is three times as likely to be offered in the 3299 high schools in the country with enrollments of 1000 or over as in the 3189 high schools with enrollments of 99 or under.[12] A second is the obstacle of slow learners in a program that, after the second year, is conceived primarily for the chosen few. As indicated earlier in the chapter, high schools are vulnerable when channeling the slow too casually out of the academic curriculum into the applied-arts vocational curriculum. Why should not a more extensive science curriculum be developed that is suited for slow as well as fast learners.

A final issue, touched on only lightly here, grows out of two questions: What should be the status of large-scale curriculum innovations conceived and developed at the national level?; Should they be guides or controls at local levels? Curriculum planning unquestionably can and should take place at almost every possible geographical and professional level. However, in respect to any given classroom situation, I state again that only a knowledgeable, insightful teacher should decide specifically what the curriculum should be. It thus follows, I believe, that large-scale curriculum innovations should be *guides*, not *controls*.

[12] Grace S. Wright, *Subject Offerings and Enrollments in Public Secondary Schools*, pp. 28–29.

Innovations Since 1956, the year that the Physical Science Study Committee came into being, large-scale innovations, usually at the national level, have dominated curriculum experimentation in the natural sciences. In physics, biology, and chemistry, to cite just three, the sequence of experimentation took the following course: science scholars prepared preliminary curriculum materials; selected teachers tried them out in the schools; the materials underwent revision once or several times more; teachers tried them out once or several times again; finally, two, three, or four years later, the materials appeared as textbooks, teacher manuals, test manuals, and audiovisual guides.

In biology, three groups proceeded independently. The major product of one was the so-called Blue Version textbook: *Biological Science: Molecules to Man*, 1963, its central theme being genetic development. The major product of the second was the Yellow Version: *Biological Science: An Inquiry into Life*, 1963, its central theme being cellular development. The major product of the third was the Green Version: *High School Biology: BSCS Green Version*, 1963, its central theme being life in an ecological setting. In chemistry, the researchers divided two ways, one group working on the Chemical Bond Approach Project, the other on the Chemical Education Materials Study. In physics, a single group formed the basic task force. In addition to these major experimental groups, dozens of others at district or regional levels have been active in all the science fields. Their goal has been for students to acquire knowledge by self-discovery and the process of transmission rather than by transmission alone. The combined outcomes of the large-scale experiments have been noteworthy, despite their frequent infringement on local curriculum control.

Mathematics

Like science, mathematics has undergone substantial curriculum revision in high schools during the past several decades.

Objectives The goals embrace both product and process. Apropos of the former, pupils study mathematics to acquire the tools they will need to meet the computational demands of life. For some, these are as simple as making change or, at a more difficult level, of completing and understanding a mortgage arrangement. For the physicist-engineer, they

might be as complex as ascertaining the power potential of a dam or determining the effect on flying objects of thermal conditions in outer space. It is apparent that mathematics operates both as general and special education, serving causes as diverse as education and industry, as transmitted knowledge and discovery learning.

Curriculum offerings In recent years, particularly since Sputnik's 1957 orbit, registrations in mathematics have increased significantly. Public high schools in 1961 reported 125 different titles for mathematics courses.[13] The subjects in grades 9–12 that attracted the greatest enrollments were the following, in the order named: elementary algebra, elementary general mathematics, plane geometry, advanced algebra, advanced general mathematics, trigonometry, solid geometry, and advanced college mathematics.[14] Some of the newer course titles include probability and statistics, analytical geometry, calculus, and mathematical analysis. Approximately two-thirds of all high school students enroll in algebra as their first mathematics course, one-third in general mathematics. This arrangement is one of many employed by high schools to meet the ever-present problem of student differences.

Issues Of the many issues inherent in any high school mathematics curriculum, two stand out as chronic. The more basic of the two centers in the need for mathematics programs to stress memory learning and deductive truth less, conceptual understanding and discovery learning more. Many students are able, almost effortlessly, to expand the algebraic element $(A + B)^3$ to the response: $A^3 + 3A^2B + 3AB^2 + B^3$. But too few of them understand the functional purpose of the algebraic element. In effect, mathematics curricula traditionally have announced to students: "Here are the mathematical truths of the ages." Learn them and apply them. Modern mathematics curricula, in contrast, are imbuing teachers more and more with the necessity for learners to discover selected mathematical truths for themselves; to learn from inductive as well as deductive methods.

A second issue relates to the mathematics curriculum for slow learners. Specifically, what constitutes meaningful content for the general mathematics course, in which one-third of all ninth graders enroll?

---

[13] Grace S. Wright, *Subject Offerings and Enrollments in Public Secondary School,* p. 7.

[14] Simon and Grant, p. 34.

Or for a tenth-grade sequel to it? High schools continue to grope for a satisfactory answer. As often as not, the general mathematics course is no more than a monotonous review of junior high school mathematics. As a partial solution to the problem, I endorse the practice of drawing content for the general mathematics course functionally from the world of the practical. Such content might well, for instance, embrace the following: measures of central tendency, stock market analysis, mortgage plans, time-payment purchasing, credit associations, budgeting, interest versus dividend accounts, income tax problems, and so forth. High schools unquestionably are culpable when allowing mathematics courses to bog down in meaningless abstraction and/or pointless repetition. The problem may best be answered at the classroom level in the persons of stimulating teachers who, because they enjoy working with the slow, can breathe life into a curriculum allowed for too long to wander aimlessly.

Innovations   Projects at institutional, state, and national levels aimed at the innovational in mathematics are numerous and far-reaching. The projects or sponsoring groups responsible for them include the following:

> The School Mathematics Study Group (Yale University)
> University of Illinois Committee on School Mathematics
> Stanford University Institute for Mathematics in the Social Sciences
> Committee on Mathematics of the College Entrance Examination Board
> University of Maryland Mathematics Projects
> Advanced Placement Program Mathematics Curriculum

In general, current research findings in mathematics give support to the following practices:

1. The twelfth-grade course to assume greater sophistication, drawing content, for instance, from such advanced concepts or areas as calculus, circular functions, and probability
2. Plane and solid geometry to combine into a single year-long sequence
3. Advanced algebra and trigonometry to combine into a single year-long sequence
4. Mathematics at the junior high school level to assume more sophistication
5. Discovery learning to recieve emphasis at all levels
6. Memory training to lead habitually into conceptual understanding

250

HEALTH AND PHYSICAL EDUCATION

The academic curriculum, fundamental though it is in education at all levels, is no more fundamental than the curriculum of health and physical education. The latter is important both in its own right and as a contributer to academic growth. If man cannot live by bread alone, students cannot live exclusively on a diet of cognition.

Objectives The overall outcome toward which the curriculum of health and physical education aspires is a student body that measures up to its optimum of physical and emotional health. The specific emphases of this curriculum are:

1. Body hygiene
2. Defensible health habits
3. Disease-prevention, disease-detection, and first-aid treatment
4. Sex hygiene and social living
5. Physical endurance
6. Games, skills, and rhythms
7. Sportsmanship
8. Accident prevention
9. Self-acceptance

Curriculum offerings All public high schools have health and physical education programs of some kind. They customarily divide along lines of medical services; courses in health, safety, and hygiene; and courses in physical education. The medical (or nursing) services generally con-

251

sist of first-aid treatment; administration of routine examinations—for example, sight and hearing; home-school liaison activities; and in-service education of faculty and student body. The course health, safety, and hygiene is sometimes discrete, sometimes a part of the physical education component. Driver training invariably is separate. Physical education *per se*, although a part of the curricula of all public high schools, slowly declines in importance after grade 9. In grade 10, for instance, 8 percent of the schools do not schedule it at all, and approximately 20 percent include it for only one or two periods per week. In grade 11, comparable percentages are 15 and 19. In grade 12, they are 18 and 20. Although these statistics relate only to boys, their counterparts for girls differ little.[15]

Issues   The primary issue of health and physical education today is the same as it was a half century ago: the issue of varsity athletics versus a balanced health-fitness program. Because too many critics have already made this issue a whipping boy, I leave it with this observation: the larger high schools have room for both programs; in the smaller schools that do not, the balanced health-fitness program should always be the hands-down winner.

A second issue relates to the traditional course in health and hygiene. Ordinarily a physical-education instructor teaches it, drawing heavily on physiology for content and on memory for learning method. Yet students who enroll in this course customarily enroll in biology also during one of their four high school years. The result not infrequently is an unnecessary duplication of effort. In respect to this issue, I have long felt that the course in health and hygiene should be a combined science-physical education responsibility. The marriage of the theoretical and the practical would result in improvement in both. It would also result in better curriculum integration and, conceivably, in improved instruction.

Innovations   Probably the most significant innovations in the health-physical education area are those contained in the recommendations made in 1961 by the Presidents Council on Physical Fitness. Most actually are less innovative than they are strong affirmations of what enlightened physical education teachers have long believed and advo-

[15] George E. Collins and J. Scott Hunter, *Physical Achievement and the Schools,* OE-28008, Bulletin No. 13 (Washington, D.C.: U.S. Department of Health, Education, and Welfare, 1965), pp. 14–16.

EDUCATION AS AN OPERATIONAL PROCESS

cated. One unspectacular recommendation, for instance, is that the physical education course meet one period daily, or that, when this is not feasible, it meet 15 minutes daily, during which students participate "in developmental activities and conditioning exercises designed to build vigor, strength, flexibility, endurance, and balance." The council was more innovative in respect to the highly organized program it proposed, including the administration by schools of the standardized test AAHPER (American Association for Health, Physical Education, and Recreation) as a means of assessing the program's results. The test assesses performance in seven activities: pullups (modified for girls), situps, shuttle run, standing broad jump, 50-yard dash, softball throw for distance, and the 600-yard run-walk. Norms were developed and made available to schools for each event or activity. In 1964, 60 percent of all youth tested were rated satisfactory.

THE PRACTICAL ARTS

With little doubt, of all the divisions of the curriculum of secondary education, the practical-arts segment is the most controversial. Under it, we include all subjects and subject areas that make a direct vocational appeal to students.

Objectives   The curriculum of the practical or applied arts divides two ways—general education and vocational education. The *general-education* part includes content that has common appeal and for which there is a common need. Courses illustrative of such content might include consumer education, wood shop, and typing. The *vocational-education* part includes content that serves the specialized needs of a selected group. The objectives of the practical arts thus are as comprehensive as are the combined objectives of general education and of the several vocational fields contained in the curriculum of any high school.

Curriculum offerings   The practical arts, collectively, include the fields of business education, industrial arts, home economics, and agriculture. High schools customarily categorize the industrial arts (woods, metals, home economics, graphic arts, and so on) separately from the vocational trades (auto shop, welding, cosmetology, masonry, and so on). The latter generally look to the Smith-Hughes Act for organization and support; the former do not. I see no point, however, in such a distinction.

253

Courses in business education offered in grades 9–12 by the greatest number of high schools throughout the country are, in the order listed: typing, bookkeeping, shorthand, office practice, general business, distributive education, business arithmetic, and business law. Their counterparts in industrial-arts education are woodworking, mechanical drawing, general shop, metalworking, and electricity. Their counterparts in home economics are family living, textiles, foods and nutrition, and home management. And their counterparts in agriculture are Agriculture 1, 2, 3, and 4.

Issues   The most basic of all issues in vocational education is the one elaborated in the first part of the chapter under the title "Special Education." It is how much vocational specialism should any high school allow? My answer, in summary, is that all high schools need to guard against the error of overspecialization. They do this by limiting the number of course hours allowed a student in a given vocational field. This limit, as stated previously, should rarely exceed one-third of all hours required for graduation.

A second issue relates to the almost habitual failure of high schools to keep their vocational programs current. The Chicago school system, for instance, still offers Pitman shorthand. And along a different dimension, the majority of high schools seem oblivious to the demands imposed on them by the electronics revolution. The answer to this problem of keeping current is for education to make continuing studies of the world of work; be conversant with data contained in existing occupational studies; decide what occupations or occupational areas are in short supply; decide whether it is feasible and defensible for high schools to prepare students to fill jobs in these areas; and finally, develop a curriculum to conform to the findings thus uncovered.

What high school curriculum planners should never forget is that general education is broadly vocational as well as broadly cultural, and that business and industry generally prefer the academically educated student to the vocationally trained one. Thus these curriculum planners need to develop for the lower ability range of students not only an up-to-date vocational curriculum *per se*, but an academic curriculum that is comparably up to date.

An important innovation   In my opinion, the progressive migration of vocational education out of the high school into business and industry constitutes the single most important recent innovation in the voca-

tional field. Work-study programs in the distributive occupations are decades old. But with the passage in 1963 of Public Law 88–210 (The Vocational Education Act), the base of such programs broadened to include an almost unlimited assortment of industrial, business, and office occupations. The act likewise broadened the base of enrollment eligibility. It authorized "vocational education programs for persons in high school, for those out of high school available for full-time study, for persons who are unemployed or underemployed, and for persons who have academic or socioeconomic handicaps . . ." The law allows students to work 15 hours in any week and to earn up to $45 in any one month while earning educational credit in an approved area training center.

To the extent the law accomplishes its manifest training goals in an industrial or business setting without sacrificing academic goals in an approved educational setting, the program will have served a highly useful purpose.

THE FINE ARTS

The fine arts in secondary education attest to society's recognition that students need fulfillment esthetically as well as cognitively and practically. At the elementary school level, the basic content of art, rhythms, and music constitute a part of general education. At the secondary school level, related content is less easily classified. Offerings in the esthetic subjects generally appear under three organizational arrangements: (1) as survey courses, usually in grades 7, 8, or 9, for which a unit of credit is granted for each; (2) as music or art activities that meet once or twice weekly, in which participation is required but for which no credit is granted; (3) and as out-and-out electives for students with specialized interests in a given fine-arts field.

Objectives The goals of the esthetic subjects in the high school (as well as at other levels) consist selectively of the following:

1. Enhanced sensitivity to the beautiful
2. Increased knowledge of the accomplishments of past and present artistic "greats"
3. Refined taste for the excellent
4. Emotional fulfillment
5. Social fulfillment
6. Enrichment of leisure-time interests

255

Curriculum offerings In music, curriculum components divide between the two areas of performance and theory. In respect to the first, 73 percent of all four-year high schools in the country have marching bands, 55 percent have choral groups, 13 percent have orchestras, and 12 percent have instrumental assemblies. In respect to theory, only 9 percent offer courses in general music and/or music appreciation.[16] Unquestionably, performance is where the high schools place their blue chips.

In art, 32 percent of all four-year high schools offer courses in general art, 8 percent in general crafts, 4 percent in art appreciation and history, 4 percent in commercial art, 3 percent in ceramics, and 2 percent in drawing and painting.[17] The obvious implication of these percentages is that art programs in the many small high schools in the country are minuscule or nonexistent.

Issues The most fundamental issue pertaining to the fine arts concerns the relative importance they should have in a high school curriculum. Proponents of the cognitive position, such as Barzun and Conant, relegate them to a place of secondary, or even tertiary, importance. In contrast, proponents of the total-personality position hold them to be intrinsically important. I subscribe to this second point of view. However, beyond grade 8, and certainly beyond grade 9, I view them as electives primarily for students with keen interests in, and with special aptitudes for, their subject-matter content. Schools that make them dumping grounds for slow learners have a distorted perspective, to say the least.

A second issue of significance relates to the fine arts in their performance roles. Within this context, what should constitute the standards of excellence: reactions of popular viewing audiences, opinions of professionals, or emotional fulfillment of the performers? With the first, the outcome too often is slickness. With the second, the outcome invariably is performance restricted to the highly talented. With the third, the outcome is an important step down the path of personality growth. The current trend is toward slickness: in marching bands, choral groups, and art fairs. If properly controlled, this appeal to public interest has its place; but it never should dominate. Performance by the talented few, with high standards the criterion, rises above criti-

[16] Grace S. Wright, *Subject Offerings and Enrollments in Public Secondary School,* p. 28.

256 [17] Wright, p. 28.

cism. But this facet should be merely one part of a balanced program for all. In the last analysis, however, the ultimate in any program of music and art should be a curriculum open to all and for the fulfillment of all.

THE EXTRACURRICULUM

The curriculum of the high school, as with that of the junior high school, does not end with course offerings; it embraces the so-called extracurriculum or cocurriculum (these are interchangeable terms) as well. Lines between the two are not at all clear-cut. For instance, dramatic performances, band activities, debate, and publication of school newspapers are curricular activities in certain schools, extracurricular in others, and both curricular and extracurricular in some. Relatedly, such cocurricular organizations as a Spanish club, a creative writing club, or a science club have attachments to both the formal and the informal curriculums.

Objectives The extracurriculum and the curriculum share identical aims: the growth of individual students intellectually, emotionally, socially, and physically. The degree of emphasis varies, of course. The extracurriculum emphasizes the social and emotional, the curriculum, the intellectual; both, in different ways, emphasize the physical. The extracurriculum functions best in the following four roles: (1) when helping students develop and practice qualities of leadership, (2) when helping them acquire and apply such social skills as self-control, courtesy, poise, and tolerance of differences, (3) when enabling them to explore individualized interests and abilities, and, in general, (4) when serving as a personality laboratory wherein active participation in a group setting is the key.

Extracurriculum offerings The extent of extracurricular activities, particularly in the larger high schools in the country, is amazing in scope. Yet, because the needs of individuals are varied, extracurricular offerings can scarcely be otherwise. Activities that make up the latter generally divide into the following categories:

1. Athletic activities: varsity, intramural, and individual
2. Curriculum clubs: for example, French, poetry, or international relations
3. Drama activities

257

4. Musical organizations: for example, band, chorus, glee club, or orchestra
5. Service clubs: for example, audiovisual, printing, photography
6. Social clubs: for example, dance or couples' club
7. Student government

Issues   All the above categories with their attendant activities have significant educational potential; yet they pose a number of knotty problems, such as: Who should participate in the extracurriculum? What steps, if any, should school authorities take to effect participation by those who need it but do not volunteer for it? The logical, but general, answer to the first question is that participation should stem from need as well as from interest. When interest alone controls, the result is a preponderance of participation by students from the middle and upper classes and only spotty participation by students from the lower socioeconomic classes. Under such an arrangement, the culturally rich get richer and the culturally poor get poorer. Some schools have attempted to solve the problem by setting aside a given class period, one to three days per week, to accommodate extracurricular activity. The collective results, however, have been far from sensational. The reason may very likely be that these schools have put too much faith in organization, which, in itself, rarely constitutes a satisfactory answer to any complex problem.

If organization *per se* is not a good answer, a climate of warmth in which school authority figures encourage students to participate in given extracurricular activities may constitute a better one. In such a setting, teacher-counselors and activity sponsors "sell" the cocurriculum to learners in need of it just as convincingly as they sell the regular curriculum.

This issue of need leads into the question of membership eligibility. Specifically, should high schools enforce a fixed grade-point average as a membership criterion for a given activity? My answer is *no* for schools that aspire to learner growth across a broad personality spectrum. In this connection, a youngster with an IQ of 75 and a correspondingly low grade-point average may need to participate in varsity football or a music activity more than in anything else the school has to offer. And for the school to make cognitive accomplishment an absolute prerequisite of personality growth makes for a strange admixture of educational values.

To Stimulate Thought

1. Review the definition of general education given at the beginning of the chapter. Then explain why a two-track mathematics arrangement in grade 9 (algebra and general mathematics) does not constitute general education within an exact definition of the term.

2. Under what circumstances, if any, might you approve of a student's enrolling in vocational subjects for half the Carnegie units of credit required for graduation purposes?

3. Debate, pro and con, my contention that the so-called academic program of the high school should be expanded for slow learners.

4. Debate Conant's recommendation that English composition should constitute 50 percent of any high school's program of English.

5. Should teachers allow students to think critically, even negatively, about democracy as a way of life? Elaborate your stand.

6. Debate, pro or con, the point of view that curriculum materials prepared by compentent scholars at the national level should serve as prescriptive blueprints for individual teachers.

7. Might selected content of the practical arts in the high school constitute general education? If so, what might the content consist of?

8. Answer question 7, with the fine arts substituted for the applied arts.

9. Take a stand on compulsory student participation in the extracurriculum. Defend your position.

REFERENCES

Alexander, William M. (ed.), *The Changing Secondary School Curriculum: Readings* (New York: Holt, Rinehart and Winston, Inc., 1967).

Alexander, William M., Vynce A. Hines, *et al., Independent Study in Secondary Schools* (New York: Holt, Rinehart and Winston, Inc., 1967).

American Association for the Advancement of Science and the Science Teaching Center, University of Maryland, *Second Report of the Information Clearing House on New Science Curricula,* 1964.

Bamman, Henry A., Ursula Hogan, and Charles E. Greene, *Reading Instruction in the Secondary Schools* (New York: David McKay Company, Inc., 1961).

Clark, Leonard H., Raymond L. Klein, and John B. Burks, *The American Secondary School Curriculum* (New York: Crowell-Collier and Macmillan, Inc., 1965).

Collins, George J., and J. Scott Hunter, *Physical Achievement and the Schools,* OE-28008, Bulletin No. 13 (Washington, D.C.: U.S. Department of Health, Education, and Welfare, 1965).

Committee on National Interest, National Council of Teachers of English, *The National Interest and the Teaching of English* (Champaign, Ill.: National Council of Teachers of English, 1961).

Evans, William H., and Jerry L. Walker, *New Trends in the Teaching of English in Secondary Schools* (Skokie, Ill.: Rand McNally & Company, 1966).

Fenton, Edward, *Teaching the New Social Studies in Secondary Schools: An Inductive Approach* (New York: Holt, Rinehart and Winston, Inc., 1966).

Fraser, Dorothy M., *Current Curriculum Studies in Academic Subjects* (Washington, D.C.: National Education Association, 1962).

Fries, Charles C., *Linguistics and Reading* (New York: Holt, Rinehart and Winston, Inc., 1963).

Gaardes, A. Bruce, "Current Experimentation in Foreign Languages," in Paul C. Rosenbloom (ed.), *Modern Viewpoints in the Curriculum* (New York: McGraw-Hill, Inc., 1964, pp. 49–56.

Gibson, John S., *New Frontiers in the Social Studies* (Medford, Mass.: Tufts University, 1965).

Greer, Edith S., and Richard M. Harbeck, *What High School Pupils Study,* OE-33025, Bulletin No. 10 (Washington, D.C.: U.S. Department of Health, Education, and Welfare, 1962).

Hook, J. N., *The Teaching of High School English* (New York: The Ronald Press Company, 1959).

Hurd, Paul De Hart, *New Directions in Secondary School Science Teaching* (Chicago: Rand McNally & Company, 1969).

Inlow, Gail M., *Maturity in High School Teaching* (Englewood Cliffs, N.J.: Prentice-Hall, Inc., 1963).

Lowenfeld, Viktor, and W. Lambert Brittain, *Creative and Mental Growth,* 4th Ed. (New York: Crowell-Collier and Macmillan, Inc., 1964).

McLendon, Jonathon C., *Readings on Social Studies in Secondary Education* (New York: Crowell-Collier and Macmillan, Inc., 1966).

Moreland, Willis D. (ed.), *Social Studies in the Senior High School* (Washington, D.C.: National Council for the Social Studies, 1965).

Muessig, Raymond H. (ed.), *Youth Education* (Washington, D.C.: Association for Supervision and Curriculum Development, 1968).

National Association of Secondary School Principals, *Student Council in the Secondary School* (Washington, D.C.: National Association of Secondary School Principals, 1955).

National Society for the Study of Education, *Basic Concepts in Music Education*, Fifty-Seventh Yearbook, Part I (Chicago: University of Chicago Press, 1958).

Parker, W. R., *The National Interest and Foreign Languages*, Department of State Publication 7324 (Washington, D.C.: U.S. Government Printing Office, 1962).

President's Council on Youth Fitness, *Youth Physical Fitness-Suggested Elements of a School-Centered Program* (Washington, D.C.: U.S. Government Printing Office, 1961).

Roberts, Roy, *Vocational and Practical Arts Education* (New York: Harper & Row, Publishers, 1957).

Rosenbloom, Paul C. (ed.), *Modern Viewpoints in the Curriculum* (New York: McGraw-Hill, Inc., 1964).

Saylor, J. Galen, and William M. Alexander, *Curriculum Planning for Modern Schools* (New York: Holt, Rinehart and Winston, Inc., 1966).

Smith, Frederick R., and C. Benjamin Cox, *New Strategies and Curriculum in Social Studies* (Chicago: Rand McNally & Company, 1969).

Starr, Wilmarth H., Mary P. Thompson, and Donald D. Walsh, *Modern Foreign Languages and the Academically Talented Student* (Washington, D.C.: National Education Association, 1960).

Sund, Robert B., and Leslie W. Trowbridge, *Teaching Science by Inquiry in the Secondary School* (Columbus, Ohio: Charles E. Merrill Books, Inc., 1967).

Trump, J. Lloyd, and Delmas F. Miller, *Secondary School Curriculum Improvement* (Boston: Allyn and Bacon, Inc., 1968).

Wright, Grace S., *Subject Offerings and Enrollments in Public Secondary Schools*, OE-24015 (Washington, D.C.: U.S. Department of Health, Education, and Welfare, 1964).

Wright, Grace S., *Requirements for High School Graduation*, OE-24003, Bulletin No. 12 (Washington, D.C.: U.S. Department of Health, Education, and Welfare, 1961).

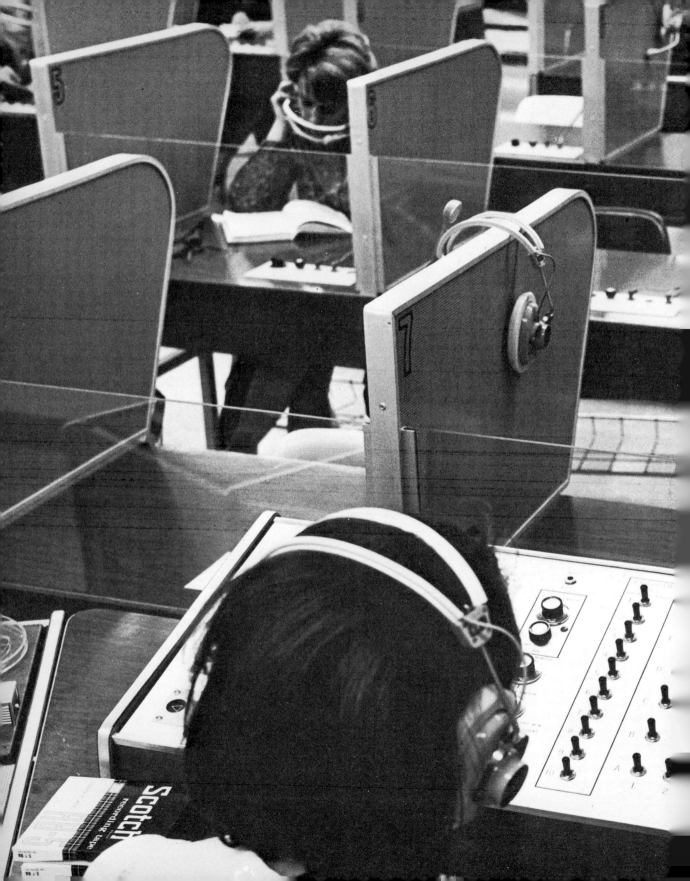

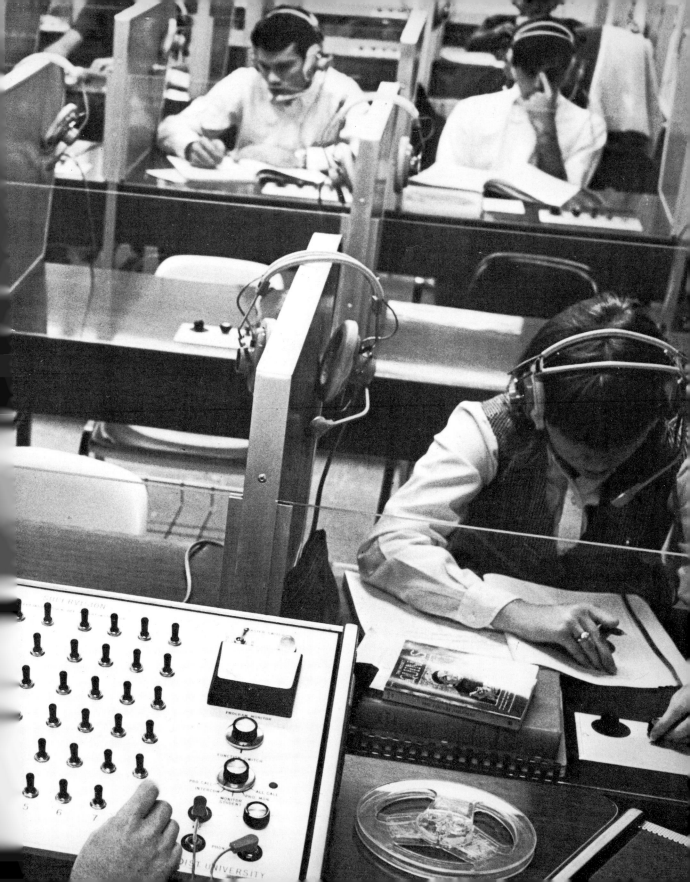

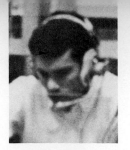

Chapter
10

**Innovations
in
Education**

The theme of this chapter is once again the topic of change. The focal emphasis is change wrought in the nation's schools by recent educational innovations. These innovations have had a marked influence on the programs of many schools, and at least some noticeable effect on the programs of all. Quite conceivably, educational innovations during the fifties and sixties were and continue to be more diversified and far-reaching than during any comparable period of the nation's history. Extensive as these innovations have been, volumes alone could do them justice. Thus selectivity needs to characterize our treatment of them in this single chapter. We deal with selected ones in the areas of (1) curriculum planning and organizational designs, (2) teacher utilization, (3) electronic teaching methods, and (4) pupil grouping.

CURRICULUM PLANNING AND ORGANIZATIONAL DESIGNS

Much of the experimentation going on in education today has to do with curriculum: who should design it, who should implement it, and what should be the methods of implementation? In this connection, a phenomenon of the second half of the present century has been curriculum conceived and designed by individuals and groups removed from schools and school systems.

Large-Scale Curriculum Projects

As developed briefly in Chapter 9, national and regional groups have recently become active in the preparation of curriculum materials, some of which ultimately reach a few or many schools. Participants in these projects customarily comprise university scholars from the various subject-matter disciplines, their counterparts in business and industry, teachers, and, to a lesser degree, professional educators. The federal government or private philanthropic foundations generally underwrite the projects.

These projects generally evolve in the following way. A power block in a given curriculum area, believing that the area needs updating, brings into being a working team constituted usually as indicated in the preceding paragraph. The team first develops curriculum materials

in draft form, then has selected teachers try them out in selected schools, repeats the process until convinced of quality, and finally has the materials published. A subsequent step is the establishing and conducting of institutes designed to ready teachers for use of the new materials.

Following are some of the better-known curriculum research groups or projects:[1]

In the natural sciences
    Physical Science Study Committee
    Biological Science Curriculum Study
    Chemical Bond Approach Project
    Chemical Education Materials Study
In mathematics
    The School Mathematics Study Group
    University of Illinois Committee on School Mathematics
    University of Maryland Mathematics Project
    Webster College Madison Project-Syracuse University
In modern foreign languages
    Foreign language Study Program of the Modern Language Association which embraced 224 projects as of 1963.
In English
    Project English, Co-operative Research Branch of the Office of Education
In social studies
    Project Social Studies, Co-operative Research Branch of the Office of Education.

Large-scale curriculum projects have at least the following two advantages. One is that knowledgeable individuals outside, as well as inside, the field of formal education contribute to the projects. In the fields of science and mathematics, this combined approach has had unquestioned merit. In fields other than science and mathematics, cooperation has taken the form primarily of university and public school personnel working together on projects of mutual interest. In most of these, leadership has come from the universities. A second advantage of the projects consists in their generous financing, which increases the possibility of a quality product without, of course, guaranteeing it.

Two counterbalancing disadvantages of large-scale curriculum pro-

[1] Heath and Rosenbloom, as cited in the chapter's bibliography, elaborate the projects engaged in by most of these groups, as well as selected projects engaged in by many other groups.

EDUCATION AS AN OPERATIONAL PROCESS

jects consist of the following. One is the disadvantage inherent in any curriculum design prepared apart from learners and superimposed, without change, on them. This procedure might be appropriate for mathematically averaged-out learners, but it is less appropriate, if at all, for flesh-and-blood students. My personal opinion on this issue, as stated in Chapter 5, is that any large-scale curriculum design should play the role only of curriculum resource, never of exact blueprint. In this connection, only the teacher of a given group of students knows them well enough to decide what the specific curriculum for them should be. This is not to imply that the classroom teacher is or should be autonomous in curriculum decision-making. But it is to suggest that within the frame of defensible curriculum structure external to the classroom, teachers should be final arbiters of curriculum relevance.

A second disadvantage resides in the likelihood of curriculum imbalance resulting when pressure groups remote from schools pursue their narrow curriculum interests without reference to breadth. As indicated previously, the humanities and social sciences are instances today of such imbalance, having been shunted aside to a disturbing degree to make way for mass experimentation in the natural sciences and mathematics.

A major goal of many of the large-scale projects, particularly those in the natural sciences and mathematics, is to advance the cause of discovery learning. Young children instinctively employ this approach as they explore the countless unknowns of life. It is the open method of induction. But it is a notoriously slow method for anyone in need of embracing large bodies of knowledge. As the verbal skills of children increase, transmitted learning tends to assume dominance over discovery learning. The former, though a faster method, also has shortcomings. By substituting symbols for things, it is always a step away from reality. It relies exclusively on authority (people and the printed word) for sanction. And in so doing, it takes initiative away from learners.

Formal education today is sensitive to the need for both transmitted and discovery learning to have places of significance in the learning scheme of any school. It is particularly desirous of protecting the status of discovery learning in the upper elementary grades and in all the high school grades. Several of the large-scale projects are advancing this outcome in the following manner.[2] They have turned away from the deductive methods of presenting formulas and equations in mathematics or principles and generalizations in the sciences. Instead they present selected information, point it directionally, have teachers serve as guides, and assign students the task of manipulating and concluding from it. This approach, in contrast to the traditional one, relies less on teachers, more on learners; less on the inviolability of knowledge, more on the importance of students' confirming or doubting its inviolability; and less on the process of memory, more on the process of reflective thought. The intent is not to exchange transmission for discovery, but to accord the latter more operational importance.

Project Head Start

The focus shifts now to a nationwide curriculum innovation, Project Head Start, whose dimensions are unique in the annals of formal education. Given legal and financial status by the Economic Opportunity Act of 1964, the project's widespread record of success has sustained it. Project Head Start is unique in the following ways: (1) its learning population consists of prekindergarten children who are socioeconomically underprivileged; (2) its goal is to enrich early so as to prevent

[2] The Chemical Bond Approach Project and The School Mathematics Study Group are illustrative of this emphasis on discovery learning.

impoverishment later; (3) its functional setting is a child development center, not a conventional classroom; and (4) teachers, parents, medical personnel, dentists, and social workers share responsibility for its educational outcomes. The following statement that introduces all issues of *Project Head Start*, published by the Office of Economic Opportunity, constitutes an excellent summary of the project's program.

> The Child Development Center is both a concept and a community facility. In concept it represents the drawing together of all those resources—family, community and professional—which can contribute to the child's total development. It draws heavily on the professional skills of persons in nutrition, health, education, psychology, social work, and recreation. It recognizes that both paid and volunteer non-professionals can make important contributions. Finally the concept emphasizes [that] the family is fundamental to the child's development. Parents should play an important role in developing policies; will work in the Centers and participate in the programs.

> As a community facility the Child Development Center is organized around its classroom and outdoor play areas. Ideally it should also provide a program for health services, parent interviews and counseling, feeding of the children, and meetings of parents and other residents of the community. The space is arranged so as to permit working in small groups or individually with the children. Where some activities are performed at other locations, the staff should function as an integral part of the Center.[3]

Project Head Start underwrites a summer program of eight week's duration. Conceived in November of 1964, the project got underway in the summer of 1965. In this first period of functional operation, the program drew 550,000 children into 2500 child development centers manned by 100,000 adults. The pupil-teacher ratio was 13:1, and the pupil-adult ratio was 5:1. The more conventional aspects of the program comprised art experiences, stories, directed play, visits to community facilities, show-and-tell activities, and science activities. Supplementing these, but no less important, were medical examinations and referral treatment, dental diagnoses and follow-up correction, parent interviews, psychological analyses, and a hot meal per child per day.

Project Head Start is still going strong. In fact, of all the educational experimentation initiated or supported during the past decade or two by the federal government and private foundations, Project Head Start is one of the most, if not the most, promising.

---

[3] See any issue of *Project Head Start,* Office of Economic Opportunity, Washington, D.C.

Higher Horizons Project

Yet another social-educational project with strong curriculum implications is the Higher Horizons Project of New York City, a forerunner to the Great Cities Program of the 1960s, which will be elaborated on later in Chapter 14. The project got its start in 1956 as Demonstration Guidance Project, a title that was changed to Higher Horizons Project in 1959. The operational hypothesis of the experiment was as simple as this, namely, that cultural enrichment is a curriculum essential for youth who are culturally deprived. To test out the hypothesis, the experimenters (teachers from the George Washington High School of Harlem) worked with a sample of 375 graduates from Harlem's Junior High School No. 43. The sample members consisted of students from the upper half of the graduating classes of 1957, 1958, and 1959, respectively. They had a mean IQ of 90 and were retarded in reading on an average of a year and a half. Junior High School No. 43 had a population that was 48 percent Negro, 38 percent Puerto Rican, 2 percent other Spanish-speaking, 1 percent Oriental, and 11 percent white. The population of the George Washington High School itself was significantly more diversified.[4]

The most innovative feature of the curriculum for these 375 youth consisted of frequent trips to community agencies and events—universities, government agencies, musical performances, museums, industrial plants, libraries, and even major-league baseball games. Equally innovative was the extensive involvement of parents in the project. More or less innovative were such features as these: each teacher, irrespective of the subject taught, being a teacher of reading a few minutes daily; remedial-reading classes with small enrollments; conventional subject-matter classes with small enrollments; strong emphasis placed on individual counseling; and, not surprisingly, an increase in educational expenditure of up to 40 percent per pupil. By the year 1962, the sample members had increased from 375 to 25,000.

The most noteworthy result of the experiment was a dramatic gain in IQ by a majority of the students. Of the original sample group, for instance, boys gained 17 points on an average and girls gained 11 points. In 1960, 58 percent of the sample had IQs of 110 or higher. Other significant results were a gain of approximately 250 percent in enrollments

[4] Frederick Shaw, "Educating Culturally Deprived Youth in Urban Centers," *Phi Delta Kappan,* 45 (November 1963), p. 94.

in academic courses, and of over 300 percent in post-high school enrollments of various kinds.[5]

Many of the educational gains undoubtedly were results of the Hawthorne Effect, that is, students of the sample responded positively to the warmth and interest manifested by teachers in the experiment. Yet the results seemingly were so positive that the Project upheld the experimental hypothesis of cultural deprivation responding favorably to cultural enrichment.

INNOVATIONS IN TEACHER UTILIZATION

A second category of innovations has teacher utilization as its focal theme. Probably the best overall single source of information on this topic consists of the January issues of *The Bulletin*, for the years 1958–1962, published by the National Association of Secondary-School Principals. For purposes of this section, we have selected for coverage two innovations in teacher utilization, namely, team teaching and the use of noncertified personnel.

Team Teaching

The first of these, team teaching, in a literal interpretation of the term, is not innovational at all. For instance, in any elementary school when a specialist teacher (of art, music, or creative dramatics) joins hands with a generalist classroom teacher, the two constitute a team. So too do a teacher at any educational level and a student teacher when, in a co-operative arrangement, they teach a given body of learners. There was team teaching, too, in the Lancastrian-Bell school of 1800, where the teacher and his student helpers shared the instructional role.

As of the mid-1950s, the term team teaching began to take on specific meaning. It became increasingly descriptive of an instructional situation in which two or more certified teachers had protracted daily responsibility for a single group of learners—this in contrast to the teachers having individual responsibility for their own respective

---

[5] Daniel Schrieber, "The Dropout and the Delinquent: Promising Practices Gleaned from a Year of Study," in *Secondary Schools Today: Readings for Educators,* edited by Frederick R. Smith and R. Bruce McQuigg (Boston: Houghton Mifflin Company, 1965), pp. 201–202.

groups and casually combining them from time to time. Under the first arrangement, a given team of four teachers, for instance, would have composite responsibility for 100 to 120 learners, rather than each of the four having individual responsibility for a given class-sized group of 25 to 30 learners, which might be fused into a larger group on occasion. The closer arrangement commits teachers on any team to a high level of co-operation in such essentials as curriculum planning, organization of learning groups, determination and implementation of instructional methods, and evaluation of learning results.

Team patterns vary extensively among schools. The Franklin Elementary School of Lexington, Massachusetts, a pioneer in the movement, has employed team teaching both with single and multigrade learning groups. The Norwalk, Connecticut School System, on the other hand, has employed it exclusively with two or more grade levels combined. In the Andrew Hill High School of San José, California, two teachers have common responsibility daily for 75 students in an English class. The Evanston Township High School of Evanston, Illinois, from the mid-1950s, has also employed the single-discipline approach. In contrast, junior high schools which employ the block-scheduling plan of necessity take the multidiscipline approach.

Advantages   The several hundred school systems that, since its inception in or around 1954, have had firsthand experience with team teaching report these advantages, among others:

1. It permits grouping flexibility. Homogeneous grouping, for instance, may constitute the grouping arrangement in one learning situation; heterogeneous grouping, in another. Flexibility applies also to class size. Learners may meet as a combined group of 120; as evenly divided subgroups of 30 each; or as unevenly divided subgroups of 90-20-5-5, or 50-50-10-10, or even 117-1-1-1.

2. It exploits specialized teacher competencies. Three third-grade teachers, for example, with specialized competencies in reading, audio-visual instruction, and counseling, respectively, are able to spread these competencies more widely under a team plan than under a single-teacher plan. So too are three teachers of a ninth-grade class in general science with specialized competencies in physics, chemistry, and astronomy, respectively.

3. It has a built-in check-and-balance system. That the team must pass collective judgment on all important curriculum and organizational matters tends to upgrade the many aspects of the learning

process. Professional inadequacy is, or at least may be, neutralized as a result.

4. In-service education is a frequent by-product. Teachers through the act of mutually sharing ideas, debating curriculum issues, and observing one another in the many phases of the instructional process tend to grow professionally as a result.

Disadvantages   Significant though these advantages are, they are offset, in part, by the following disadvantages.

1. Most fundamental of all, cooperative effort is not easy for teaching teams to achieve and sustain. In fact, it is tantalizingly elusive. The magnitude of the tasks involved constitutes one reason for its elusiveness. In this connection, cooperation is essential in the planning phase, in the implementation phase, and also in the evaluation phase. And none of these is narrowly dimensioned or patently simple. Cooperative planning of a year's curriculum; group decision-making on matters of instructional method, class size, and teacher roles; and agreement on ways to evaluate learning outcomes, all demand the professional best from teachers.

These demand the teachers' personal best as well. Cooperative endeavor works when teachers on a team are flexible, tolerant of disagreement, objective, and not excessively self-centered. However, when teachers fail in these qualities, cooperative endeavor fails. A surprising number of teaching teams throughout the country, unable to meet these important but taxing personality requisites, have had short lives.

Yet a third requirement of team teaching in the area of cooperation is planning time. Teachers who make wise choices in such areas as curriculum, instruction, and evaluation are those who engage in professional dialogue until satisfied with the results. And this is a time-consuming process, so time-consuming that schools unwilling to lighten the loads of team teachers should, conceivably, not attempt team teaching at all.

2. A second disadvantage of team teaching resides in the burden it places on facilities. Classrooms designed to seat from 25 to 35 pupils characterize most schools. Yet facilities capable of accommodating as many as 120 to 150 pupils characterize the needs of most team-teaching arrangements. Conventionally constructed schools generally surmount this obstacle by pre-empting, for large-group purposes, lunchrooms, gymnasiums, and assembly halls. These areas are rarely satisfactory, however. The ideal is for school systems, at the time of construction,

273

to build buildings around anticipated team-teaching needs. Some schools that have done this are Englewood Elementary School of Englewood, Florida; the Grove Street Elementary School of Lexington, Massachusetts; and the Marie Creighton Junior High School of Jefferson County, Colorado. Without proper physical plants, team teaching tends to suffer.

3. A third disadvantage of team teaching lies in the possibility of detachment as a result of pupils' too often being part of a large group. However, teachers aware of this possibility need not let it become reality. Thus the disadvantage may be more theoretical than actual.

Use of Noncertified Teaching Personnel

The use in schools of paid noncertified teaching personnel constitutes still another innovation in teacher utilization. It was a product of the teacher shortage of the 1950s. The justification usually given for the innovation is that certain duties performed by teachers are at a professional level whereas others are not; teachers are able to perform the former more adequately when noncertified personnel perform the latter.

Paid noncertified teaching assistants divide into the two categories of *semiprofessionals* and *subprofessionals*. The first engage in activities such as reading and evaluating English themes, serving as assistants in science laboratories, serving as members of teaching teams, supervising selected extracurricular activities, and supervising or assisting in study

halls. These semiprofessionals customarily have college degrees and specialties that serve specific needs in formal education. The subprofessionals perform: (1) housekeeping duties, such as care of blackboards, plants, and supplies; (2) clerical duties, such as taking roll, handling funds and messages, typing, and grading objective tests; (3) supervisory duties, such as assisting in the loading and unloading of buses, and supervising in lunchrooms and on playgrounds; (4) personal-service duties, such as helping young children with wraps and overshoes, and making routine health checks; and (5) nonprofessional instructional duties, such as arranging for field trips, arranging for audiovisual materials and equipment, and preparing selected learning materials.[6]

The pioneer experiment in the use of paid noncertified teaching personnel was the one carried on in the 1950s in Bay City, Michigan. It was an experiment in the use of teacher aides in elementary school classrooms. The 1955 report[7] in regard to it made many headlines, but the study itself made few converts. The Fairfield-Yale study, although primarily a job analysis of the duties performed by elementary school teachers, casts important light on the teacher-aide issue. It revealed, in this connection, that teachers spend approximately 20 percent of their professional time performing tasks that nonprofessional personnel might perform. Since around 1960, the high schools of Newton, Massachusetts, and Evanston, Illinois—as two examples only—have made the services of lay readers available to selected teachers of English. And the Norwalk, Connecticut, school system, since around 1958, has had noncertified personnel as members of teaching teams.

Despite the reported success of many pilot projects involving non-certified teacher aides, formal education remains unconvinced about their practicality and effectiveness. One reason resides in education's inability to distinguish sharply between important and unimportant teaching duties. A second reason lies in the irregular time demands that subprofessional tasks tend to impose on teacher assistants. Helping children with wraps, collecting gifts for various causes, cleaning the blackboard, watering plants, and performing related tasks do not fit neatly into a packaged work period of a day or half day. A third reason

[6] This topic of nonprofessional teaching personnel is elaborated by Robert H. Anderson in *Teaching in a World of Change* (New York: Harcourt, Brace & World, Inc., 1966), pp. 110–121.

[7] *A Co-operative Study for the Better Utilization of Teacher Competencies.* Second Printed Report, 1955 (Mount Pleasant, Michigan: Central Michigan College, 1955), 32 pp.

resides in the reluctance of teachers to relinquish certain of their duties for fear of losing rapport and pupil insight as a result.

In view of the foregoing, this concluding statement seems warranted. Experiments in the utilization by schools of noncertified teacher assistants are inconclusive, with the verdict on their effectiveness being far from in. It will probably remain undetermined for a long time.

ELECTRONIC METHODS

The innovations to be covered in this section[8] share a common involvement with electronics. The first three—television instruction, programmed learning, and the language laboratory—are methods media. The fourth, the computer, is primarily an administrative research medium.

Television Instruction

The sensational success of commercial television (CTV) in the thirties made the advent of instructional television a foregone conclusion. CTV itself, broadly viewed, is an educational servant, despite the fact that viewer pleasure and dollar profit tend to obscure educational purposes. Educational Television (ETV) and Closed Circuit Television (CCTV) serve education in a more direct way.

ETV is a term reserved for stations licensed specifically for educational purposes. In 1953, the Federal Communications Commission brought into being the first ETV station, licensing it to the University of Houston. Ten years later, 79 of these stations were in existence in 32 states and the District of Columbia. Of these 79 stations, 26 were licensed to colleges and universities, 20 to public educational institutions, and the remaining 33 to assorted public agencies or civic groups. ETV's viewing audience is estimated at 20 million, with 8.5 million fairly regular viewers. Programs consist of formal course offerings and informal educational broadcasts.

The problems of ETV are many, consisting selectively of the following: limited financing, performers of uneven quality, little prime program time, and limited range of ultra high frequency bands. Further-

---

[8] Some of the material covered in this section comes from Gail M. Inlow, *The Emergent in Curriculum* (New York: John Wiley & Sons, Inc., 1966), Chap. 8.

more, it directs its efforts primarily at adults.[9] For these and other reasons, educational television defers to closed circuit television as the more functional school medium.

CCTV is not only functional but also relatively uncomplex. Its mechanical requirements are four in number: a place of origin for programming, a system of coaxial cables, sizable receiving sets, and places for student viewing. Ideally, all but the sets themselves should be built into a school at the time of its construction. The noteworthy advantage of CCTV over ETV lies in its greater adaptability to local curriculum needs. Schools or school systems themselves determine what instructional programs should go into the medium. And the latter can go in live or via teletapes. In either instance, those closest to the intended learners are in control of the curriculum.

CCTV accomplishes, or at least is capable of accomplishing, the following outcomes: (1) extending the influence of capable instructional leaders to larger audiences; (2) extending the reach of key school events; (3) contributing to close-up viewing, as, for instance, of a science demonstrtion; (4) serving the needs of a team-teaching situation; (5) making large-group seating space less essential; and (6) performing intercom functions. In serving these purposes, CCTV exploits its strengths as a tell-and-show medium. It is an agent of verbal learning and of demonstration. In both roles, it is capable of meeting many of the less sophisticated demands of cognitive learning.

However, it has the following intrinsic limitations. It keeps learners passive by denying them (except in a few isolated instances) the opportunity to talk back. It is authority-centered, denying learners the opportunity to individualize. It fails the demands of critical thinking and problem-solving at advanced levels. Furthermore, it operates almost completely outside the social and emotional purviews of education. Specifically, it cannot lead a seminar, it cannot discover what a learner is thinking or feeling, it cannot counsel, it cannot socialize. What is more, it cannot, and should not, replace a teacher for any protracted time period. Television in either educational form, ETV or CCTV, is a methods supplement, a teacher supplement. It serves education best when enriching without replacing. Most important of all, schools should employ it only for those curriculum purposes for which it is best suited.

---

[9] An exception, in this regard, was the Midwest Program on Airborne Television Instruction (MPATI), which transmitted packaged lessons to various classrooms in six Midwestern states. After an impressive start in 1959, MPATI steadily declined in influence.

277

Programmed Learning

Programmed learning may use either machines or books. The teaching machine, interestingly, has captured the headlines, despite the fact that the heart of the learning involved lies not in the machine but in the program. The intent of this section is not to cover the topic of programmed learning in detail, for book-length treatment alone could do that. Rather, the intent is to provide readers with a crisp description of the topic, one designed to introduce them to its vocabulary and concepts, and thus to encourage them to investigate it further.

A program customarily embraces the following characteristics

1. It presents learners with questions or problems.
2. Learners respond to them in some overt way: by writing in answers or by checking multiple-choice answers.
3. The program informs learners as to whether their responses are correct or incorrect. This process is variably called reinforcement or feedback.
4. The program, at all times, controls the sequence of the stimulus items.
5. Learners proceed through a program at their own respective rates.

Programs generally consist of two types: (1) linear and (2) branched (or scrambled). The former, with B. F. Skinner the creator and staunch advocate, guides learners down a straight path that leads inexorably from fixed step to fixed step. The following example is typical. Each stimulus item with its elicited response constitutes a frame. The learner, it should be noted, writes in his responses.

Frame 1
S. Grammar is a study of language. It may be either formal or functional. Irrespective of category, however, grammar should be regarded as a (_____).
R. (study of language)

Frame 2
S. Grammar, when formal, is not necessarily an integral part of the spoken or written word. When functional, the reverse is true. Thus when a teacher asks for a definition of a part of speech, his approach is that of (_____) grammar.
R. (formal)

Frame 3
S. The linguistic approach, because it adheres closely to the spoken or written word, conversely is an instance of (_____) grammar.
R. (functional)

The branched (or scrambled) type, with Norman A. Crowder the creator and advocate, guides learners down varying and more circuitous paths, the nature of the path depending on the nature of a given individual's responses. The following example is typical. The learner, in this instance, checks a multiple-choice answer rather than writing in one of his own. This is a feature of the branched type. Then he receives some sort of feedback. Finally, he receives instructions as to the next course of action.

Frame 1

Grammar is a study of language. It may be either formal or functional. It is formal when not an integral part of written or spoken expression. It is functional when the reverse is true. Thus a teacher who asks a slow learner to define a noun: (Check one of the following)

( ) A. Is being unreasonable.
( ) B. Is following the approach of formal grammar.
( ) C. Is following the approach of functional grammar.

Frame 2

So you pressed button A because you thought the teacher to be unreasonable. Whether he was or not is not pertinent to the issue at hand. Now press the button for Frame 1 and try again.

Frame 3

You correctly noted that teachers who require learners to define a part of speech operate in the traditions of formal grammar. Good work! Now press the button for Frame 5 and move on.

Frame 4

You pressed button C, implying by your response that a definition of a part of speech is essential to its usage. Yet infants say "Mama" without being able to define the concept noun. We suggest that you press the button for Frame 1, reassess the terms functional and integral, and then try again.

As previously indicated, a program may take the form of a book or may appear in some other form that will fit into a teaching machine. If the former, the learner moves from place to place in the book in response to verbal instructions. If the latter, the machine manipulates the program in response to manual stimuli superimposed by the learner. In any event, programs are meticulously ordered; highly verbal; individually, albeit methodically, paced; designed to teach the student, not to fail him; and characterized by feedback throughout.

A consensus evaluation of programmed-learning methods is that when carefully conceived and implemented, they possess substantial

learning value. Yet they have serious limitations as well. Some of these are as follows: (1) they handicap poor readers, (2) they retard the learning pace of fast learners, (3) their effectiveness is restricted mostly to the area of cognitive learning, and to the more elementary cognitive processes at that, (4) they keep learners closely tied to authority-determined content, (5) programs tend to become prematurely dated, and (6) both programs and machine conceivably may sedate as much as teach, once their novelty has worn thin. In conclusion, a wise suggestion is for schools to regard them as experimental, select programs only after careful screening, employ programs and/or machines discriminately in terms of the cognitive things they do best, and restrict their use to abbreviated time periods.

The Language Laboratory

The language laboratory, a classroom configuration conceived to advance the cause of modern foreign-language instruction, constitutes yet a third electronic approach to elicit comment in this chapter. The configuration made its initial appearance in higher education in 1947; in secondary education, a little more than a decade later. In 1958, 64 language laboratories existed in the schools; in 1962, 5000; today, reportedly several thousand more exist. The National Defense Education Act of 1958 supplied the growth impetus. Title III of the Act subsidized on a matching basis the purchase and installation by schools of language-laboratory paraphernalia. Title VI provided for the in-service education for teachers who were to use them.

A language laboratory, in brief, is a learning area consisting[10]

> of mechanical and electronic equipment by means of which students, individually or in a group, hear and respond to material prerecorded in a foreign language. They may listen with headset and hear their own voices, either simultaneously as they speak into the microphone, or by recording on a disc or tape and then playing back their own recording.

The electronic hardware of a language laboratory comprises the following essentials: (1) a master control console equipped with headphones, microphones, tape recorders, and monitoring jacks, the latter connected to all pupil booths or stations; and (2) pupil booths or sta-

---

[10] Marjorie C. Johnson and Catherine C. Seerley, *Foreign Language Laboratories in Schools and Colleges* (Washington, D.C.: Department of Health, Education, and Welfare Bulletin No. 3, 1958), p. 6.

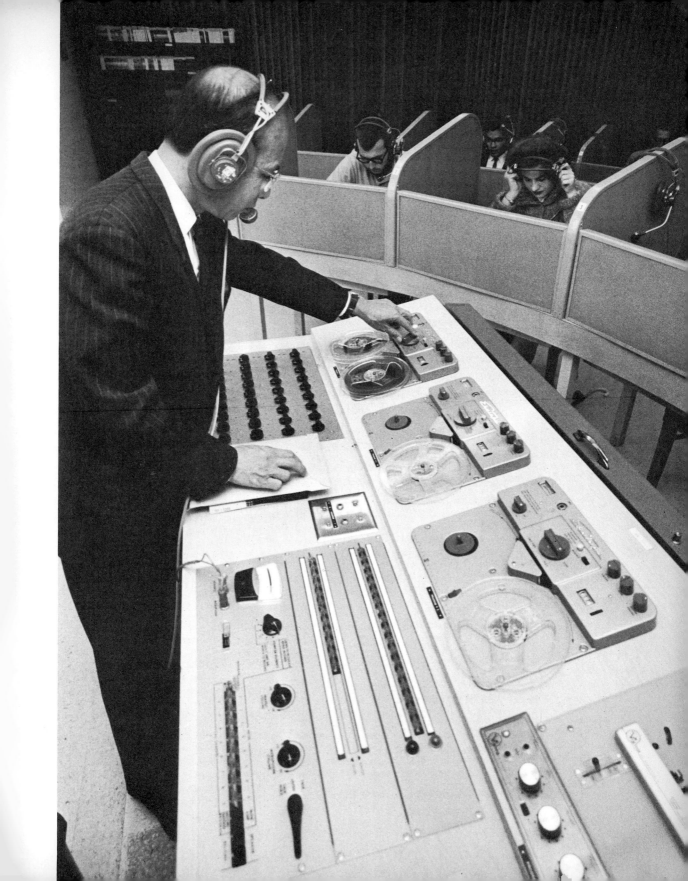

tions, acoustically insulated, also equipped with headphones, microphones, and tape recorders. The primary learning media are also twofold: (1) tapes on which language spoken with native fidelity has been reproduced; and (2) knowledgeable and flexible teachers capable of integrating their own resources with those recorded on the tapes.

The language laboratory has its operational center in the aural-oral (listening-speaking, or audio-lingual) approach to language learning. As indicated in Chapter 9, the rationale is that students learn a language best by hearing it spoken authentically and often. In the laboratory they listen to recordings, repeat to a teacher or tape what they think they hear, compare the two, and through a progression of effort move ever closer to the outcome of oral fidelity. As stated by one source.[11] ". . . the oral approach should be primary . . . fluency is more important than perfection." The aural-oral approach obviously postpones language syntax—sometimes for only weeks or months, sometimes for as long as a semester or even a year.

In the last analysis, the language laboratory will earn its mark to the degree that (1) the aural-oral approach proves its superiority over the memory-syntax-translate approach, (2) tapes (that are analogous to programs in teaching machines) exist in sufficient number and quality to meet the needs of learners who differ widely, and (3) teachers are able and willing to serve the rather exacting demands of the laboratory. Many laboratories today stand idle, or only partially used, because of teacher inertia, fear of the new, lack of mechanical ability, or inadequacy of in-service preparation.

The Computer in Education

A relative newcomer to the field of electronics in education is the computer. Its functions are threefold: to receive input data, to manipulate the data received, and to produce output data. These three functions, combined, comprise what is technically known as EDP or Electronic Data Processing. The number base of digital computers is the binary, not the decimal, system: in other words, its base is 2, not 10.

Electricity constitutes the energy of a computer, which has no mova-

---

[11] Elton Hocking, "Future Prospects of Language Teaching with the Use of the Language Laboratory" in Felix J. Oinas (ed.), *Language Teaching Today: Report of the Language Laboratory Conference Held at Indiana University January 22–23, 1960* (Bloomington: Indiana University, 1960), p. 14.

ble parts. It is capable of adding and subtracting only; yet this limitation, for two reasons, imposes no serious handicap. For one reason, the processes of multiplication and subtraction are actually contrived methods, respectively, of addition and subtraction; for a second reason, the tremendous operating speed of which computers are capable compensates many times over for this limitation. One source states that the speed of present-day computers is comparable to Tolstoy's writing *War and Peace* "in about 2 seconds."[12]

Computerized research may be as uncomplicated as a set of punched cards processed in a manual sorting-recording machine or as complicated as a detailed research program fed into and interpreted by a sophisticated electronic computer. Simplicity generally characterizes the computer activities of most schools and school systems.

Schools tend to employ computer methods mostly in the fields of counseling and school administration, and to a limited extent in the field of curriculum. In the guidance area, such data as school marks, IQ scores, achievement-test scores, home-and-family information, and health data customarily are card-punched and machine-processed. In the area of school administration, the computer serves in such areas as class scheduling (particularly when the module is the basic unit), budgetary matters, pupil attendance, and comparisons among classes and schools. The world of electronics, including computers, has not revolutionized education, but it has certainly enhanced its effectiveness.

INNOVATIONS IN PUPIL GROUPING

In this final section of the chapter, the focus shifts from electronic phenomena to the more prosaic topic of pupil grouping. The latter began to assume importance when education ceased being a privilege of the socioeconomic establishment and became a right of the masses. My intent here is not to cover the topic in breadth or depth, but to cover some aspects of it briefly, and only the innovative ones at that. The following four topics have been selected for treatment: (1) innovations in class size, (2) the nongraded classroom, (3) the Advanced Placement Program, and (4) the dual-enrollment plan.

[12] Murray Tondow, "Computers: Concepts and Hardware," in John W. Loughary, *et al, Man-Machine Systems in Education* (New York: Harper & Row, Publishers, 1966), p. 24. The entire book was helpful to me as I wrote this section.

Innovations in Class Size

For well over a half century, the American public has required children, except for the retarded exceptional, to stay in school until the age of fourteen, fifteen, or sixteen. Age sixteen is the controlling one at the moment. This requirement commits education to effect class groupings that work a hardship neither on taxpayers nor on students.

For years, the number 25 was the uncontested compromise in regard to class size. Yet when educational researchers sought to validate it, they could find only subjective evidence to support it. The issue of class size became increasingly acute in the 1940s and 1950s when the World War II babies enrolled in the schools at a time when teachers were in critically short supply. Overcrowding was one obvious result. Experimentation with learning groups of various sizes was a second less obvious result. The latter was usually a by-product of experiments connected with television instruction and team teaching. Although these took place at all educational levels, secondary education became the most actively involved of all educational echelons in investigating the issue of class size. It was one of several issues investigated and reported on by the commission on the Experimental Study of the Utilization of the Staff in the Secondary School, an agency of the National Association of Secondary School Principals.

The report of the commission, published in 1961, was replete with such categorical pronouncements as the following—all alleged to characterize "tomorrow's schools."

> The organization of instruction in tomorrow's schools will provide many more opportunities for individual students' *independent study*, inside schools as well as outside, during school hours as well as after them. . . . Generally speaking, however, independent study will average 40 percent of the school's schedule for students.[13]

and

> Tomorrow's schools will assemble large classes of from 100 to 500 students or more whenever the education purpose calls for it. If a class is to hear a presentation by a teacher or some other speaker on a face-to-face basis, 150 students probably will be the maximum class size. If the purpose, however, is to view a film or a television program, the number may range up to 300 students or more. . . . Combined, these purposes

[13] J. Lloyd Trump and Dorsey Baynham, *Guide to Better Schools: Focus on Change* (Skokie, Ill.: Rand McNally & Company, 1961), p. 27.

suggest that about 40 percent of a student's time will be spent in large classes.[14]

The work of the commission and its report were nothing if not controversial. Some schools took the recommendations at face value and began almost immediately to implement them. Conceivably, the report was partially responsible for such schools as the Brigham Young Laboratory School, Provo, Utah, and the Theodore High School, Theodore, Alabama, moving toward a strongly oriented independent-study plan. Hundreds of schools, through the media of television and team teaching, moved toward the large-group learning plan.

The greatest merit of the commission's work was that it emboldened certain schools to experiment with the problem of class size. The greatest limitation of the commission's work lay in the pretense that it had absolute answers (the 40:40:20 ratio, for instance) whereas it had only opinions. Thus the issue of class size is still far from being resolved. Logically, there is no one ideal class size. Memory-cognitive learning of factual and simple conceptual content may not be a function of class size. But dialogue, reflective thinking, problem-solving, creativity, social growth, and emotional growth are very much functions of class size. Thus the need is for schools to articulate goals first, and only then to make decisions regarding the size of learning groups. The flexibility in class size that team teaching allows may well be education's best single answer.

The Nongraded Classroom

Though the nongraded classroom dates back to the 1930s, it is still regarded as innovational in its current use. In early America, instruction involved a tutorial relationship between a teacher and a single pupil or small cluster of pupils. Then came the approach of the little red schoolhouse with a number of children of widely divergent ages, abilities, and backgrounds brought and kept together in a common learning space. Next came the approach of grading which, in 1848, Horace Mann as the theoretician and John Philbrick as the practitioner pioneered in the Quincy School of Boston. The graded plan had its origin in 1537 when John Sturum introduced it into Strasburg, Germany. The theory of grading is that pupils upon reaching a predetermined age

---

[14] Trump and Baynham, p. 29.

will enroll in school and then move from grade to grade if capable of meeting the standards of each advanced grade. When unable to do so, they remain in a given grade until demonstrating enough proficiency to move upward. In actual practice, age rather than demonstrated ability acts as the controlling standard, with extensive learner heterogeneity along many lines being the customary result.

Education's counter to grading has been, in at least certain instances, the nongraded classroom. First implemented by Western Springs, Illinois, in 1934, it since has become an organizational pattern in over 50 school systems and 550 schools.[15] Its setting has been grades 1–3 primarily, grades 4–6 on occasions, and grades higher than 6 only rarely. Our comments here apply exclusively to its role in elementary education. The ensuing features are composite characteristics of the nongraded plan.

1. It keeps children together for three years rather than one, usually throughout the period of the primary grades—on occasions, as previously indicated, also throughout the period of the intermediate grades.

2. During either of these three-year periods, sequential progress of all pupils up a progressive curriculum ladder is the projected goal. Each pupil, at least in theory, starts where he is and moves vertically from curriculum step to step.

3. When learning takes place in small groups, learned ability rather than age is the criterion. Thus, several eight-year-olds might well be in a first-level remedial-reading group; and a few six-year-olds might well be in an advanced science project customarily regarded as appropriate only for eight-year-olds.

4. Teachers customarily remain with a given group for three years, but they may change groups from year to year. The former plan is more logically defensible when the teacher is reasonably competent; it is not at all defensible when the teacher is significantly less competent than his colleagues. Pupils should not be exposed to a "weak" teacher for three years.

5. Decisions to promote or retard are customarily made at the end of a three-year period; in this way, teachers are able to accumulate more clinical data to back up their decisions than when making them at the end of one year. An occasional gifted child may move on after two years; most children do so after three years; a few are not ready for the next rung until after four years.

[15] John I. Goodlad and Robert H. Anderson, *The Nongraded Elementary School* (New York: Harcourt, Brace & World, Inc., 1963), p. 55.

My personal opinion is that the conventional graded plan, if integrated and conducted with clinical care, is capable of achieving all the outcomes claimed for the nongraded plan. Fundamental to both are curriculum integration, learner individualization, teacher competency, and administrative support. In this regard, the glowing success reported for nongrading may well be as much the product of effort expended by teachers in preparing for the plan than of the intrinsic advantages of the plan itself. Yet if nongrading is a better catalyst for in-service growth than grading, this may make it educationally superior.[16]

The Advanced Placement Program

The topic of this section, the Advanced Placement Program, is a phenomenon of secondary and higher education. A creation of the College Entrance Examination Board, the Educational Testing Service has been a co-partner in its growth, and the Ford Foundation a co-partner in its financing. The basic purposes of the program are threefold: (1) to assure talented students a curriculum commensurate with their needs and abilities; (2) to help high schools formulate and implement such a curriculum; and (3) to help high schools select appropriate students for the program. Although the program establishes no IQ criterion for admission, a score of 120, generally constitutes a practical minimum. Other criteria consist of a desire on the part of student participants to excel, a willingness to work long hours, and the interest of parents in the program. Teachers in the program need to meet standards generally comparable to those required of teachers of college freshmen. Advanced Placement Program classes are conducted along homogeneous lines in most participating high schools, but homogeneity is not a stipulated requirement.

Though the primary purpose of the program, allegedly, is to provide high school seniors (sometimes juniors) with a curriculum that will challenge them, a strong competing purpose is to ready students for advanced curriculum placement when they enroll in a college or university. The latter, depending on institutional policy, may or may not award course credit to them. In any event, course credit is granted only to students who do satisfactory work on examinations administered by

[16] The topic of the nongraded classroom, and the next one of the Advanced Placement Program, are developed in greater detail in Gail M. Inlow, *The Emergent in Curriculum,* Chaps. 15 and 16, respectively.

the College Entrance Examination Board. These examinations are usually held in May. Harvard University, in 1962, awarded such credit to 130 of 500 entering Advanced Placement students.

The Advanced Placement Program has many positive attributes, with curriculum updating uppermost. Yet it is vulnerable when guilty, as it often or even customarily is, of the following questionable practices: (1) emphasizing the cognitive in learning to the neglect of such other outcomes as mental health, social growth, and value building; (2) paying undue attention to the intellectually favored to the neglect of the average and slow; (3) overemphasizing the academic subjects to the neglect of the applied- and fine-arts subjects; and (4) transferring an unwarranted amount of curriculum control from high schools to colleges and universities. These faults generally are more extrinsic than intrinsic. Yet they are serious enough to give high schools pause, and, hopefully, to precipitate aggressive counter-action against them.

Dual Enrollment

Yet a fourth innovation in pupil-grouping, dual enrollment, is as basic as the issue of the right of private education to utilize the curriculum and facilities of public education. Dual enrollment constitutes an arrangement whereby students attend a private school for part of a school day and a public school for the remaining part.

The National Education Association, in 1963, made a status study of dual-enrollment practices in the nation's schools. In 1965, it published its findings, which included a description of dual-enrollment practices in nine representative communities.[17] Specifically, the NEA sent postcards to the 12,366 public school systems having enrollments of over 300, asking if they shared their programs and facilities with nonpublic school children. Responses came from 7410 systems, of which 280 in 35 states answered in the affirmative. The sharing venture, however, was of significant proportions in only 183 of the 280 systems. From these 183, the NEA selected nine for case-study purposes. Of these, three (categorized as Class I) accommodated nonpublic school children for four to five, or fewer, class periods per week; and six (categorized as Class II) accommodated such children for a half day (or just short of that) five days per week. The three communities consisted of Cabell County, West Virginia; Hartford, Connecticut; and Pittsburgh, Pennsylvania. The six consisted of Allegheny County, Pennsylvania; Cherry Hill, Michigan; Flint, Michigan; Kearsley, Michigan; Kimberly, Wisconsin; and Warren, Michigan.

In the three systems categorized as Class I, nonpublic school children were enrolled in homemaking and industrial-arts classes. In addition, those from one school were enrolled in swimming; and from another, in drafting. In the six systems categorized as Class II, nonpublic school children relatedly were enrolled in homemaking and industrial arts; additionally, in science, mathematics, a modern foreign language, art, and music. The dual relationship for the three Class I systems dated back, at the earliest, to 1914 in the case of Pittsburgh; at the latest, to 1934 in the case of Hartford. The dual relationship for the six Class II systems dated back only to 1963. Thus, it follows that any extensive utilization by nonpublic school children of public school facilities and curriculum is definitely a recent phenomenon.

The advantages of the dual-enrollment plan reside almost exclusively in the educational enrichment that redounds, as a result, to nonpublic school pupils. And that these advantages are significant is an understatement. The disadvantages comprise the following: curriculum components forced to serve divergent educational philosophies, indefinite legal status of the plan, divided administrative authority, divided student loyalties with the resulting extracurriculum complications, and the

[17] James E. Gibbs, *et al., Dual Enrollment in Public and Nonpublic Schools: Case Studies of Nine Communities* (Washington, D.C.: U.S. Department of Health, Education, and Welfare, 1965).

strain placed on public school facilities by the unpredictability of non-public school demands.

The dual-enrollment plan unquestionably is on trial. That children now enrolled in nonpublic schools have the legal right to transfer to public schools goes without saying. The real issue, however, is whether children and schools can divide their allegiances without both the children and education being losers. Continued experimentation with the plan alone holds the answer.

To Stimulate Thought

1. Identify and elaborate the pros and cons of a curriculum design prepared at the national level and channeled to local teachers to follow verbatim.

2. Conceive a school oriented exclusively to discovery learning. What serious problems would it face?

3. Identify and describe what you believe to be the major strengths of the Head Start Program.

4. A truism in education is that pupils bring meaning to the printed page as well as extracting meaning from it. Relate this truism to the Higher Horizons Project of New York City.

5. As a means of self-analysis, project yourself into the future as a member of a teaching team in your major field; in such a role, identify what you think your greatest strengths and weaknesses might be.

6. What tasks do you think a teacher aide might perform in your teaching field? Analyze each in terms of whether its performance by another might weaken your bond with students.

7. As yet another means of self-analysis, project yourself into the role of on-camera performer in a closed circuit television project. Identify what you think your greatest strengths and weaknesses might be.

8. Psychological reinforcement is alleged to be perhaps the most outstanding feature of programmed learning. Do you assess this feature to be highly significant? Defend your stand.

9. Evaluate what you believe to be the advantages and shortcomings of the aural-oral approach to language instruction.

10. List the learning activities in your major field that you think could be taught to large groups of learners.

11. List the characteristics of the nongraded classroom, identifying those, if any, that you regard as unique to it.

12. Develop the theme: "Students who do college-level work in high school should receive college credit for it."

13. Evaluate the pros and cons of the dual-enrollment plan.

290

REFERENCES

Anderson, Robert H., *Teaching in a World of Change* (New York: Harcourt, Brace & World, Inc., 1966), Chap. 6.

Association for Supervision and Curriculum Development, *Educational Leadership*, 23 (November 1965). This highlights the Head Start Program.

Brown, B. Frank, *The Nongraded High School* (Englewood Cliffs, N.J.: Prentice-Hall, Inc., 1963).

DeCecco, John P. (ed.), *Educational Technology* (New York: Holt, Rinehart and Winston, Inc., 1964).

Diamond, Robert (ed.), *A Guide to Instructional Television* (New York: McGraw-Hill, Inc., 1964).

Educational Technology. Interested readers should keep abreast of this journal published twice monthly.

Frymier, Jack, *Fostering Educational Change* (Columbus, Ohio: Charles E. Merrill Publishing Co., 1969).

Gibbs, James E., *et al*, *Dual Enrollment in Public and Nonpublic Schools: Case Studies of Nine Communities* (Washington, D.C.: U.S. Department of Health, Education, and Welfare, 1965).

Goodlad, John I., and Robert H. Anderson, *The Nongraded Elementary School* (New York: Harcourt, Brace & World, Inc., 1963).

Heath, Robert W. (ed.), *New Curricula.* New York: Harper & Row, Publishers, 1964.

Hocking, Elton, *Language Laboratory and Language Learning* (Washington, D.C.: National Education Association, 1964).

Hutchinson, Joseph C., *Modern Foreign Languages in High School: The Language Laboratory* (Washington, D.C.: U.S. Department of Health, Education, and Welfare, 1961).

Inlow, Gail M., *The Emergent in Curriculum* (New York: John Wiley & Sons, Inc., 1966), Chaps. 7, 8, 9, 14, 15, and 16.

Rosenbloom, Paul C. (ed.), *Modern Viewpoints in the Curriculum* (New York: McGraw-Hill, Inc., 1964).

Rossi, Peter H., and Bruce J. Biddle, *The New Media and Education* (Chicago, Ill.: Aldine Publishing Company, 1966).

Shaplin, Judson T., and Henry F. Olds (eds.), *Team Teaching* (New York: Harper & Row, Publishers, 1964).

The Institute for Communication Research, *Educational Television The Next Ten Years* (Stanford, Calif.: Stanford University Press, 1962).

Trump, J. Lloyd, and Dorsey Baynham, *Guide to Better Schools: Focus on Change* (Skokie, Ill.: Rand McNally & Company, 1961).

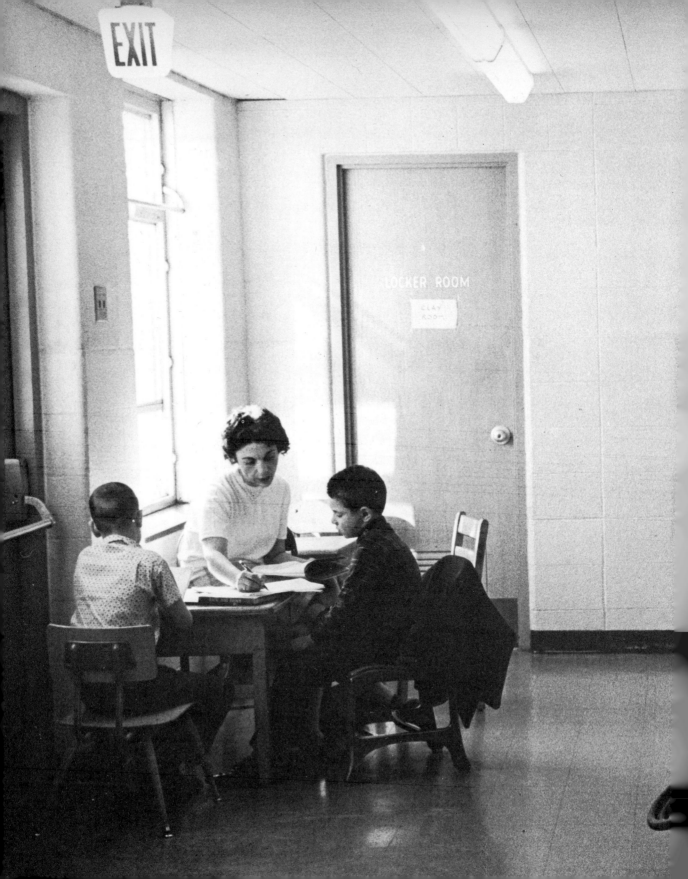

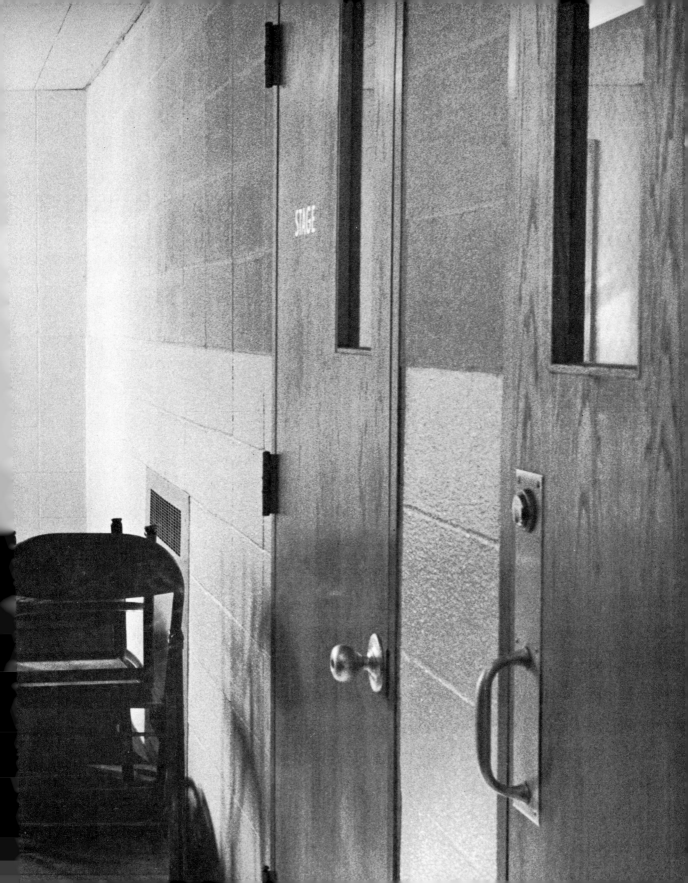

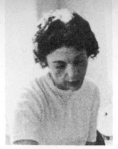

Chapter
11

Guidance
and
Counseling

The modern Rip Van Winkle, who after a sixty-year sleep (blame inflation for the increase), wandered into a modern school, would be in for a number of surprises. One would be the guidance and counseling program, with its many attendant activities. Such terms as objective testing, personality inventory, stanine, Advanced Placement Program, projection, unconscious motivation, and statistical significance would ring strangely in his ears. So too would such job titles as psychometrician, child-guidance counselor, vocational-guidance counselor, and school psychologist. And, conceivably, a few of the teachers he met— the more conservative and detached, at least—might share his astonishment. Some teachers are oblivious to the fact that curriculum, which at the turn of the century was academically oriented exclusively, is today socially and personally oriented as well.

Schools today pursue student growth along at least these four avenues: course offerings, extracurricular activities, library services, and student personnel services. In respect to the last term, I submit the following taxonomy to assure that writer and reader are communicating in the same terms.

1. *Student personnel services* of any school subsume the three specific services of pupil accounting, health, and guidance. The primary concern of each is the student as an individual, not students in groups or en masse.

2. *Guidance services* of any school exist to help students achieve self-identity, from which base of reality they are better able to formulate and attain meaningful life goals. Guidance services divide into categories of the emotional (or psychological), of the vocational, and of the educational. The goal of the first is emotional maturity; of the second, wise choice of vocation; of the third, intelligent planning for the educational present and for the post-high school future.

3. *Counseling* is a phase of guidance that brings counselor and student together in a special relationship. The counselor relates to the counselee with the purpose of understanding him and his problems and of affording him supportive assistance as he attempts to solve his problems. The counseling process involves data gathering, data analysis, face-to-face meetings, and follow-up activities—any or all of these.

4. *The interview* is that part of the counseling process characterized by a face-to-face confrontation between a counselor and a counselee.

The various instructional services stand out in contrast to the guid-

ance services in that they are oriented more in authority figures, more in subject matter, and more in learning groups. The instructional services, furthermore, contribute to student growth more by the avenue of knowledge; the guidance services, more by the avenue of personalities. The instructional services deal primarily with the rational aspects of behavior; guidance services deal with both the rational and the nonrational aspects.

THE RAISON D'ETRE OF GUIDANCE

The guidance movement came into being in response to a number of influences, of which the following four were particularly significant: (1) the increasing complexity of industry as an outgrowth of the Industrial Revolution, (2) the growing diversity of the student population, a phenemenon that began to reach crisis proportions shortly after the turn of the century, (3) the increasing applicability of the concepts and methods of psychology and psychiatry, and (4) the mounting realization that education could accomplish its goals in a reasonably satisfactory way only when complementing group methods with individual ones.

Increasing Complexity of Industry

Guidance originated in the vocational area. Industrialization and technology made it inevitable; job specialization precipitated it. Frank Parsons is generally considered its father. In 1908 he established, and became the first director of, the Vocational Guidance Bureau in Boston. Such was the origin of vocational guidance which education, before long, incorporated into its mainstream.

Vocational guidance came into being as a social need: jobs in the marketplace had become so numerous and complex that young people needed help in planning for them. Approaches to vocational guidance in the schools, since its inception, have been many and varied, including such media as formal courses in vocations, vocational-interest inventories, special aptitude tests, exploratory job employment, work-study arrangements, and personal interviewing. In addition to the 1908 date, two other important dates stand out in the history of vocational guidance—1913, which marks the establishment of the National

EDUCATION AS AN OPERATIONAL PROCESS

Vocation Guidance Association and 1939, which marks the advent of the *Dictionary of Occupational Titles,* a product of the United States Employment Service.

Diversity of the High School Population

The growing diversity of school population stands as yet another raison d'être for the guidance movement. During the last decade of the nine-

For every 10 pupils in the 5th grade in 1959–60

9.7 entered the 9th grade in 1963–64

8.5 entered the 11th grade in 1965–66

7.2 graduated from high school in 1967

4.0 entered college in fall 1967

2.0 are likely to earn 4-year degrees in 1971

Estimated retention rates, fifth grade through college graduation: United States, 1959 to 1971.
Source: Kenneth Simon and W. Vance Grant, Digest of Educational Statistics, OE-10024-67 (Washington, D.C. U. S. Department of Health, Education and Welfare, 1967), p. 8.

teenth century, although most children attended elementary school, only 5 to 10 percent of the eligible youth in this country attended high school. Today, approximately 90 percent attend high school. This dramatic increase, although a social boon, creates problems for high schools: overcrowded classrooms, less individual attention, a greater range of student abilities, a comparably greater range of social differences, and an increased awareness of student needs which, without a guidance program, might go unnoticed and unattended. Mass education inevitably multiplies the likelihood that the individual student will become depersonalized. Guidance services operate to counter this eventuality.

Insights of the Mental-Health Orientations

The increasing applicability of the concepts and methods of the several mental-health orientations — clinical psychology, neuropsychiatry, psychoanalysis, and social work — have made this counter all the stronger. The year 1908 is significant here for an event of far greater social significance, in my opinion, than the opening of Frank Parson's Vocation Bureau. I refer to the publication of Clifford W. Beers' *The Mind That Found Itself*. Beers wrote autobiographically about his experiences with schizophrenia (then called *dementia praecox*). His frightening institutional experiences included lashings, enchained confinement, and other sadistic affronts to his humanity. That these were commonplace in most mental-health institutions of Beers's day made the account all the more credible and moving. Beers's poignant story won sympathy from millions of readers and the support of the noted psychiatrist Adolph Meyer, whose interest led, in that same year, to the founding of the National Committee for Mental Hygiene. This committee has since become the National Association for Mental Health.

The thought-provoking message of the mental-health-oriented systems is basically this. Man is a creature of both heredity and environment. Genetic predispositions, home influences, school experiences, teachings of the church or synagogue—in fact, all the influences of life that bear on him—combine to narrow his field of independence and choice. Yet he is only partially a victim of circumstances; he also is a creature of volition. Within a delimited range, he is committed to choose and to live by his choices.

298

The related message to education is that learners cannot necessarily become what external authority may want them to become or what they themselves may want to become. Expectations for them need to be realistic. Neurotic disorders, in fact, are often the result of the failure of authority figures to accept this principle. The message even more fundamentally is that learners are individuals who vary greatly in terms of almost any given trait. They are organisms who vary in terms of cognitive abilities, mental health, physical health, social maturity, and moral values. Because students differ this widely, schools, with the aid of guidance services, have a mandate to discover what the differences specifically are, and to program discerningly in respect to them.

Need for Clinical Approaches

As schools become involved in the many tasks of programming, they soon come to realize the shortcomings of group methods as a realistic approach to many of the problems of student differences. Such instructional methods as the lecture, question-answer, discussion, textbook, round table, and student committees share the limitations of all group methods: they are much more expedient than clinically effective. These group methods are barely adequate when the goal is cognitive growth. They are usually inadequate when the goal is emotional and social growth or vocational insight. Thus the recognized need for schools to employ more individual and small-group approaches to student growth constitutes one more reason for the inception and rapid growth of the guidance movement. Guidance is dedicated to studying students as individuals, to pinpointing their problems and needs, and to helping them resolve their problems and fulfill their needs.

THREE FOCAL CONCERNS OF GUIDANCE

As mentioned at the beginning of the chapter in the definition of guidance services, guidance has focal concerns in the three areas of the *emotional, vocational,* and *educational.* All are important, all are related, none has a convincing claim to exclusiveness. And if the concerns themselves are three in number, so too are the approaches to them, which a number of writer-commentators identify as (1) remedial or

299

corrective, (2) preventive or adjustive, and (3) promotional or developmental.[1] Actually, these are ingredients of education at all levels, namely: remedial help for students who have observable problems, careful before-the-fact planning and programming to head off problems before they occur, and assistance for students to grow progressively toward their potentials.

Emotional Concerns

Our society is, in general, sympathetic toward all guidance concerns, but it is uncertain about the degree of support it should give the one in the specific area of the emotional. As with motherhood and progress, few question the desirability of such personality outcomes as self-acceptance, self-reliance, reality contact, emotional consistency, and wholesome human relationships; but many question the methods employed by the various therapeutic systems in achieving them. Also, many question whether any aspect of therapy should lie within the purview of formal education *per se*. Schools are rarely subject to attack when relying on subject matter as an avenue to emotional maturity, despite the fact that cognition *per se* has been found wanting for centuries. However, critics, particularly those of a conservative bent, become increasingly apprehensive when the schools enter into the sensitive area of counseling.

Yet the number of schools entering this province is on the increase, for several reasons. For one, as mentioned in the last paragraph, cognitive learning content itself has proved to be an unpredictable therapist. For another, the combined systems of psychiatry, psychoanalysis, clinical psychology, and social work have endowed guidance with a hard core of psychological theory and therapeutic methods that, when discerningly employer, have demonstrated their practial worth. For a third, the dangers to the world that reside in maladjusted individuals seem more ominous today than they have ever been. Ghengis Khan's power to harm was great, and Adolph Hitler's even greater, but the power potential of a maniacal leader in today's push-button world has

[1] Lawrence H. Stewart and Charles F. Warmath employ the terminology of *remedial, preventive,* and *promotional* in *The Counselor and Society* (Boston: Houghton Mifflin Company, 1965), pp. 35–43. Joseph W. and Lucile U. Hollis employ the parallel terminology of *corrective, adjustive,* and *developmental* in *Organizing for Effective Guidance* (Chicago: Science Research Associates, Inc., 1965), p. 13.

awesome dimensions. For these fundamental reasons, if for no other, schools of the present and future may have no choice but to educate for healthy emotions as well as for informed minds.

The avenues that lead toward this affective outcome consist of the following; only the first two are relatively uncontroversial.

1. *The subject-matter curriculum.* Cognition, while no guarantor of mental health, is a valuable ally. Cognition is most valuable, however, when teachers, sensitive to its potentials, relate appropriate curriculum content to the emotional lives of student learners. Great literature, for instance, as a mirror of life's universals, has exciting therapeutic possibilities. So does much of the content of the social studies, of the fine and applied arts, and of the natural sciences. The therapeutic possibilities are there; they will go untapped, however, if teachers fail to exploit them.

2. *Teachers who are mentally healthy.* A curriculum rises to its cognitive and affective apex under the leadership of teachers who themselves are emotionally healthy. Mental health, like its pathological opposite, breeds in kind. Thus, schools unquestionably educate for the healthy emotions through the example of teachers who bring healthy emotions to the classroom. Teacher education, unfortunately, is slow to recognize and program for this outcome.

3. *Therapy through direct teaching about mental-health concepts.* A number of schools incorporate the content of mental health into the curriculum. The underlying hypothesis is that teaching about mental-health concepts at appropriate readiness levels will act to prevent or alleviate emotional disorders at some later time. This hypothesis, in the opinion of some, is tenuous. But is it any more tenuous than when schools, for instance, teach the rules of fair play in a given sport in hope that students will incorporate the rules into their lives? Or when social-studies teachers teach about the freedoms in the hope of engendering an undying allegiance to them? Or when a professional therapist employs oral exchange in the hope of effecting an emotional change in a disturbed client? Verbal symbols, while not an open avenue to the emotions, constitute at least a promising one.

Several years ago, I asked this question of a sizable group of professional therapists: Should the schools make a verbal approach to the content of mental health?[2] Of the 82 who responded, approximately 60

---

[2] Gail M. Inlow, "Can the School Curriculum Make A Frontal Approach to Mental Health," *The Journal of Educational Research,* 56, No. 8 (April 1963), pp. 395–402.

percent were strongly in favor, 12 percent were undecided, and 28 percent were opposed. Topics proposed most often for curriculum inclusion were these: defense mechanisms, emotions and their effect on behavior, interpersonal relationships, the self-image, sex, and unconscious motivation. These topics, they opined, should be dealt with informally in the elementary school grades when readiness manifested itself and should be dealt with both formally and informally in the high school grades, with a meaningful course in psychology serving to pull them together.

Counseling procedures   Counseling constitutes yet a fourth approach employed by schools to help the young grow toward their emotional potentials. The counseling process, it is to be recalled, involves data gathering, data analysis, and face-to-face confrontations between counselors and counselees. The theme of the latter may at times be as uncomplicated as a minor behavior problem, or at other times as complex as neurotic or even psychotic behavior. Few find fault with counseling when it does not go beyond a teacher's or counselor's engaging in informal observation, consulting cumulative records, interviewing students in regard to academic or disciplinary matters, or interviewing parents about the problems of their children. But many question the process when it has deeper clinical implications.

With society and education itself not ready to underwrite counseling in depth, the compromise in many schools is a program that goes up to but not beyond psychological first aid. This commits a school to engage in supportive activities with disturbed pupils but not to administer anything resembling specialized, long-term therapy. The school, while being supportive to disturbed students, usually becomes involved with parents and/or appropriate community agencies to arrange the next steps in the counseling process.

Vocational Concerns

Students' emotional problems not infrequently have correlates in vocational problems. These latter, as stated early in the chapter, constituted the reason why formal education, shortly after 1908, introjected vocational guidance into its mainstream. The classical definition of vocational guidance as the process of matching people with jobs is as valid today as it ever was. However, it works effectively only when those responsible for it view people and vocations as complex and

302

Put your answers to this page in Column 1

a. Take special notice of people when you are traveling

b. Take special notice of the scenery when you are traveling

c. Take special notice of the crops when you are traveling

d. Read lessons to a blind student

e. Keep a record of traffic past a certain point

f. Interview people in a survey of public opinion

g. Go to the amusements at a country fair

h. See the exhibits of canned goods at a country fair

j. See the livestock at a country fair

k. Exercise in a gymnasium

l. Go fishing

m. Play baseball

n. Browse in a library

p. Watch a rehearsal of a large orchestra

q. Visit an aquarium

r. Collect the signatures of famous people

s. Collect butterflies

t. Collect pieces of different kinds of wood

u. Visit an exhibit of famous paintings

v. Visit an exhibit of various means of transportation

w. Visit an exhibit of laboratory equipment

x. Sell vegetables

y. Be a _____ ist

Source: From Kuder Preference Record Vocational Form CH by G. Frederic Kuder. Copyright 1948, by G. Frederic Kuder. Reprinted by permission of the publisher, Science Research Associates, Inc., Chicago, Illinois.

dynamic. The concise message to the employed of the future is this. First, have or develop a realistic understanding of yourself, including your abilities, interests, skills, and personality characteristics. Second, view the vocational world as a changing one in which job categories and job clusters, not single jobs, are the essential considerations. Within this frame, ready yourself in general education as extensively

303

Source: From the Strong Vocational Interest Blank for Women, Form TW 398, 1968; reproduced with permission of the copyright holder and publisher, Stanford University Press.

as you can, for that is the single most important requirement of most vocations.

Both vocational education and vocational guidance have had to broaden their horizons in the past several decades to keep pace with changes brought on by the electronics revolution. The central change has been an ever-increasing demand for more highly skilled workers. From 1947 until 1964, for instance, the ranks of white-collar workers rose from 34.9 to 42.2 percent. During the same period, the ranks of blue-collar workers, not including farmers, declined from 40.7 to 36.3 percent. The decline in farm workers was a dramatic one of from 14 to 6.3 percent.[3]

[3] National Commission on Technology, Automation, and Economic Progress, *Technology and the American Economy,* Vol. 1 (1966), p. 22.

EDUCATION AS AN OPERATIONAL PROCESS

Education regards vocational guidance as a long-term process, and because meaningless without self-understanding, its operating base, understandably, is general education. Vocational-guidance personnel in high schools, while operating from this nontechnical base, nonetheless engage in certain specialized activities. They administer pencil-and-paper instruments such as vocational interest inventories, personality inventories, and tests of special aptitude. They plan and conduct career-day conferences at which invited representatives from business, industry, and the professions counsel with interested student groups. They hold interviews with students about their vocational concerns. All these have the purpose of helping students learn more about themselves, particularly about their vocational interests and aptitudes.

At a more concrete level, vocational-guidance workers encourage children and youth to perform household chores, and high school youth to work summers and perhaps part-time during the later school years. They encourage high school graduates, depending on circumstances, either to continue their education or to get into occupations that match their personality profiles.

The traditionally popular course in vocations has gone by the board. So too have most other oversimplified approaches to vocational guidance. And society is the winner, for both individuals and industry have become too complex for simple methods to be meaningful, assuming they ever were.

Educational Concerns

The third major category, educational guidance, is the fastest-growing in educational circles today. The factor that more than any other has contributed to its growth is the almost obsessive interest of many, both inside and outside the ranks of formal education, in the welfare of superior learners. In 1957, Americans became almost pathologically frightened over the Sputnik affair, and since then have turned increasingly to the gifted to keep the nation strong. A sequel to Sputnik was the allocation by the National Defense Education Act, 1958, of 15 million dollars, not for guidance in general, but for educational guidance in particular, with "able students" the major beneficiaries. The guidance program that Conant proposed in *The American High School Today*, 1959, was also anchored primarily in the academics and slanted one-sidedly toward the gifted.

305

A second important contributor to the growth of educational guidance has been the mounting interest of the society in the welfare of culturally deprived children. The latter bring many specialized problems to the schools, high on the list of which are difficulties in the area of language communication. Educational guidance unquestionably has an important contribution to make in this particular area.

In the last analysis, however, the guidance program that performs its educational mission creditably is one that is involved with the educational concerns of all learners. These concerns include, but are not limited to, the administration of standardized tests, the careful interpretation of test results, and the application of the results to curriculum situations. The concerns embrace or impinge on processes as diverse as those associated with academic achievement, grade placement, homogeneous grouping, scheduling, failure, promotion, and college planning. Generally speaking, educational guidance has two centers of interest. One is the elementary and secondary schools themselves. The concerns of this center are meaningful learning activities tailored to the specialized needs of all students and the efforts of all students to measure up to their potentials. The second center is post-high school education. Its concerns are college attendance, selectively determined, for all students capable of profiting from it, and appropriate next steps, also selectively determined, for the remainder of the high school population.

I conclude by emphasizing that educational guidance is the right of all students, of the nonexceptional as well as the exceptional, just as education in America is the right of all.

ORGANIZATIONAL SCHEMES

Schools throughout the country perform their guidance functions in the context of many organizational arrangements. These tend to divide into the following four patterns: classroom-centered, homeroom-centered, specialist-centered, and combined teacher-specialist-centered.

Classroom-Centered Guidance

The most traditional of the four is one in which classroom teachers are the only, or, at least, the focal figures in a given school's guidance program. The cliché, or truism, as the case may be, that every teacher

EDUCATION AS AN OPERATIONAL PROCESS

is a guidance worker certainly takes on validity in this organizational scheme. When the scheme is other than nominal, teachers have no choice but to be counselors as well as subject-matter academicians. If anyone administers the program of standardized testing, they do. They are the ones who counsel students, who interview parents, who staff cases. In fact, irrespective of the nature of pupils' problems—whether emotional, vocational, or educational—classroom teachers are key guidance personalities. The charm of the approach is that it brings pedagogy and guidance together in the persons of single individuals. However, it is a more congenial combination in the self-contained classroom of the elementary school than in the departmentalized classroom of the secondary school. In the former, a teacher is responsible usually for not more than 25 to 30 learners; in the latter, for as many as 125 to 200. Guidance in the latter instance is inevitably a loser to the weight of numbers. And apart from numbers, the pedogogical-guidance combination, when it ascends to technical levels, imposes an impossible burden on teachers in terms of the knowledge and skills it requires.

Homeroom-Centered Guidance

The homeroom organization for guidance represents secondary education's effort to remove some of the guidance burden from classroom teachers. At the junior high school level, as developed in Chapter 7, it frequently takes the form of the block-time class in which English, social studies, and guidance activities constitute the responsibilities of a single teacher. In the senior high school, the homeroom, if it exists, is customarily a separate organizational entity that meets from once weekly to daily for varying periods of time. To be effective, the homeroom plan should meet the following criteria:

1. Utilize the services only of teachers who are knowledgeable about and interested in guidance concerns and activities
2. Meet often enough and long enough for guidance to become operational [A reasonable target is two 40-minute period per week.]
3. Lighten the teaching load of homeroom teachers in recognition of their guidance efforts
4. Follow a guidance-curriculum arrangement that possesses at least a modicum of structure
5. Restrict homeroom enrollments to manageable numbers

307

Specialist-Centered Guidance

Schools that recognize the guidance limitations of the typical classroom or homeroom and that desire to rise above them usually adopt some kind of centralized organizational plan. In it, guidance workers may not be classroom teachers at all. Instead, they may be full-time "generalist" counselors, vocational counselors *per se*, psychometricians, visiting teachers, school psychologists, or individuals with other titles too numerous to be detailed here. The number of guidance specialists in any given school and the specific duties any or all may perform are ever a function of the philosophy, needs, and financial structure of a given school.

The advantages of a school's having one or more qualified specialists in the guidance area are considerable. The most basic advantage is the greater depth of technical insight that such individuals are able to bring to a school. A second one is the release of classroom teachers from guidance responsibilities for which they may be inadequately qualified. A third one is the greater accessibility of counseling services to students. Balanced against these advantages, however, is the possible disadvantage of classroom teaching and counseling becoming too widely separate, the result being teachers who are one-sidedly academic and who refer atypical cases too casually; and, relatedly, specialist counselors who are one-sidedly clinical and who operate too far outside the academic mainstream of education. The ideal, of course, is for both teachers and specialists to play their respective roles co-operatively and sensitively to the end of an articulated professional effort.

Combined Teacher-specialist Guidance

A fourth organizational approach is one in which selected teachers with specialized guidance qualifications combine the two roles of teaching and centralized counseling. One teacher, for instance, might teach three high school classes and also serve as the school's vocational counselor. A second teacher might instruct in a block-time class in a junior high school and also be the school's emotional counselor or testing technician. This combined teaching-counselor arrangement works best in a departmental school setting; least well in a self-contained classroom school setting. Its major advantage is that it keeps teaching and counsel-

308

ing together. Its major disadvantage is that specialized guidance skills in classroom teachers are not usually present in sufficient quantity or quality.

GUIDANCE PRINCIPLES

Irrespective of the differential organizational shapes of school guidance programs, the same body of principles generally governs all of them. This body, selectively, embraces the following: (1) individualism is the central value; (2) guidance is a two-way process; (3) problem causality invariably is multidimensioned; and (4) guidance takes place at different operational levels.

Individualism as the Central Value

Guidance, like all other educational processes, starts and ends with individualism as the central value. Guidance shares this principle with social forces as exalted as the Constitution of the United States, the Judeo-Christian ethic, and most therapeutic systems. Each in its own way posits humanness as a supreme value but also as a demanding taskmaster. In this latter role, at least at the level of the ideal, it is satisfied only when individuals realize their potentials. The goal thus is optimum development of individuals in the several areas of the cognitive, the affective, and the psychomotor. Rugged individualism falls short of this goal for reason of its egocentricity. But so too does "other-directed" conformity for reason of its value sterility. Within a frame of individualism maturely conceived, "the status quo is no more or no less than a point of departure for change. The *what is* continuously concedes to the *what should be*."[4]

Guidance as a Two-way Process

As students strive to realize their potentials, the proper role of guidance personnel is as partners with students. In this role, they gather information about pupils, collate and relate it to problems, give emotional support to pupils as called for, and assist in the formulation of solutions to their problems.

A decade or two ago, one of the more controversial issues in education was whether counselors should play detached, unassertive roles or active, assertive ones. The issue invariably pitted Carl Rogers and his nondirective system of counseling against a diverse group devoted to direct counseling methods. The debate, for the most part, was an exercise in futility, however. For one reason, the debaters generally argued as if counseling had the same dimensions in all situations, which it does not. For a second reason, each misrepresented the position of the opposition. The nondirectivists were depicted as doing and saying almost nothing at all in counseling situations. And the directivists were depicted as advising almost to a point of ordering clients to act.

Most today assume a middle position that includes the following tenets. The focal center of all counseling, irrespective of circumstances,

[4] Gail M. Inlow, *The Emergent in Curriculum* (New York: John Wiley & Sons, Inc., 1966), p. 5.

is always the counselee. Counseling approaches and methods are situational, never stereotyped. Generally speaking, the true role of any counselor is to help counselees to help themselves. A counselor does this best when he observes carefully, when he is an informed resource person, when he is empathic. He listens, he volunteers, he questions, he articulates, he summarizes, he assesses. In the last analysis, however, it is the counselee who makes final decisions and takes action based on them. And even more important, it is the counselee who has to assume responsibility for whatever action he elects to take.

In the area of educational guidance, counselors tend to be somewhat more assertive than in other guidance areas. They not infrequently, for instance, take firm stands on whether or not a student needs to repeat a grade or subject, whether or not he enrolls in an honors or a remedial class, whether or not he participates in many extracurricular activities or in just a few. In the area of vocational guidance, counselors tend to be relatively unassertive. They may explain, they may interpret, but they usually resist the temptation of giving "superior" advice. In the area of the emotional, counselors predicably are unassertive. Yet the posture they assume even in it is always a function of the case at hand. Thus it, too, resists stereotyping. Counseling, we repeat, is a two-way relationship, with the roles of counselors and counselees inevitably differing from situation to situation.

Multidimensioned Problems

In most counseling situations, problems tend to appear initially as unadulterated and simple; once understood, however, they tend to take on more complex dimensions. Thus they rarely are discreetly academic, or emotional, or physical, or social; more often, they constitute a syndrome that comprises several or all of these. A given student, for instance, may be failing a course as much for emotional reasons as for academic ones. And another may be maladaptive not because of unsocial tendencies but because of an antipathy toward physical changes associated with the onset of adolescence.

This tendency of problems to have complex roots and characteristics constitutes an important reason why schools should not sharply divide the responsibility for guidance among narrowly oriented specialists. Specialization, in fact, in any area of life easily loses perspective when not built on a solid general base. Thus, guidance workers, **311**

ideally, should be reasonably effective in all phases of school guidance even though organizationally and functionally slanted perhaps more toward one phase than toward others.

Guidance as a Function of Levels

As already established in the section on organizational schemes, guidance takes place at different levels. It takes place in the school at the level of the classroom or homeroom teacher and of the guidance specialist. It takes place outside the school at the level of any therapist. The important requirement, in this connection, is for guidance personnel at every level to operate within the frame of reasonable expectations. Classroom teachers usually are not personnel specialists, and personnel specialists may not be classroom teachers. Yet each customarily has an important niche in a school's guidance program.

Classroom teachers constitute the first line of defense. This is true whether they are with pupils five to six hours daily, as in most elementary schools, or for only a single period, as in most secondary

312

schools. They perform their guidance functions in a number of ways, their goal being the better understanding of pupils and enhancement of their growth. Teachers study pupils in a wide variety of ways, utilizing selectively the following techniques or methods: informal observation, formal observation, tests, inventories, home questionnaires, pupil interviews, parent interviews, sociometric devices, anecdotes, written work, oral work, the health record, the academic record, and the occasional case study. Many teachers are masters of none of these, but all teachers, because they are *de facto* guidance workers, should understand and use at least some of them routinely.

I state again that classroom teachers do not have to be, and most are not, guidance experts. But they are parent surrogates who have moved through a sequence of professional experiences designed to make them more than subject-matter academicians. They assuredly are guidance workers. And when they play their roles conscientiously and sensitively, the magnitude of their contributions to student growth can be inestimable.

The homeroom or block-time teacher is usually somewhat more specialized in guidance know-how and practices than most classroom teachers, but the difference is not customarily great. The difference becomes greater, however, when centralized specialists (either at the system or school level) constitute the base of comparison. These, whether in areas of emotional, vocational, or educational counseling, have to meet—at least in certain states—professional standards high enough to exclude academic generalists from their ranks. Although specialists, most have also been teachers; thus they tend to retain their academic skills and interests while performing specialized functions. This is as it should be.

When guidance problems become acute or prolonged, schools generally recommend that parents seek help outside the school. Under such circumstances, school guidance personnel serve as referral agents. And because the majority of serious cases have emotional causality, referrals customarily are made to private therapists, hospital clinics, or public-health and family agencies.

MEDIA OF APPRAISAL

As classroom teachers, homeroom teachers and specialist counselors engage in the complex task of pupil appraisal, they usually have at their

313

disposal, and thus tend to employ, an extensive assortment of methods and techniques. I have selected ten of the most frequently employed of these for brief development in this section, deliberately passing over, because of space limitations, such methods and techniques as the autobiography, the formal anecdote, sociometric devices, and the diary. The ten to be treated subsequently consist of the following:

1. Observation
2. Standardized tests
3. Personality and interest inventories
4. Home questionnaire
5. Interview
6. Health record
7. Academic record
8. Home visit
9. Case study
10. Follow-up of school graduates

Observation

Of the many appraisal media in the repertoire of guidance counselors at all levels, observation, with little question, is indispensable. Observation is psychological viewing. It is the study of such behavior manifestations as words, facial expressions, and kinesthetic reactions, all of which contribute to the insight of a knowledgeable observer. Many underestimate the value of informal observation for reason of its subjectivity. Admittedly, it is subjective, but it is not to be deprecated for that. Statesman and foreign diplomats certainly do not deprecate it. Neither do knowledgeable individuals in such other service pursuits as social work, medicine, and personnel interviewing. The rational and affective processes embrace the tangibles of body chemistry, neurons, glands, and organs. But these, because they express themselves psychologically as well as physiologically, lend themselves both to subjective and objective assessment. Thus informal observation plays an important role in almost all guidance situations.

Standardized Tests

This second guidance tool, standardized testing, is as intrinsically objective as informal observation is intrinsically subjective; yet neither is exclusively one or the other. Irrespective of this issue, standardized

314

```
    YEAR XI  (6 tests, 2 months each; or 4 tests, 3 months each)
[  ]   1. *Memory for designs I   (same as IX, 3)   (1½+)   [  ]
[  ]   2. *Verbal absurdities IV   (2+)   [  ]
            a).................................................................................................
            b).................................................................................................
            c).................................................................................................
[  ]   3. *Abstract words II   (same as XIII, 2)   (3+)   [  ]
            a) Connection.................................................................................
            b) Compare.....................................................................................
            c) Conquer......................................................................................
            d) Obedience...................................................................................
            e) Revenge......................................................................................
[  ]   4. Memory for sentences II   (1+)   [  ]
            a) At the summer camp the children get up early in the morning to go swimming.
            b) Yesterday we went for a ride in our car along the road that crosses the bridge.
[  ]   5. Problem situation II   (±)   [  ]
[  ]   6. *Similarities: Three things   (3+)   [  ]
            a) Snake — cow — sparrow.............................................................
            b) Rose — potato — tree.................................................................
            c) Wool — cotton — leather............................................................
            d) Knifeblade — penny — piece of wire...........................................
            e) Book — teacher — newspaper.....................................................
.......  Alternate. Finding reasons II   (2+)   [  ]
            a).................................................................................................
            b).................................................................................................
_____  Mos. credit at Year XI
```

Source: Sample page from Stanford-Binet Intelligence Scale, Form L-M (Boston: Houghton-Mifflin Company, 1960). Reprinted by permission.

testing made its advent in 1905 when Binet and Simon presented to the world its first intelligence test. That event precipitated a movement that, before long, was to assume dramatic proportions. *The Sixth Mental Measurements Yearbook,* for instance, includes a listing of 1219 tests and 795 test reviews prepared by 396 reviewers.[5]

A test that is standardized is one that meets the following criteria.

1. It has been prepared with professional care and precision.
2. It is valid: that is, it tests essentially what it is supposed to test.
3. It is reliable: that is, it leads essentially to the same testing outcomes each time it, or a comparable instrument, is administered to a given group.
4. It has statistical norms that permit the conversion of raw scores to relative scores. The relative base might consist, for instance, of

[5] Oscar K. Buros (ed.), *The Fifth Mental Measurements Yearbook* (Highland Park, N.J.: Gryphon Press, 1965), p. xxx.

percentile scores, grade-placement scores, age-equivalent scores, or quartile scores. A raw score of 170, when converted, might thus appear as a derived score at the 80th percentile; as a score of 15 years, 6 months; or as one in the first quartile. The advantage of this arrangement is obvious: guidance personnel and testees themselves are able to interpret test results on a comparative as well as absolute basis.

The three most common categories of standardized tests used in schools today are achievement, intelligence, and special aptitude. Some of the better-known instruments in the first two categories (inclusion of the third would require too much detail) consist of the following:

1a. Achievement (elementary and junior high school)
California Achievement Tests
Iowa Tests of Basic Skills
Metropolitan Achievement Tests
Sequential Tests of Educational Progress
Stanford Achievement Test

1b. Achievement (senior high school)
Co-operative Achievement Tests
Iowa Tests of Educational Development
Sequential Tests of Educational Progress

2. Intelligence (various levels)
California Test of Mental Maturity, Long Form, group (kindergarten-college)
Kuhlmann-Anderson Test, Booklets G and H, group (grades 7–12)
Lorge-Thorndike Intelligence Tests, group (K–12)
Revised Stanford-Binet Intelligence Tests, Form L-M, individual (age two to adulthood)
SRA Primary Mental Abilities Tests, group (ages five to seventeen)
Wechsler Intelligence Scales, individual, Children's Scale, WISC (ages five to fifteen); adult Scale, WAIS individual (ages sixteen and over)

Standardized testing, in essence, is a controlled method of observation. It enables guidance personnel to study students individually and in groups. Specifically, it enables them to ascertain intellectual ability and potential, to assess performance against both, and to act on the data that such analysis provides. Standardized testing is not an exact

process; definitely not a panacea. But guidance and education would be tremendous losers without it.

Inventories

Inventories, although belonging in a general way to the category of standardized tests, differ sufficiently to receive separate treatment here. The essential difference is that responses to *test* items are right or wrong, with an external standard always the criterion. Responses to *inventory* items, in contrast, are neither right nor wrong; instead, they are mirrors of personality intangibles and vary with individuals. Two types of inventories, personality and vocational interest, are the ones most often employed in schools.

Personality inventories By eliciting responses from an individual across a broad range of concerns, this type of inventory purports to weave a personality profile from the results. Personality inventories contain such items as the following:

> I daydream a lot.
> I feel that people steal my important ideas.
> Thoughts about sex upset me.
> I like people.
> Life has been kind to me.
> I get apprehensive in crowds.

Educators and psychologists, although attracted by the possibilities that reside in personality inventories, are, at present, skeptical about their validity. The basic question is whether pencil-and-paper items are capable of opening the doors of personality in any significant way. A related question is whether individuals are capable of being sufficiently objective about themselves to give honest answers to stimulus items. A third related one is whether individuals withhold answers that go against the social grain of the culture. And a fourth is whether schools have an ethical right to probe into the personalities of students. Until these questions receive satisfactory answers, schools need to move cautiously in this clinical direction.

Vocational-interest inventories This type of inventory has evolved in two developmental ways. The Strong Vocational Interest Blanks (a separate one for men and women) are illustrative of one way. Their creator, E. K. Strong, studied the interests of men in 56 occupational

317

categories and of women in 30. Then he constructed two inventories, each of which contains 400 items covering a wide range of human interests. Testees answer each of the items with a response of Like, Indifferent, or Dislike. Testees ultimately receive grades of C, C+, B−, B, B+, or A as indicators of how closely their expressed interests correspond to those of members of each of the many occupational groups. The assumption is that an affinity of interests in general is a valid predictor of vocational interests in particular. Only grades of A or B+ are regarded as valid indicators.

The Kuder Preference Record is illustrative of the second approach. The creator, C. F. Kuder, started out by dividing the occupational world into the following ten categories: outdoor, mechanical, computational, scientific, persuasive, artistic, literary, musical, social service, and clerical. Then he developed items and grouped them in clusters of three, having testees indicate which interest in each category they would like to pursue *most* and *least*. One cluster, for example, contains the following three alternatives: Visit an art gallery, browse in a library, visit a museum. A preference for the first presumably indicates an artistic interest; for the second, a literary interest; for the third, a scientific interest. The ultimate result of the Kuder Preference Record is a profile that, in percentiles, indicates the relative interests of testees in each of the ten occupational categories.

Interest inventories, generally speaking, are more stable than personality inventories. Thus they tend to have greater stature in the guidance programs of most schools.

Home Questionnaire

The home and family questionnaire serves as yet another valuable source of information about pupils. A parent or guardian customarily completes it when a child enters kindergarten and then updates it periodically. The home questionnaire customarily elicits, under the following headings, data pertaining to appropriate members, young and old alike, of all cooperating households.

1. names
2. educational status
3. occupational status
4. special talents
5. whether home is owned or rented

6. leisure-time interests
7. languages spoken
8. publications subscribed to
9. organizational affiliations
10. special interests in school affairs

EDUCATION AS AN OPERATIONAL PROCESS

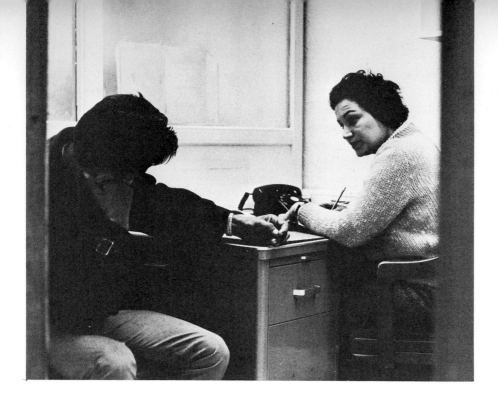

Interview

As mentioned several times previously, the interview has a place of importance in any counselor's storehouse of personnel methods. We conceive the interview in the present context as involving a face-to-face, give-and-take relationship between two individuals in which both have a high degree of functional autonomy and freedom. The content of the interview in any defensible guidance frame is never rigidly structured. It has more structure in some situations and less in others, but in all it evolves from the dynamics of the face-to-face confrontation itself.

All interviews, irrespective of their exact dimensions, succeed or fail depending on two factors: (1) whether a given counselor and counselee are able to establish a comfortable professional relationship, and (2) whether they have the combined ability and desire to identify, understand, and solve problems. In respect to the first, the counselor is always the one on whom responsibility falls for establishing and maintaining rapport. This he does by projecting warmth, by being interested and helpful, and by being permissive. In respect to the second, "the problem is the thing." And problem-solving always demands careful identification of problems; mature understanding of the problems; and

319

the deriving of solutions that are first conceptualized, then tried out, and finally evaluated.

Throughout this problem-solving process, the counselor, even though one of two partners, plays a specialized role. In it, he accepts, clarifies, guides, questions, and even, at times, contributes his own ideas. But he refuses to accept final responsibility for decision-making. Rather, he places the onus for that upon the counselee, where it belongs. Within that frame, he plays the role of supporting, helping personality. As I have stated elsewhere,[6]

> . . . the principles of the interview have this message for counselors at any level; help students with problems by providing necessary information, by correcting obvious errors of substance, and by generally sharpening up issues, but don't dictate future action. . . . The over-all goal of independence is, at best, never easy to reach . . . [In this regard,] it is better that there should be an occasional error of student choice than that he . . . not have the right to make it.

Health Record

The medical record that in one form or another almost all schools maintain on children and youth has guidance value conceivably too obvious to require discussion here. The record is important for the story that it tells about physical health. It is important also for the story that it communicates, at least occasionally, in regard to the psychosomatic disorders of students. In either event, it constitutes one more significant source of information for guidance workers.

Academic Record

Like the health record, the academic record has obvious guidance value. It provides interested classroom teachers and specialized counselors with a picture of any student's academic performance over a period of time. It assumes particular significance when revealing phenomena such as inconsistency of pupil performance within any given time period, achievement that belies ability, achievement with noticeable variation from subject-matter area to subject-matter area, and achievement that makes college plans stand out as reasonable or unreasonable.

[6] Gail M. Inlow, *Maturity in High School Teaching* 2d Ed. (Englewood Cliffs, N.J.: Prentice-Hall, Inc., 1970).

The academic record is more than a bare account of course marks earned or given over a period of time. Much more than that, it may well be the door to valuable insights in breadth.

Home Visit

Visits to the homes of students stand high on the list of desirable personnel practices. However, such visits, at the practical level, pose a number of hard-to-resolve problems. For elementary school teachers to visit the homes of 25 to 30 pupils is not an easy task. And for high school teachers to visit the homes of 125 to 150 pupils is virtually an impossible one. Most schools thus resort to the home visit selectively. They send specialist counselors to the homes of pupils who are having more than their share of adjustment problems. This method, while admittedly bringing school and home more closely together, is not preventative, treating problems only after they have come to light.

The compromise in most elementary schools is for the home to come to the school, rather than the reverse. Parents confer with teachers periodically in the classrooms where their children are enrolled. The compromise of the New Trier Township High School of Winnetka, Illinois, however, is to retain the home-visit script but to implement it in a specialized way. At this high school, the chairman of each freshman advisory room visits the homes of all students assigned to his room. Matthew Gaffney, an outstanding superintendent of an earlier generation, initiated this procedure almost a half century ago, and it is one that the high school still follows today. Mass education keeps even the New Trier High School from attaining the home-school ideal, though the New Trier school strikes at least a reasonable compromise with it.

Case Study

The case study is yet another guidance technique that contributes to the cause of pupil understanding and, hence, pupil adjustment. Because of its detailed nature, centralized personnel staffs are more likely than classroom teachers to employ it. Furthermore, such staffs tend to employ it most in instances of highly disturbed pupils. In District 108 of Highland Park, Illinois, for example, the technique fits into the follow-

ing organizational arrangement. Any teacher who, after conscientious and persistent effort, is unable to "reach" a given pupil asks the central guidance office for assistance. The teacher presents relevant facts and articulates the central issue. The guidance office counters with a case study developed around that issue.

A few years back, a first-grade teacher in the Shaker Heights, Ohio, school system was conscious of failing the needs of a six-year-old pupil. The academic work the youngster did he did outstandingly well. But during most of every school day, he was autistic and detached. A case study revealed an IQ of 170 and a curriculum that failed almost completely to challenge. Armed with this new information, the teacher, a capable one, enriched the curriculum for the boy, involved him more purposefully in it, and thus soon got the problem under control.

The case study, in effect, entails a problem-solving approach. The essentials are observation, sensing the problem, gathering and pinpointing the data, concluding from the data, and testing out the conclusions. Some case studies are intricately elaborate because they deal with problems that are commensurately elaborate. Other ones are uncomplicated because the problems dealt with are uncomplicated.

Follow-up Studies

Certain schools interested in, and financially capable of, doing so regularly or often conduct follow-up studies of graduates. The data-gatherings methods customarily employed consist of questionnaires, letters, and interviews. Such studies constitute one source of possible insight into the effectiveness of the curriculums and instructional programs of the schools involved. Although not magnifying the importance of such studies, we see definite value in them. The chief obstacle to their employment is time and research costs. Yet these generally are not prohibitive.

THE CENTRAL GUIDANCE ISSUE

The central issue of guidance is the same as that of education itself: guidance or education for what purposes, guidance or education toward what ends? The answer of some is a *cultural model* constructed in the image of social norms and societal expectations. Such a model has the

322

advantage associated with social "status quoism" along any dimension —the security of changelessness. But if it has this advantage, it also has two disadvantages: one is the sterility of changelessness and the other is the loss of individualism to social sanction when the latter becomes the sole guiding force.

The answer of others is a *developmental model* to reflect growth expectancy at sequential stages of chronological development. Such a model, however, needs to resist the tendency of holding up group averages as a goal of all individuals in a particular age category. When it resists this tendency, it has merit.

The answer of still a third group—and one that I personally endorse —is the *individual model*. This latter is not discrete in the sense that it operates completely outside the frame of social and developmental expectancy. Such would be impossible as well as defeating. Rather, it uses cultural and developmental expectancy as a growth base, while building toward the ultimate of individual growth. This ultimate is total personality fulfillment, which comes closest to attainment in a world where freedom, healthy emotions, healthy social relationships, knowledgeability, reflective thought, and a satisfying code of living stand as towering values. Comparably, it comes closest to attainment in an educational-guidance setting which helps individuals to free themselves from undue dependence on external authority, from self-centeredness, from social withdrawal, from false fears, from ignorance, from unreasonable aspirations, and from ill-conceived life values.

In brief, the center of guidance is the individual. The goal is a combined one of self-identity and fulfillment. The scope embraces both the rational and the irrational components. Thus a movement that had only a vocational base in 1908 has a base today that is as broad as personality itself.

To
Stimulate
Thought

1. The following statement appears early in the chapter: Learners cannot necessarily become what external authority wants them to become. Relate this statement to fixed curriculum standards that pupils have to meet to be eligible for promotion. Do you regard such an approach as tenable?

2. Take a stand and defend it, pro or con, on the statement: Schools should have the staff services of clinical psychologists and/or psychiatrists, whose responsibility it is to administer to the emotional needs of students.

3. Also take a stand and defend it, pro or con, on the statement: Schools should employ cognitive approaches only in attempting to meet the emotional needs of students.

4. Develop the theme that mental health, like its pathological opposite, breeds in kind.

5. Should high schools include a course in psychology as part of their general-education curriculum? Why or why not? If your answer is yes, describe broadly what the nature of the content should be.

6. General education is the single most important approach to most vocations. Elaborate this statement, pro or con.

7. Should the gifted receive more attention proportionately in the schools than the average or slow? Defend your stand.

8. For a hypothetical school that you characterize, describe the guidance organization you think it should have.

9. Observe some individual carefully for as long a period as you practically can. Note such mannerisms as facial expression, posture, kinetic movement, speech habits, and verbal connotations. Then from these data alone, write up a thumbnail sketch of the person.

10. An adoption of the so-called *individual model* in education might well lead students to question the status quo in many areas of life. In this connection, which of the following, if any, do you think should be off limits to such questioning: school policy, home values, social customs, the democratic way, religion? Defend your answers.

REFERENCES

Arnhoff, Franklyn, Eli A. Rubenstein, and Joseph C. Speisman, *Manpower for Mental Health* (Chicago: Aldine Publishing Company, 1969).

Buros, Oscar K. (ed.), *The Sixth Measurement Yearbook* (Highland Park, N.J.: Gryphon Press, 1965).

Davis, Frederick B., *Educational Measurements and their Interpretation* (Belmont, Calif.: Wadsworth Publishing Company, Inc., 1964).

Ebel, Robert L., *Measuring Educational Achievement* (Englewood Cliffs, N.J.: Prentice-Hall, Inc., 1965).

Hollis, Joseph W., and Lucile U. Hollis, *Organizing for Effective Guidance* (Chicago: Science Research Associates, Inc., 1965).

Miller, Carroll H., *Guidance Services* (New York: Harper & Row, Publishers, 1965).

Miller, Frank W., *Guidance Principles and Services*, rev. ed. (Columbus, Ohio: Charles E. Merrill Books, Inc., 1968).

Ohlsen, Merle M., *Guidance Services in the Modern School* (New York: Harcourt, Brace & World, Inc., 1964).

Roeber, Edward C., *The School Counselor* (Washington, D.C.: The Center for Applied Research in Education, 1963).

Shakow, David, *Clinical Psychology as Science and Profession* (Chicago: Aldine Publishing Company, 1969).

Smith, Fred B., and Sam Adams, *Educational Measurement for the Classroom Teacher* (New York: Harper & Row, Publishers, 1966).

Stewart, Lawrence H., and Charles F. Warmath, *The Counselor and Society* (Boston: Houghton Mifflin Company, 1965).

Tyler, Leona E., *The Work of the Counselor*, 2nd Ed. (New York: Appleton-Century-Crofts, 1961).

Weinberg, Carl, *Social Foundations of Educational Guidance* (Glencoe, Ill.: The Free Press, 1969).

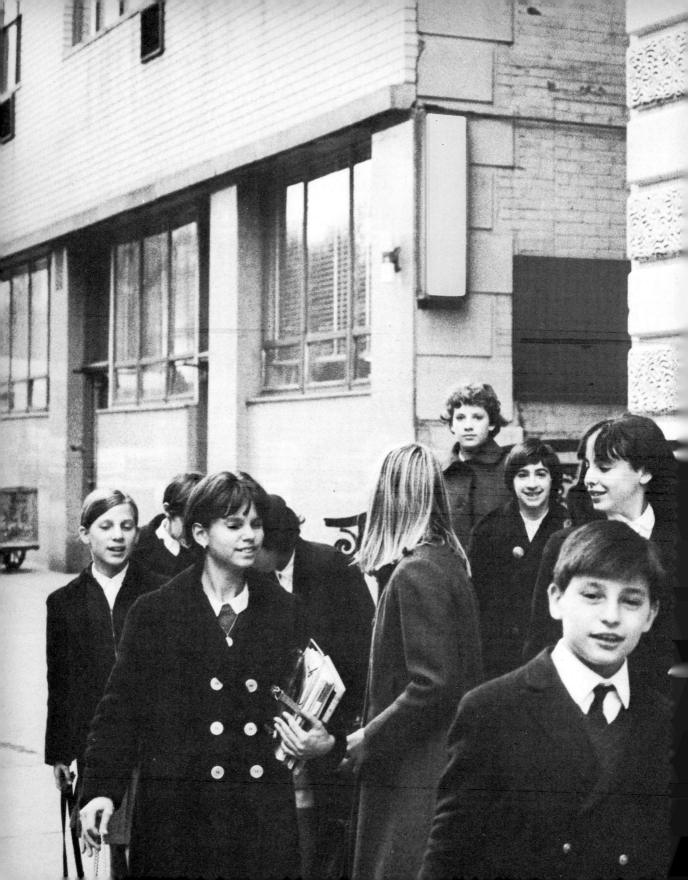

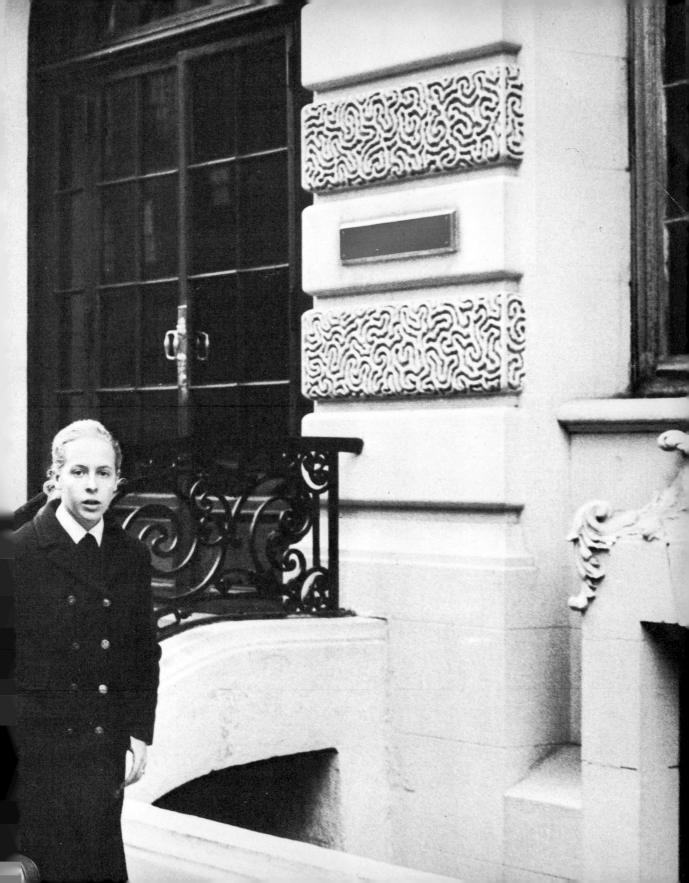

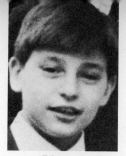

Chapter
12

**Nonpublic
Education**

1742: Moravian Seminary (for girls), Germantown, Pennsylvania
1751: Benjamin Franklin's Academy (for boys), Philadelphia
1778: Andover Academy, Andover, Massachusetts
1781: Phillips Exeter Academy, Exeter, New Hampshire
1821: Emma Willard School, Middlebury, Vermont
1837: Mount Holyoke Seminary, South Hadley, Massachusetts
1860: Staunton Military School, Staunton, Virginia (the first military school)
1897: Gilman School, Baltimore, Maryland (the first country day school)

These and hundreds of other independent schools kept America literate prior to the advent of universal public education. Once public education became dominant in the country, parochial and private schools, for a half century or more, lived through a period of considerable uncertainty. During this period, even their right to exist was chronically in doubt. The issue, as indicated in Chapter 4, was categorically resolved in 1925 at the federal Supreme Court level. The situation that led to a resolution of the issue was as follows. In 1922, the State of Oregon passed a law requiring all children to attend public schools, directing that the transition from nonpublic to public schools be completed by not later than September 1, 1926. The Catholic Church, in the now famous case of *Pierce et al v. Society of Sisters*, 268 U.S. 510 (1925), challenged the Oregon law all the way to the Supreme Court, which, in 1925, handed down the following precedent-setting decision:

The fundamental theory of liberty upon which all governments in this Union repose excludes any general power of the State to standardize its children by forcing them to accept instruction from public teachers only. The child is not the mere creature of the State; those who nurture him and direct his destiny have the right, coupled with the high duty, to recognize

and prepare him for additional obligations . . . [However], no question is raised concerning the power of the State reasonably to regulate all schools, to inspect, supervise, and examine them, their teachers, and pupils. . . .

This significant pronouncement, made by the highest legal body in the land, established for the future the legal right of parochial and private schools to exist. Certain details of their relationship to the respective states, however, remained for subsequent laws and court enactments to decide. We are living through, and will continue for decades to live through, this important period of decision making. Certain aspects of it will be covered later in the chapter in the section pertaining to law and the independent school.

SOME STATISTICS

Nonpublic schools, as the following current statistics attest, is big business on many counts.

TABLE 12.1

Number of schools, by level	elementary	15,340†
	secondary	4,606†
		19,946†
Number of schools, by type	day schools	18,700*
	boarding schools	800*
		19,500
Pupil enrollments	elementary	4,600,000
	secondary	1,400,000
	(13.5 percent of all enrollments)	6,000,000‡
Number of teachers (full-time and part-time)		231,000
Operating expenditure	3.5 billion yearly compared with 21 billion yearly for public education.**	

* Figures are approximate.
† Kenneth A. Simon and W. Vance Grant, *Digest of Educational Statistics 1968* (Washington, D.C.: U.S. Department of Health, Education, and Welfare, 1968), p. 6. Figures are approximate.
‡ Simon and Grant, p. 31.
** J. Marion Snapper, "Contributions of Independent Education," in McGarry and Ward, p. 104.

In 1962, boarding schools, exclusive of those for physically or psychologically handicapped children, divided by number into the following categories as indicated.

Boys' elementary schools	40
Boys' secondary schools	213
Boys' elementary and secondary schools	24
Military and naval schools, elementary and/or secondary	86
Girls' elementary schools	12
Girls' secondary schools	196
Girls' elementary and secondary schools	58
Coeducational elementary schools	31
Coeducational secondary schools	122
Coeducational elementary and secondary schools	37
	819[2]

In respect once again to pupil enrollments, totals for both church-related and nonchurch-related schools are essentially as presented in Table 12.2 (see the footnote to that table).

The following two generalizations emerge from Table 12.2. The first is that nonpublic education in this country is predominantly sectarian. Of the 6,304,772 students enrolled in nonpublic schools in 1965–1966, 5,963,502, or 94.59 percent, made up the student bodies of church-related schools.

A second generalization explicit in Table 12.2 is that nonpublic education is not only predominantly sectarian but also predominantly Roman Catholic sectarian. Of all nonpublic school students in the country in 1965–1966, the 5,481,325 enrolled in Roman Catholic schools made up 86.94 percent of the total: 88.69 percent in elementary education, 80.74 percent in secondary education. The Lutheran and Seventh Day Adventist churches held second and third places, respectively, in enrollment totals.

Other data of at least some significance include the following. The ten states with the greatest number of nonpublic school enrollments consist, in the order listed, of New York, Pennsylvania, Illinois, Ohio, Michigan, New Jersey, California, Massachusetts, Wisconsin, and Missouri. Combined, they account for 70 percent of nonpublic enrollment totals in the nation. Furthermore, in the eight states of Rhode Island,

[2] Totals were extrapolated from Paul Bauer, *The Boarding School Directory of the United States*, Vol. 2, 1966–1969 (Chicago: Educational Bureau, Inc., 1966).

TABLE 12.2   ENROLLMENTS IN NONPUBLIC SCHOOLS, 1965–1966, BY TYPE OF ORGANIZATIONAL CONTROL OF THE SCHOOLS*

		Elementary	Secondary	Totals
A.	Church-related			
	1. Baptist	19,287	5,902	25,189
	2. Christian Reformed	30,065	12,210	42,275
	3. Friends	5,533	5,039	10,572
	4. Jewish	42,091	10,498	52,589
	5. Lutheran	171,598	16,923	188,521
	6. Methodist	3,528	2,094	5,622
	7. Presbyterian	2,795	1,971	4,766
	8. Protestant Episcopal	30,633	17,949	48,582
	9. Catholic (Roman)	4,370,277	1,111,048	5,481,325
	10. Seventh Day Adventist	44,487	18,116	62,603
	11. Other	26,766	14,692	41,458
	Subtotals	4,747,060	1,216,442	5,963,502
B.	Nonchurch-related	181,622	159,648	341,270
	Totals	4,928,682	1,376,090	6,304,772

* Simon and Grant, . . . p. 32. Selected totals presented in Table 12.2 differ somewhat from their counterparts presented previously in Table 12.1. The totals for pupil enrollments presented in Table 12.1 (4,600,000 elementary and 1,400,000 secondary) are for the year 1968–1969; furthermore, they are only approximations. The comparable totals presented in Table 12.1 (4,928,682 elementary and 1,376,090 secondary) are for the year 1965–1966; they too are only close approximations.

New Hampshire, New York, Wisconsin, Massachusetts, New Jersey, Illinois, and Pennsylvania, nonpublic school enrollments are in excess of 20 percent of all enrollment totals in each of the states. Rhode Island is highest with 29.22 percent; Pennsylvania is eighth with 20.22 percent.

SOME CHARACTERISTICS OF PRIVATE SCHOOLS

Private schools in this country, viewed collectively, go back to the founding Colonies, and, before that, to their historically famous English counterparts. The concept of private schooling rests comfortably in the nation's traditions of individualism, this despite the class consciousness of some of the schools themselves. The fact of their existence attests to the willingness of a democracy, whenever possible, to offer people

social choices, including educational ones. As indicated in Table 12.2, private schools in the country enroll approximately 340,000 students. This total, however, is far from commensurate with the importance of private education as a social influence in the American culture.

Private schools vary widely in type and scope. They exist differentially as schools for boys, schools for girls, or schools for both sexes. They exist as elementary schools, as secondary schools, or as both types. They exist and operate as country day schools, residential schools, small-family schools, large highly structured ones, Latin schools, military schools, farm schools, and college-preparatory schools —these are just some of the many.

Within this frame of difference, however, they share many common features. An obvious one is the requirement of tuition payments from most enrollees. As of 1959–1960, tuition rates in the Middle Atlantic region, selectively, were as follows: for sixth-grade girls in day schools, a median of $675 yearly, with a range of $460 to $1,100; for for sixth-grade boys, a median of $750 yearly, with a range of $565 to $1,000. Comparable rates for girls and boys, respectively, for the twelfth grade were $837, and $600 to $1,150; $875, and $570 to $1,250.[3] An educated guess is that most tuition rates have increased from 20 to 25 percent in the interim period. For students in attendance at private boarding schools, total costs rarely fall below $2,000 per year and not infrequently exceed $3,000.

A number of private schools today, desirous of extending the range of social and economic heterogeneity in their student populations, are granting scholarships in increasing numbers to students eligible in all but financial ways. This practice understandably accentuates funding as a critical requirement in at least some private schools. In respect to this issue of financial structure, private schools, according to one estimate, derive income from the following sources: 85.3 percent from tuition, 4 percent from special gifts, 3.6 percent from endowments and 7.1 percent from "other sources."[4]

In addition to their funding similarities, private schools, within the range of admitted variability, share a number of curriculum similarities. For the most part, they, more than their public school counterparts, tend to assign the academic subjects a more dominant role, and the

[3] Roger F. Murray, III, "Financing the School" in William Johnson (ed.), *A Handbook for Independent School Operation* (Princeton, N.J.: D. Van Nostrand Company, Inc., 1961), p. 185.

[4] Murray, p. 192.

fine- and applied-arts subjects, a less dominant one. And because they are more traditionally oriented, private schools engage less in curriculum experimentation, and accordingly are slower to make changes in curriculum practices dictated by such experimentation.

Yet despite this tendency of private schools to perpetuate time-honored patterns and practices, a growing number today are resisting it at the action level. These schools are the ones that, in my opinion, are making the private school what it properly should be; namely, a place where honest doubt about controversial educational practices should find articulate expression—a human laboratory for educational experimentation. Such a stirring of liberalism had recent expression in a curriculum survey conducted during the school year 1959–1960 by the National Council of Independent Schools. The survey uncovered a number of innovational practices that the council deemed significant enough to explicate and publish in book format.[5] Its purpose was to encourage curriculum change by giving visibility to past and ongoing experimentation.

Teachers in private schools, although constituting far from a distinctive breed, differ from their public school counterparts in a number of respects. Generally speaking, while varying extensively from school to school and individual to individual, they are more academically oriented, less pedagogically oriented, more diverse in social backgrounds, and more likely to have used some interest outside the teaching field as a springboard to teaching. As will be developed later in the chapter, law encourages diversity within their ranks by holding them but loosely in most states to existing patterns of teacher certification. Other identifying characteristics are lighter teaching loads, closer parent relationships, smaller classes, lower salaries, and varied tenure rights.

Private school pupils, like their instructional leaders, also differ without constituting a distinctive breed of individuals. Their most distinguishing feature is a greater homogeneity along socioeconomic lines than is characteristic of public school pupils. Class exclusiveness, indeed, is frequently, if not habitually, in evidence. Along other than socioeconomic lines, however, private school pupils, in the composite, differ little from their public school counterparts. Even in regard to the factor of academic ability, although small-group comparisons often reveal significant differences, large-group comparisons customarily reveal few, if any.

[5] I refer here to David Mallery, *New Approaches in Education* (Boston, Mass.: National Council of Independent Schools, 1961).

EDUCATION AS AN OPERATIONAL PROCESS

A concluding statement here is that private schools generally have the legal right to be more creatively different than they actually are. In practice, the more creative public schools, particularly affluent suburban ones, tend to outdo most of their private school counterparts in the areas of curriculum innovation, instructional method, and program breadth.

AN OVERVIEW OF ROMAN CATHOLIC EDUCATION

Private schools unquestionably exert a powerful influence in the American social order. In respect to size, however, they are no match for church-related schools in general and for Roman Catholic schools, in particular. Of all elementary and secondary school students in the country in 1965–1966: private schools enrolled 0.56 percent; non-Catholic church-related schools, 0.88 percent; Catholic church-related schools, 11.94 percent; and public schools, 86.62 percent.

In deference to the quantitative importance of Roman Catholic schools among independent schools, I submit here a brief synopsis of the Catholic educational position. The controlling concept identifies God as the ultimate of all values: he is personal, noncontingent, purposeful, and perfect. Man, God's conscious creation, comes into the world committed, a priori, by the natural as well as the divine order, to become his divine potential. The Catholic Church is the instrument conceived and chosen by God to help man achieve this outcome. Its methods are theology, the liturgies, pastoral counseling, and formal education. Within this conceptual frame, the immediate concedes to the ultimate and the natural to the supernatural.

Three social institutions influence all Roman Catholics. One is the *family* which, as viewed by the Church, has as its primal function the generation and education of children. In respect to this function, the rights of the family are conceived as taking priority over those of the civil authority.

> If God has given the family the obligation to educate its children, it must have given the family the right to educate them. This right cannot be transferred or taken away because the obligation cannot be transferred or taken away.[6]

[6] Pius XI, *This Is Training,* The Encyclical "Divini Illius Magistri" (Bristol, Engl.: Burleigh Press, 1946), p. 5.

A second social institution that impinges on Roman Catholics is the *Church*. In Roman Catholicism, the Church reigns omniscient in the supernatural order: "She alone has and always will have the whole of mortal truth."[7]

The third social institution that impinges on Roman Catholics is the *state*. In this connection, the Catholic Church "renders to Caesar" the things that, in its view, belong to Caesar: the temporal welfare of all the people, the maintenance of a climate in which individualism can have wholesome expression, in effect, responsibility for all "earthly matters."

Formal education in Roman Catholicism, apparent from the foregoing, is inseparable from the religious mainstream of the Church. As stated by Britt:[8]

> A special spirit pervades the total school situation where religion is not only seen as the central discipline, but as a unifying and integrating principle of the entire curricular and extracurricular offerings. Instead of lessening the reality and the content of any discipline, religion augments and perfects this knowledge within the child.

Pope Pius XI makes his case for the unity of education and religion by denying the possibility of religious neutralism in education:

> So-called "neutral" schools, from which religion is excluded, go against the basic principles of education. In any case, there are no such things as "neutral" schools. In practice they become irreligious schools.[9]

Throughout the last half of the nineteenth century, the Catholic Church made a concerted effort to secure tax support for its schools. The effort, however, had too few political supporters for it to be successful. Undaunted, the Church at the Third Plenary Catholic Council of Baltimore, in 1884, blueprinted an educational plan for the future:

> Near each church, where it does not exist, a parochial school is to be erected within two years from the Promulgation of this Council, and is to be maintained *in perpetuum*, unless the bishop on account of grave difficulties, judges that a postponement be allowed . . . we exhort Catholic parents to procure for their beloved offspring . . . a truly Christian and Catholic education.

[7] Pius XI, p. 9.

[8] John F. Britt, "Rights and Roles of Parents, Church, and State in Education" in McGarry and Ward, *Educational Freedom and the Case for Government in Independent Schools*, p. 54.

338 [9] Pius XI, p. 36.

Thus Roman Catholicism conceives education as a means to religious ends. It is a conception that, to Catholics, lies outside the purview of debate. The issue of how Catholic schools are to be financed, however, is very much a topic of debate. It is one of several social-legal issues that merit attention in the next section dealing with law and nonpublic schools.

LAW AND NONPUBLIC SCHOOLS

The most germinal of all legal decisions regarding nonpublic schools was the one handed down by the Supreme Court in the 1925 *Pierce v. Oregon* case—the one cited earlier in the chapter. It endowed the independent school with legal status. It said, in effect: Your right to exist is inalienable; you have both legal and social respectability in the highest meaning of the terms. However, the Pierce case dealt only with the fundamental right of the independent school to exist. The specifics of its operational existence have become focal in other legal dicta and legislative enactments.

Irrespective of contrasting labels, organizations, and operational details, the nonpublic school, like its public counterpart, is an agency serving the public interest. Thus it is subject to certain public controls. These divide into the following two categories: (1) controls exercised over nonpublic schools because, in a very real sense of the term, they are public institutions; (2) controls, nonfinancial and financial, exercised because nonpublic schools are educational institutions serving a significant segment of the public.

Nonpublic Schools as Public Institutions

Law in its several forms impinges on independent schools just as it does, for example, on apartment buildings, factories, or chain stores. Because independent schools are housed in buildings, building codes apply. Because independent schools are employers, employer-employee regulations apply. When independent schools are run by corporate bodies, corporation laws apply—in respect, for example, to contracts, fiscal responsibility, and property rights. And in respect to schools that operate for financial profit, laws pertaining to profit-making organizations apply.

Nonpublic Schools as Educational Institutions

As educational institutions *per se*, independent schools are subject to many of the same controls that state authorities exercise over public schools. One such control is compulsory-school attendance, along with required records and reports, such attendance constituting a legal requirement in all states. It is no respecter of school type. Another mutually shared control is that which exempts approved schools from tax assessments. The position of church-related schools, in this regard, is as follows:

> Every state in the Union, either by statute or constitutional provision, exempts religious property from taxation; there are specific provisions to this effect in the constitutions of 32 states, in 15 of which the exemption is mandatory.[10]

[10] David Fellman, "Separation of Church and State in the United States, a Summary View," *Wisconsin Law Review*, No. 3 (May 1950), p. 454.

A third control that makes no distinction between nonpublic and public schools consists of curriculum content made compulsory by state laws. Many, if not most, states require all schools, irrespective of type, to make curriculum coverage of the following selected topics: the communication skills, patriotism, principles of representative government, Constitution of the United States and of the individual state, proper display of the flag, Australian ballot system, health and physical education, nature and effect of alcoholic drinks and narcotics, communicable diseases, honesty and moral courage, humane treatment of birds and animals, safety education, history of the United States, and conservation of resources.

Nonfinancial Controls of Nonpublic Schools

Three important areas in which state control applies differently to non-public than to public schools consist of the teaching of religion, school accreditation, and teacher certification. In respect to the first, parochial schools, by definition, have the legal right to indoctrinate pupils with religious dogma; in fact, that is their primary *raison d'etre*. Private schools may, if they so desire, engage in such indoctrination. Public schools, in contrast, may not. Law, as indicated previously in several other contexts, prohibits their indoctrination of pupils in strictly denominational dogma, including that associated with *Bible* reading and prayer.

Nonpublic and public schools also differ from state to state in regard to school accreditation. As the reader may recall, school accreditation is a function of two agencies: an individual state and a regional accrediting association (for example, the New England Association). In respect to the first, state accreditation varies extensively throughout the country. In researching for this chapter, I was surprised to discover that two states, Hawaii and Utah, have no legal provisions for the accreditation of public schools at either the elementary or secondary level. Seventeen additional states have no such provisions for the accreditation of elementary schools.[11] Yet even in those states in which direct accreditation provisions are absent, indirect accreditation takes place through such activities as school inspections, screening for state-aid outlays, enforcement of compulsory attendance laws, auditing of

[11] William B. Rich, *Approval and Accreditation of Public Schools,* OE-20013, Misc. No. 36 (Washington, D.C.: U.S. Office of Health, Education, and Welfare, 1960), p. 3.

school funds, and approval of school districts in lieu of approval of schools themselves. And if state accreditation practices vary widely in regard to public schools, they vary even more widely in regard to independent schools. In general, state legislation is more permissive in regard to the accreditation of independent than of public schools. Among the fifty states, only seven—Alabama, Connecticut, Louisiana, Kentucky, Michigan, Nebraska, and Nevada,—are narrowly prescriptive.[12] In Washington, the right of accreditation is delegated by law to the county superintendent of schools.

The state of Illinois operates its program of parochial and private schools in accordance with dicta laid down in Circular Series A, No. 160, 1964. The title is *Evaluation, Supervision and Recognition of Independent, Parochial, and Private Schools*. The spirit of the circular is evident in the following:

> The Office of the Superintendent of Public Instruction feels that each Independent, Parochial, Private School, or school system, should be judged \in terms of its stated goals and its total educational program. Reasonable variation will be permitted in the application of established recognition standards, if adequate evidence is presented by the school to justify such variation (p. 2).

Regional agencies (which exercise control only over high schools) are even further removed from the accreditation function in regard to nonpublic schools than are the states themselves. In 1960, for instance, as the following figures reveal, only about one independent high school in seven was regionally accredited in the eight states standing first in alphabetical order.[13]

Alabama	12 of 37
Alaska	2 of 10
Arizona	0 of 26
Arkansas	4 of 21
California	0 of 279
Colorado	12 of 42
Connecticut	39 of 101
Delaware	8 of 18

[12] Fred F. Beach and Robert F. Will, *The State and Nonpublic Schools*, Misc. No. 28 (Washington, D.C.: U.S. Department of Health, Education, and Welfare, 1958), pp. 23–25.

[13] Diane B. Gertler and Leah W. Ramsey, *Nonpublic Secondary Schools, Directory 1960–1961*, OE-20043 (Washington, D.C.: U.S. Department of Health, Education, and Welfare, 1961), pp. 11–23.

EDUCATION AS AN OPERATIONAL PROCESS

Teacher certification constitutes yet a third area in which nonpublic and public schools differ. And, as in the case of school accreditation, law is more permissive toward nonpublic school than toward public school teachers. In respect to the latter, all states license public school teachers; and all comparably establish, in one form or another, minimum qualifying standards. Statutory law in approximately half the states delimits comment about teacher certification to public school teachers only. In West Virginia and Texas, respectively, the wording of the applicable statutes is as follows:

> W. Va.: The state superintendent of free schools shall have authority to issue certificates valid in the public schools of the State, in accordance with standards and requirements approved by the state board of education.

> Tex.: The State board of education . . . shall prescribe rules and regulations for the certification of teachers and for the system of examining applicants for teachers' certificates and otherwise granting certificates for teaching in the public schools of the state. . . .

Only in the four states of Alabama, Nebraska, North Dakota, and Michigan do certification laws, by specific wording, require comparable preparation on the part of both nonpublic and public school teachers. In 23 other states, certification laws, by inference, call for comparable preparation from the two groups.[14] Irrespective of legal wording, however, certification laws in practice are less binding on nonpublic than on public school teachers. Thus nonpublic schools, particularly private schools, often hire individuals who, despite serious certification deficiencies, give professional promise of becoming effective teachers. Cases in point include poets, musicians, widely traveled individuals, and scientists from industry. Such individuals, once hired, then work off their certification deficiencies during a four- or five-year in-service period.

The aforementioned Illinois Circular Series A, No. 160 sets forth the following as professional-education requirements for teachers in nonpublic schools.[15] The extensive latitude within each section is readily apparent.

[14] In Fred F. Beach and Robert F. Will, *The State and Nonpublic Schools*, pp. 31–152, statutory and constitutional provisions, by state, are provided on such topics as state aid, curriculum requirements, certification, records and reports, compulsory attendance, etc.

[15] The Office of the Superintendent of Public Instruction, *The Illinois Program for Evaluation, Supervision and Recognition of Independent, Parochial and Private Schools*, Circular Series A, No. 160 (Springfield, Ill.: 1964), pp. 3–4.

These teachers shall have at the time of undertaking their responsibilities, or within five years from the date of initial employment:

1. A course in the Psychology of the Individual as: Adolescent Psychology, Educational Psychology, Psychology of Learning, Learning and Motivation, Counseling, and other similar courses
2. A course in the Psychology of the Group as: Introduction to Social Psychology, Group Dynamics, advanced courses in Social Psychology, and other similar courses
3. A course in the Philosophy of Education as: Philosophy of Education, Comparative Education, The Educational Classics
4. Teaching experience under supervision as: a collegiate practice teaching program, or a year's experience under the school's supervision which provides:

   a. time for observation of other teachers
   b. systematic visitation by a designated experienced teacher
   c. conferences between the experienced teacher and the student teacher

And if the basic requirements themselves are flexible, the "Equivalencies in Professional Education" are even more so. For instance:[16]

1. Two years of successful foreign service in the Peace Corps may be considered equivalent to one course in Group Psychology or Teaching under Supervision.
2. A course in Cultural Anthropology may be considered equivalent to one course in Social Psychology.
3. One year of teaching experience in a foreign land may be considered equivalent to one course in Educational Philosophy.
4. One year of clinical experience, working with youth in an approved social agency, may be considered equivalent to either one course in Social Psychology, Individual Psychology, or Teaching under Supervision.

Public Support for Nonpublic Schools

Public financial support for independent education constitutes one of the major social issues of the day. The volatile aspect of the issue is not support for independent education in general but support for religious education in particular. The federal government spoke out indirectly on the issue by declaring in the First Amendment: "Congress shall make no law respecting an establishment of religion . . ." This single-purposed statement became prologue to the more general doc-

[16] The Office of the Superintendent of Public Instruction, *The Illinois Program*, p. 7.

trine of separation of church and state. This doctrine, although inviolate in theory for almost two centuries, has not had comparable inviolability in practice.

In essence, the issue is whether public financial support for religious education categorically constitutes a violation of the separation of church and state doctrine. A realistic answer has to be an unequivocal "No." Thus the more functional question is what kinds of public financial support are legal and what kinds are not. Most answers to this second question are far from categorical, as the subsequent development of the topic will reveal.

Proponents of public financial support for independent education have historical precedent on their side. In the early Colonial days, Virginia gave state support to Anglican schools; Massachusetts, to Puritan-run schools. In fact, the political and the religious were inseparable in most of the Colonies throughout the entire seventeenth century and well into the eighteenth century. However, a cleavage between state and church that was evident in the pre-Revolutionary war period became increasingly noticeable during the next hundred years. The rise of free public schools deepened the rift, which continues to exist today.

The following synopsis constitutes, in my opinion, an accurate overview of the status of nonpublic education in respect to public financial support. Specifically, all states take a stand constitutionally or legislatively, or both, in respect to financial support for sectarian causes, including parochial schools. Seven states forbid public grants to schools not under their exclusive control. Sixteen allow public funds to be used only for the support of "common" or "free" public schools. Twenty-two states forbid public appropriations to sectarian institutions of any kind. And the remaining states, irrespective of legal nomenclature, assume a similar position.[17] Some states, however—notably Alabama, Georgia, and Virginia—recognize state support for nonsectarian schools as being legal.[18]

Despite legal opposition throughout the country to tax support for sectarian schools, all states, as previously indicated, make nonpublic school property tax exempt. What is this but an instance of public support for nonpublic schools?

The case of *Cochran v. Louisiana State Board of Education*, 281 U.S. 370 (1930) constitutes a more specific instance. In this connection, a 1928 Louisiana law had authorized the state to issue free textbooks to all pupils in the state, regardless of whether the school they attended was public or nonpublic. In 1930, via the appellate process, the case reached the United States Supreme Court, which upheld the legality of the aforementioned Louisiana law. The Court announced: "The schools . . . are not the beneficiaries of these appropriations. They obtain nothing from them, nor are they relieved of a single obligation because of them. The school children and the state alone are the bene-

[17] For positions assumed by individual states, we invite attention to James R. Brown, "State Constitutions and Religion in Education" in McGarry and Ward, *Educational Freedom and the Case for Government Aid to Students in Independent Schools,* Chapter X.

[18] Beach and Will, *The State and Nonpublic Schools,* p. 15.

EDUCATION AS AN OPERATIONAL PROCESS

ficiaries." This decision established precedent for the so-called child-benefit principle, under which guise public tax monies may go to independent schools whenever children, not the schools, are the primary beneficiaries. What is perplexing, in this connection, however, is that the dividing line between child benefit and school or denominational benefit is not easily identifiable.

The case of *Everson v. Board of Education,* 330 U.S. 1 (1947) constitutes a second specific instance of the application of the child-benefit principle. The case emanated from the objection raised by a New Jersey citizen over the state's transportation of children to and from Catholic schools. The Court upheld New Jersey's right to engage in this practice:

> . . . we cannot say that the First Amendment prohibits New Jersey from spending tax-raised funds to pay the bus fares of parochial school pupils as a part of a general program under which it pays the fares of pupils attending public and other schools . . . The First Amendment . . . requires the state to be a neutral in its relations with groups of religious believers and nonbelievers; it does not require the state to be their adversary. State power is no more to be used so as to handicap religions than it is to favor them.

In respect to this case, the Supreme Court upheld New Jersey's legal right to provide transportation for nonpublic school pupils. It did not, however, make the practice mandatory. For this reason, the seven states of Alaska, New Mexico, Oklahoma, Oregon, Vermont, Washington, and Wisconsin which, by statute, forbid free transportation to nonpublic school pupils are within their legal rights in so doing.[19] Indeed, law on this issue of transportation varies from state to state.

During the past several decades, federal legislation has made a number of significant financial concessions to nonpublic schools. The following are selected instances. The GI Bill of Rights of 1944 was no respecter of school category; neither was the National School Lunch Act of 1946. The National Defense Education Act currently authorizes loans to nonprofit elementary and secondary schools for equipment deemed essential to the learning process. The loans may be used for the several curriculum areas of "science, mathematics, history, civics, geography, economics, modern foreign languages, English, reading, other humanities, and the arts." Applications for loans go to the U.S. Office of Education, Washington, D.C., 20202. They are covered by Title III, Section 305 of the NDEA, amended.[20]

[19] James R. Brown in McGarry and Ward, p. 174.

[20] U.S. Department of Health, Education, and Welfare, *Loans to Nonprofit Private*

The Elementary and Secondary Education Act of 1965, PL 89–10, is yet another instance of recent concessions made by the federal government to independent schools.

Several opportunities are afforded local public educational agencies to meet the special educational needs of elementary and secondary school pupils, whether enrolled in public or nonpublic schools, through supplementary services authorized under Title I. These could include broadened health services, school breakfasts for poor children, and guidance and counseling services, as well as special educational services per se.

. . .

Title II of the bill provides $100 million in Federal funds for allotment to states to buy textbooks, library books and other resources, and various instructional materials for the benefit of all children no matter whether they attend public or private schools. . . . The textbooks and library materials, with ownership remaining with a public agency, will be made available to nonpublic schools on a loan basis.

. . .

Title III authorizes Federal funds to start a five-year program for establishment and development of community educational and cultural centers (and similar supplementary services). The centers and services would be open and available to both public and private school students and to out-of-school youths and adults as well.[21]

Scholarship programs of the various states likewise draw no lines between public and nonpublic collegiate institutions attended by scholarship recipients. And the amounts expended in such programs are considerable. In 1962–1963, New York, for example, granted more than 50,000 state scholarships and fellowships, the stipend range extending from $200 to $700. In 1963–1964, California granted 4480 scholarships and fellowships, with awards ranging from $300 to $900 for students who attended private colleges and universities.[22] And these states are merely two instances of the 50.

A concluding statement here is that although public financial support for independent schools is slowly gaining favor, it has not yet penetrated deeply into their programs. It relates to textbooks, bus transpor-

Elementary and Secondary Schools, S-31 (Washington, D.C.: U.S. Government Printing Office, 1966).

[21] U.S. Department of Health, Education, and Welfare, Office of the Assistant Secretary (for Legislation), *PL 89–10: The Nation's First Elementary and Secondary Education Act* (Washington, D.C.: U.S. Government Printing Office, 1965), pp. 12–15.

[22] James R. Brown in McGarry and Ward, p. 180.

tation, and minor school facilities, all of which have legitimacy under the child-benefit principle. Yet why do teachers not have comparable legitimacy, or comparable science laboratories, or comparable school buildings?

In the logic of some, the child-benefit principle should embrace formal education, at least the secular part of it, in its entirety. To these, a logical next step would be public financial support for all aspects of learning that, irrespective of school auspices, take place outside the frame of sectarian religion. Reasonable though this position may be to advocates of this view, it is anathema to those who oppose it. And irrespective of the logic or illogic of the position, the culture as a whole is opposed to direct tax support for denominational religion in any direct guise. Thus, for the foreseeable future, patrons of independent schools will continue to pay twice for the education of their children: once through taxation and a second time through tuition outlays. Even as debate goes on over the seeming unfairness of this financial burden, the social forces that produce it continue to operate as a realistic fact of American life.

To Stimulate Thought

1. Identify the central theme of the Pierce case of 1925. Describe and critically appraise it.

2. In instances where nonpublic schools are recognized to be inferior to competing public schools, what steps, if any, should the state take to upgrade the former? What conceivably would be the sensitive points in the involvement?

3. Defend the position that private schools which are profit-making should not be allowed to exist and operate.

4. Assume the position that public financial support should be provided nonpublic schools for all nonreligious aspects of their programs. Then identify and discuss the major problems, if any, that such an arrangement would create.

5. Take and defend a position on the proposition that certification requirements for nonpublic school teachers should be more flexible than those for public school teachers.

6. Debate the proposition that the child-benefit principle can embrace teacher salaries as logically as it can textbooks and transportation costs. **349**

REFERENCES

Bauer, Paul (ed.), *The Boarding School Directory of the United States*, Vol. 2, 1966–1969 (Chicago: Educational Bureau, Inc., 1966).

Beach, Fred F., and Robert F. Will, *The State and Nonpublic Schools*, Misc. No. 28 (Washington, D.C.: U.S. Department of Health, Education, and Welfare, 1958).

Burns, James A., *The Catholic School System in the United States* (New York: Benziger Brothers, Inc., 1909).

Burns, James A., and Bernard J. Kohlbrenner, *A History of Catholic Education in the United States* (New York: Benziger Brothers, Inc., 1937).

Chamberlain, Ernest B., *Our Independent Schools: The Private School in American Education* (New York: American Book Company, 1944).

Ferrer, Terry, *The Independent School: Its Role in American Education*, Public Affairs Pamphlet No. 238 (New York: Public Affairs Committee, Inc., 1956).

Fichter, Joseph H., *The Parochial School* (Notre Dame, Ind.: University of Notre Dame Press, 1958).

Fund for the Republic, *Religion and the Schools* (New York: The Fund, 1959).

Gertler, Diane B., and Leah W. Ramsey, *Nonpublic Secondary Schools, Directory 1960–1961*, OE-20043 (Washington, D.C.: U.S. Office of Health, Education, and Welfare, 1961).

Greeley, Andrew M., *The Education of Catholic Americans* (Chicago: Aldine Publishing Company, 1966).

Johnson, William (ed.), *A Handbook for Independent School Operation* (Princeton, N.J.: D. Van Nostrand Company, Inc., 1961).

LaNoue, George R., *Public Funds for Parochial Schools?* (New York: National Council of the Churches of Christ in the U.S.A., 1963).

Mallery, David, *New Approaches in Education* (Boston: National Council of Independent Schools, 1961).

McGarry, Daniel D., and Leo Ward (eds.), *Educational Freedom and the Case for Government Aid to Students in Independent Schools* (Milwaukee: The Bruce Publishing Company, 1966).

McLaughlin, Sister Raymond, *A History of State Legislation Affecting Private Elementary and Secondary Schools in the United States, 1870–1945* (Washington, D.C.: The Catholic University of America Press, 1946).

Neuwein, Reginal A. (ed.), *Catholic Schools in Action* (South Bend, Ind.: University of Notre Dame Press, 1966).

U.S. Department of Health, Education, and Welfare, *Church-Related Boards Responsible for Higher Education*, Bulletin 1964, No. 13, OE-53021 (Washington, D.C.: U.S. Government Printing Office, 1964).

U.S. Department of Health, Education, and Welfare, *Loans to Nonprofit Private Elementary and Secondary Schools*, S-31 (Washington, D.C.: U.S. Government Printing Office, 1966).

Ward, Leo, *Federal Aid to Private Schools* (Westminster, Ind.: Newman Press, 1964).

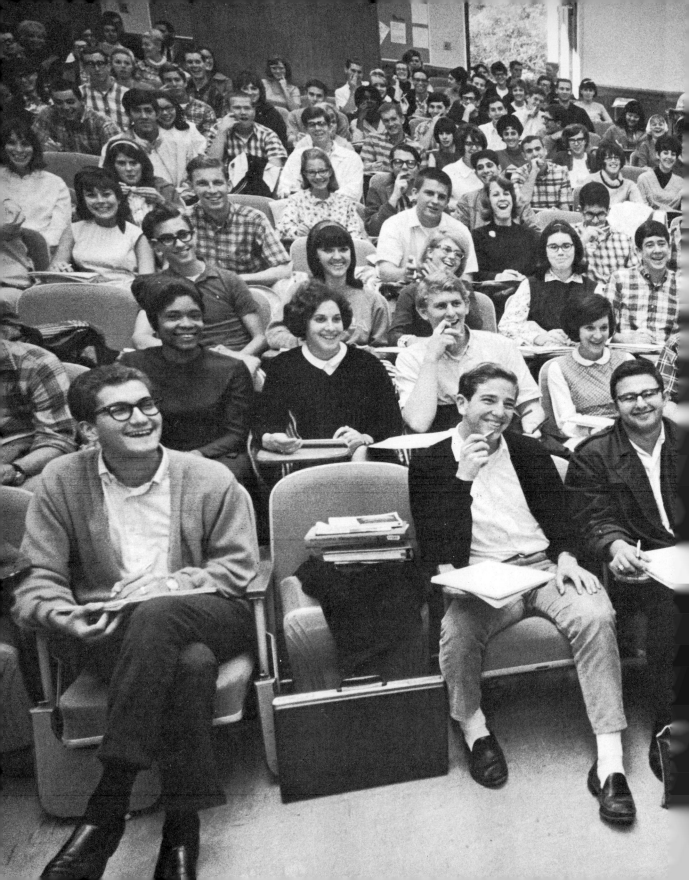

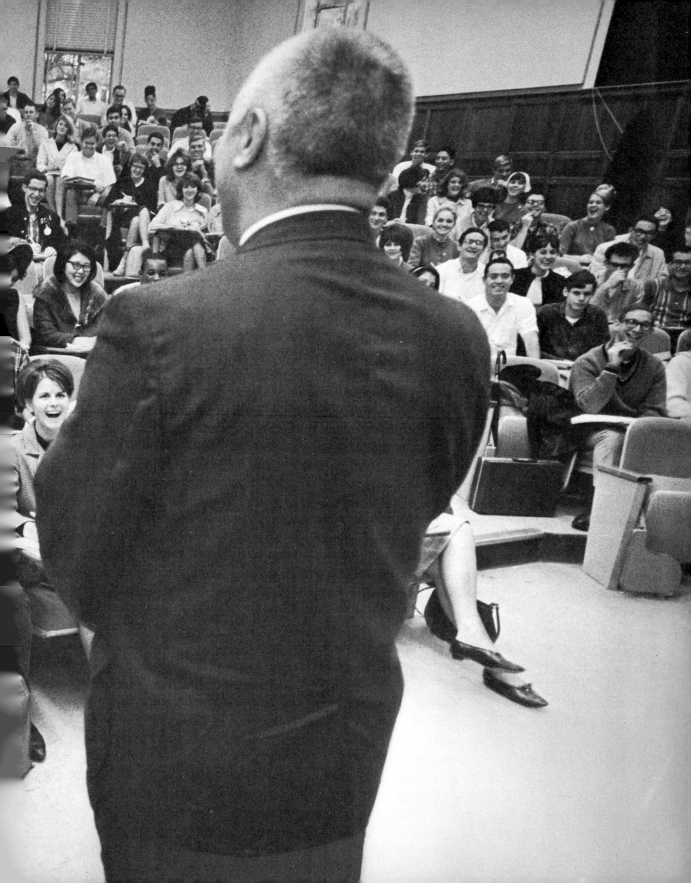

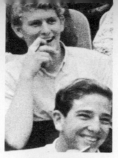

Chapter

13

*Higher
Education*

Formal education in the United States reaches its zenith in the college or university. When the latter does its job well, society profits because more of its members have experienced significant change. They leave the college or university more knowledgeable, more adept in basic skills, and generally more mature. They come to higher education with one set of values and leave with another.

Harvard College, founded in 1636, was the first institution of higher learning in the United States. Other colleges to open their doors during the Colonial period were William and Mary in 1693, Yale in 1701, Princeton in 1746, Kings (now Columbia University) in 1754, Brown in 1764, Rutgers in 1766, and Dartmouth in 1769.

For two hundred years, the college, rather than the university, dominated higher education in this country. The curriculum customarily consisted of the seven liberal arts (except for music), Greek, Latin, and philosophy. It was essentially the same curriculum for all students, irrespective of their future goals. When these goals were professional in nature, apprenticeship training following college graduation was the customary road to competence.

The university in the United States is a phenomenon of the latter half of the nineteenth century. A throwback to the Middle Ages, its immediate origins are England and Germany. From England, via the traditions of Oxford and Cambridge, the American university inherited the Renaissance ideal of the man of many parts—the forerunner of the modern-day "whole man." The Oxford or the Cambridge scholar had his inevitable bouts with knowledge and ideas, but these did not preclude others in the province of the social, the physical, and the esthetic. All were deemed essential to his development. From Germany, via the traditions of the University of Berlin, the American university inherited the concept of knowledge for its own sake. These two influences—social breadth and scholarship in depth—continue to make themselves felt in American higher education today.

Universities in America have evolved in two ways. One has been by way of evolutionary growth, the starting point being pre-existing colleges. In the nineteenth century, liberal arts colleges, such as Harvard or Kings, constituted the primary root sources. In the past several decades of the present century, pre-existent teachers' colleges have

constituted another important root source. The second source of universities has been direct origin. Most state universities are outgrowths of this direct-origin. So too are such eminent private universities as Johns Hopkins (opened in 1876) and the University of Chicago (opened in 1892).

The direct-origin process, in respect to both colleges and universities, has been a distinguishing characteristic of higher education since 1960. During the first four years of the 1960s, 146 institutions of higher learning had their advents, and the number continues to increase.[1]

SOME STATISTICS

Higher education in the United States is big business today in terms of almost any criterion. It is multipurposed, multidimensional, and multi-organizational. But its most obvious characteristic is its size.

Enrollments in Institutions of Higher Education

A major index of size is student enrollment, details of which appear in Table 13.1. The table reveals that in the fall of 1967, 6,911,748 under-graduate and graduate students were enrolled in the many institutions of higher learning throughout the country. Included in this total were an estimated 40 percent of all high school graduates of the class of 1966–1967. The 1967–1968 total of 6,911,748 students will, according to conservative estimates, increase to approximately 11,000,000 students in 1975.

Publicly controlled colleges and universities enroll approximately 70 percent of all students in 1967 and are expected to enroll well in excess of that in 1975. Males, who constituted 59.8 percent of the 1967 enroll-ment total, will continue their dominance for years to come. Of the more than 6,000,000 undergraduates in 1967, in excess of 17 percent were enrolled in junior colleges.

Miscellaneous Institutional Data

The approximately seven million students in attendance at colleges and universities in 1967 were enrolled in 2537 institutions.[2] Of this

[1] Lewis B. Mayhew, "The New Colleges," in Samuel Baskin (ed.), *Higher Education: Some New Developments* (New York: McGraw-Hill, Inc., 1965), pp. 1–16.

[2] National Center for Educational Studies, *Higher Education Educational Directory,* Part 3 (Washington, D.C.: U.S. Department of Health, Education, and Welfare, 1968), p. 6.

TABLE 13.1 TOTAL ENROLLMENTS IN INSTITUTIONS OF HIGHER
EDUCATION BY SEX, CATEGORY, AND INSTITUTIONAL CONTROL,
FALL 1967

				Totals
A.	Sex	Male:	4,132,800	
		Female:	2,778,948	
				6,911,748
B.	Category	Resident:	6,621,239	
		Extension:	290,509	
				6,911,748
C.	Control	Public		
		State:	3,349,518	
		Local:*	1,466,510	
			4,816,028	
		Private		
		Nonchurch:	1,120,093	
		Protestant:	482,211	
		Roman Catholic:	447,531	
		Other Denominations:	45,885	
			2,095,720	
				6,911,748

Source: Kenneth A. Simon and W. Vance Grant, *Digest of Educational Statistics,*
1968 Edition (Washington, D.C.: U.S. Department of Health, Education, and Welfare,
1968), pp. 64, 66.
* Local only, or local and state combined.

total, slightly fewer than 700 were junior colleges.[3] Of the 2537 institutions, 1037 were publicly controlled, and the remaining 1500 were non-
publicly controlled.

Enrollments in publicly controlled institutions are considerably larger
than those in privately- or church-controlled institutions. The University
of Minnesota, for example, enrolls approximately 40,000 students; the
University of California, 90,000 on its seven campuses. This factor of
size, characteristic of many, if not most, publicly controlled institutions
of higher education, explains why they enroll 70 percent of the nation's
student body, although constituting only 40 percent of the total number
of institutions.

In 1968, the nation's 2537 colleges and universities had the equivalent of 504,000 full-time teaching personnel with the rank of instructor

[3] *Ibid.,* p. 6.

or higher. This total included teachers of degree-credit courses only. It notably exceeded that of a decade earlier: the comparable total for 1957–1958 was 206,486.[4] The indication is that college teachers in the foreseeable future will unquestionably be much sought-after. This is good news, particularly for males, who constitute 82 percent of university and four-year college faculties, and 68 percent of junior college faculties.[5]

In 1966–1967, the nation's universities and four-year colleges awarded 550,000 baccalaureate degrees, 147,000 master of arts or master of science degrees, and 19,809 doctor of philosophy degrees. Impressive though these totals are, they fall short of the needs for trained manpower in the fields of education, government, business, and industry.

INSTITUTIONAL TYPES

Institutions of higher education divide into at least the following four categories: (1) the junior college, (2) the liberal arts college, (3) the land-grant college or university, and (4) the multipurpose university. Each receives brief treatment here.

The Junior College

Of the four categories, the junior college and the land-grant college are native. One writer describes the junior college "as the only educational institution which can truly be stamped 'made in the United States of America.' "[6] The junior college is also the newest of the four. It came into being in 1892 when the University of Chicago divided its program into a lower two-year block designated the academic college, and into a higher two-year block designated the university college.[7] In 1900 an estimated eight junior colleges existed in the country, all privately controlled. By 1930 the total number, private and public, had risen to

[4] Simon and Grant, 1968, pp. 5, 79.

[5] National Education Association, *NEA Research Bulletin,* Vol. 44, No. 2 (May 1966), p. 40.

[6] Edmund J. Gleazer, Jr., *American Junior Colleges,* 6th ed. (Washington, D.C.: American Council on Education, 1963), p. 3.

[7] R. Freeman Butts and Lawrence A. Cremin, *A History of Education in American Culture* (New York: Holt, Rinehart and Winston, Inc., 1953), p. 424.

400, and by 1967, to almost 700. The first public junior college opened its doors in Joliet, Illinois, in 1901.

Junior colleges serve a number of purposes. In respect to program, all but the strictly technical institutions offer lower-division academic courses for students who intend to earn baccalaureate degrees later. Most junior colleges, in addition, offer terminal education for non-college-bound students. Many, if not most, provide guidance and counseling services to students and sometimes to nonstudent community members as well.

In respect to the student populations of junior colleges, most are indigenous to the communities in which the colleges are located. Many junior colleges, in fact, bear the label *Community College*. As stated by Medsker: "The term connotes a close interrelationship of the college and the life of the community: the college looks to the community for suggestions in programming and the community looks to the college for many different services to many different people."[8]

Generally speaking, junior colleges perform their academic functions better than they do their terminal-education functions. For one reason, the former is endowed with greater prestige than the latter. For a second reason, the relationship between terminal-education offerings and student or community needs is often too approximate to result in transfer. The newness of terminal-education programs may constitute yet a third reason. In respect to the guidance function, it too has a long way to go to achieve its intended purposes.

Despite its shortcomings, however, the junior college is becoming an increasingly valuable component of higher education. Its chief claim to merit is that it serves the needs of many to whom formal education beyond high school would otherwise be denied.

The Liberal Arts College

The liberal arts college has the deepest roots of all institutions of higher learning anywhere in the world. In medieval days, its curriculum consisted of the traditional liberal arts. With the passage of time, the curriculum has kept pace with social change, absorbing selected aspects into the three fields of the humanities, the social sciences, and the natural sciences.

[8] Leland L. Medsker, *The Junior College: Progress and Prospect* (New York: McGraw-Hill, Inc., 1960), p. 16.

Purposes of the liberal arts college are to transmit the hard core of knowledge and values that man needs in order to become and remain human; to eliminate biases, superstitions, and other instances of provincialism; to provide a background that will give perspective to specialization; and to lay the groundwork for a lifetime of continuing

education. These purposes are indeed unassailable. The curriculum designed to achieve them, however, is rarely as unassailable. It often is highly abstract and symbolic; oriented very much in the past, very little in the present; resistant to change; and oblivious to the practical needs of submarginal cultural groups. Yet my indictment here is not so much of curriculum designs *per se* as of man's collective inability to decide what experiences make man human. In my opinion, the best answer comes from those planners who, while orienting a curriculum to the most valid of the past, remain sensitive to the issues and values of the present, and incorporate them into the curriculum.

Liberal arts colleges in the country total approximately 800. Most are privately controlled; proportionately fewer are publicly or church-controlled. Enrollments in liberal arts colleges are typically small, ranging in most instances from 200 to 500. Until almost the turn of the nineteenth century, as stated previously, the liberal arts college was the dominant single force in higher education in the United States. Since that time, however, the university has assumed dominance.[9]

Land-grant Colleges

Like the junior college, the land-grant college is a native-born institution. The Morrill Act of 1862 brought it into being. Under provisions of the act, the federal government granted to each state for each congressman 30,000 acres of land, or the monetary equivalent thereof, with the stipulation that the proceeds go to the establishing of colleges of agriculture and of mechanical arts. The governing principle was that higher education should be practical as well as theoretical, should be for immediate as well as ultimate application. Some of the evolving institutions became independent state colleges; however, most of these later became specialized universities. Others emerged as parts of all-purpose state universities. Iowa State University at Ames, and Purdue University at West Lafayette, Indiana, are instances of the first. The University of California, Berkeley, and the University of Missouri, Columbia, are instances of the second. A second Morrill Act, in 1890, led to the establishing of colleges for Negroes throughout the country.

[9] An excellent source of additional information on the liberal arts college is by Earl J. McGrath and L. Richard Meeth (eds.), *Co-operative Long-Range Planning for the Liberal-Arts Colleges* (New York: Teachers College Press, Teachers College, Columbia University, 1964).

Irrespective of organization or student population, the land-grant college has actively advanced the causes of agriculture, engineering, home economics, and the industrial arts. It has consistently been an institution close to the common man and his interests. Not eschewing the liberal arts, it has employed them to advance the causes of the immediate and practical as well as the delayed and ultimate.

The Multipurpose University

The multipurpose university, coined the *multiversity* by Clark Kerr, former president of the University of California, at Berkeley, is an academic community that embraces within its confines a number of independent schools and colleges. The nucleus of every university is a liberal arts college that functions both autonomously and contingently: autonomously, in that it functions as a college in its own right; contingently, in that it serves the general-education needs of a university's specialized schools and colleges. These latter, in the smaller universities, often consist only of business, education, and a graduate school. In the larger universities, they consist additionally of one or more of the following: agriculture, architecture, dentistry, engineering, hotel management, journalism, law, medicine, music, nursing, public administration, and speech.

The modern-day university has a diversified ancestry that goes back to the first medieval universities of the twelfth century, such as those at Bologna, Oxford, and Paris. By 1500 approximately 80 universities were in existence in the Western world.[10] They customarily divided into faculties of arts, law, medicine, and theology. The curriculum of these early universities, however, was more comfortable in the areas of the seven liberal arts than in the various professional areas—except for theology.

A second germinal source, as indicated earlier, was the German university of the nineteenth century, with its guiding tenet of knowledge for its own sake. This source accorded legitimacy to pure science, so-called, and assigned to research a place of higher priority than it did to teaching.

Practical sources were the Industrial Revolution, with its growing demand for knowledge and techniques of applied science; Darwinian theory, with its emergent demand for advanced theoretical science;

[10] H. G. Good, *A History of Western Education,* 2nd ed. (New York: Crowell-Collier and Macmillan, Inc., 1960), p. 103.

the advent of certain new professions, with their attendant specialized demands; the need for updating most of the old professions; and a mounting loss of confidence in the ability of a classical curriculum to ready learners for the many complex demands of a rapidly changing social order. These forces, because often in conflict, placed universities in crossfires. Each institution sooner or later had to take a stand on such issues as: classical learning versus nonclassical learning; the province of theory versus the province of application; research versus teaching; and science versus the humanities and the social sciences. That universities assumed differing stances in regard to these issues revealed American individualism once more at work.

Despite differences in approaches and emphases, most universities today subscribe to and advance the following significant purposes.

Instruction   Though the instructional function is an obvious one, it should not be taken for granted. Faculty members, irrespective of their other professional obligations, have an inescapable responsibility to teach students. Their methods may vary widely, but the responsibility itself is a universal one.

General education   Universities create an ethos within student bodies by broadening an already substantial base of general education and authenticating its content. In this connection, the elective system in higher education had almost no limits in the last half of the nineteenth century. President Eliot of Harvard was the system's ardent champion. Around the turn of the century, however, universities moved increasingly toward a core of curriculum constants (or choices within curriculum areas) to be required of all students, irrespective of their professional goals. The University of Chicago, at that time, led the way by making this core the curriculum of its Lower School. The University of Minnesota, in the 1930s, made it the curriculum of its General College which, like the Lower School of the University of Chicago, reached up through grade 14. And other universities, in their own ways, established or re-established general education as foundational to all other outcomes in higher education. There was a trend back to the wide-open elective system starting in the 1920s, but it is currently in the process of reversing itself, at least somewhat.

Vocational education   Universities educate both indirectly and directly for vocational outcomes. The liberal arts college constitutes the indirect

364

moving force. Professional schools combine to constitute the direct moving force.

The archival function Universities collect, preserve, and display, original documents, relics, and anatomical specimens; they maintain libraries and art collections; and they serve as storehouses of records and reports.

The productive-creative function To many, the single most important function of a university is to produce or create. Universities engaged in implementing this function customarily employ the methods of experimentation, research, scholarly writing, and creation in the esthetic areas of art, music, dance, and drama. This function is the source of the "publish-or-perish" debate that waxes from warm to hot in all universities. I postpone discussion of this issue until later in the chapter. Suffice it to say here that the issue is not creativity versus noncreativity; it is the degree of emphasis that universities should place on either single function.

The service function The function has to do with the contribution that institutions of higher learning believe they need to make to social, business, and governmental groups. A start of an answer is that colleges and universities vary widely in regard to this function. Generally speaking, colleges and private universities are less service-oriented; public universities are more so. Yet having said this, we hasten to add that the University of Chicago and Harvard University are every bit as service-oriented as two of their outstanding public counterparts, the Universities of Michigan and Wisconsin.

The service function has many faces. It takes the form, for instance, of work-study programs in certain engineering schools, wherein students alternate activities between industry and the university. It takes the form of school surveys conducted by schools of education. And since 1940, it most often has taken the form of research-and-development projects performed by colleges and universities for the federal government. This topic too is developed later in the chapter.

CURRICULUM TRENDS IN HIGHER EDUCATION

The overwhelming scope of curriculum issues and designs in higher education mitigates against their extensive coverage in a book of this general nature. Thus, I have elected to cover in this section some innovational developments and trends in curriculum: first, those that are manifesting themselves in independent and university-related liberal arts colleges; and second, those that are manifesting themselves in **366** professional schools of universities.

Developments and Trends in Liberal Arts Colleges

Increased cooperation among related departments of at least certain liberal arts colleges stands out as a current phenomenon of great importance. For almost a century, departmental discreteness was routinely accepted by faculties as an inecapable fact of academic life. Sociologists had only nodding acquaintance with anthropologists, biologists rarely had dialogue with chemists, and professors of education virtually sealed themselves off from their counterparts in the other behavioral sciences, and vice versa. The elective system, with its propensity for subject-matter specialization, constituted one reason for these walls of separation. The knowledge explosion constituted another. Irrespective of reasons, the liberal arts college traditionally has been more a cluster of unrelated divisions than a complex of integrated divisions held together by common purposes and joined together in cooperative endeavor.

Today, departmental integration, although still far from commonplace, is more prevalent than it was a few decades ago. One of its products is the general major that broadly reaches into several departmental areas rather than narrowly and intensively into only one. In colleges that offer general majors, some students have the option of electing, for example, a general literature major rather than an English major. At Muhlenberg College, they may elect a general-science major that includes several sciences rather than a conventional science major that is narrowly limited.

A second product of departmental integration is research mutually engaged in by specialists from different but related fields. Research that combines biology and chemistry, sociology and psychology, or economics and political science is illustrative.

The high priority currently assigned by liberal arts colleges to non-Western cultures and affairs constitutes yet another significant curriculum innovation. This step in the direction of broadly conceived world affairs is one that the country has long needed. For three centuries American colleges ironically called themselves *liberal*, while walking a narrow and provincial path. The result was that graduates, upon leaving their alma maters, departed with half-truths or untruths about many peoples of the world, about many places and events remote from themselves, and about many international issues. That America's global posture suffered from this naïvete goes without saying.

367

Today colleges in increasing numbers are countering this long-standing tradition of global isolation. One commonly employed approach is through curriculum additions which focus on non-Western problems and affairs. The liberal arts college of Harvard, for example, has added a course entitled Far Eastern Civilization; of Northwestern University, courses entitled African Studies, and World History in Modern Times; of Columbia University, a course entitled, Oriental Civilization; and of Colgate University, a course entitled Non-Western Area Studies. As stated by one source:[11]

> . . . the non-Western cultures of the Orient, Africa, and the Middle East have emerged as possibly the most potent forces in the world, and certainly of such influence as to demand educational attention. The collegiate response has been to create non-Western emphases through changes in the substance of existing courses, through new courses on Oriental or African culture, and through the enrichment of the extraclass life of the college with non-Western art, lectures, and collections of readings.

A second counter to provincialism is student residence or travel outside the confines of English-speaking countries. Foreign-study programs generally cite such objectives as the following: "(1) the general education of the student, (2) the intellectual and professional development of the student in his specialized field of study, and (3) the furthering of international understanding."[12]

Foreign-study programs are on the increase, so much so that they no longer are a rarity. For example, the liberal arts colleges of Columbia, Harvard, and Cornell Universities and of the University of Illinois sponsor anthropology programs in Latin American countries. Stanford has an exchange arrangement with the Universities of Taipei and Tokyo. Princeton sends students to Lebanon to study Arabic languages. Wisconsin gives undergraduate credit for a year's work in India. Smith College is well known for its junior year abroad.[13] And these examples are just a few of the many that might have been cited.

Independent study constitutes yet a third significant innovation. Independent study, as a departure from the traditional lecture-dominated or discussion-dominated class, customarily embraces these features: considerable latitude of student choice of subject matter, depth pene-

[11] Hugh S. Brown and Lewis B. Mayhew, *American Higher Education* (New York: The Center for Applied Research, in Education, Inc., 1965), p. 79.

[12] Irwin Abrams, "The Student Abroad," in Samuel Baskin (ed.), *Higher Education: Some Newer Developments* (New York: McGraw-Hill, Inc., 1965), p. 80.

[13] Abrams, pp. 82–84.

tration by students into a few learning areas in lieu of superficial coverage of more, and curriculum direction provided by a tutorial adviser-guide. Independent study, in effect, substitutes learner discovery of knowledge for authority-ordered transmission of knowledge. Essentials to its success are adviser-guides, who structure enough rather than too little or too much, and learners mature enough to rise to the program's almost unlimited possibilities.

In many institutions, independent study is for honors students only. In a growing number, it is for average students as well. And early though limited reports from these institutions are sanguine about the program's effectiveness with learners of average ability.[14] These students, too, are apparently able to reap the benefits of greater freedom.

The increasingly close relationship between colleges and secondary schools is a fourth significant innovation. It is a relationship with an interesting history. Secondary education initially came into being to improve the preparation of those students who were to attend college. Cast in this role, secondary education had to work closely with higher education, and vice versa. With the coming of the twentieth century, secondary education opened its doors to the masses. The resulting change in composition of the student body precipitated curriculum changes of telling significance. One fact stood out clearly: the traditional college-preparatory program was plainly not functional for many of this newer group. Thus, curriculum change became the standing order of the day.

In attempting to meet the needs of the slow and average, secondary education unquestionably failed, at times, the needs of the talented. And in the eyes of colleges and universities, the extent of the failure was often deplorable. Thus a wall between secondary and higher education began to mount, a wall that became increasingly formidable with the passage of time. And it was not until 1951, as elaborated in Chapter 10, that the wall began to crumble, the Advanced Placement Program being in large part responsible. The program's goal from the start was a curriculum tailored to the evolving needs of talented students as they progressed through the later years of secondary education into the early years of higher education. Students who are successful in the Program customarily start their college work in sophomore-level rather than freshman-level classes. Whether or not they receive academic credit

[14] One such report comes from the Committee on Utilization of College Teaching Resources, *Better Utilization of College Teaching Resources* (New York: Fund for the Advancement of Education, May, 1959).

for the freshman-level courses waived depends on institutional policy.

The Advanced Placement Program, along with its admitted successes, has frequently been guilty of giving disproportionate attention to cognitive outcomes, to academic subjects, and to talented learners at the expense, respectively, of affective outcomes, of nonacademic subjects, and of average or below-average learners. It also has resulted, at times, in an excessive amount of prescription by colleges over high school programs.

Irrespective of these shortcomings, however, the Advanced Placement Program has been effective in bringing liberal arts colleges and high schools into a closer relationship. Their meeting point has been gifted students. The outcome of the working alliance has often been the transplantation, intact, of first-year college courses into high school programs. What is needed instead is for college and secondary school personnel mutually to evaluate and revise, not just transplant. Such a step, however, commits college personnel to learn more than they presently know about secondary education. At present, even though assuming leadership roles, most college personnel are comfortable only around the outer fringes of secondary education. To be operationally effective, they need first-hand knowledge of the inner workings of secondary education and penetrating insight into its programs and problems. Though colleges and high schools are moving closer together, they have a long way to go to become truly integrated.

Developmental Trends in Professional Schools

Like liberal arts colleges, professional schools are also in a fluid state. They are characteristically dynamic, ever mirroring innovations and changes occurring in the professions they serve. Thus curriculum change, not curriculum constancy, is the hallmark of excellence in any first-rate professional school. Deliberately avoiding the specialized aspects of each of the several professional schools, we identify and briefly develop here two innovations that increasingly characterize the curriculum of most, if not all, of them.

The first is the increased amount of general education being required of students enrolled in professional schools. In this connection, history conceivably may record the mid-twentieth century as the era of the specialist in such fields, among others, as law, medicine, dentistry, business, government, and industry. And that specialization in many

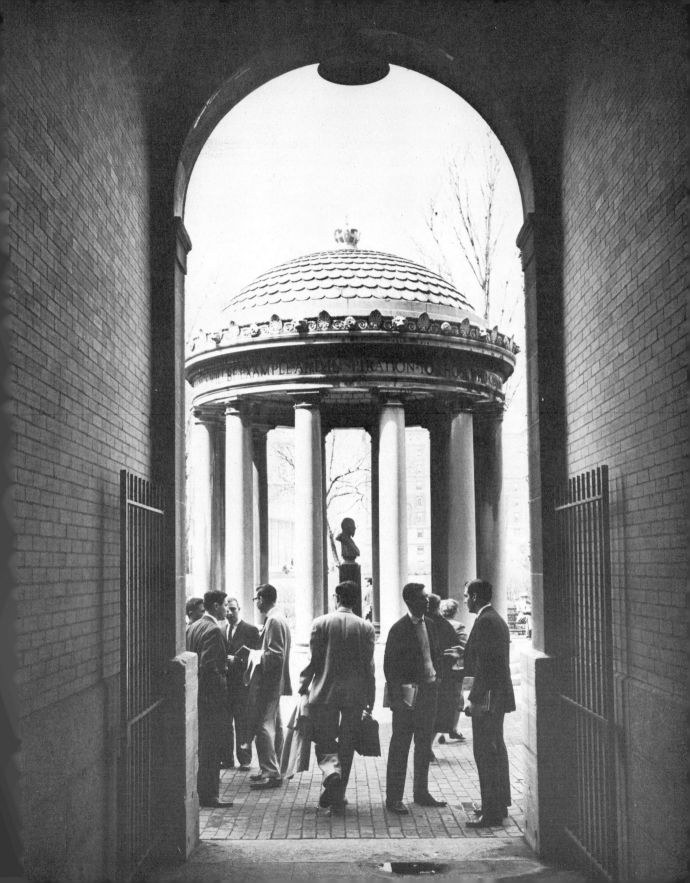

of life's concerns is a basic essential goes without saying. Yet specialization not grounded in general knowledge and insight easily undergoes distortion for reason of its narrowness. In the opinion of many, professional schools through the fifties moved too sharply in the direction of specialization with general education the loser. In the sixties, the trend began to reverse itself. A consensus view today is that a broad base in the academic disciplines is an "essential not only for an informed citizenry and a satisfying personal life but also . . . for professional competency and success."[15]

The question of just how much general education constitutes a broad base is a moot one. A number of professional schools, however, are moving toward the goal of requiring two years of general education at the undergraduate level. And they generally prefer it to accompany special education over a longer enrollment period in preference to its exclusive concentration in the first two college years.

A second innovational feature of the curriculums of most professional schools is the requirement of a core of professional subject matter to serve as a balance wheel for subsequent specialization. Under this and the previously discussed arrangement, a professional curriculum thus pyramids from general education, to a professional core, to specialization. The core in a school of business conceivably might embrace, for instance, accounting, marketing, finance, and industrial or personnel management. Under such a design, students would first enroll in at least one course in each of these before specializing later in any one. The core in engineering conceivably would consist of physics, general chemistry, computer fundamentals, and calculus. In music, it might consist of theory and composition, vocal performance, and instrumental performance. In speech, it might consist of public address, group communication, speech disorders, and electronics media.

ISSUES IN HIGHER EDUCATION

Because universities and colleges are dedicated to complex missions, have fluid organizational structures, have highly individualized faculties, and enroll students with a wide variety of needs and personalities, it is no wonder that issues of almost every size and kind arise to plague them. From the welter, we have selected four for development here,

[15] Earl J. McGrath, and L. Richard Meeth, "Organizing for Teaching and Learning: The Curriculum, in Baskin, p. 43.

the first two of which received passing comment earlier in the chapter. The four selected are these: (1) the productive function versus the instructional function, (2) higher education and the federal government, (3) the problem of the wall between instructional faculties and governing boards, and (4) the student-power movement.

The Productive versus Instructional Function

Under the term *productive function*, I broadly include such activities as experimentation (performed, for example, in laboratories, clinics, and classrooms), library research, the writing of manuscripts, and creativity at work in, for instance, art, music, the dance, and literature. All have validation of the existent or creation of the new as their purposes. Experimentation employs firsthand discovery to bring new knowledge into being or to validate old knowledge. Library research and the writing of manuscripts utilize the methods of data gathering, analysis, synthesis, and rational interpretation to accomplish essentially the same outcomes. Esthetic creativity at work taps the wellsprings of imagination for its products. The productive function of higher education has a long and respected tradition that reaches back at least as far as the Middle Ages.[16]

That the productive function—research and creative endeavor—is an important one is too universally accepted to elicit debate. Whether or not it is the primary function of any institution of higher learning, however, is very much a topic of debate. Vying with it for top priority is the instructional function. A survey of current practice would reveal private and public universities, particularly the larger ones, insistent that faculty members research, write, or produce in some other creative way, or conceivably face professional nonentity as a consequence of failure to do so. These large universities encourage productive output by keeping faculty loads fairly small. Responsibility for not more than two class assignments daily, the sponsoring of two to five doctoral candidates yearly, the advising of perhaps from 20 to 25 undergraduates or masters candidates per term, and responsibility for one or two faculty-committee assignments generally combine with productive-

---

[16] Two excellent comprehensive treatments of graduate education *per se* are Bernard Berelson, *Graduate Education in the United States* (New York: McGraw-Hill, Inc., 1960) and Everett Walters, *Graduate Education Today* (Washington, D.C.: American Council on Education, 1965).

creative activities to constitute par for the professional work load. The same survey would reveal that most independent colleges, as well as selected of the emerging universities, attach greater importance to quality teaching than they do to the research-productive function. Some, more than others, might prod professors to "produce," but few would issue them a one-way ticket to academic oblivion if they resisted the prodding. Characteristically larger teaching and advisement loads in these colleges and small universities make research or creative outcomes more difficult for faculty members to achieve. In this connection, responsibility for three to four classes daily is not exactly conducive to the achievement of such outcomes.

To those holding the position that creation and instruction are mutually reinforcing, the issue is completely academic. Such individuals contend that creative work heightens instructional quality; conversely, that instruction gives perspective to creation. To them, the issue is not one of either-or but of how much of each.

The logic of this position is so persuasive to me that I regard the researcher-teacher or creator-teacher as the ideal. Yet because individuals differ widely in their interests and abilities, and because institutions differ just as widely in their purposes and programs, higher education needs to find room both for faculty members who are skilled teachers but lackluster creators, and for their opposites who are unskilled teachers but talented creators. Ideally, the dichotomy between research and teaching, or creative endeavor and teaching, should not exist; but because it often does, higher education can ill afford to lose specialized talent for sake of an arbitrary ideal.

In line with this reasoning, the publish-or-perish dictum might logically convert, in certain instances, to a teach-or-perish dictum. Better still, both might convert to a dictum to research well, to publish well, to teach well, to create well, or to counsel well. In other words, the communication to faculty members conceivably would go something like this: excel in one or more talents that higher education holds to be important, but do not feel compelled to be what you cannot be. If only a fair researcher but an effective teacher, align yourself with a college that places premium value on teaching. If a talented researcher but only a passably effective teacher, align yourself with a university that will put your specialized talent to work while holding your teaching responsibilities to a minimum. In either event, work hard on your weakness to the end, hopefully, of its becoming a modest asset to your specialized talent, or, at least, ceasing to be a liability to it.

374

Higher Education and the Federal Government

We turn now from the individual faculty member and his problem of role identity in an institution of higher education to a related problem of the role identity of the federal government in higher education. Historically, there was no problem: the federal government underwrote higher education with land and monetary grants, but took care to remain operationally remote. In 1917, this posture changed somewhat when the Smith-Hughes Act, as the first of many to follow, cast the government in the role of sponsor of vocational causes. The posture changed yet again in the 1930s when the government, through the National Youth Administration, assumed responsibility for seeing that the unemployed were educated. The most dramatic change of all, however, took place during and after World War II, in which period the base of

the federal government's involvement in education became significantly broadened. Throughout the war, the government utilized the resources of colleges and universities on matters of strategy, logistics, propaganda, and intelligence. In a very real sense, higher education became a tool of national survival.

During and since World War II, universities and colleges have been important recruitment sources of specialist personnel in government. These institutions additionally have assumed responsibility for, and successfully completed an extensive assortment of, research-and-development projects. In effect, in addition to their other functions, they have increasingly become governmental laboratories. In this new relationship, the federal government and higher education both have played as much by ear as by the notes. The latter, in fact, have usually not been written.

Discordant features of the relationship have consisted selectively of the following.[17]

1. The federal government does not have an agency to coordinate its many relationships with educational institutions. As a result, any university with a sizable number of government projects often has to work with any or all of the ensuing: Department of Defense, Public Health Service, National Science Foundation, Atomic Energy Commission, Department of Agriculture, National Aeronautics and Space Agency, and Department of Health, Education and Welfare. That this lack of coordination often results in inefficiency and unnecessary confusion is unquestionably an indictment of loose organization.

2. Because the vast majority of federal projects in higher education, from the time of the NDEA Act of 1958, have been in the applied sciences, the three areas of the social sciences, the humanities, and the pure sciences have suffered as a consequence. For instance, in 1965 the ratio of federal appropriation for research and development was approximately 35 to 1 between the sciences and social sciences, and substantially greater than that between the sciences and the humanities. The 1964 revision of NDEA and the many acts of the 1960s dealing with problems of the culturally deprived narrowed both ratios slightly, but the humanities and the social sciences still receive short shrift from the federal government.

[17] For much of the content of this section, I give credit to William Clyde DeVane, *Higher Education in Twentieth-Century America* (Cambridge, Mass.: Harvard University Press, 1965), Chap. VI.

A personal anecdote strikes me as appropriate here. In the fall of 1967, two of my colleagues in Northwestern University's Engineering School and I were debating the pros and cons of sponsoring a Ph.D. candidate in the combined areas of curriculum and systems analysis. When the issue of funding arose, I was pessimistic, from past experience, about securing federal support for the project. My two engineer colleagues, however, were mildly amused at my negativism, informing me that they could virtually guarantee federal support. Their response was that "science today is practically writing its own ticket." My hope is that science, while writing its own ticket, is not witnessing a serious decline of humanistic and social concerns in the culture. Unquestionably, any excessive investment of time and monies in any one or a limited number of curriculum areas leads to a proportionate neglect of the remaining areas.

3. And if a few curriculum areas have been the primary beneficiaries of federal research support, a few institutions of higher education comparably have been the primary beneficiaries of such support. The result is that the already affluent institutions, such as Harvard, the University of Chicago, and the University of California, are getting richer and the poor ones are getting poorer. The top 25 universities, in fact, receive more federal monies than all the other approximately 2500 colleges and universities put together. (See Table 13.2.)

4. With many, if not most, government projects having to do with national defense, the problem of secrecy is becoming increasingly troublesome. In this connection, higher education has long prided itself on an open posture before knowledge, both as to its acquisition and its dissemination. Today, this openness is giving way to increasingly tight security and close secrecy.

5. The uneven dissemination of government projects among faculty members of any given institution inevitably results in salary imbalances. The crux of the problem is that the government's salary schedules are almost always more favorable to professors than are non-government schedules. Thus when certain professors in an institution "work for the government" and others do not, faculty morale often suffers from the resulting salary inequities.

6. The federal government's penchant for getting things done in a hurry constitutes one of the most serious problems of all. Much too often the result is carelessness in one or more phases of planning, implementation, and assessment.

377

TABLE 13.2   FEDERAL OBLIGATIONS FOR RESEARCH AND DEVELOPMENT TO 25 UNIVERSITIES AND COLLEGES RECEIVING THE LARGEST AMOUNTS, 1964-1966

[Dollar amounts in thousands]

Institution (in order of R. & D Obligations, 1966)	1964		1965		1966		Percent of Ph.D. Degrees in the Sciences and Engineering, 1964-1965
	Amount	Percent of U.S. total	Amount	Percent of U.S. total	Amount	Percent of U.S. total	
1. Massachusetts Institute of Technology	63,206	6.61	52,460	4.87	57,227	4.55	3.23
2. University of Michigan	33,907	3.55	37,992	3.53	46,362	3.69	2.29
3. Stanford University	27,645	2.89	29,544	2.74	43,348	3.45	2.63
4. Columbia University	30,188	3.16	35,645	3.31	40,429	3.21	2.06
5. University of California—Los Angeles	24,640	2.58	27,577	2.56	36,067	2.87	1.94
6. University of Illinois	22,964	2.40	25,871	2.40	35,315	2.81	3.48
7. Harvard University	26,676	2.79	28,995	2.69	31,159	2.48	2.34
8. University of California—Berkeley	22,792	2.38	26,849	2.49	29,949	2.38	4.18
9. University of Chicago	24,076	2.52	24,474	2.27	27,033	2.15	1.62
10. University of Pennsylvania	17,942	1.88	19,534	1.81	25,755	2.05	1.51
11. University of Wisconsin—Madison	18,181	1.90	22,803	2.12	23,392	1.86	3.06
12. Cornell University	16,359	1.71	22,665	2.11	23,015	1.83	2.15
13. New York University	17,740	1.86	20,074	1.86	22,356	1.78	1.58
14. University of Washington	16,506	1.73	15,927	1.48	21,262	1.69	1.45
15. University of Texas	15,482	1.62	19,228	1.79	20,930	1.66	1.48
16. Johns Hopkins University	17,877	1.87	19,323	1.79	20,294	1.61	.98
17. University of Minnesota—Minneapolis-St. Paul	15,611	1.63	20,462	1.90	19,251	1.53	2.63
18. Yale University	14,117	1.48	15,719	1.46	17,422	1.38	1.61
19. University of California—San Diego	7,189	.75	8,935	.83	15,406	1.22	.21
20. Ohio State University	12,908	1.35	14,798	1.37	15,170	1.21	2.41
21. University of Maryland	10,922	1.14	12,603	1.17	14,130	1.12	1.29
22. Purdue University	7,758	.81	10,663	.99	13,905	1.11	2.67
23. Washington University	8,847	.93	10,457	.97	13,512	1.07	.47
24. University of Pittsburgh	10,818	1.13	12,048	1.12	13,394	1.06	.90
25. California Institute of Technology	10,972	1.15	13,007	1.21	13,162	1.05	.97

Source: National Science Foundation, Federal Support for Academic Science and Other Educational Activities in Universities and Colleges (Washington, D.C.: U.S. Government Printing Office, 1967, pp. 38–39.

7. Finally, colleges and universities are customarily at loggerheads with the federal government over how much overhead costs the latter should assume for projects performed by the former. Rule-of-thumb percentages are constantly a bone of serious contention.

In respect to these seven issues, as well as others that might have been included, I confess to considerable ambivalence. Yet certain convictions arise above the ambivalence. One of these is that colleges and universities for the foreseeable future will, at least in part, be in the service of the federal government. In fact, as social agencies, they will not be able to remain uninvolved. Without them, the government would be unable to perform many of its research-and-development functions.

Thus, with the federal government and higher education destined to be working partners for years to come, an agency to coordinate their mutual interests and activities needs to come into being. A theoretical model for such an agency was sketched by John W. Gardner, when he was President of the Carnegie Foundation, in his booklet *AID and the Universities* (1964). The plan was an outgrowth of Gardner's seven-month study of steps the Agency for International Development and cooperating universities might take to improve their working relationship.

AID is an organization of the federal government. Along with the Department of State, it is the agency most involved

in bringing students, faculty, and research scholars to the United States from other countries, and in sending American citizens abroad for study, teaching, research, and advisory services in education.

. . .

Under Federal Programs, approximately 23,500 American citizens have gone abroad and 58,000 foreign nationals have come to the United States for university study, advanced research, teaching, lecturing, and educational consultations of various kinds.[18]

Financial backing for the government's international development program started with the Fulbright Act of 1946. In the interim, the program's base has been enlarged by a number of other federal acts, the most recent one at the time of this writing being the International Education Act of 1966. At the end of 1963, "seventy-two universities in the United States were performing technical assistance tasks under 129

[18] American Council on Education, *Higher Education in the United States,* a reprint from Allan M. Cartter (ed.), *American Universities and Colleges* (Washington, D.C.: American Council on Education, 1964), p. 61.

separate contracts with AID. More than $158 million was involved in those contracts."[19]

Gardner's organizational proposal, in this connection, was for the establishment of a semiautonomous government institute which "would handle certain aspects of technical assistance, particularly those aspects dealt with by the universities." The name of the agency, according to Gardner, would be the National Institute for Educational and Technical Co-operation (NIETC). He elaborates as follows:

> It would be a separate corporate entity under its own board of trustees and would have an independent budget, but would be ultimately responsible to the AID Administrator. It would have its own career merit system and the right to establish its own levels of compensation guided by the comparability principle; and it would be so constituted that personnel of other government agencies, universities, or foundations could move in and out of it as the situation required without loss of perquisites attached to their normal employment.[20]

It is this kind of agency that the government needs to coordinate its domestic as well as its international relationships with universities. With hundreds of millions currently at stake, and billions ultimately at stake, the existing patchquilt of disorganization is both incredible and intolerable.

As colleges and universities take on increasingly important roles in governmental affairs at home and abroad, it is essential, however, that they not depart from their two primary functions, namely, instructing students and advancing knowledge. Failure in these areas will inevitably lead to individual and cultural regression across a broad front. Not only that, but government itself will fail to receive the assistance it needs from higher education. We thus end by affirming that government work must only supplement, never replace, higher education's fundamental purposes. Only through the preservation of these purposes will individualism flower, society mature, and government itself receive the assistance from higher education that it needs.

The issue of secrecy is the knottiest one of all. My personal reaction to it is as follows. Basically, colleges and universities should be open books. Practically, however, under the duress of unusual circumstances, they occasionally have to turn from this ideal. But the departure should be temporary; and under no circumstances should it be allowed to

[19] John W. Gardner, *AID and the Universities* (New York: Education and World Affairs, 1964), p. 1.

380 [20] Gardner, pp. 45–46.

harden into a pattern. The hope of the future is that man and cultures will mature to a point where padlocked secrecy in colleges and universities, even as a measure of expediency, will be unnecessary; where "cloak-and-dagger" behavior in national and international affairs will find its way back into fiction.

The Wall between Instructional Faculties and Governing Boards

As individual professors search for their proper professional identities, and as higher education collectively searches for its proper relational role with government, college and university faculties search for their proper governing roles in the institutions they serve. The basic problem is the civilization-old one of who will, or should, govern whom when a group of individuals work together in pursuit of commonly held purposes.[21] The three groups that in any college or university are legally or professionally endowed with official power are the following: (1) boards of trustees in private institutions or boards of regents in public ones, (2) administrative officials, and (3) teaching faculties.

An assessment of the power inherent in any of the three groups is dependent on answers to the questions: Should colleges and universities be line organizations patterned after industry; or should they be democratic communities? If democratic communities, do members of the three groups have enough in common to work together democratically, and, if so, what should their respective roles be? If industry-patterned organizations, then is the conservative's conception of colleges and universities as line organizations governed exclusively, or almost exclusively, by ruling boards and administrative functionaries a sound one? Under such an arrangement, a board of trustees and its executive officers would be in character when unilaterally decreeing, for instance, that a student-admissions policy, or a faculty-tenure policy, or an institutional-research policy should be of a given kind. The teaching faculty would have little or no policy voice.

In contrast to this conservative position, the liberal position conceives colleges and universities as democratic communities in which

---

[21] Some of the concepts discussed in this section come from R. Freeman Butt's excellent chapter "Formulation of Policy in American Colleges and Universities," in *The Year Book of Education 1959: Higher Education,* edited by George Z. F. Bereday and Joseph A. Lauwerys.

policy decisions are properly reached only when democratic processes are employed. Under such an arrangement—one that I wholeheartedly endorse—the governing principle is for individuals who are most affected by an impending decision to act as a controlling, but not as an exclusive, force in its formulation. This is, at one and the same time, both a sound democratic principle and an equally sound liberal business-management principle.

The question of whether board members, administrators, and teaching-faculty members have enough in common to work together co-operatively is a moot one. And the answer to it differs from institution to institution and from time to time within any given institution. In general, the greatest block to democratic cooperation is the fact that trustees or regents tend to constitute a different breed from instructional personnel. In private institutions, they are customarily affluent men of affairs. In public institutions, they may be successful politicians as well. In both private and public institutions, board members tend to be politically and socially conservative in their beliefs and in the causes they support. Instructional faculty members, in contrast, although not indigent, are rarely affluent. Furthermore, they tend to be politically and socially liberal in their beliefs and in the causes they support.

Juxtaposed between the two groups is the college or university president who, more often than not, has greater affinity with his board associates than with the teaching faculty. And juxtaposed between him and the teaching faculty is the dean or vice-president in charge of faculties who, more often than not, has more affinity with the teaching faculty than with the administrative superiors. Yet he cannot consistently side with the former lest he antagonize the "powers that be." His position truly is an unenviable one in higher education, embedded as it customarily is in organizational schizophrenia.

The following are characteristic features of staff relationships in most colleges and universities throughout the country. Channels of communication between faculty and boards of trustees or regents are more often closed than open. Faculties only rarely participate in the selection of incoming presidents. The faculty members concerned customarily have no voice in the selection of incoming deans or department heads. Faculty members of departments or related organizational units customarily have no voice in the hiring or dismissing of faculty members or in budget matters that affect a faculty as a whole. There is a collective trend toward more faculty self-government, but it is a very

382

slight one. Self-government finds greatest expression in large public institutions and in small, private liberal arts colleges.[22]

I conclude this section with a position statement on the relative policy-making roles that board members, administrators, and teaching faculties should, in my opinion, play in any college or university. A fundamental first need is for an institution to identify the functional spheres of influence of each power-wielding group. In the case of a teaching faculty, the primary sphere should embrace the academic program and the personnel involved in its implementation. A secondary sphere should embrace business concerns that impinge on the primary sphere. In the case of the board of trustees or board of regents, the primary sphere should encompass the business program, including the financial structure of the institution. A secondary sphere should encompass, at a broad level, the academic program. In the case of the president, deans, and other administrative officials, the primary sphere should include policy recommendation and policy implementation, once it has been approved by the controlling interest group. A secondary sphere should include check-and-balance functions exercised over other power-wielding groups.

Once an institution has identified the primary spheres of each power-wielding group, the obvious need is for authority within each group to be allowed to operate. In most instances, functional spheres overlap. Faculty staffing, for instance, is a combined faculty-administrative board concern. Professional involvements are greatest for the faculty and administration; financial involvements are greatest for the board and administration. The nature of any institution's admissions policy is yet another instance of a combined concern. A faculty generally assesses the policy from an academic point of view; a board and an administration assess it from a financial point of view as well.

Because of the inevitable overlap of policy issues, it is essential that colleges and universities establish and keep open all channels of communication among the three power-wielding groups. The channels should always be two-way or three-way. In such a scheme, unilateral action should be rarity.

Administrative power in practice often becomes excessive, sometimes capricious, with faculty power being the frequent loser. Individual faculty members are not necessarily harmed personally by this imbalance, shielded as most are by tenure rights and, in critical instances,

---

[22] Butts, pp. 254–255.

by the American Association of University Professors, organizational champion of academic freedom. However, if faculty members as individuals are not seriously harmed by it, faculty members collectively, and education as a whole, are seriously harmed by it. They are harmed by the mismanagement that inevitably results when a function is performed under the leadership of persons not qualified to lead. Mismanagement is held to a minimum, however, when colleges and universities decentralize operational powers to functional interest groups and, in the process, commission them to lead both knowledgeably and cooperatively.

Student Power

The most volatile issue in higher education today is the one posed by the student power movement. The current wave of student-protest marches, disruption of academic classes, interference with campus assemblies, "sit-ins," and occasional arson are instances of student resistance to constituted authority. Recent widely-publicized victims of this resistance include the University of California, the University of Wisconsin, Columbia University, San Francisco State College, and the University of Chicago.

Exactly who the student militants are in these and other collegiate institutions is at least partially conjectural. They seem, however, to divide into three categories. One category includes a small hard core of anarchists who, while desirous of destroying the status quo, lack a program to fill the vacuum thereby created. Selected members of The Students for a Democratic Society are cases in point. A second category consists of members of selected ethnic minority groups: Negroes, Puerto Ricans, and Mexican-Americans, for example, who have definitive social causes to advance. The goals of these ethnic groups are (1) compensatory education at the college level to atone for decades of socially enforced second-rate education at the elementary and secondary-school levels; (2) student bodies that increasingly include more of their ethnic-group members; (3) faculties that increasingly include more of their ethnic-group members; (4) curriculums that more comprehensively embrace their ethnic origins and traditions; and (5) administrations that include them more actively in the many processes of decision making. A third category includes that vast body of young **384** people who, like their almost countless counterparts through the ages,

desire social change and gravitate toward those who champion it. Individuals in this third category are mostly followers, not leaders, in the student power movement.

Coverage that would do justice to the movement would require volumes. It involves factors that are as comprehensive and complex as our basic political documents, as their inadequate translation into social action, as the difficulty of succeeding generations to understand one another, as the mind and emotions of man himself. Thus we admit to oversimplification in the ensuing summary statement.

We postulate that the fundamental cause of student unrest in colleges and universities resides in the legitimate desire by the younger generation to precipitate change in the social order. Yet this desire is not at all novel. It is, rather, a desire shared by idealized youth of every new generation. An innovative feature, however, is its urgency—a product of many causal factors, selected of which are (1) the increased visibility accorded social action by the mass-communications media; (2) the denial to youth of access to conventional channels of communication; (3) the unpopular conflict in Viet Nam; (4) the futility created by man's power to obliterate himself and civilization; and (5) a long history of indignities heaped on Negroes and other minority groups. These forces have projected social inequities into the open while strengthening the hands of young social actionists who are attempting to rectify them. That attempts at rectification have precipitated many instances of over-action and over-reaction is obvious to most.

If the fundamental cause of student unrest is a legitimate desire for peaceful change, a secondary cause is the irrational desire by a few militant dissidents to effect social change by violent means. But violence is not, per se, categorically, a social evil—as the American Revolution, for example, demonstrated. Destructive violence, however, without a positive plan or program to replace what is to be destroyed, constitutes anarchy. Unfortunately, at least a few colleges and universities throughout the country are recipients of this kind of violence, violence that is unaccompanied by any plan of positive action. Thus it constitutes nothing less than rebellion.

Institutional responses to the student power movement should consist, in our opinion, of the following measures. First and foremost, college administrations and faculties, without abdicating their leadership roles in essential academic matters, should learn and practice the art of listening to students. In the process, they should regard and treat students as young, thinking adults, not as troublesome children. Re-

385

latedly, administrations, faculties, and students should join frequently, even systematically, in collective forums wherein common problems and grievances are ventilated and resolved. Collective "reasoning together" often prevents problems from rigidifying into issues. Within this frame, however, administrations and faculties should identify and give visibility to those concerns and responsibilities that are uniquely theirs, and only theirs, thus serving notice that outside interference by students will result only in futility and failure.

When colleges and universities designate those areas in which issues are negotiable and those in which they are not, openness, flexibility, and integrity tend to characterize discussions of negotiable issues. Relatedly, forthright explanation and reasonable resistance to pressure should characterize confrontations over issues that are not negotiable. Colleges and universities need, more than they have in the past, to include students in important decision-making matters. But they should not, cannot, in fact, abdicate their legal and professional roles and functions.

Fundamentally, colleges and universities are social-academic institutions committed to serve the needs of all students. Thus they cannot, with impunity, concede narrowly to the demands of a few unreasonable militants. In fact, they have no choice but to resist these demands when they or their advocates are immoderate. Still it is most important, at the same time, for colleges and universities, in some systematic way, to include students actively in decisions that vitally affect them.

A CLOSING WORD

In any age, greatness in higher education—for that matter, in life itself —is as much a product of nonconformity as conformity. Neither of these is intrinsically good or bad; each is good or bad only in terms of purposes and situations. Conformity is the protector of the status quo which, when value-oriented, quite properly needs a protector. Nonconformity, in contrast, is the champion of defensible change; thus it holds the key to progress. The first is usually the path of ease; the second is usually the path of discomfort.

Traditionally, many colleges and universities have chosen the path of ease, have rested comfortably in the status quo. The great ones, however, after assessing the status quo and finding it wanting, have gone **386** the way of change. The great ones today are those in which diversified

research is taking place, in which open dialogue is the vogue, in which instruction is exciting, in which faculties and materials of learning keep pace with needs, in which authority serves not itself but the cause of scholarship and learners. The criteria of excellence in these great colleges and universities are skepticism more than acceptance, pursuit of the unknown more than preservation of the known, and justified protest more than patterned compliance.

Of course, no institution of higher education is capable of satisfying all these criteria. Yet those institutions that most nearly satisfy the criteria are higher education's leaders today and will continue to be their leaders in the future.

To Stimulate Thought

1. Many junior colleges have nonacademically oriented programs for youth and adults. Of what, in your opinion, should these programs consist? And what purposes should they serve?

2. Take a stand, and defend it, on the issue of colleges and universities requiring all students to complete a year's course in world history or its equivalent.

3. Develop the theme that a specialist to be effective needs first to be a well-rounded generalist.

4. Admitting that college professors ideally should be researchers as well as teachers, what is the case, if any, for teacher-counselors who do not do research?

5. Take a stand, and develop it, on the issue: The federal government is going counter to America's traditions by actively advancing science at the expense of the social sciences and the humanities.

6. Debate the issue: Colleges and universities should accept secret projects from the federal government.

7. Develop the theme, pro or con, that colleges and universities become great, at least in part, when they bring to their teaching and research faculties individuals with divergent interests and points of view.

REFERENCES

American Council on Education, *Higher Education in the United States* (Washington, D.C.: American Council on Education, 1965).

387

Babbidge, Homer D., Jr., and Robert M. Rosenzweig, *The Federal Interest in Higher Education* (New York: McGraw-Hill, Inc., 1962).

Baskin, Samuel (ed.), *Higher Education: Some Newer Developments* (New York: McGraw-Hill, Inc., 1965).

Benjamin, Harold R. W., *Higher Education in the American Republics* (New York: McGraw-Hill, Inc., 1965).

Berelsen, Bernard, *Graduate Education in the United States* (New York: McGraw-Hill, Inc., 1960).

Brown, Hugh S., and Lewis B. Mayhew, *American Higher Education* (New York: The Center for Applied Research in Education, Inc., 1965).

DeVane, William Clyde, *Higher Education in Twentieth Century America* (Cambridge, Mass.: Harvard University Press, 1965).

Dodds, Harold W., *The Academic President: Educator or Caretaker?* (New York: McGraw-Hill, Inc., 1962).

Dressel, Paul L., *The Undergraduate Curriculum in Higher Education* (Washington, D.C.: The Center for Applied Research in Education, Inc., 1963).

Educational Research Corporation, *College Admissions Data Service* (Cambridge, Mass.: Educational Research Corp., 1966–1967).

Freeman, Stephen A., *Undergraduate Study Abroad: Report of the Consultative Service on U.S. Undergraduate Study Abroad* (New York: Institute of International Education, 1964).

Gleazer, Edmund J., Jr., *American Junior Colleges*, 6th Ed. (Washington, D.C.: American Council on Education, 1963).

Hutchins, Robert Maynard, *Higher Learning in America* (New Haven: Yale University Press, 1963).

Kerr, Clark, *The Uses of the University* (Cambridge, Mass.: Harvard University Press, 1963).

Lovejoy, Clarence E., *Lovejoy's College Guide* (New York: Simon and Schuster, Inc., 1966).

Mayhew, Lewis B., *General Education: An Account and Appraisal* (New York: Harper & Row, Publishers, 1960).

McGrath, Earl J. (ed.), *Cooperative Long-Range Planning in Liberal Arts Colleges* (New York: Bureau of Publications, Teachers College, Columbia University, 1964).

Medsker, Leland L., *The Junior College: Progress and Prospect* (New York: McGraw-Hill, Inc., 1960).

Meeth, L. Richard, *Selected Issues in Higher Education: An Annotated Bibliography* (New York: Bureau of Publications, Teachers College, Columbia University, 1965).

Messersmith, James C., *Church-Related Boards Responsible for Higher Education*, OE-53021, No. 13 (Washington, D.C.: U.S. Department of Health, Education, and Welfare, 1964).

EDUCATION AS AN OPERATIONAL PROCESS

Morrison, D. G., and Clinette F. Witherspoon, *Procedures for the Establishment of Public 2-Year Colleges,* OE-57006, No. 14 (Washington, D.C.: U.S. Department of Health, Education, and Welfare, 1966).

Morrison, Robert S. (ed.), *The Contemporary University:* U.S.A. (Boston: Houghton Mifflin Company, 1966).

Muskin, Selma J., *Economics of Higher Education,* Bulletin 5, 1962 (Washington, D.C.: U.S. Department of Health, Education, and Welfare, 1962).

Orlans, Harold, *The Effects of Federal Programs on Higher Education: A Study of 36 Institutions* (Washington, D.C.: The Brookings Institute, 1962).

Sanford, Nevitt (ed.), *The American College: A Psychological and Social Interpretation of the Higher Learning* (New York: John Wiley & Sons, Inc., 1962).

Selden, William K., *Accreditation: A Struggle Over Standards in Higher Education* (New York: Harper & Row, Publishers, 1960).

Smith, G. Kerry (ed.), *Stress and Campus Response* (San Francisco: Jossey-Bass, Inc., Publishers, 1968).

Stoke, Harold W., *The American College President* (New York: Harper & Row, Publishers, 1959).

Sutherland, Robert L., *et al.* (eds.), *Personality Factors on the College Campus* (Austin, Tex.: The Hogg Foundation for Mental Health, 1962).

Tickton, Sidney G., *The Year-round Campus Catches On* (New York: Fund for the Advancement of Education, 1963).

Tiedt, Sidney W., *The Role of the Federal Government in Education* (New York: Oxford University Press, 1966).

Trent, James W. and Leland L. Medsker, *Beyond High School* (San Francisco: Jossey-Bass, Inc., Publishers, 1968).

U.S. Department of Health, Education, and Welfare, *Education Directory—Part 3: Higher Education* (Washington, D.C.: U.S. Government Printing Office, 1966).

Veblen, Thorstein, *The Higher Learning in America* (New York: B. W. Huebsch, 1918).

Wilson, Logan (ed.), *Emerging Patterns in American Higher Education* (Washington, D.C.: American Council on Education, 1965).

Part Four
Exceptional Learners
in
Education

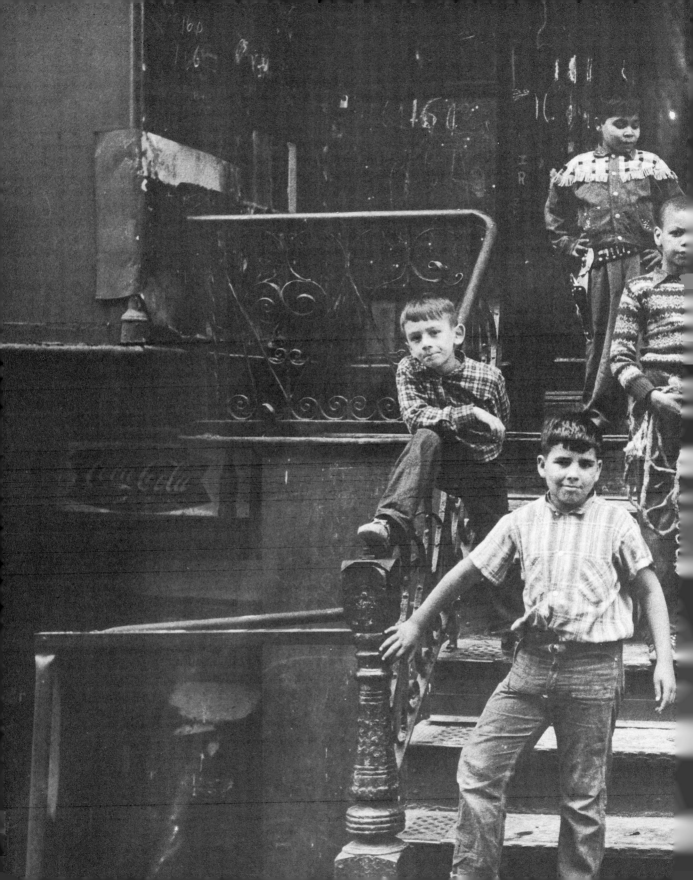

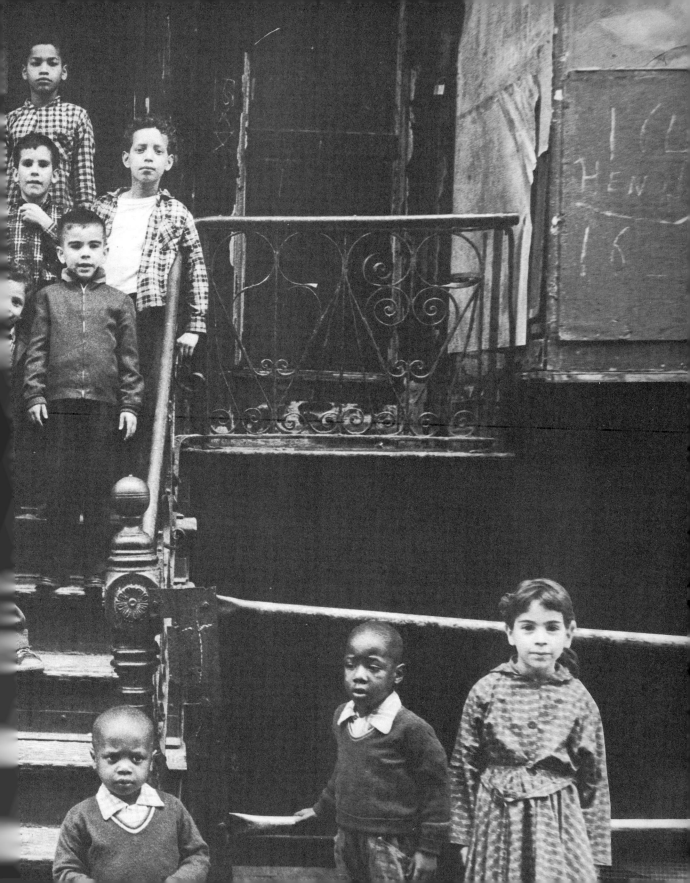

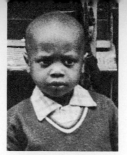

Chapter
14

Culturally Deprived Learners

At this juncture, the book makes a directional turn from educational program to student learners. And in view of the coverage already made of so-called normal learners in Chapters 6 to 8, the shift here is to exceptional learners: specifically, (1) to the culturally deprived, (2) to the gifted, and (3) to the physically handicapped. The first constitutes the theme of the present chapter; the next two, of the ensuing two chapters.

The term *culturally deprived* (or *culturally disadvantaged,* or *culturally underprivileged*) is one customarily employed to describe individuals deficient in the social experiences that the majority in the society routinely enjoy. These individuals do not lack a culture, obviously; yet their falls short of the standards that apply to the dominant middle-class culture. It falls short in such material components as employment, income, housing, travel, and medical care; and in such psycho-social components as self-worth, belonging, acceptance, mores, language, and attitude toward the society's institutions and general way of life.

The so-called culturally deprived are not in the least a single-entitied, discrete group. Ethnically (in a loose employment of the term), they include in their ranks people of all races and ethnic groups: notably; Negroes, Caucasians, Puerto Ricans, Mexicans, Southern Europeans, and reservation Indians. Negroes are undoubtedly among the most deprived, and nonwhites, collectively, are even *more so.* In respect to habitat, Negroes live mostly in large cities and Southern rural areas. Deprived Caucasians or "poor whites," including Southern European immigrants, live mostly in large cities, in Appalachia, or on farms in the South. Puerto Ricans cluster mostly in New York City. Mexicans inhabit Los Angeles and San Francisco primarily. And American Indians are indigents of reservations located, for the most part, in the West. In respect to their combined numbers, estimates rarely go as low as

15 percent and usually go as high as 20 percent of the total population. In respect to financial status, most of the culturally deprived live on estimated family incomes of $3,000 annually, or less.

Havighurst responds as follows[1] to his self-addressed question: Who are the socially disadvantaged?

1. They are at the bottom of the American society in terms of income.
2. They have a rural background.
3. They suffer from social and economic discrimination at the hands of the majority of the society.
4. They are widely distributed in the United States. While they are most visible in the big cities, they are present in all except the very high income communities. There are many of them in rural areas, especially in the southern and southwestern states.

Other responses to the same question could well include the following noneducational characteristics.

1. They desire their fundamental constitutional rights: to vote; to enjoy free speech; to have open access to such public facilities as hotels, restaurants, parks, and swimming pools; to buy property they can afford; to secure jobs they are capable of filling, to be recipients of legal justice; to be free of fear; and, in general, to have rights equal to those enjoyed by all other citizens. And they increasingly demand not just their rights, but even more, equal results from their efforts. In effect, their goal is to attain at least an equitable cross section of the many good things of life that American society affords.

2. They are oriented to the physical here and now: for instance, to the essentials of everyday living, to the job of the moment, to the amount of spending money in the pocket, to the cop on the beat, to places of entertainment in the neighborhood.

3. Because so oriented, they react less than adequately to the abstract; thus are unable to cope as meaningfully as the average person with concepts and generalizations.

4. Not part of the dominant culture, and feeling alienated as a result, they compensate by withdrawing into themselves or by lashing out aggressively at individuals and forces that, in their opinion, fence them in.

5. If Negro, families are usually very much, if not completely, ma-

[1] From Robert J. Havighurst, "Introduction," in John M. Beck and Richard W. Saxe (eds.), *Teaching the Culturally Disadvantaged Pupil* (Springfield, Ill.: Charles C Thomas, Publisher, 1965), pp. ix–x. Courtesy of Charles C Thomas, Publisher, Springfield, Illinois.

ternally controlled; if other than Negro, families are usually paternally oriented and controlled.

6. If families are Negro and live on incomes of under $2,000 annually, they have, on an average, 5.3 children, contrasted with 2.9 children in families that are Negro and live on incomes of over $10,000.[2]

7. They receive less than adequate medical care, and for this reason, among others, they have higher than average death rates.[3]

8. Most fundamental of all, they are human beings: each an individual, none a stereotype. And being human, they are, in great part, products of their environments. Thus they introject a way of life that irrespective of its exact characteristics sets them apart from the dominant controlling culture.

FEDERAL LEGISLATION
AIMED AT THE CULTURALLY DEPRIVED

During the past several decades, the federal government has championed the cause of the culturally deprived, both adults and children, in an increasingly pervasive way. The first thrust was the School Lunch Act of 1946 which, since its passage, has assured indigent children of at least one hot meal per day, either at low cost or at no cost at all. Other more recent federal legislation comprises the following.

1. The Welfare Amendments of 1962 (PL 87-543) expanded the Social Security Act by extending aid, mostly in the form of vocational education, to children under 18 years of age from families on public relief. The amendments, in addition, subsidized the cost of day-care centers for working mothers whose spouses are unemployed and on relief.

2. The Manpower Development and Training Act of 1962, and amendments to it in 1963, established and underwrote a vocational program for out-of-school youth unemployed or underemployed, also a literacy program of 22-weeks duration for those, including functional illiterates, in need of it. Since 1965, the act has provided educational opportunity and employment for youth at Opportunity Centers.

3. The Vocational Education Act of 1963 (PL 88-210) also provides

[2] Journal of the American Academy of Arts and Sciences, *Daedalus*, 94 (Fall, 1965), p. 758.

[3] *Daedalus*, pp. 761–764.

for the vocational education of disadvantaged persons. Eligibility includes individuals still in school or out of school who are in need of vocational training or retraining. The act divides into the categories of Work-Study Provisions, Residential Vocational Schools, Area-Vocational Schools, and the Commissioner's Role—both administrative and financial.

4. The Economic Opportunity Act of 1964 (President Johnson's so-called Anti-Poverty Bill) which has the two-pronged goal of providing vocational education for disadvantaged youth aged 12 to 21; and preschool education, broadly conceived, for disadvantaged children aged four to five. In respect to the former, the act provides for a Job Corps whose goal is to upgrade the work and study skills of the youth enrolled. The hoped-for result is a greater readiness by youth for gainful employment in the world of business and industry. The government underwrites their living expenses during the program and compensates them at the rate of $50 monthly. In respect to the latter, the act has underwritten for preschool children the Head Start program, beginning with the summer of 1965 and continuing to the time of this writing. As stated in Chapter 10, of the many federal programs designed to help the culturally deprived, Project Head Start is one of the most, if not the single most, successful.

Built into the act is VISTA, or Volunteers in Service to America. These volunteers, some 5000 in number in 1965, are, in effect, domestic Peace Corps members. Their duties are instructional and administrative. Their salaries are a modest $50 monthly, exclusive of living allowance or its equivalent.

5. A 1964 revision of the National Defense Education Act which broadened the 1958 version by including the teaching of disadvantaged children as one of its new provisions.

6. The Elementary and Secondary Education Act of 1965 which was enacted for the purpose of improving the education of approximately 5 million children from families with annual incomes of under $2,000. In the words of President Johnson on April 11, 1965, "By passing this bill, we bridge the gap between helplessness and hope for more than five million educationally deprived children in America." A total of $1.06 billion was appropriated by the act for the causes of educational programming, instruction, and construction. Specific outcomes have been an upgrading of instructional resources including libraries, textbooks, audiovisual aids and materials, and in-service growth of teachers. Once more in the words of President Johnson: "I believe deeply no

law I have signed or will ever sign means more to the future of America." In the process of implementation, the act, as might be expected, has fallen short of these high hopes. Yet it is the type of legislation the country needs desperately as it struggles for victory in the social revolution of the times.

7. The Higher Education Act of 1965 was enacted to strengthen the community service programs of colleges and universities "so as to assist in the solution of community programs such as housing, poverty, government, recreation, employment, youth opportunities, transportation, health, and land use." This act stands as yet another landmark in the nation's war on poverty and on associated manifestations of human deprivation.

EDUCATIONAL PROJECTS
RELATING TO THE CULTURALLY DEPRIVED

Emanating, at least in part, from the aforementioned legislation are educational projects and programs inclusive of the following. Literally hundreds might have been included, but only a few have been. Some have been discussed in other parts of the book, but have been included again here for purpose of completeness.

1. *The Higher Horizons Project,* a forerunner to the Great Cities Program, was initiated in New York City in 1956 as an experiment in curriculum enrichment for socially disadvantaged children. As described in Chapter 10, disadvantaged secondary school students were transported into the greater New York City community for purposes of cultural enrichment. A consistently reported result was a significant increase in their IQs.

2. *The Banneker Project,* initiated in St. Louis, Missouri, in 1957, is a home-school experiment in elementary school education. The Project learners are 97 percent Negroes who attend exclusively slum schools in the downtown area of the city. Teachers and administrators, bolstered by an extra appropriation of $200 per pupil per year, make frequent visits to the homes of the children, urging parents both to make school visits and to maintain close contact in a variety of ways with school personnel throughout the period of their children's school enrollment. On the surface, the project seems to have little new to offer. The veneer, however, conceals a forthright approach employed by school personnel that might hold the key to the Project's success. **399**

Dr. Samuel Shepard, as the project's chief administrator and also the Assistant Superintendent of Schools, has said to parents:[4]

If your child stays home to pay the bill collector, he won't be in school. If he has to baby sit, he won't be in school. You can't send him around the corner to get bread and milk at 10 minutes to 9 and expect him to be at school on time.

School personnel other than Shepard who work in the project reportedly understand the life styles of the community adults and their children, impose reality on them, and solicit their support in a straightforward manner.

3. *The Great Cities Program,* first implemented in 1959 in Detroit, Michigan, constitutes a massive attempt by the large cities of the country to improve educational programs for the culturally deprived. The cities, 15 in number, are Baltimore, Boston, Buffalo, Chicago, Cleveland, Detroit, Houston, Los Angeles, Milwaukee, New York, Philadelphia, Pittsburgh, St. Louis, San Francisco, and Washington, D.C. The 15 cities subscribe in common to the so-called central hypothesis[5] that the problems of children with limited backgrounds can be effectively and economically solved by:

1. Development of a program of education adapted to the needs of these children
2. Modifications in the organizational patterns within the school
3. Proper selection and utilization of personnel
4. Improved utilization of instructional equipment and materials
5. Involvement of parents and of the community in the educational program

The Great Cities Program in the process of implementation utilizes the services of individuals from the following categories: multidiscipline consultants from sociology, anthropology, social and clinical psychology, psychiatry, and public administration; school-community representatives to coordinate the activities of the several institutions involved; and visiting teachers to strengthen the bonds between school and home. Other characteristics of the implementation process consist of curriculum materials carefully selected and discerningly applied, instruction that meets high standards, and school expenditures that ex-

[4] Harold Baron, "Samuel Shepard and the Banneker Project" in Meyer Weinberg (ed.), *Learning Together: A Book on Integrated Education* (Chicago: Integrated Education Associates, 1964), p. 47.

[5] Carl A. Marburger, "Considerations for Educational Planning," in A. Harry Passow (ed.), *Education in Depressed Areas* (New York: Bureau of Publications, Teachers College, Columbia University, 1963), p. 80.

ceed the normative by 5 to 15 percent. In readying personnel for the program, the 15 cities have consistently relied on intimate involvement of teachers (or teacher trainees) in problems of the culturally deprived, on in-service workshops, and on informal consultant services when deemed essential.

4. *Project ABLE* is a statewide program, initiated by New York State in 1961, developed along lines of the Higher Horizons Project of New York City. It was, and continues to be, an attempt by New York to extend this project to other cities, villages and suburban communities of the state. Under Project ABLE, the state of New York provides $200,000 annually, on a matching basis, to designated school systems interested in a Higher Horizons type of program. Since 1961, four other states: Maine, Pennsylvania, Rhode Island, and California have been planning, or have completed plans, for a similar program. The State of California recently appropriated $324,000 for such a program.[6]

5. *Project Head Start,* which got underway in 1965, warrants no further comment here in view of the treatment accorded it earlier in this chapter and in Chapter 10, as well.

6. A number of colleges and universities throughout the country have revised their admissions policies downward to permit the enrollment of selected marginal graduates of inner-city high schools. The underlying rationale is that admissions standards such as minimum IQ or CEEB (College Entrance Examination Board) scores are not valid criteria when applied to culturally deprived students. Some universities currently involved in this experimental approach include the following: Brown, Dillard, Harvard, Northwestern, and Southern (Baton Rouge); colleges include Rhode Island and Whitworth (Spokane).

7. Selected colleges and universities have developed, or are in the process of developing, innovational teacher-education programs designed to ready teachers for instruction of culturally deprived children and youth. Hunter College and Queens College of New York City are two cases in point. One writer describes the Hunter College program as follows:

Student volunteers are assigned to a particular school in a depressed neighborhood, usually in Harlem. They familiarize themselves not only with the schools but with the community as well. They visit Negro homes, read Negro newspapers, confer with community leaders, talk with local ministers, and inspect local housing projects, hospitals, and police stations. They

[6] Bernard A. Kaplan, "Issues in Educating the Culturally Disadvantaged," *Phi Delta Kappan* (November 1963), pp. 70–76.

observe teachers for two weeks before they gradually "break in" to a regular classroom assignment.[7]

Queens College is known for its Bridge Project: "Building Resources of Instruction for Disadvantaged Groups in Education."

CHARACTERISTICS OF CULTURALLY DEPRIVED CHILDREN

Early in the chapter we sketched a panoramic picture of culturally disadvantaged adults and their families. Characterizing the word picture were such descriptive terms as poverty, objects of discrimination, desire for an equitable share of the good things of life, pre-occupation with the physical and the present, alienation, and unfulfilled basic needs. But towering over all others was the descriptive term *human*.

Now we proceed to sketch a personal-socioeducational picture of the children and youth who live as family members with deprived adults. These children and youth are also customarily poor, living on substandard subsistence quotas, living in substandard housing, wearing substandard clothing, and bending to substandard norms of health and hygiene. Furthermore, imbued with a kind of Robin Hood logic, they exhibit less than adequate respect for the personal and property rights of middle-class individuals and institutions. Like their adult counterparts, they live in narrowly circumscribed physical environments. To most, a distance of three or four miles from home is a long way.

These children and youth are victims not only of physical but of psychological deprivation. They live in squalor but are very much aware of how the other three-fourths live. And such knowledge raises doubts in their minds about their own basic adequacy. Contrasts between the inner city and the suburb, between the run-down rural hovel and the spacious, well-kept farmhouse; in fact, sharp contrasts along any physical dimension invariably breed psychological problems that exceed the bounds of physical difference. Thus when the culturally deprived child asks such probing, but understandable, questions about himself as: Who am I? How worthwhile am I? What is my destiny?, he receives the psychologically disturbing answers: You are a child of poverty. In the eyes of many, you are not as good as others. Your future may well be no more than an extension of your present lot.

[7] Frederick Shaw, "Educating Culturally Deprived Youth in Urban Centers," in Joe L. Frost and Glenn R. Hawkes (eds.), *The Disadvantaged Child: Issues and Innovations* (Boston: Houghton Mifflin Company, 1966), p. 235.

He receives these defeating answers because the social order has denied him the minimum recognition that a wholesome self-image requires. For an individual, in any social category, to respect himself, others need to respect him. And, conversely, for an individual to respect others, he needs first to respect himself. Unfortunately, in this connection, the culturally deprived child tends to fall short on both these counts. He fails on the first count because the middle-class culture has "learned" from previous generations to misunderstand and deprecate him and because his own culture is entangled too much in the stresses of everyday living to give him the psychological support and sustenance he needs. He fails on the second count as a victim of circumstances: deprived of adequate social recognition, he is incapable of relating positively, much less altruistically, to others.

Enlightenment alone can provide an escape from this deeply etched and circular groove of defeatism. And enlightenment resides in the dominant culture's cumulative store of knowledge about man and his environment. Recent significant contributions to this store have come from the fields of sociology, psychology, anthropology, psychiatry, and socially-oriented religious groups. Collectively these reveal the culturally deprived, both young and old, to be inheritors, as well as active perpetrators, of life's influences; to be individuals who, more than anything else, need self-worth; to be individuals who, when imbued with a feeling of self-worth, will advance the cause of human welfare as well as reap its benefits. Conversely, these reveal that individuals tend to become and to remain pathological when denied the feeling of self-worth.

All these physical, personal, and social limitations accompany culturally deprived children to school, making the already complex processes of teaching and learning even more complex. The most serious limitation of all is that these children who are nonsymbolically oriented have to compete in the most symbolically oriented institution known to man. They come from homes where conversation is conspicuous by its rarity, and, when engaged in by family members, is characterized more by brevity, monosyllables, and kinetic movement than by significant verbal exchanges. As a group, they respond unevenly to reading instruction, they listen more courteously than comprehendingly, and they rarely talk without being prodded.

A factor that makes the language problem even more of an obstacle is the fact that they speak and listen to a nonstandard pattern of English in their homes and communities while being exposed to a different one

—so-called standard English—in the schools. The nonstandard pattern differs widely from group to group, with faulty syntax constituting the only common characteristic. Pronounciation, enunciation, and sentence structure vary extensively.

Yet another contributing factor to the school language problem is the narrow experience range of culturally deprived children. To the young who have not been to a zoo, the word *elephant* is only as meaningful as the primer picture is able to make it. To pupils who have seen mostly run-down slum or rural dwellings, the clean, shiny white building of the school book is an academic fancy. And because most culturally deprived children in the eighth or ninth grade conceive law and order as a composite of the policeman visible in their neighborhood and "The Man" up there somewhere, a civics unit on "Our local government" has but limited meaning. Applicable to the culturally deprived child, if to anyone, is the basic, though hackneyed, truism that a reader has to bring meaning to the printed page if he hopes to extract meaning from it. That is to say, the more extensive and graphic the life pattern, the more meaningful are the messages that word symbols convey. For the culturally deprived child, these messages either do not come through at all or come through blurred—and for the two reasons just given: first,

404

the language may be that of a "foreign" group; and second, provincial life experiences are unlikely catalysts of refined meaning.

AN EDUCATIONAL PROGRAM
FOR THE CULTURALLY DEPRIVED

Against the background of detail about the millions of culturally deprived in the American society, we now sketch an educational program that, at least in part, holds promise of ameliorating their condition. The goals of the program neither are, nor should they be, different from those conceived for learners in the composite. Thus the program espouses outcomes that lie along emotional, physical, social, and cognitive dimensions. Even though the goals in composite do not differ, qualitative emphases among them do. In Project Head Start, for example, of the 560,000 children enrolled in the program in 1965, 110,000 needed glasses, 50,000 were partially deaf, 75,000 needed shots, and 25,-000 suffered from malnutrition.[8] These health statistics compelled education, at least at the start, to highlight the physical dimension. Man cannot live by bread alone, but without bread he cannot live at all. Yet again, emotionally disturbed children may need mental health, and socially retarded ones may need socializing experiences at least as much as they need cognitive learning. And in the single area of the cognitive itself, culturally deprived children customarily have more specialized learning needs, particularly in the category of language communication, than do the majority of their culturally different associates.

For positive learning along any dimension to take place, unlearning often has to precede. In this connection, however, what is learning but the replacement of old patterns with new ones? And how can education better effect the exchange of old for new than by bringing learners into the educational fold early and retaining all of them, or almost all, at least through high school, and many beyond high school?

Preschool Programs

If the culturally deprived are to remain in and realize optimum benefit from school, formal education unquestionably needs to reach them as early as practically possible. This it is currently doing in Project Head

[8] Joe L. Frost and Glenn R. Hawkes, (eds.), p. 9.

Start. This it does in any community when it actively campaigns for parents to enroll their children in kindergarten even though law does not require such attendance. This it does when, once children are in the primary grades, it remains dissatisfied unless reaching them with telling effect. Preschool education is both a cultural bridge to, and a readying ground for, academic growth. It is the former in that it leads children reassuringly, and surefootedly, into a new cultural world. It is the latter in that teachers help children in that new world to understand a different-sounding language, introduce them to exploratory and manipulative things, help them to distinguish between what is mine and what is yours, encourage children to tell about themselves and their experiences, and impress on children the importance of personal hygiene. In effect, the goal is functional learning in the immediate present and readiness for functional learning in the long-term future. A similar picture is painted by Martin Deutsch in the following:[9]

> The use of the preschool experience as both a bridge between the two cultures with which the child must deal and as a stimulant to his development, dictates that its program be carefully planned to accomplish these goals. There must be a balance between the social and the cognitive; between the cultural and the emotional. I must say at the outset categorically that planning by educators does not mean regimenting the children. It means organizing a program that will best accomplish the ends in view by supplying the most effective bridge and the most effective early stimulation.

The goal of education in working with children marginal to the dominant culture unquestionably should be to reach them early before life habits and patterns have hardened. Such a step is an investment in the future both of the individuals reached by it and of the culture itself.

Child Study as an Essential Part of the Curriculum

For educational personnel to reap maximum dividends from this investment, they need to study learners as diligently as they do curriculum and instructional methodology. As stated by one source:[10]

[9] Martin Deutsch, "Nursery Education: The Influence of Social Programming on Early Development," in John M. Beck and Richard W. Saxe, (eds.), *Teaching the Culturally Disadvantaged Pupil,* 1965, p. 147. Courtesy of Charles C Thomas, Publisher, Springfield, Illinois.

[10] Joe L. Frost and Glenn R. Hawkes, "The Disadvantaged Child: Overview and Recommendations," p. 8.

Such study should emphasize techniques for evaluation of the child's social, emotional, physical, and intellectual development, with subsequent practical implementation in the classroom. Evidence of levels of development, achievement motivation, experiential background, and special strengths and weaknesses, compiled from careful observation of the child in varied situations should be used in assessment. Teaching should then proceed on the basis of *diagnosis* of individual and group needs.

Similarly stated by another source:[11]

In short, we believe that good teaching means taking a group "where they are," whatever the criteria used to establish this fact, and then proceeding in *any and all* directions necessary to build upon and extend the capabilities of these students.

Educational personnel, if they truly are to take culturally deprived children "where they are," need to be clinicians in the finest sense of the term. Medical and dental personnel need to take appropriate action in respect to health needs; psychologists, psychiatrists, and social workers, in respect to emotional needs; and teachers and psychologists, combined, in respect to both social and academic needs. Culturally deprived children, even more than culturally favored ones who also need it, require attention across a broad spectrum of growth. The academic-cognitive approach will not suffice; as often as not it has proved self-defeating.

Language Skills Paramount

Among the many needs that educational personnel customarily discover as they make clinical studies of the culturally deprived, none, as indicated earlier in the chapter, stands out more prominently than those in the area of language. Language has low status value in the typical submiddle-class home or community. "Us ain't go no" may be every bit as acceptable as "We do not have any."

In settings outside the home and community, however, nonstandard language almost habitually creates obstacles, sometimes serious ones. For one, nonstandard language is not always understandable to listeners who speak the so-called standard dialect of the dominant culture. The above illustration is more understandable than, for instance, "My wido ceel is bus" (my windowsill is busted). Language like this

[11] Loretta B. Jones and Richard Wisniewski, "Curriculum Needs of Slow Learners" in August Kerber and Barbara Bommarito, *The Schools and the Urban Crisis: A Book of Readings* (New York: Holt, Rinehart and Winston, Inc., 1965), p. 337.

that fails to communicate any meaning at all obviously fails its most basic purpose. A second obstacle erected by nonstandard language is that even when it communicates meaning in general it does not necessarily do so with linguistic refinement. For a teen-ager to categorize all constituted authority as "The Man" performs, to say the least, a disservice to communication specificity. A third obstacle is purely social —nonstandard language erects a barrier for individuals interested in climbing the upward-mobility ladder of the "standard" culture. All who seek socioeconomic advancement do not necessarily have to wear the same brand and cut of suits or speak in identical dialects; but if realistic in their expectations, they had better conform, within reason, to existing norms. As graphically stated by one writer:[12]

> In a most realistic sense, we cannot save the fifty million economically and culturally disadvantaged human beings who are drowning in the sea of our national affluence until we have taught them, beginning in their earliest childhood, to speak, to read, and in some measure, to write the words and forms of English that are acceptable to our society.

The educational ideal is for schools to launch children, preferably not later than at ages four or five, into language experiences. For the first few years after the launching, up through grade four or five, the goal should be an extensive employment of oral language. For emotional and social, as well as for semantic reasons, culturally deprived children need to talk. Coming from nonverbal worlds, they require a rich diet of compensatory verbal experiences in the school as a means of readying them for school itself and for the verbal world outside the school. And, in this connection, language theorists hold that efforts by teachers to change the nonstandard language patterns of young children should rely, for the most part, on indirection, very little on direction. These same theorists, however, advocate that a systematic approach to language development begin in grade four or five, but under two conditions: one, that teachers meticulously refrain from disparaging any aspect of the nonstandard language employed by pupils; the other, that teachers play down the formalities of traditional grammar. Requiring pupils to intone: "A verb is a word that depicts action or state of being," or to underline all subordinate conjunctions in a given paragraph rarely has functional value.

In respect to the disparagement issue, a recommended approach for

---

[12] Richard Corbin, "Literacy, Literature, and the Disadvantaged," in Richard Corbin and Muriel Crosby, *Language Programs for the Disadvantaged* (Champaign, Ill.: National Council of Teachers of English, 1965), p. 4.

the teacher might well take the form of an explanation such as the following:

> I have observed that some in our class pronounce the word *you* as if it were spelled *yo*; *going to* as if it were spelled *gonter*; *because* as if it were spelled *cuz*; and *harm* as if it were spelled *hawm* with no r sound in it. (The teacher writes all the forms on the board). In some parts of the country, your pronunciations would be entirely acceptable. In many parts, however, they would stand out as different from the customary. Thus I suggest that while in school you pronounce words as do most people in the country. To the extent you succeed, you will have an easier time in the future engaging in job interviews, talking to strangers, and being understood by people, almost irrespective of where they come from or what they do.

Any program for the culturally deprived, thus, should involve them extensively in language usage: in speaking and listening from the time of initial school entrance, in reading and writing when they are ready— hopefully by not later than grade one, in their nonstandard dialects in the earlier stages, increasingly in the standard dialect as they reveal a readiness for the changeover. Learner interest, a basic requirement of any language program, is in great part a product of teacher ingenuity and curriculum appropriateness. When interest is absent, inertia sabotages; when interest is present, a language program is well on its way toward achieving its important goals.

In respect to the issue of curriculum appropriateness, learning materials need to be carefully screened and selected against the important criterion of cultural relevance. Primary-grade primers for all learners, and unequivocally for the culturally deprived, should include characters who are Negro, Puerto Rican, Mexican, and American Indian as well as white. And they should relate to themes and situations that are as credible to the submiddle class as to the middle class. The preparation of intercultural curriculum materials is slow in developing, however, as attested to by the following provocative statement. "For 277 years—from 1685 until 1962—no Negro characters appeared in first-grade basic readers used in American schools . . . the Caucasian culture depicted was steadily refined until, in most instances, it became upper middle class."[13] Yet noteworthy progress has been made during the past few years—one instance being in the Great Cities Project—in providing learners with books that are multiracial in characters and content.

[13] Gertrude Whipple, "Multicultural Primers for Today's Children," in Frost and Hawkes, p. 301.

The factor of reading interest, however, reaches beyond racial veneer into such fundamental components as plot credibility, characterization, language usage, and preferences of individual readers. *Silas Marner*, for instance, has unbelievably soporific powers over culturally deprived high school students (perhaps over nondeprived students also). *Kon Tiki* is a preferable substitute. For readers less advanced in language, *The Red Pony* or *Mutiny on the Bounty* or *The Oxbow Incident* has merit. Learners need to read up to their ability levels, to be sure, but such an outcome is academic if they do not read at all. Interest at least motivates them to read.

The IQ Issue

In any educational program for the culturally deprived, the IQ issue is a pivotal one. It poses, among other questions, the following two basic ones: (1) Is intelligence a genetic trait relatively unresponsive to environmental influences, or is it one that responds viably to such influences? (2) To what extent are IQ tests valid indicators of innate ability and valid predictors of learning outcomes?

The phenomenon of differences in school performance among social groups of various kinds has precipitated extensive research in regard to the first of the two questions. Researchers, literally by the hundreds, have sought to determine whether certain groups differ innately in intelligence or whether manifest differences among them in school performance are products of environmental influences.

The traditional position depicts intelligence as a fixed-genetic trait; furthermore, it espouses the view that Caucasians are more intelligent than non-Caucasians.[14] The most unequivocal proponents of this "Scientific-Racist" position includes *Carleton Putnam*: white supremacist, author of *Race and Reason* (1961), and the controlling force in the National Putnam Letters Committee; Frank McGurk of Villanova University, whose article "Psychological Tests: A Scientist's Report on Racial Differences," in *U.S. News and World Report* (September 21, 1956) made world headlines; Henry Garrett, psychologist who in "The Equalitarian Dogma," *Mankind Quarterly* (1960), accused the opposition of perpetrating "the scientific hoax of the century;" and Audrey Shuey, psy-

[14] I give credit here to Thomas F. Pettigrew, whose book, *A Profile of the Negro American* (Princeton, N.J.: D. Van Norstrand Company, Inc., 1964) is of unquestioned merit; and whose chapter, pp. 100–135, on "Negro American Intelligence" is particularly noteworthy.

chologist at Randolph Macon College and author of *The Testing of Negro Intelligence* (1958) who, in my opinion, ignores all research that runs counter to her bias.

The majority position of the day, one that is becoming increasingly dominant with the passage of time, posits intelligence as a functional process that responds to environmental influences. As stated by Pettigrew,[15]

> Intelligence is a plastic product of inherited structure developed by environmental stimulation and opportunity, an alloy of endowment and experience. It can be measured and studied only by inference, through observing behavior defined as "intelligent" in terms of particular cultural content and values.

To the extent intelligence is plastic and viable, it resists those who would express it as a single IQ statistic. In this connection, most learning theorists view intelligence as fluctuating along a continuum, with the composite of environmental experiences ascertaining the specific resting point at any given time. The limits of the continuum, however, are ever a topic of conjecture. Bloom, for instance, postulates as follows:[16]

> A conservative estimate of the effect of extreme environments on intelligence is about 20 I.Q. points. This could mean the difference between a life in an institution for the feeble-minded or a productive life in society.

Kirk, also viewing intelligence as a product of environmental influences, conceives the limits somewhat differently:[17]

> Perhaps we should say that an individual has an I.Q.—not of 80 or 60 or 120—but of 80 to 120 or 120 to 160, and that how the individual develops after birth is dependent on the interaction of the organism with the environment. So this individual may have an I.Q. of 80 with a poor environment or 120 with a good environment.

To the question, "How valid are intelligence tests as indicators of innate ability?" the answer is "Not very"; in respect to the Negro race and many other minority groups, the answer is "Scarcely valid at all." Validity suffers when nonverbal individuals have to perform

[15] Thomas F. Pettigrew, "Negro American Intelligence: A New Look at an Old Controversy," in Frost and Hawkes, p. 114.

[16] Benjamin S. Bloom, *Stability and Change in Human Characteristics* (New York: John Wiley & Sons, Inc., 1964), p. 89.

[17] Samuel A. Kirk, "Language, Intelligence, and the Educability of the Disadvantaged," in Corbin and Crosby, p. 250.

in verbal situations; when test items, appropriate for one cultural group, are not appropriate for other groups; when selected testees are less "test-wise" than others; and when some are less highly motivated than others. Because minority-group members fall short in each of these four respects, the IQ is not a valid measure of their intellectual potential. Instructional figures thus need to assess IQs as mere approximations; and, above all else, not to allow the IQ to act as a self-fulfilling predictor. As a guide, it has merit; as a prophet, it is a poor one.

Specifics in Organization and Curriculum

An educational program that reaches the culturally deprived during their impressionable years, that emphasizes language development, and that assesses intelligence realistically, possesses the essential requirements for success. Success mounts, however, when the program features the following specifics in organization and curriculum.

1. *Small classes.* A rule of thumb for the culturally deprived is a 20 to 25 percent reduction in normal class size. With fewer pupils, teachers are better able to identify and give attention to individual needs and interests.

2. *Auxiliary professional staff.* Ideally, classroom teachers of the culturally deprived should have the assistance of such auxiliary professional personnel as the following: school psychologist or adjustment counselor, reading specialist, nurse, speech pathologist, school-home-community coordinator, librarian, supernumerary master teacher, and specialists in such activity fields as physical education, art, and music.

3. *Nonprofessional staff.* To free teachers for their more professional responsibilities, staff aides, as required, should perform such nonprofessional tasks as hall supervision, lunchroom supervision, mimeographing, classroom housekeeping, and clerical work. Teachers themselves, however, in my opinion, should grade papers, supervise study halls, and perform all other duties that are directly, or even tangentially, professional. By performing instead of delegating these duties, they get better acquainted with their young associates; as a result, they are better able to integrate their instructional efforts.

4. *School-home cooperation.* With foundational reasons for the educational retardation of pupils residing in home and community influences, school personnel should work closely with parents to the desired end of enlisting their support for the cause of education. In the Ban-

412

neker Project of St. Louis, Missouri, it is to be recalled, school personnel have been aggressive in their solicitation of parental support—and the results reportedly have been gratifying. School-home cooperation unquestionably is an elusive goal; yet its importance may well justify all the energy expended to attain it.

5. *School-community agency cooperation*. Nor is school-community agency cooperation any less a goal than school-home cooperation. Any approach to cultural deprivation hopeful of success needs to involve a diverse assortment of agencies and individuals, both public and private, in a cooperative effort. These comprise, selectively, school personnel, public administrative bodies, inspectors of sanitation, inspectors of buildings, health personnel, policemen and other law-enforcing personnel, juvenile courts and judges, social workers, recreational agencies and their leaders, community-house personnel, YMCA and YWCA workers, and clergymen of diverse affiliations. Schools that work closely with other community agencies report, almost without exception, resulting educational gains. A noteworthy example is the

Passaic, New Jersey, cooperative arrangement that is presently in its fourth decade of existence.[18]

6. *The school as a community center.* One organizational approach that advances the cause both of educational outcomes *per se* and of school-community agency cooperation is a school that serves both as a center of learning conventionally conceived and as a neighborhood center as well. In the latter role, the school remains open late afternoons and evenings, Saturdays, also, in selected instances, to serve the educational and recreational needs of the old and young alike. Programs under such an organizational arrangement customarily include activities in the fields of the communication skills, the practical arts, the fine arts, and health.

7. *Summer programs.* An educational program that extends through the summer is a logical counter both to cultural retardation and to its accomplice, educational retardation. Havighurst speaks to this issue in the following categorical manner.[19]

> Summer programs in areas serving culturally deprived children should be as extensive as possible. Ideally, all schools in the compensatory program should be open 12 hours a day 12 months in the year. This would promote more economical use of the many fine new buildings, reduce wasteful repetition of grades, provide constructive summer activities, and permit a variety of special programs to meet special talents and needs.

8. *Cultural enrichment.* As already attested to almost beyond the point of question in the Higher Horizons Project of New York City and the Great Cities Project throughout the nation, culturally deprived children need the enrichment that experiences outside the frame of their own narrow cultures are capable of providing. Thus, great though their need for abstract learning may be, it responds best in a setting of enriched concrete reinforcement. Forearmed with this knowledge, school personnel should methodically, yet imaginatively, earmark places, people, and events that hold promise of enriching the lives of the culturally deprived; then incorporate these into the school's curriculum.

As the reader may already have concluded, such items as smaller-

[18] The Passaic, New Jersey, school system in the late 1930s joined hands with law enforcement agencies to combat juvenile delinquency and its attendant educational evils. The reported results are heart-warming. For a more detailed report, see Gail M. Inlow, *The Emergent in Curriculum* (New York: John Wiley & Sons, Inc., 1966), pp. 255–256; also John P. Gower, *What One Community Has Done for its Children* (Passaic, N.J.: Passaic Public Schools, 1961).

[19] Robert J. Havighurst, *The Public Schools of Chicago* (Chicago: Board of Education, 1964), p. 78.

than-average class size, expansion of auxiliary staffs, home visits, close school-community cooperation, schools that serve as neighborhood centers, and curriculums that reach outside local communities have financial implications. And I have no pat recommendation for the monetary source(s) from which an additional $50, $100, or maybe $150 per pupil per year should come. The federal and state governments, however, are the most likely possibilities. Irrespective of source, the society's long history of neglect of the culturally deprived commits it to compensatory efforts in their behalf. In the long run, all additional expenditures will pay for themselves, many times over, in such outcomes as greater human productivity, increased industrial output, lower crime rates, and fewer admittances to public hospitals and clinics.

TEACHERS OF THE CULTURALLY DEPRIVED

The most important single requisite of education for the culturally deprived is teachers who are professionally and personally qualified to work productively with them. Educational facilities, materials of instruction, teaching method, and school organizational practices approximate their potentials only when qualified teachers approximate theirs.

Essential Characteristics

Successful teachers of the culturally deprived possess most or all of the following attributes.

1. First and foremost, the factor of personal desire, not arbitrary administrative edict, is the dominant reason for their assignments in submarginal-community schools. A high degree of dedication and altruism, such as that evidenced by Peace Corps or Job Corps members, constitutes the controlling motivator. Such individuals have social consciences that extend well beyond the veneer limits of sympathy; they are idealists who find fulfillment in reality.

2. Scholarly competence reinforces their personal dedication. Missionary zeal apart from knowledge and insight is a questionable asset; reinforced by knowledge and insight, it constitutes an invaluable asset.

3. These teachers, because they are students of people as well as knowledge, acquaint themselves with the backgrounds, values, customs,

and attitudes of the local population—old and young alike—with whom they work. In this connection, Hauser recommends that all Chicago teachers in "high student turnover" schools bring to their assignments an understanding of: "the history of minority groups in America and the world at large . . . the content and method of teaching children of different cultural heritages . . . [and] human relations practices." He goes on to say that "In a society ethnically and racially pluralistic, it is imperative that all staff members achieve knowledge, understanding, and appreciation of the contributions of every group."[20] Possessed of such knowledge and insight, successful teachers of the disadvantaged take the latter "where they are," relate to them as social equals, and, looking beyond their poverty and cultural emptiness, perceive their innate qualities of human dignity.

4. These teachers—irrespective of their subject-matter majors, if secondary school-oriented; or of their many curriculum responsibilities, if elementary school-oriented—are capable teachers of language. All, in fact, who work professionally with the culturally deprived should be both students and teachers of language.

5. In the same way, they should be students of sociology and psychology.

6. They should be versatile in the area of teaching method, not fearing to experiment with the new and untried.

7. Finally, successful teachers of the culturally deprived, while retaining their generally middle-class values, do not expect their young associates to accept those same values unadulterated and to subscribe to them automatically. These teachers hold fast to a hard core of universal values that are capable of being implemented—for instance, social responsibility, civic responsibility, basic honesty, dependability, self-acceptance, self-reliance, problem-solving in the immediate, and altruism. Of necessity, however, they concede in respect to certain other values which, even though highly important, are almost impossible to instill in certain submarginal learners—for instance, education for delayed benefits, impeccable neatness, social graces, avoidance of aggression, and absolute respect for constituted authority. In a very real sense, successful teachers of the culturally deprived are pragmatists. Although usually value-oriented themselves, they accept without prejudice the values of their young associates which are known to be imper-

[20] Philip M. Hauser, *Report to the Board of Education, City of Chicago* (Chicago: Board of Education, March 31, 1964), p. 32.

vious to change. While accepting provincial values, however, they do not concede universal ones. Instead, they bide their time until learner readiness gives evidence of becoming a reinforcing ally.[21]

The above composite, although admittedly an ideal, is one that prospective teachers of the culturally deprived should seek to approximate. Such recruitment incentives as small classes, board-provided in-service education and transportation, teacher aides, more extensive than average instruction resources, and extended police protection go only so far. What is needed fundamentally is competent teachers motivated by social empathy to help the culturally deprived to realize their potentials.

To Stimulate Thought

1. List and briefly develop what you believe to be the causes for the existence of from 30 to 40 million culturally deprived individuals in the United States.

2. Next, analyze each stated cause, identifying in the process steps society might take to eliminate it.

3. Defend the assertion: Of all the antipoverty programs currently underwritten by the federal government, Project Head Start holds promise of being the most productive.

4. Develop the theme that cultural enrichment precipitates an increase in the IQ.

5. Build a case, for or against, the practice employed by selected colleges and universities of enrolling culturally deprived students whose IQ or CEEB scores fall below minimum institutional standards.

6. Develop the concept: Readers need to bring learning to the printed page.

7. In your opinion, should education of the culturally deprived embrace medical, psychological, and sociological services? Develop your response in some detail.

8. Elaborate the statement: Irrespective of organizational level or subject-matter area, all teachers of the culturally deprived should be teachers of reading.

9. Identify and describe the specific contributions that selected community agencies should make to public schools and the pupils they serve.

[21] James E. Heald takes an interesting stand on the present topic of discussion in "In Defense of Middle Class Values," *Phi Delta Kappan* (October 1964), pp. 81–83.

10. Conceive yourself as a teacher in an inner-city "slum" school. What personal-social attitudes, skills, and knowledge do you think you would need that you do not now possess; and what negative attitudes might you have to overcome?

REFERENCES

Beck, John M., and Richard W. Saxe (ed.), *Teaching the Culturally Disadvantaged Pupil* (Springfield, Ill.: Charles C Thomas, Publisher, 1965).

Chilman, Catherine S., *Growing Up Poor* (Washington, D.C.: U.S. Department of Health, Education, and Welfare, 1966).

Corbin, Richard, and Muriel Crosby (eds.), *Language Programs for the Disadvantaged* (Champaign, Ill.: National Council of Teachers of English, 1965).

Crain, Robert L., *The Politics of School Desegragation* (Chicago: Aldine Publishing Company, 1968).

Crosby, Muriel, *An Adventure in Human Relations* (Chicago: Follet Publishing Company, 1965).

Daedalus, "The American Negro." (Fall 1965).

Duker, Sam, *Listening Bibliography* (New York: Scarecrow Press, Inc., 1964).

Educational Research Information Center, *Catalog of Selected Documents on the Disadvantaged* (Washington, D.C.: U.S. Department of Health, Education and Welfare, 1966).

Frost, Joe L., and Glenn R. Hawkes (eds.), *The Disadvantaged Child: Issues and Innovations* (Boston: Houghton Mifflin Company, 1966).

Fusco, Gene, *School-Home Partnership in Depressed Urban Neighborhoods: OE-31008* (Washington, D.C.: U.S. Department of Health, Education, and Welfare, 1964).

Goldstein, Bernard, *Low Income Youth in Urban Areas* (New York: Holt, Rinehart and Winston, Inc., 1967).

Graham, Grace, *The Public School in the New Society* (New York: Harper and Row Publishers, 1969).

Havighurst, Robert J., *The Public Schools of Chicago* (Chicago: Board of Education, 1964).

Jewett, Arno, Joseph Mersand, and Doris Gunderson (eds.), *Improving the English Skills of Culturally Different Youth* (Washington, D.C.: U.S. Department of Health, Education, and Welfare, 1964).

Kvaraceus, William C., John S. Gibson, and Thomas J. Curtin (eds.), *Poverty, Education, and Race Relations* (Boston: Allyn and Bacon, Inc., 1967).

Muse, Benjamin, *The American Negro Revolution* (Bloomington, Ind.: University of Indiana Press, 1968).

418

Passow, Harry A., Miriam L. Goldberg, and Abraham J. Tannebaum (eds.), *Education of the Disadvantaged: A Book of Readings* (New York: Holt, Rinehart and Winston, Inc., 1967).

Pettigrew, Thomas F., *A Profile of the Negro American* (Princeton, N.J.: D. Van Nostrand Company, 1964).

Riessman, Frank, *The Culturally Deprived Child* (New York: Harper & Row, Publishers, 1964).

Shuy, Roger W. (ed.), *Social Dialects and Language Learning* (Champaign, Ill.: National Council of Teachers of English, 1965).

Stauffer, Russell G. (ed.), *Language and the Higher Thought Processes* (Champaign, Ill.: National Council of Teachers of English, 1965).

United States Commission on Civil Rights, *Racial Isolation in the Public Schools* (Washington, D.C.: U.S. Government Printing Office, 1967).

U.S. Department of Labor, *The Negroes in the United States: Their Economic and Social Situation*, Bulletin No. 1511 (Washington, D.C.: U.S. Government Printing Office, June, 1966).

Watt, Lois B., *Literature for Disadvantaged Children: A Bibliography* (Washington, D.C.: U.S. Department of Health, Education, and Welfare, 1968).

Weinberg, Meyer (ed.), *Learning Together: A Book on Integrated Education* (Chicago: Integrated Education Associates, 1964).

Woodward, C. Vann, "The Hidden Sources of Negro History," *Saturday Review* (January 18, 1969), pp. 29-32.

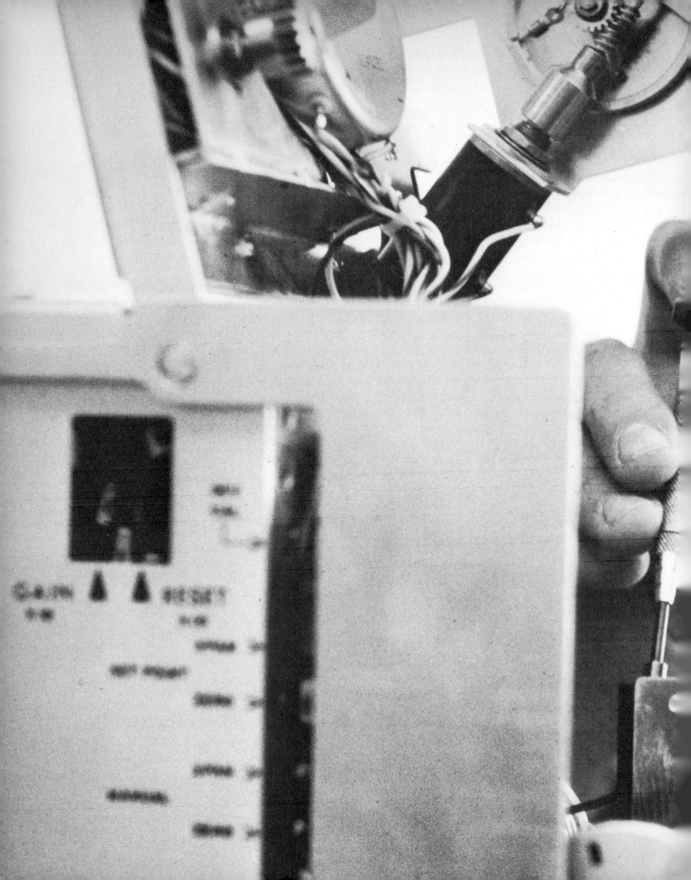

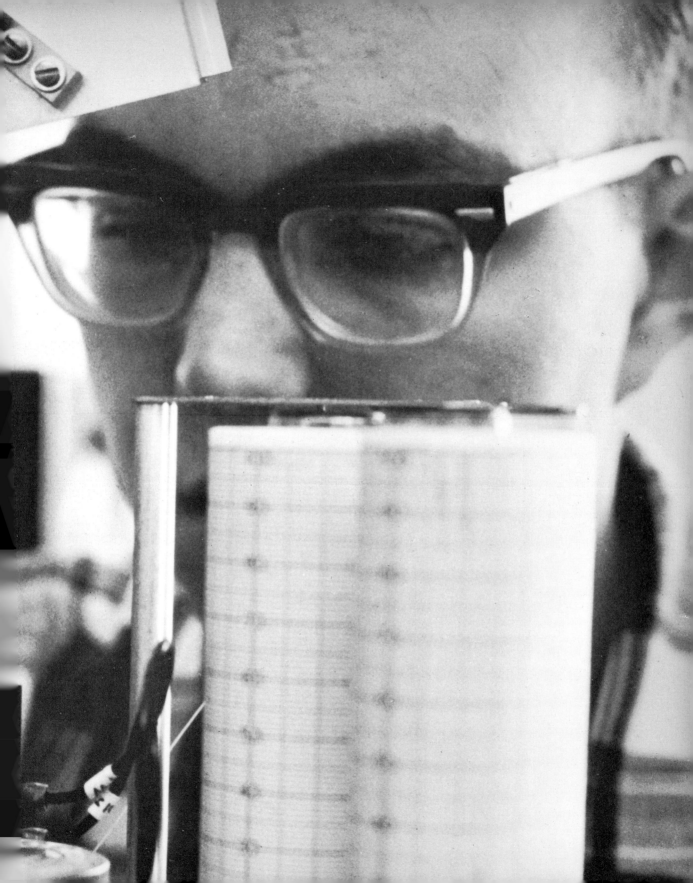

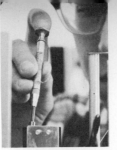

Chapter

15

Academically Talented Learners

The society's current concern for the educational welfare of culturally deprived learners parallels, without at all detracting from, its historical concern for the educational welfare of academically talented learners. The affinity between formal education and talented learners, indeed, is too great for any competitive force to threaten it seriously. Unquestionably, the talented today are in the spotlight of formal education, more so in certain respects than they have ever been before.

The academically talented, by definition, are adept in a world of abstraction; their forte is verbal symbolization. Their native abilities, however, often go undeveloped, even unnoticed, when formal education fails to search them out actively and to cultivate them. In times past, society was satisfied for schools simply to meet the needs of the visibly talented, most of whom came from middle-class and upper-middle-class families. Today, in contrast, society expects schools to be searchers after, as well as developers of, academic talent, wherever it resides.

Reasons for the nation's mounting interest in the academically talented reside in both moral and practical considerations. In respect to the first, America's humanistic orientation commits it to help all learners—fast, average, and slow—to become their potentials. Ability is a commodity too priceless to go unnourished. In respect to the second, the complex world of social affairs makes academic talent an increasingly necessary and valuable asset. The electronics revolution, for instance, would not have occurred in the first place, or, having occurred, would have been short-lived, had it not been for the trained minds developed in the schools. America's requirements as a world power and the increasing sophistication within the professions constitute two further reasons why society needs to put to maximum use all the academic talent it can find.

Sputnik's orbit in 1957 was, at one and the same time, an engineering feat of staggering proportions and a motivator of almost unbelievable educational change in the United States. Its message to the country and to formal education was starkly simple: "The electronic age is here. Are you ready for it?" The reply of perturbed realists was a categorical *No*. A nation that had performed near-miracles during four years of

war had become too relaxed in the early days of peace. A nation that had come to take its educational superiority in the world for granted suddenly developed misgivings. America in 1957 was a perplexed and apprehensive nation, in need of knowledge and power it did not possess.

When it took audit, it uncovered many reasons for this lack, one residing in the educational system. The system was operating not only with an outdated curriculum, but with a personnel policy that reflected a national indifference toward talent. As of 1954, for instance, colleges and universities were educating not more than two-fifths of the top quarter of high school students.[1] Another fifth of the top quarter did not even graduate from high school.[2] What was this but a profligate waste of brain power and an unpardonable loss of humanistic talent? The first of the two above-mentioned statistics underwrites the growing conviction that college attendance should be not a privilege, but a right for all who are qualified, the underlying thesis being that ability is too essential to go uncultivated.

The past several decades of scientific and social change, troublesome though they have been, unquestionably have cast mental ability in a new light. Today more than ever before it is perceived as power. When harnessed and channeled pathologically, it has awesome possibilities. It is capable of destroying nations, of making falsehood appear as truth, and, in fact, of dehumanizing people in bizarre and terrible ways. Yet when harnessed and channeled the right way, it can be a veritable boon to mankind. It is capable of refining man's personal and social values, of giving him more creature comforts, of making him more physically and emotionally healthy, in general, of making him more humane.

Because of its humanizing potential, mental ability is a quality that civilized societies are mandated to cultivate. This they do best in a social frame wherein formal education, and the society itself, accord all learners equal worth, irrespective of differences in mental ability. Thus, the position I take in the chapter is that the academically talented are special in an educational sense and are thus deserving of special educational attention. They are not, however, intrinsically better than, or worse than, their less talented counterparts.

[1] Lyle M. Spencer, "New Directions in Academic Talent Hunting," in Bruce Shertzer, *Working with Superior Students: Theories and Practices* (Chicago: Science Research Associates, Inc., 1960), p. 7.

[2] Henry Ehlers and Gordon C. Lee, *Crucial Issues in Education* (New York: Holt, Rinehart and Winston, Inc., 1964), p. 262.

WHO ARE THE ACADEMICALLY TALENTED?

Name designations and definitions constitute a major problem for anyone writing or reading about the academically advantaged. For instance, the sample of Terman's *Genetic Studies of Genius*, Vol. I, 1925, consisted of children whose IQs were 140 or higher. Terman's sample of geniuses thus was a highly selective one. In later studies, he used 137 as a cutoff point. Gallagher employs the term *highly gifted* to describe children with IQ scores (Binet) of 148 or higher; the term *gifted* to describe children with IQ scores of 132 and higher; and the term *academically talented* to describe children with IQ scores of 116 and higher. He estimates that one child in a typical population of 1000 is highly gifted, two children in 100 are gifted or *highly gifted*, and 16 in 100 are academically talented, gifted, or highly gifted.[3] An Illinois Office of Education study employs the terms highly gifted and gifted in the manner of Gallagher, but substitutes *moderately gifted* for Gallagher's academically talented.[4] The Abington Pennsylvania school system uses an IQ of 120 to separate the so-called *academically gifted* from the nongifted.[5]

Witty avoids the IQ issue completely by identifying "any child gifted whose performance in a potentially valuable line of human activity is consistently remarkable."[6] Conant, although ambiguously referring to the gifted as those capable of handling "stiff" courses, reveals unambiguously that his primary interest is in the 15 percent of the most *academically able* students.[7]

I employ the term *academically talented* to describe the children and youth who constitute the theme of this chapter. Their IQs start at 115 to 120. They make up from 15 to 20 percent of a normally distributed population. From time to time, I refer to the more capable among them

[3] James J. Gallagher, *Teaching the Gifted Child* (Boston: Allyn and Bacon, Inc., 1964), p. 11.

[4] The Office of the Superintendent of Public Instruction, *Education for the Gifted Pupils in Illinois Schools,* Circular Series A 145. (Springfield, Ill.: Office of the Superintendent, 1961), p. 12.

[5] School District of Abington Township, *A Program for the Academically Gifted* (Abington, Penna.: Abington Township, March 1965), p. 6.

[6] Paul Witty, "Who Are the Gifted?" *Fifty-Seventh Yearbook of the National Society for the Study of Education,* Part II (Chicago: University of Chicago Press, 1958), p. 62.

[7] James B. Conant, *The American High School Today* (New York: McGraw-Hill, Inc., 1959), p. 22.

as *gifted*. Throughout the chapter, the reader needs to keep in mind that the academically talented, though characterized by many similarities, are too different for stereotyping to be proper. Their differences, in fact, almost without exception, are greater than their similarities. First and foremost, they are individuals. Group descriptions of them, including the one in the next section, are only as authentic as central tendencies (averages) are capable of making them.

CHARACTERISTICS OF THE ACADEMICALLY TALENTED

The vast majority of the academically talented, however, despite their many differences, tend to share the following characteristics. These characteristics have undergone validation many times by such well-known observers in the field as Lewis Terman, Paul Witty, J. P. Guilford, James Gallagher, E. Paul Torrance, Calvin Taylor and others.

1. Above all else, the academically talented live in an abstract world: of symbols, of ideas, of concepts, of generalizations.

2. Living in this world, they tend to make critical assessments of life and its problems. Far from being satisfied with the *what*, they probe analytically into the *why*. They are divergent thinkers who, employing the status quo merely as a point of departure, challenge established patterns of values and behavior.

3. Being symbolically oriented, they learn to read early, and they go through life reading widely. They are customarily two to four grade levels ahead of their classes in such reading categories as vocabulary size, paragraph meaning, and reading speed. In this single area of reading, in fact, the academically talented have the greatest relative superiority over their peers.

4. It follows from the above, as well as from definition, that the academically talented are rapid learners. With formal education, a symbolically oriented institution, and the academically talented, symbolically oriented individuals, rapid learning is a foregone result.

5. They are not only rapid learners but are highly retentive of what they learn.

6. Furthermore, they are able to concentrate for long periods, to give sustained attention even to complex tasks.

7. Their interests in life are many and varied; they are ever exploring, ever opening new vistas of interest. Terman and Oden, although writing specifically about the gifted, not the academically talented in

general, comment that their interests are "many-sided and spontaneous, . . . they make numerous collections, cultivate many kinds of hobbies, and acquire far more knowledge of plays and games than the average child."[8] In general, they are more creative than their peers.

8. The academically talented hold more than their share of leadership positions both in and out of school.

9. They tend to be somewhat better physical specimens and to be somewhat more stable emotionally than average children. The Terman study supports these allegations most convincingly.

10. Interestingly, academically talented children, the more gifted in particular, tend to be relatively further advanced in reading, social studies, and science than in arithmetic. Terman, Gallagher, and Crowder all attest to this phenomenon.[9]

11. The academically talented chafe or rebel when subjected to protracted routine, drill, or other repetitive learning processes that, by their very nature, lack the power to motivate and challenge.

12. Generally speaking, the academically talented excel their less talented counterparts along almost every known dimension: cognitive, social, emotional, physical, and ethical. The popular stereotype of the introverted, spectacled, nonathletic, impractical bookworm has no basis in reality. An authentic depiction, in contrast, more properly portrays the academically talented as outgoing, mentally and physically healthy, reality oriented, and interested in life along many fronts.

IDENTIFICATION OF THE ACADEMICALLY TALENTED

How to identify the academically talented, especially the more gifted within that select group, constitutes one of education's many dilemmas as it attempts to program wisely for them. Schools have employed, with varying degrees of success, the following methods or techniques of selection: scholastic aptitude (intelligence) tests, achievement-test batteries, teacher and counselor observations, school marks, and tests of creativity. The guiding principles of identification generally include the ensuing: (1) selection should go down the path of many, not just one or two, methods; (2) schools should employ a team approach, not just rely on the judgment of one or a small number of individuals;

[8] Lewis M. Terman and Melita Oden, "The Stanford Studies of the Gifted" in Paul Witty (ed.), *The Gifted Child* (Boston: D. C. Heath and Company, 1951), pp. 23–24.

[9] James Gallagher, p. 32.

(3) the process of identification should be continuous, not a first-of-the-year task that, when completed, is set aside for another year; (4) identification that involves testing should be the responsibility of individuals trained in test selection, administration, and evaluation; (5) identification procedures should be ever-changing and evolving as new insights are gained.

Many regard identification of the academically talented as a simple process. It may be simple with respect to learners who demonstrate their talents in obviously manifest ways; but it is far from simple with respect to the culturally deprived, to creative nonconformists, and to slow readers, to mention just three illustrative categories.

Scholastic Aptitude Tests

Scholastic aptitude or intelligence tests constitute what is probably the most frequently employed method of identifying the academically talented. And the frequency of their employment is matched by their usefulness. Indeed, if a holocaust destroyed all of them, education would assign high priority to the task of replacing them. Yet valuable as they undeniably are, scholastic aptitude tests are too imperfect to constitute the one and only method of identification.

Lack of uniformity of statistical results emanating from individual tests on one hand, and group tests on the other, stands out as one of the many imperfections. For example, two researchers, Martinson and Lessinger, first administered the Stanford-Binet, an individual test, to a selected group of learners, resulting in the identification of 332 academically talented ones with IQs of 130 and higher. They then administered several group tests to the same children. The tabulated results revealed that 50 percent of the sample of 332 had failed to qualify on the group tests. The individual and group tests varied least at the low end of the Binet IQ range—approximately 10 points in the 130–139 interval; most at the high end of the range—34 points in the 160–169 interval.[10]

The factor of differential heights of test ceilings (a ceiling of a test is the highest score attainable) constitutes another imperfection of scholastic aptitude tests. Significantly, if a highly gifted twelve-year-old took the following tests and completed all the items correctly, his IQ

[10] Ruth Martinson and L. M. Lessinger, "Problems in the Identification of Intellectually Gifted Pupils," *Exceptional Children*, 26 (1960), pp. 227–231, 242.

Intelligence Tests	Maximum IQ (12-year-olds)
Stanford-Binet (individual)	190
Wechsler Intelligence Scale (individual)	154
California Test of Mental Maturity (group)	157
Otis Quick Scoring Test of Mental Maturity (group)	153
Lorge-Thorndike Intelligence Test (group)	147

Source: Adapted from The Office of the Superintendent of Public Instruction, Illinois, Circular Series A 145, p. 14.

would vary as widely as indicated in the following—an astonishingly large variation, to say the least.

Irrespective of the factor of differential test ceilings, the primary advantage of individual tests, such as the Stanford-Binet and Wechsler, is that they neutralize reading deficiencies: A technician reads the items and a testee responds orally to them. The primary disadvantage is that they are expensive to administer, demanding the time and energy of a professional testing staff.

The primary advantage of group tests resides in their ability to reach large bodies of students in a single test situation: thus they have great appeal for budget-minded school administrators. Their major disadvantages consist selectively of the following three. One, as already indicated, is their inappropriateness for learners with reading problems. In such situations, low IQs are often more symptomatic of difficulties in reading than of any deficiency in innate intelligence. A second disadvantage of group-intelligence tests, as developed in the preceding chapter, lies in their inappropriateness for the culturally deprived. Test items drawn from a middle-class culture and expressed in standard English communicate inadequately to individuals from many subcultures. A third disadvantage is that group-intelligence tests—even more than individual ones—evaluate memory learning more than conceptual understanding, factual responses more than reflective thought and creativity.

For these reasons, I reject the logic of those who casually conclude that the academically talented, almost without exception, are individuals who score high on scholastic aptitude tests. Conant is a case in point. Schools, he says, should administer a scholastic aptitude test to students in grades 7, 8, or 9 as a means of identifying the upper 15 percent of the nation's top learners. These, he continues, would, with one possible exception, constitute the academically talented. The ex-

ception would consist of learners who, even though not in the upper 15 percent, received "high-honor grades" in the beginning algebra course.[11] Conant oversimplifies the issue by placing too much faith in scholastic aptitude tests. By so doing, he improperly excludes many bright children who, although unable to cope with his primary method of selection, meet other criteria of giftedness.

Achievement-Test Batteries

A second type of standardized test employed by most schools in identifying the academically talented is the achievement test or achievement-test battery. These run the gamut of the various academic subjects: reading, language arts (in addition to reading), science, mathematics, social studies, and foreign languages. Many of the same shortcomings inherent in intelligence tests are comparably inherent in these. Intrinsically verbal, they are inaccurate evaluators of individuals who are inherently nonverbal. Furthermore, they consistently fail to identify bright low-achievers. Their chief asset is that they measure what students actually have learned, not what they are intrinsically capable of learning.

Teacher and Counselor Observations

Most schools, aware of the limitations of exclusively objective media of identification, look to teacher, and occasionally to counselor, observations as yet another method. Common practice is for schools to employ intelligence and achievement tests as the basic controlling techniques, observation as a supplemental technique. Under such an arrangement, observers are expected to add, but not to remove, names from any preformulated roster submitted to them. Additions tend to be innately intelligent pupils who are culturally deprived, emotionally maladaptive, or relatively nonverbal for reasons unknown. The accuracy of subjective observation admittedly varies widely from individual to individual. Yet when engaged in by clinically trained observers, observation often fits many important pieces into the jigsaw puzzle of identification.

[11] James B. Conant, *The American High School Today* (New York: McGraw-Hill, Inc., 1959), pp. 113, 134–135.

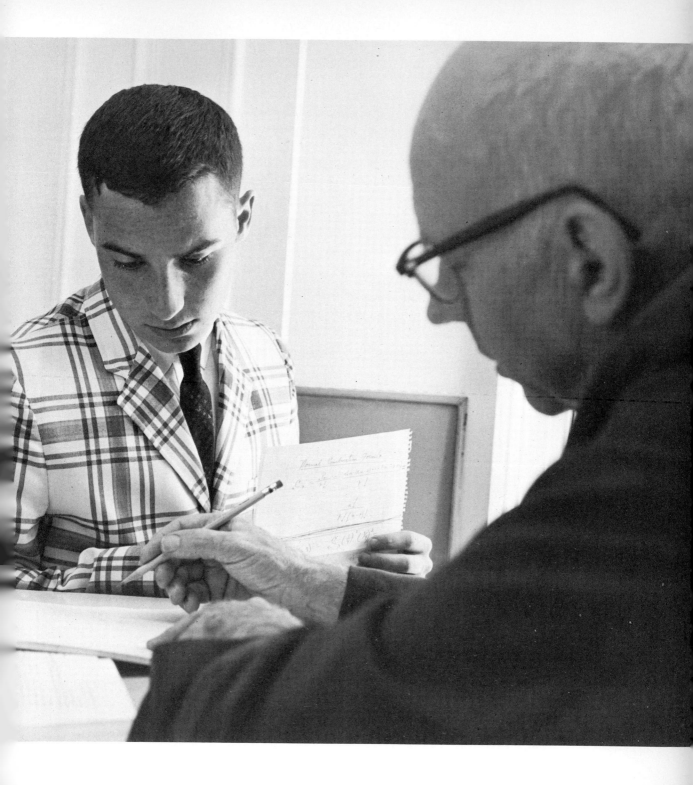

School Marks

Schools customarily employ marks or grades as still another index of academic talent. School marks, in effect, are the subjective equivalents of standardized achievement test scores. They are vulnerable in that they bear the stamp of teacher subjectivity, are notoriously unanalytical because usually condensed into single symbols, and often mirror social behavior as much as cognitive learning. Despite their recognized fallability, however, they are justifiable elements in the mosaic of identification. Generally speaking, though, they should be supplementary, not primary, elements.

Measures of Creativity

In at least some schools, individuals responsible for identifying the academically talented weave measures of creativity into the indentification mosaic. They generally are part of an evolving group whose members, disenchanted with the imitative-response nature of existing intelligence tests, search for flexibility in the world of the nonconformist creative. A pioneer in this group is J. P. Guilford, of the University of Southern California, Los Angeles, whose research on creativity has influenced many studies of creativity made during the sixties. Contending that intelligence extends beyond repetitive learning into creative learning, Guilford has developed, and has attempted to refine, a number of instruments that purportedly evaluate this important added dimension. One such instrument commits testees to make as many associations as possible to given stimulus words. The word *bark*, for instance, might elicit the responses of bark (of a dog), bark (on a tree), bark (of an irritable person), bark or barque (as a sailing vessel), and so forth. Another such instrument calls for testees to complete an open-ended episode (a "Lady or the Tiger" type of episode), with creativity inferred from the responses made. A third confronts testees with various number combinations from which, within a given time limit, they are asked to formulate as many mathematical problems as possible.

A research study conducted by Getzels and Jackson at the University of Chicago laboratory school in the early sixties gave widespread visibility to the topic of creativity. The sample of the study consisted of two groups of students drawn from grades 6 through 12. One group characterized as the "High Intelligence Group" embraced 28 sample members whose mean IQ was 150, but who scored low on selected

432

measures of creativity. The second characterized as the "High Creativity Group" embraced 26 members whose mean IQ was 127, and who scored high on the aforementioned measures of creativity. The school behavior pattern, in profile, of the two sample groups reveals the following.

(1) The High Creative Group, despite their appreciably lower IQs, excelled the High Intelligence Group in academic achievement.

(2) Teachers, however, preferred working with the High Intelligence Group.

(3) The High Intelligence Group members were conformist whereas their High Creative counterparts were nonconformist with respect to social relationships, adherence to school standards, and vocational interests. The High Creativity Group members, in general, were more capricious and offbeat in their behavior and attitudes.[12]

With due regard for the interest that Getzels and Jackson have precipitated in the area of creativity, their sample was too limited, their research design too approximate, and their measures of creativity too debatable for anyone to draw hard and fast conclusions from the reported findings. Nor should anyone draw hard and fast conclusions from the findings of any other research studies on creativity.[13]

In respect to the topic of this section, creativity unquestionably is an important criterion for individuals to consider when engaged in identifying the academically talented. Unfortunately, however, instruments to measure it are not sufficiently refined for schools to place great faith in them. Quite conceivably, then, teacher observation rather than instrumentation should constitute the primary medium of creativity assessment.

A Closing Word on Identification

The following question is basic to the identification issue: Of the several identification media covered—intelligence tests, achievement tests, observation, school marks, and measures of creativity—what is the relative merit of each? As the reader has probably already inferred, the question has no single answer. An indirect answer is that a broad

[12] Jacob W. Getzels and Philip W. Jackson, *Creativity and Intelligence* (New York: John Wiley & Sons, Inc., 1962), pp. 56–61.

[13] For a compact synopsis on the topic of creativity see Gail M. Inlow, *The Emergent in Curriculum* (New York: John Wiley & Sons, Inc., 1966), Chap. 5.

criterion base is almost always preferable to a narrow one. And in any broad base, intelligence-test results, achievement-test results, and teacher opinions should be the basic ingredients.

A foregone conclusion in respect to the many criteria is that they always will differ in the way they identify academic talent. Attesting to this phenomenon is a study of gifted children reported by Pegnato and Birch in 1959. The two researchers, employing an individual intelligence test and using an IQ of 136 as the cutting edge, identified as gifted 91 junior high school children out of a total possible sample of 1400. When other methods of identification were subsequently employed, the results differed significantly. The Otis Group Intelligence Test, for example, identified as gifted only 20 of the 91; teacher opinion, only 41; the school honor roll, 67; and group achievement tests, 72.[14] These results admittedly may not be typical, but they are not surprising.

PROGRAMMING FOR THE ACADEMICALLY TALENTED

Once a school has arrived at a definition of the academically talented and has employed defensible methods to identify them, only then will it be ready to program for them. And the task of implementation will inevitably pose more complex problems than did the preliminaries.

The foundational principles of education, however, will remain essentially the same, because they apply to all pupils irrespective of their known differences. One guiding principle is that learning, to be effective, needs to start with any individual where he is and relate to him developmentally from that point on: to his abilities, his needs, and his interests. This it does within the frame of the controlling social pattern. This principle thus commits a school, within the limits of its capabilities, to study each academically talented student (as it should all students) and program for him as an individual.

To the extent the student conforms to the composite sketched early in the chapter, a curriculum will take shape with the following characteristics. It will be oriented, although not exclusively so, to the symbolic abstract: proportionately more so in the secondary school, proportionately less so in the elementary school. While developing the fundamental skills, while transmitting essential knowledge of the past, and

[14] Carl W. Pegnato and Jack W. Birch, "Locating Gifted Children in Junior High Schools, a Comparison of Methods," *Exceptional Children* 25 (March 1959), pp. 300–304.

while engendering important attitudes and values of the present, it will encourage the student to question, to probe, to be skeptical—in effect, to be open before life. A closed, restricted environment provincializes; an open, expanding one, sophisticates. In deference to the student's ability to learn rapidly, the curriculum for him will be quantitatively greater than for the average. In deference to his long attention span, it will not hesitate to engage him in learning tasks, in depth, for relatively long periods. Yet in recognition of his variety of interests, the curriculum will allow him to diversify as well as intensify. In recognition of his leadership potentials, it will involve him in situations, both curricular and extracurricular, where these may undergo development. And the curriculum will include only a necessary minimum of learning routine such as drill.

A second guiding principle of education is that all learners should feel successful in their academic work. Thus for the composite academically talented student in question, the curriculum would need to be at his level. If too far below, it would bore him. If too far above, it would frustrate him. In effect, it should challenge but not overtax him. Apropos of current practice in many schools today, "honor" students often have to meet standards that are too demanding, content that is overtaxing, and homework that keeps them studying into the proverbial "wee-small" hours. Such demands constitute an overchallenge, with health and social interests often suffering as a result. Yet the opposite extreme of gifted children being held down by, and thus bored with, curriculum trivia is every bit as objectionable. The proper approach lies somewhere between these polarities.

The issue of students achieving success in the curriculum raises a related question of whether school personnel should acquaint the academically talented with the fact of their greater-than-average ability. A surprising number of writers on the subject encourage the practice on grounds that such knowledge inspires the academically talented to attain greater heights. But they habitually avoid comment on the possible adverse effects such encouragement might have on the personalities of these talented youngsters and on the morale of others who fail to receive such encouragement. My opinion on this issue is that schools should emphasize optimum growth of all students, irrespective of ability level or potential, avoiding as much as possible comparisons—even implied ones—of individuals. To me, this is the more mature and wholesome approach: take each individual where he is, help him to grow, and don't be overly concerned about whether he excels or falls short of

435

others. The issue may even be academic in view of the fact that talent, by its very nature, is generally aware of itself. In any event, the goal should be mature understanding and acceptance, self-inspired, not externally implanted.

Enrichment

Throughout the combined organizational levels of education, the approach of curriculum enrichment is the one most commonly employed by teachers of the academically talented. As a trade term, it generally relates more to specialized curriculum practices employed in heterogeneously grouped than in homogeneously grouped classes. In the single-subject organization of the secondary school, the approach of enrichment is a lesser task than it is in the self-contained classroom organization of the elementary school. In the latter, a single teacher has the responsibility of individualizing for the academically talented in all subjects included in the curriculum.

Curriculum enrichment generally takes the form of the following three plans. In one, academically talented students in any given year first complete the standard curriculum as rapidly as possible; then move into learning experiences that challenge by their greater breadth and depth. Under a second plan, academically talented students, without getting quantitatively ahead of their less talented counterparts, pursue each curriculum element in greater qualitative depth. Under a third plan, academically talented students do not follow a standard curriculum at all, engaging instead in learning experiences deliberately tailored to their abilities, needs, and interests. This is more the plan of homogeneous than of heterogeneous grouping, however.

The curriculum guide of the Abington Township School District, Abington, Pennsylvania suggests the following enrichment possibilities. They are paraphrased and modified selectively here.[15]

In the elementary school: leadership in classroom activities, leadership in out-of-class activities such as assemblies and student government, science demonstrations, creative writing (including skits, short stories, or poems), independent reading, editing, or writing for the class or school paper, making community surveys, pursuing art or music in depth, taking extra field trips, and engaging in extracurriculum activities.

[15] School District of Abington Township, pp. 29–30, 32–33, 35–36.

In the junior high school: studying foreign language in some depth, engaging in stepped-up independent study and research, extensive independent reading, viewing and reporting on selected television programs, performing advanced projects in the industrial arts, participating in science fairs, managing assembly programs and social events, wise selection of elective subjects, and engaging in many or most of the activities listed for the elementary school but not listed here.

In the senior high school: independent study and research appreciably stepped up, weekend visits to institutes and museums, active involvement in life of the community, active but selective participation in the extra-curriculum, and engaging in many or most of the activities listed for the junior high school but not listed here.

Acceleration

Enrichment, as previously stated, generally implies a traditional arrangement wherein teachers guide the academically talented down paths somewhat specialized, but not organizationally different, from those followed by their less talented counterparts. *Acceleration,* in contrast, generally implies some kind of significant departure from traditional admission or classroom-organizational arrangements. The combined goal is a more appropriate curriculum and earlier graduation from a given school level.

Early enrollment in kindergarten or first grade Acceleration takes place, in one instance, when schools, after careful clinical screening,   **437**

admit into kindergarten or first grade selected children who are younger than the established minimum age. Law in most states requires schools to admit into first grade those children, except for the handicapped abnormal, who will be six years old not later than December 1 following the date of their September enrollment. Law customarily is permissive toward schools which, for sound reasons, elect to enroll children younger than the legally approved age. Thus most schools, from time to time, admit selected younger-than-average children whom they deem sufficiently mature emotionally and socially, as well as sufficiently capable intellectually, to do satisfactory work in the first school rung, either kindergarten or first grade.

Double promotion Acceleration assumes yet another face when schools promote pupils two grades instead of one. This practice is called double promotion or grade skipping. Casually accepted as defensible educational practice until 1925 or 1930, it has undergone increasingly close scrutiny since. The twofold purpose of double promotions is to get gifted pupils into a more appropriate curriculum, and to project them into post-school life earlier by reducing the length of their formal education.

Grade skipping, however, raises a number of provocative and controversial questions. One is whether a child who misses a curriculum year will be seriously handicapped by the loss. A second is whether a child cognitively capable of advancing two years is equally capable emotionally and socially. A third is whether double promotions are as defensible at certain levels as at others.

The consensus story on double promotions goes something like this. The academic world is divided attitudinally toward the practice. Teachers and educational theorists are more anti than pro; textbook writers and at least a few researchers are more pro than anti. Terman and Oden, for instance, come out forthrightly in favor of it.[16]

> It is our opinion that nearly all children of 135 I.Q. or higher should be promoted sufficiently to permit college entrance by the age of 17 at least, and that the majority of this group would be better off entering at age 16. Acceleration of this extent is especially desirable for those who plan to complete two or more years of graduate study in preparation for a professional career.

All, however, irrespective of their other possible differences, agree that a year's void created in a carefully graduated curriculum is harmful. Thus, double promotions should be made only for pupils who, mature along many lines, have been able to work ahead; or, when once promoted, are able to make up the important curriculum experiences missed. This qualification rules out double promotions conceived on the spur of the moment and hurriedly implemented. Knowledgeable observers agree also that double promotions are most objectionable and harmful at a time when the skills of communication constitute the heart of the curriculum. In terms of recommended practice, then, no grade skipping at all should take place in the primary grades unless the curriculum, as in an ungraded organizational arrangement, is graduated vertically so as to enable a bright youngster to work ahead and thus to complete three years of work in two. Even in the upper-elementary and junior-high-school grades, pupils should cover all important curriculum content in a condensed time period rather than skipping it entirely.

Provisions in the high school for acceleration In the high school, acceleration takes place in several ways. The occasional school allows selected students to carry overloads and attend summer sessions to the end of their earlier graduation. The practice, however, has several

[16] L. M. Terman and Melita Oden, *The Gifted Child Grows Up—IV*, (Stanford, Calif.: Stanford University Press, 1960), p. 275.

drawbacks. One is the chronological loss of a half year or year of formal education for the early graduate who does not attend college. The extra work taken in anticipation of this outcome does not necessarily compensate for the time loss. Formal education is a phenomenon not just of curriculum exposure but of the experiences and mature insights that learners bring to it. Thus curriculum coverage over a shorter period may not necessarily be as beneficial as related coverage over a longer period. The practice is also vulnerable, particularly the overload part, to the extent it accentuates the quantitative aspects of education at the expense of the qualitative.

This discussion of early graduation through overload arrangements is largely academic, however, in view of the limited role that such arrangements play in high school programs throughout the country. In fact, they and almost all other approaches to acceleration are overshadowed by the Advanced Placement Program which plays the starring role. By way of review, we cover a few of its attributes here.

A creation of the College Entrance Examination Board, its purpose is to accelerate the academically talented through college in a shorter-than-average period of time. It does this by guiding them into selected college-level courses during the period of their high school enrollment. The more gifted sometimes complete as many as four of these courses during their junior and senior years, thus enabling them later to graduate from selected colleges and universities in three years. The less gifted among the academically talented generally complete not more than one or two such courses while in high school. Then by carrying overloads or enrolling in summer-school programs once in college, they, too, often graduate in less than four years.

In my opinion, however, curriculum enrichment rather than student acceleration is the Program's most commendable feature. But it is commendable only when high school and college personnel reject the easy alternative of transplanting existing college curriculum designs into high schools, and, instead, enmesh themselves in the arduous process of curriculum development. When they do this latter, the assured advantage of curriculum improvement in the high school will tend to outweigh the sometimes questionable advantage of earlier-than-average graduation of students from college.

Secondary education, however, while exploiting the curriculum benefits of the Advanced Placement Program for the academically talented, should work equally hard to provide a comparably adequate program for the average and slow. Balance needs to characterize the whole

approach. And under no circumstances should secondary education forsake the cherished goal of total developmental growth for all learners.

A POSITION STATEMENT

Civilized societies worthy of the name should have a pervasive interest in talent in all approved categories. Wherever they find it, they should help it to become its potential. Talent differs in quality and amount from individual to individual, but the right to develop it does not differ.

Certain individuals are talented academically: that is, they are capable of achieving noteworthy success in a world of abstract symbols and concepts. One feeling is that because of their unusal ability, particularly because of their greater-than-average autonomy, they require only a modicum of help form instructional figures. And the position has the position has enough logic to make it appear convincing, at least on the surface. Second, it is thought that the academically talented, because they have more to offer the society than others, are entitled to, and thus should receive, greater-than-average attention from authority figures. This position also has a base of logic. A third idea, one that I hold, is that the academicall talented should receive special attention from instructional figures, but not for reason of their having greater social worth; rather for reason of their having specialized academic interests and needs. Good education is one that meets learners where they are, that tailors a curriculum to their uniqueness, and that guides them toward the goal of optimum fulfillment.

Consistent with this point of view, then, the social order, including formal education, needs to seek out academic talent wherever it may be found: in the poverty of submarginal social classes and in the affluence of the middle and upper-middle social classes. And when the academically talented are discovered, formal education has a mandate to administer in specialized ways to their unique interests and needs.

To Stimulate Thought

1. Defend the statement: Relatively speaking, the gifted in any culture are more deserving than the less gifted of a complete education.

441

2. In your opinion, should the nation subsidize the college education of high school graduates who, although intellectually capable of attending college, are financially unable to do so? Justify your reasons.

3. Elaborate the statement: The academically talented are divergent thinkers who, employing the status quo merely as a point of departure, need to challenge established patterns of values and behavior.

4. Why is it possible for certain individuals to score high on individual intelligence tests and considerably lower, proportionately, on group tests?

5. Criticize the assumption of many that the academically talented are those who score in the top 15 to 20 percent on tests of scholastic aptitude.

6. Review the paragraph on the Pegnato and Birch study presented several pages back. Then list as many reasons as you can why the more frequently employed methods of selecting academic talent vary as widely as they do.

7. Identify and develop the pros and cons of a school's informing academically talented learners of the existence and dimensions of their talents.

8. Identify and elaborate the pros and cons of double promotions as a method of acceleration.

9. Develop the statement: Fewer courses intensified quite conceivably are preferable to more courses less intensified.

10. Assume a highly gifted student with a Stanford-Binet IQ of 180. Further assume him to be a student in a sophisticated suburban high school that offers the equivalent of one and one-half years of work in college-level courses. In the event the student in question completed all this work and received credit for it when enrolling in a given university, what problems, academic and social, might he have to face in the university that other "more normal" students would not similarly have to face?

REFERENCES

Anderson, Kenneth E., *Research on the Academically Talented Student* (Washington, D.C.: NEA, 1961).

Bishop, William E., "Successful Teachers of the Gifted," *Exceptional Children* 34 (January 1968), 317–325.

Committee on Education of Exceptional Children, "Education of Exceptional Children," *Review of Educational Research* 39 (February 1969), the entire issue.

DeHaan, Robert F., and Robert J. Havighurst, *Educating Gifted Children* (Chicago: University of Chicago Press, 1961).

Durr, William K., *The Gifted Student* (New York: Oxford University Press, 1964).

Fliegler, Louis A. (ed.), *Curriculum Planning for the Gifted* (Englewood Cliffs, N.J.: Prentice-Hall, Inc., 1964).

Gallagher, James J., *Teaching the Gifted Child* (Boston: Allyn and Bacon, Inc., 1964).

Getzels, Jacob W., and Philip W. Jackson, *Creativity and Intelligence* (New York: John Wiley & Sons, Inc., 1962).

Inlow, Gail M., *The Emergent in Curriculum* (New York: John Wiley & Sons, Inc., 1966), Chaps. 5, 16.

Martinson, Ruth A. and May V. Segal, *The Abilities of Young Children* (Washington, D.C.: Council for Exceptional Children, 1967).

Noffsinger, Thomas, "Creativity: A Critique," *Science Education*, 1969.

Raph, Jane Beasley, Miriam L. Goldberg, and A. Harry Passow, *Bright Underachievers: Studies of Scholastic Underachievement Among Intellectually Superior High School Students* (New York: Bureau of Publications, Columbia Teachers College Press, 1966).

Sands, Theodore, Charles R. Hicklin, and others, *The Development and Testing of Instructional Materials for Gifted Primary Pupils* (Normal, Ill.: Illinois State Normal University, 1965).

School District of the Abington Township, *A Program for the Academically Talented* (Abington, Penna.: School District, 1965).

Shertzer, Bruce (ed.), *Working with Superior Students* (Chicago: Science Research Associates, Inc., 1960).

Terman, Lewis M., and Melita Oden, *Genetic Studies of Genius—IV. The Gifted Child Grows Up* (Stanford, Calif.: Stanford University Press, 1947).

Torrance, E. Paul, and Robert E. Myers, *Teaching Gifted Elementary Pupils How to Do Research* (Minneapolis: Perceptive Publishing Company, 1962).

U.S. Department of Health, Education, and Welfare, *State and Local Provisions for Talented Students: An Annotated Bibliography*, Bulletin No. 5, OE 35069 (Washington, D.C.: Superintendent of Documents, 1966).

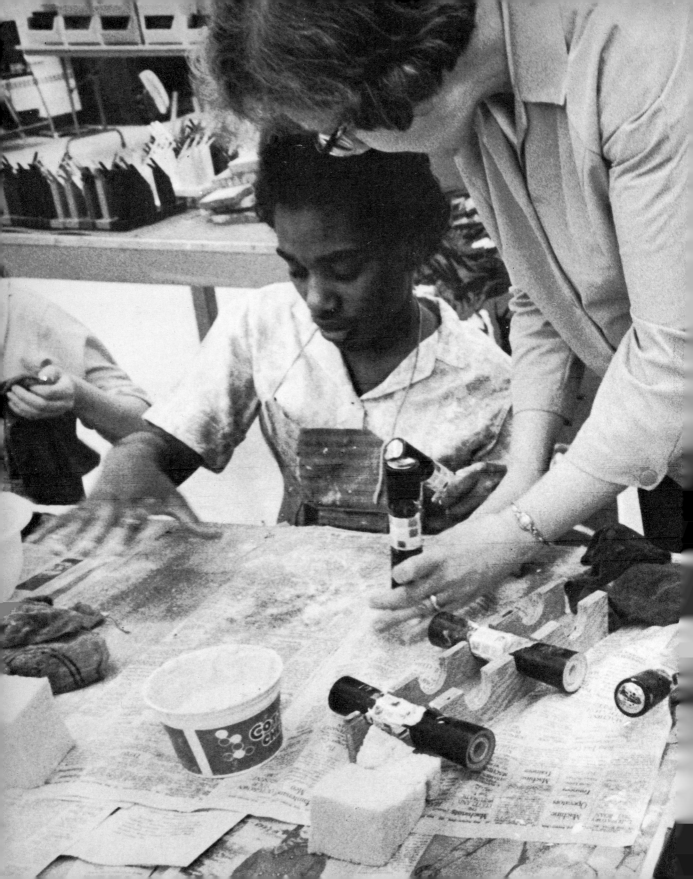

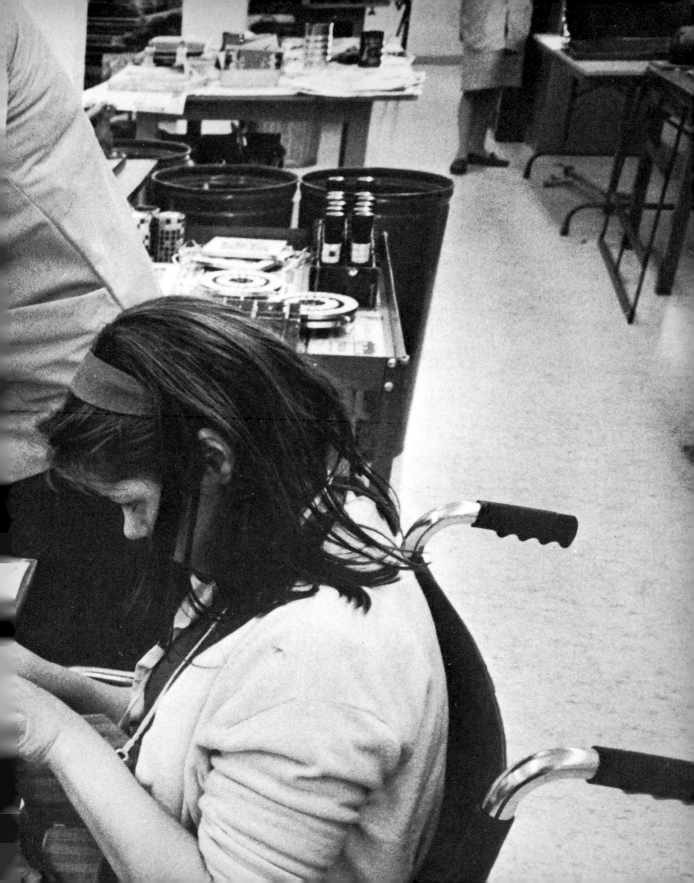

Chapter
16

Mentally, Emotionally, Physically Handicapped Learners

The central theme of Chapter 14 was the culturally deprived; of Chapter 15, the academically talented. The central theme of this chapter reverts to the deprived, but, in the present context, focuses on children deprived in other than socioeconomic ways. Specific coverage is made of three categories of deprived learners: the mentally handicapped, the emotionally-socially handicapped, and the physically handicapped. These with their never-ending problems continually test the nation's humanistic claims and traditions.

Historically, severely handicapped persons as, for instance, mental defectives, psychotics, the cerebral palsied, or the blind have either been demeaned or pitied, but not often helped. Today, the approved approach is one of neither debasement nor pity; instead, it is one of acceptance, understanding, and help. The thesis is that the handicapped, being human, share with all other human beings the right to become their potentials.

History reveals that until recently individual families or clans had to bear the major responsibility for care of the severely handicapped. The contrasting trend today is for government to assume some or much of this responsibility. And this new social arrangement represents yet another important gain for the have-nots of the world. Human dignity is a mockery, however, under a governmental system that supports individualism for some but not for all. Nor is it any more authentic when a governmental system conceives individualism as capable of realization apart from a social group. As already stated or implied a number of times in the book, humanism's ultimate is individualism with altruism its goal.

My definition of the handicapped child is as follows: he is one who deviates so much from the so-called normal child that school patterns and practices need to undergo substantial change in order to accommodate his uniqueness. For specific purposes of this chapter, he is the mentally retarded, the emotionally-socially maladjusted, the speech-impaired, the visually handicapped, the deaf and hard of hearing, and the crippled or otherwise physically impaired. He could also be the multihandicapped or the bed-ridden child ill for a variety of medical reasons.

The incidence of handicapped children and youth in the United

States, although only approximately known, is disturbingly high. Table 16.1 supports this conclusion.

With the gifted deleted from Table 16.1, the totals emerge as 3,638,000, or 10.7 percent, handicapped out of a total school-age population in 1954 of 34 million. These are sobering figures, although in all probability, most of the 3,638,000 were able to live fairly productive lives. Most of them were also enrolled in so-called regular classes in school.

A more recent 1966 study, detailed in Table 16.2, reveals the number of exceptional children actually enrolled in special programs in regular public schools or in public and private residential schools.

The two tables contain convincing evidence that the handicapped in and outside the frame of formal education constitute a sizable group of young individuals. The human worth of the 3,638,000 children of school age, who, in 1954, were handicapped, and the 2,106,200 children of school age who, in 1966, were enrolled in special education programs, is inestimable. Beyond debate, the American society and its institution of formal education have an inescapable obligation to help the handicapped become their potentials. This chapter's overview will help the reader determine how well either or both have succeeded in assuming this obligation.

TABLE 16.1 ESTIMATE OF INCIDENCE OF EXCEPTIONAL CHILDREN OF SCHOOL AGE

Areas of Exceptionality	Percent of Incidence	Estimated Number of School-aged Children
Visually handicapped	0.20	
Blind		10,000
Partially seeing		58,000
Crippled	1.50	510,000
Special health problems	1.50	510,000
Deaf and hard of hearing	1.50	510,000
Speech-handicapped	2.00	680,000
Socially maladjusted	2.00	680,000
Mentally retarded	2.00	680,000
Gifted	2.00	680,000
Total	12.70	4,318,000

Source: Romaine P. Mackie and Lloyd M. Dunn, *College and University Programs for the Preparation of Teachers of Exceptional Children,* U.S. Office of Education Bulletin No. 13 (Washington, D.C.: U.S. Government Printing Office, 1954). Certain of these totals differ from others given later in the chapter, the reasons residing in the diagnostic, and data-gathering variables.

TABLE 16.2 ENROLLMENT IN SPECIAL EDUCATION PROGRAMS FOR EXCEPTIONAL CHILDREN: UNITED STATES, FEBRUARY, 1966

Area of Exceptionality*	Total enrollment	Local public schools	Public and private residential schools
1	2	3	4
Total	2,106,200	1,978,900	127,300
Visually handicapped	23,300	15,400	7,900
Deaf and hard of hearing	51,400	32,700	18,700
Speech-impaired	987,000	987,000	—†
Crippled and special health problems	69,400	69,400	—†
Emotionally and socially maladjusted	120,400	64,700	55,700‡
Mentally retarded	540,100	495,100	45,000
Other handicapping conditions	2,500	2,500	—†
Gifted	312,100	312,100	—†

Source: Kenneth A. Simon, *Digest of Educational Statistics,* OE-10024-68 (Washington, D.C.: U.S. Department of Health, Education, and Welfare, 1968), p. 33.

* Pupils are reported according to the major type of exceptionality for which they are receiving special education.

† Not included in survey of residential schools.

‡ Includes education programs in public hospitals for the mentally ill.

THE MENTALLY HANDICAPPED

First in order of treatment are the mentally handicapped, a sizable group, who, by whatever name, either are innately less intelligent than their more favored counterparts or have developed their intellectual powers to a lesser degree. The issue is one of genetic versus environmental causality, of nature versus nurture. Until approximately a half century ago, the genetic explanation dominated. Those who espoused it based their conclusions primarily on selected studies of families which, when researched within the frame of limited controls, revealed a long history of mentally defective offspring. One such family was that of a Martin Kallikak who, during the Revolutionary War, was reported to have mated with a mentally defective barmaid.[1] From this union came an unsavory group of offspring, approximately 80 percent of whom allegedly were both social misfits and mental defectives. Following this misalliance, Martin Kallikak reportedly married a socially respected, intelligent woman from which union emanated a line of pre-

[1] H. H. Goddard, *The Kallikak Family* (New York: Crowell-Collier and Macmillan, Inc., 1912).

dominantly intellectual offspring. The conclusion from this and related studies was that mental development, for the most part, is an inherited characteristic.

Although genetic factors establish the absolute limits of intelligence, we realize today that environmental factors determine the degree to which individuals will develop their intellectual potentials. When the environment is barren, as with many of the culturally deprived, the IQ over a period of years may experience losses as great as 10 to 20 gradients. When the environment changes from meager to enriched, however, the IQ may well show gains of comparable proportions.

Irrespective of causality, the mentally handicapped are slower than average in their cognitive and social responses; consequently, they are late arrivers at almost all stations of intellectual growth. Yet they are far from being homogeneous. Even on the trait of intelligence itself, they differ extensively. Specifically, depending on the orientations and trade vocabularies of individual writers and researchers, they differ as indicated in Table 16.3.

TABLE 16.3 CATEGORIES OF THE MENTALLY HANDICAPPED

Dimensions	Category 1	Category 2	Category 3
1. The IQ dimension	50 to 70 or 75	25–49	24 or less
2. The mental deficiency dimension	moron	imbecile	idiot
3. The educability dimension	educable mentally handicapped	trainable mentally handicapped	costodial mentally handicapped
4. The autonomy dimension	semiindependent	semidependent	dependent
5. The numerical ratio dimension (approximations)	25 in 1000	3 to 4 in 1000	1 in 1000

The Educable Mentally Handicapped

The so-called morons of the first quarter of the present century are today's educable mentally handicapped (EMH). The change involves more than just one of nomenclature: it reveals a directional shift from their mental deficiency (a negative approach) to their educability (a positive approach). As indicated in Table 16.3, the educable mentally handicapped constitute about 2.5 percent of the total school population.

450

The specific educational objectives for this category of learners lie in the five areas of the emotional, the academic, the social, the vocational, and the psychomotor. The composite objective is to make these individuals as autonomous as they are capable of becoming in the world of the self, the world of communication, the world of people, and the world of work.

The educable mentally handicapped have IQs that range from 50 to 70 or 75. Held down by this limitation, the mental ages of even the most capable among them rarely exceed nine or ten, and their academic achievement rarely goes beyond the fourth- or fifth-grade level. In respect to the ones with IQs of 50 to 55, a mental age of six or seven and academic achievement at the level of grade 1 or grade 2 are likely eventualities.[2] It follows, then, that EMH children are slow to grasp abstractions of all kinds and are completely incapable of grasping the more complex ones. This deficiency comes with them to school and stays with them usually for life. Because of it, their progress in such abstract tasks as reading, writing, spelling, listening, and computing is relatively slow and halting—more so with some, less so with others. Even the brighter, however, are rarely ready for such tasks until they reach the latter part of the second or the third grade.

The following traits typify them. They have short attention spans, a direct result of symbolic and cognitive limitations. They require special learning materials in school such as the following: a wide variety of reading and arithmetic readiness materials in the primary grades, a rich diet of learning concretions in all grades, diversified audio-visual learning materials, and books that although geared to their ability levels do not bear grade designations. Their play interests are at the level of their mental rather than chronological ages. Thus for a fourteen-year-old girl with a mental age of seven or eight to play with dolls is developmentally predicated. EMH children also tend to have lower-than-average frustration tolerances, conceivably because too many authority figures and peers with whom they associate expect more of them than they are capable of producing. In respect to vocational potential, the brighter EMH children, if carefully trained and closely supervised, are capable of performing semiskilled tasks in business and industry; the less bright, however, do not progress beyond unskilled routines. Spe-

[2] The mental age of a child divided by his chronological age results in the IQ. Thus a child aged sixteen mentally and twelve chronogically has an IQ of 133. A child aged twelve, with a mental age of six, has an IQ of 50.

cifically, the educable mentally handicapped tend to become packers in stockrooms, dishwashers, busboys, nurses' aides, messengers, elevator operators, porters, laundry workers, or production-line factory workers—these among many others.

The curriculum for EMH children in the elementary school concentrates, for the most part, on the skills of communication and computation, on personal hygiene and grooming, on self-acceptance, on social and citizenship skills, on wholesome leisure-time activities, and on a simplified body of facts and concepts. The curriculum in the junior high school and the high school likewise embraces content in the fundamental skills, developmentally related, to be sure, to the abilities of the learners. In addition, the secondary school curriculum embraces a variety of activities in home economics and the mechanical arts, focusing throughout on problems associated with the theme of getting and keeping a job.

Formal education employs a variety of organizational arrangements as it strives to meet the needs of the educable mentally handicapped. The most common one is the ungraded special class, suited particularly well to the small school or school system that enrolls a very limited number of EMH pupils. A school system with a population of 500, for example, would be likely to have 10 to 15 such pupils enrolled. The ungraded class, although administratively expedient, is pedagogically vulnerable. Like the little red schoolhouse of old, it brings together so much pupil diversity that learner outcomes are often adversely affected. An age range of eight years and an ability range of 25 IQ gradients are not uncommon. These ranges are tolerable in small class-sized groupings. Yet, even then, academic, personal and social outcomes suffer from the lack of homogeneity of the learners.

A second organizational arrangement is one wherein EMH pupils meet in special classes part of a school day and in regular classes for the remainder of the day. The skill subjects make up the heart of the curriculum in the former; the applied-arts subjects, the heart of the curriculum in the latter. My personal feeling is that schools which employ this combined scheme should expand it to include EMH students not only in the "regular" curriculum of the applied arts but in that of the social studies and, on occasions, in that of science and the cocurriculum as well. My reason is that inasmuch as EMH students are destined to be a part of the "normal" world—not to be set apart from it by close parental or institutionalized care—they should be as much a part of the normal school world as possible.

452

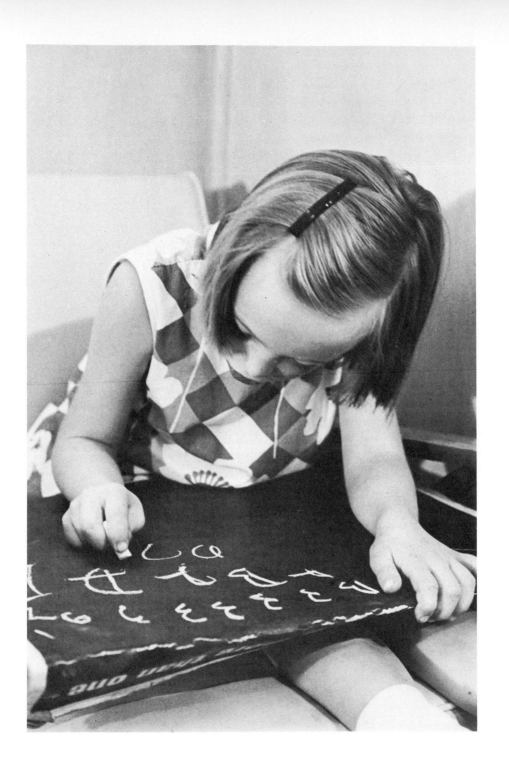

A third arrangement is the homogeneous class of EMH pupils. In such a setting, numbers permitting, the desired goal is a chronological-age range of not more than two to four years, and a mental-age range of half that amount. This reduction in heterogeneity over that characteristic of the ungraded class tends to pay off in increased teaching and learning effectiveness.

Two other organizational arrangements consist of the segregated school that enrolls only EMH pupils, and the itinerant teacher who moves from school to school, or from classroom to classroom in any one school, working with individual EMH pupils in regular classes. Neither scheme is very effective and, fortunately, neither one is very popular. The former, a vestige from Europe,[3] has two primary shortcomings. For one, it sets the EMH too much apart from life in general. For a second, it adds to the social stigma of children who attend—a stigma that results from the thoughtlessness of a society that, as yet, only partially understands the problems and feelings of the EMH. In this arrangement, the rational component once more takes precedence over the humanistic personal; the man of greater reason over the man of lesser reason.

The Trainable Mentally Handicapped

Mentally handicapped children and youth whose IQs range from approximately 25 to 50 constitute the central theme of this section. Until recently, they bore the nondescriptive and somewhat offensive label of imbecile; today, they bear the more descriptive and less offensive label of trainable mentally handicapped (TMH). Although estimates of their number vary, an emerging consensus attests to the existence of three to four of them in every 1000 children of school age. Of the total group, approximately two-thirds live at home and one-third live in special residential institutions, public and private.[4]

The primary characteristic manifested by all trainable handicapped children is their inability to grow out of childhood. Their bodies make fairly normal progress, but their minds, emotions, and social skills stay immature.

[3] International Bureau of Education, *Organization of Special Education for Mentally Deficient Children* (Geneva, Switzerland: The Bureau, 1960).

[4] Samuel A. Kirk, *Educating Exceptional Children* (Boston: Houghton Mifflin Company, 1962), pp. 133–135. I cite this book here as one of the more exceptional ones on the topic of the exceptional.

An appropriate curriculum for them, then, is one that administers to their elemental needs. Its goals are to help them learn such basic fundamentals as (1) to take care of themselves—dress, eat, become toilet-trained, and stay presentable; (2) to relate in a reasonably acceptable way to associates by distinguishing between mine and yours, by taking turns, and by avoiding aggressive body contact with others; and (3) to become occupationally useful at simple, routine tasks performed in a sheltered environment.

Desired "academic" outcomes of the curriculum consist of the following fundamentals:

1. In reading, to recognize their names and such other important symbols as stop and go, men and women, entrance and exit, open and shut, and danger. Even the brighter TMH pupils are rarely able to read first-grade primers.

2. In arithmetic, to count to 10, tell time, know their ages, and make simple change; also to distinguish between more and less, great and small, high and low, many and few.

3. In physical hygiene, to learn values and skills related to foods, dental care, washing and bathing, toilet training, safety, and posture.

4. In the fine and applied arts, to color, draw, paint, use simple tools, construct simple objects, help with home tasks, perform housekeeping tasks in the classroom, and participate in musical events.

5. In the content subjects, to learn a few basic facts and concepts of social studies and science.

The society is more certain about an appropriate curriculum for the trainable mentally handicapped than it is about the agency responsible for implementing it. The issue brings two groups face to face: those who hold the public schools to be responsible and those who do not. The first contend that formal education is responsible because it alone is qualified to assume the responsibility. The second differs on grounds that the proper purview of formal public education is curriculum content at a level of the conceptual, not at a level of the trainable repetitive.

I personally side with the public-education advocates. Theirs is a point of view that gives every appearance of being the emerging one. For instance, in[5]

the fall of 1958, 10 states had mandatory legislation and 15 had permissive legislation for the inclusion in the public schools of the trainable mentally

---

[5] I. Ignacy Goldberg and William M. Cruickshank, "Trainable but Noneducable," *National Educational Association Journal*, 47 (December 1958), p. 622.

retarded. Four additional states interpreted the existing statutes for exceptional children to include the trainable without further legislation. . . .

One alternative to this point of view might be community schools and classes under the care of a specialized local or state agency of some kind. Such an agency conceivably, however, would be less capable of exerting leadership than would the institution of education. A totally unacceptable alternative would be the denial of formal education to the TMH.

Irrespective of agency responsibility, I agree with the following statement made in a recent public document, namely, that[6]

the mentally retarded are entitled to all the privileges, dignities and respect we expect for ourselves and others in our society . . . the retarded, because of their handicaps, are properly entitled to a sympathetic understanding and a deep concern for their welfare and betterment.

The Custodial Mentally Handicapped

A closing statement is in order here on the so-called custodial mentally handicapped—the atypical defectives, that is, with IQ's of less than 25. Their most characteristic feature is dependency. In fact, without constant care from others, living itself is impossible for them. Approximately one youngster in a thousand fits into the custodial-handicapped category. Because both uneducable and untrainable, however, they lie outside the scope of this book.

THE EMOTIONALLY-SOCIALLY HANDICAPPED

Very much in the scope of this book, however, are the emotionally-socially maladjusted. The more seriously disturbed among them do not attend school at all, and those who do range widely from the near-normal to the near-psychotic. The borderline cases are the most difficult for teachers and even the clinically trained to identify. Third-grade Jimmy, for instance, daydreams a lot. Is he bored with school? Is he a sensitive esthete? Or is he seriously out of contact with reality? Ninth-grade Christi makes a habit of pretending to be what she is not. Is she an adolescent poseur, or is she pathologically dissatisfied with herself?

[6] U.S. Department of Health, Education, and Welfare, Public Health Service, *Design of Facilities for the Mentally Retarded,* No. 1181-C-1 Washington, D.C.: U.S. Government Printing Office, 1966), p. 1.

Tom is a "bad actor" on the football field—losing his temper with a minimum of provocation and sounding off frequently. Is he, in common parlance, just a spoiled brat? Or is he a maladjusted boy in need of counseling, perhaps even of professional therapy?

A major reason why maladjustment resists easy identification is that its semantic opposite, adjustment, comparably resists easy identification. Normal adjustment, as defined by one source, "refers to behavior generally observed of individuals within a specific social context and generally considered appropriate."[7] I accept this criterion, even though oversimplified, in view of the general nature of the topic's treatment in this section.

With adjustment viewed in this frame, school administrators and teachers rightfully suspect maladjustment in pupils when they consistently manifest any of the following symptoms.

1. *Fixate consistently on themselves.* Maturity's progression is away from the self to an expanding world of others, with altruism the ultimate value. The most immature, failing this test, stay emotionally infantile. Symptoms might include the need for a pupil to be first in everything, callous disregard of others, rigidity of points of view, a double set of standards—one for the self and another for associates, and refusal to accept responsibility for behavior.

2. *Dislike themselves.* Maturity's progression is also away from dissatisfaction with the self to wholesome acceptance of the self. Symptoms of dissatisfaction are frequent deprecation of looks or personality, constant solicitation of praise, and carping criticism of others.

3. *Are unable to adapt to their environments.* The emotionally maladjusted customarily are environmental misfits. They move against or withdraw from others. They resent and resist authority. They tilt at windmills. They are incapable of establishing stable affective relationships. They do poorly in school. They drop out early. They are delinquency-prone.

4. *Manifest inappropriate overt emotional symptoms.* The emotional responses of maladjusted children are situationally inappropriate and excessively intense. In regard to the first, anger erupts for no apparent reason, tears fall with little provocation, and moodiness results from trifles. In regard to the second, the emotions of the maladjusted are

[7] Clarence C. and Sylvia Sherwood, "The Emotionally Disturbed Child," in Joseph S. Roucek (ed.), *The Unusual Child* (New York: Philosophical Library, Inc., 1962), pp. 51–52.

often violent and compulsive: they seemingly have to express themselves without restraint or appropriateness.

5. *Have covert correlates to overt symptoms.* Outward manifestations of emotional disturbance in the maladjusted reveal, under psychological and medical examination, internal correlates. These might be cardiac and digestive irregularities, endocrine imbalances, or chronic anxiety and tension.

6. *Do not live up to potentials.* The distorted emotions of the maladjusted tend to block progress along many growth lines. Thus the emotions should be suspect when, for instance, the bright perform significantly below capacity.

7. *Overuse the defense mechanisms to escape reality.* Individuals unable to maintain their egos when looking into the psychological mirror of life tend to bolster them by employing the so-called defense mechanisms. Normal individuals employ these also, but the difference is one of degree. The mechanisms themselves consist selectively of the following, with an illustration provided for each.

Rationalization: Bill, regularly turned down on dates, assuages his ego by deciding that girls are snobs and not worth dating.

Denial: Bob, an emotionally unstable fifth grader, has a history of failing the expectations of those around him. Ridiculed constantly for his failures but unable to prevent them, he develops a pattern of defending himself through psychological denial: "But you didn't tell me to do it," and so on. At the emotional level, he believes—because he has to believe—his own excuses.

Regression: Anita, unable to keep up with other first graders and feeling shut out as a result, reverts to infantile attention-getting behavior: whining, tantrums, and nonconstructive play.

Sublimation: Melinda, unattractive and unable to get dates, sublimates by engaging in a wide variety of group activities in and out of school. These become almost a compulsion with her.

Identification: Tom, a would-be athlete but always a poor one, compensates by identifying with the Wilt Chamberlains, Gayle Sayers, Cassius Clays, and Arnold Palmers. His behavior frequently verges on the autistic.

These symptoms and a host of others that might have been named and elaborated provide clues to emotional and social maladjustment. A major difficulty, as previously stated, is to find the dividing line between emotions that are more and those that are less normal. An over-

simplified rule of thumb is that the less normal emotions tend to be more intense, more compulsive, and more inappropriate to age and situation.

The vast majority of the emotionally disturbed are enrolled in so-called regular classrooms. Estimates of the total number of the disturbed in school range from 7 percent by Wickman to 8 percent by Ullmann, to 12 percent by Rogers.[8] Whatever the correct total, the emotionally disturbed confront education with a magnitude of problems. And it deals with them effectively only when taking seriously its responsibility for the affective as well as for the intellectual lives of all learners. As developed in Chapter 11, and thus covered only briefly here, education manifests a seriousness of purpose in this regard when it (1) has teachers who are not just knowledgeable but who are also well adjusted and empathic; (2) has teachers who relate to learners, not just to learning; (3) has a carefully conceived curriculum in which all pupils may realize success; (4) has special counseling for those in need of it; and (5) refers the more seriously disturbed to agencies outside the regular school environment.

For these latter individuals, the next stop might well be any of the following: the office of a private therapist, a special day school, or a residential school. The defeating characteristics of many special classes and schools for the emotionally disturbed is that the personnel in charge often think more in terms of truancy and delinquency than of the children's need for therapeutic care. The end result should be rehabilitation, not merely punitive retention. Commenting on the Parental School in Chicago (a residential school), Havighurst[9] writes that "no one seems able to decide what it ought to be (detention home, school, residential treatment center, nonparental institution, etc.)."

Organizational schemes for the more seriously maladjusted should follow the law of parsimony: proceed, that is, from the more casual to the more unusual. For elementary school children, regular classrooms and social-adjustment classes in schools near the homes of the children should serve as the central guidance centers. The latter should be under the aegis of trained psychologists and social workers. The focus should be more on early identification and prevention than on after-the-fact rehabilitation. For high school youth, social-adjustment day schools should be the main guidance centers for those incapable of adjusting

[8] Samuel A. Kirk, p. 246.

[9] Robert J. Havighurst, *The Public Schools of Chicago* (Chicago: The Board of Education of the City of Chicago, 1964), p. 458.

to regular high schools. Residential schools should be the line of last, or near last, resort. And the goal for the disturbed in both elementary and secondary schools should be psychological change, not punishment; personality integration, not symptom manipulation.

THE SPEECH-HANDICAPPED

Children with speech problems comprise still another sizable category of handicapped learners. In nontechnical language, they are handicapped in the sense that their speech is unpleasant in sound; inappropriate in respect to age; or unintelligible, either in part or in toto. And their problems may be either organic or functional in nature. If organic, the cause might be any of the following: neurological defects in the brain or central nervous system, cleft palate, impaired hearing, defect in the larynx (voice box), or defect in the breathing apparatus. If functional, the cause might be psychological, faulty early training, or sinusitis. Five percent of school age children have a speech handicap: three percent have functional, thus correctable, disorders; two percent have organic disorders, which are hard or impossible to correct.

Speech impairments divide into categories by percentages as indicated in Table 16.4.

TABLE 16.4   ESTIMATE OF INCIDENCE OF SPEECH DEFECTS AMONG CHILDREN IN THE UNITED STATES, AGED 5-21

Type of Problem	Percent of Children
Articulation	3.0
Stuttering	1.0
Voice	.1
Cleft palate	.1
Cerebral palsy	.1
Retarded speech development	.2
Speech problems due to impaired hearing	.5
	5.0 percent

Source: Karl C. Garrison and Dewey G. Force, Jr., *The Psychology of Exceptional Children* (New York: The Ronald Press Company, 1965), p. 187.

The functional articulation disorders take the forms of *substitutions* of sounds: for example, *thay* for *say*, or *Fweddie* for *Freddie*; of omis-

sions: mostly dropped word endings; of *distortions:* for example, the whistling "s" sound; and of *additions:* for example, *slimber* for *slimmer.*

Stuttering is in certain respects the most baffling of all the speech disorders, with comparably qualified specialists differing widely regarding its possible causes. The most frequently postulated are genetic influences, emotional factors, left-handedness, and endocrine imbalances. In my opinion, evidence is most heavily slanted in the direction of emotional causation. The handicap manifests itself in most children before they reach age nine. One in 9 is affected by it. Six boys to one girl are its victims. And the habit is a greater handicap in individual speech situations than in choral ones. In this connection, stuttering is generally so much less pronounced in a choral-singing or speaking situation, that when the stutterer shares the spotlight with a group, his handicap is noticeably diminished.[10] In view of the general nature of this book, I pass over the other five categories of speech disorders listed in Table 16.4.

Education's program aimed at the needs of the speech-handicapped has two organizational settings. One is the familiar classroom; the other is the office of the speech therapist. In the first, the classroom teacher, rarely a speech specialist, contributes significantly to the cause of amelioration by warmly accepting the speech-handicapped and thus minimizing their disorders. As stated by Murphy,[11]

> The classroom teacher will best serve handicapped children, not in terms of specific speech procedures, but on the basis of a sensitive, nurturant personal relationship with the child as both interact throughout the school year. . . . she will try to provide successful speaking experiences; acceptantly, she will hear him out; she will set the tone of the classroom by virtue of her own tolerant and accepting attitudes and reactions.

As the insightful classroom teacher relates to the speech-handicapped, he never belittles them, acts to prevent peers from doing so, and avoids such profitless but embarrassing admonitions as "Take it easy," "Pronounce your words carefully," and "Start over again." His is an accepting role, an encouraging and supporting role.

To the specialist falls the task of performing the technical functions of any speech-correction program. These consist of observing, diagnosing, assessing causality, and guiding the handicapped through a program of corrective action. The customary case load of a speech correctionist is somewhat in excess of 100 pupils. In addition to his clinical work

[10] Albert T. Murphy, "The Speech Handicapped" in Joseph S. Roucek, pp. 72–75.

[11] Murphy, pp. 82–83.

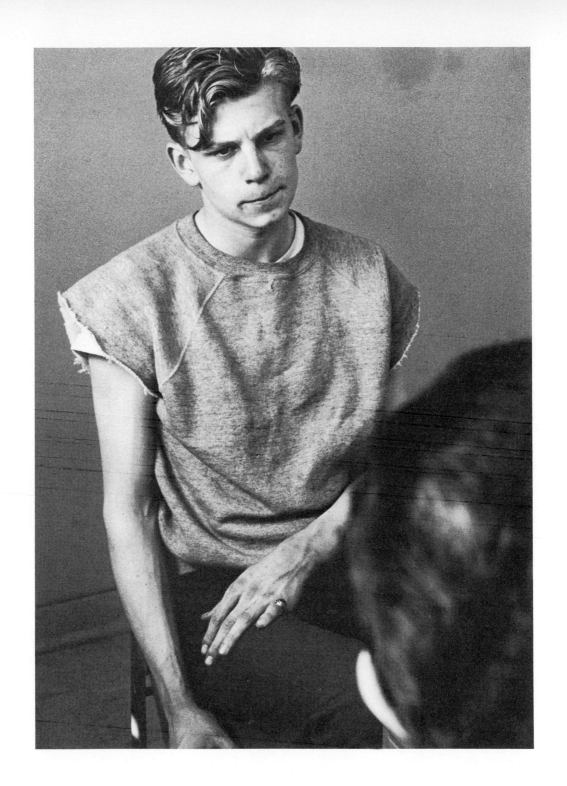

with pupils, he usually plays the role of in-service leader of the teaching faculty. As of 1960, approximately two-thirds of the states had certification standards for speech correctionists. Thus specialists and generalists are working more and more in concert as education manifests an increasing concern for the problems of the speech-handicapped.

THE VISUALLY HANDICAPPED

For purposes of this section, the visually handicapped comprise those "children who either have no vision or whose visual limitations after correction result in handicaps unless special provisions are made."[12] More specifically, they consist of the blind and partially sighted. They do not include individuals whose vision, with the aid of mechanical devices, falls within the broad range of normal. The three major causes of defective vision are these: structural defects of genetic origin in the eye or in neurological processes related thereto; these same defects of disease origin; and malfunctioning of eye muscles.

The blind, as categorized by legal authorities, consist either of individuals who do not see at all or of those who see only as well at 20 feet as individuals with normal vision see at 200 feet. Furthermore, their lateral vision has a range of 20 degrees or less. As of 1960, the blind in the United States totaled approximately 385,000, most of whom were elderly. Approximately 8000, however, were in elementary and secondary education, constituting a ratio of 1 blind pupil to 5000 visually normal ones.

The blind relate to life through their auditory, olfactory, tactile, and gustatory senses; yet these, contrary to popular opinion, are no more acute in the blind than they are in the normal. Most of the blind are retarded in motor development and measure somewhat below average in intelligence. Socially they tend to be appreciably more withdrawn than people who see. Their speech is generally louder, with the range less than normal. Gestures are inappropriate or absent. The blind read by Braille, which is a slow method, and also a delimiting one in that only selected publications have been translated into Braille. The Braille alphabet takes the form of raised marks as follows.

[12] John W. Jones, *The Visually Handicapped Child at Home and School,* OE-35045, Bulletin 1963, No. 39 (Washington, D.C.: U.S. Department of Health, Education and Welfare, 1963), p. 1.

         A   B   C

    ·   ·   ·   ·   · ·
                                ·
    ·   ·   ·   ·   ·
    ·
              ·   ·   ·   ·   ·

In 1962, the American Printing House for the Blind reported 8095 pupils in grades 1 to 12 to be Braille readers.[13]

As learners, the blind rely heavily on teacher explanation for understanding. The concept of a mountain, for instance, is only as meaningful to most of the blind as oral explanations are capable of making it. Thus a teacher would describe Pike's Peak, among other ways, as being over 14,000 feet above sea level and approximately 8000 feet above its base; as being steep at some points and rolling at others; as being covered with evergreens except for the top several thousand feet where rocks replace vegetation; as being often cloud-covered (extensive elaboration would take place here); and so forth. Teachers of the blind exploit the sense of touch in learning situations that involve, for example, geometrical figures, relief maps, linear distance, volume, and texture. They regularly employ aids: for instance, talking books, phonographs, tapes, arithmetic counters, Braille books, and Braille typewriters. In regard to the last-named aid, the goal for the blind is a Braille typing speed of from 40 to 60 words per minute.

In contrast to the blind, the partially sighted are those who, despite relatively severe sight handicaps, employ vision as their primary channel of learning. On an average, they see at 20 feet what people with normal vision see at 70. Except for selected specialized training, however, they sit in schools side by side with normally sighted learners and go through life doing most of the things that normally sighted people do.

The partially sighted learner in the composite, as depicted by Jones,[14] manifests the following symptoms:

Progresses at a rate below that which might be considered appropriate for children of approximately the same age, grade, and intelligence test scores.

Fails to complete long reading assignments or other school tasks involving extensive eye use, especially when time is limited.

[13] Jones, p. 41.

464   [14] Jones, p. 15.

Understands the basic principles involved in certain areas of study such as long division, but makes errors in the comparatively easier procedures such as addition, particularly when working with long columns of figures.

Remembers and understands material read to him better than that which he reads himself.

Confuses letters and words which look somewhat alike.

Covers or shields one eye habitually while reading.

Holds reading material at an unusual distance or angle.

Skips letters, words, or lines while reading.

Has difficulty copying from textbooks, workbooks, or chalkboards.

Tires quickly or is easily distracted while working at his desk.

Is confused by details such as those appearing on maps, charts, or diagrams.

Writes unusually small, large, or very poorly.

Appears clumsy or awkward on the playground.

Has poor eye-hand coordination.

Rubs or brushes eyes frequently.

Thrusts head forward or squints when looking at near or far objects.

Stumbles or trips often.

A widely employed school-organization arrangement for the partially sighted is one first conceived and implemented in 1913 by Dr. Robert B. Irwin. Under the Irwin plan,[15]

the child is enrolled in a special "sight-saving" class which serves as his homeroom. But he joins his normally seeing classmates in all classes except those requiring concentrated eye work. For concentrated eye work the partially seeing attend a special classroom with a teacher specially prepared to teach them. The most desired goal following from Irwin's efforts is integration of the partially seeing in regular classes of regular schools.

Any learning situation involving partially sighted pupils should be free from glare. Teachers should avoid standing in front of windows or lights. Their blackboard writing should be large and legible. And they should rely more on oral than on written expression for learning outcomes.

Selected agencies, as listed below, that publish specialized learning materials for the visually handicapped consist of the following:[16]

[15] Robert M. Frumkin and Miriam Z. Frumkin, "The Blind, Partially Seeing, and Color Weak," in Roucek, pp. 135–136.

The American Association of Instructors of the Blind, 2363 South Spring Ave., St. Louis, Mo. 63110. Proceedings of national conventions and *The International Journal for the Education of the Blind*.

The American Association of Workers for the Blind, 1511 K Street N.W., Washington, D.C. 20005. Proceedings of national conferences.

The American Foundation for the Blind, 15 West 16th St., New York, N.Y. 10011. Pamphlets on special topics and the *New Outlook for the Blind*. The Foundation also operates a lending library of more than 25,000 pieces of literature in this field.

Children's Bureau, U.S. Department of Health, Education, and Welfare, Washington, D.C. 20025. Pamphlets on selected topics.

Council for Exceptional Children, 1201 16th St., N.W., Washington, D.C. 20036. *Journal of Exceptional Children* and monographs on special topics.

Council for the Education of the Partially Seeing, Division of the Council for Exceptional Children, 1201 16th St., N.W., Washington, D.C. 20036. *Newsletter*.

Division for the Blind, Library of Congress, Washington, D.C. 20025. Catalogs, book lists, and pamphlets on selected topics.

The National Society for the Prevention of Blindness, 16 East 40th St., New York, N.Y. 10016. Catalogs of publications, films, materials, and *Sight-Saving Review*.

Office of Education, Education for Exceptional Children Branch, U.S. Department of Health, Education, and Welfare, Washington, D.C. 20025. Pamphlets on selected topics.

Office of Vocational Rehabilitation, Division of Services for the Blind, Department of Health, Education, and Welfare, Washington, D.C. 20025. Pamphlets on rehabilitation and employment opportunities.

THE DEAF AND HARD-OF-HEARING

The deaf and hard-of-hearing constitute a fifth category of learners who challenge education with the uniqueness of their handicaps. The deaf are those whose hearing, even with the help of mechanical aids, remains nonfunctional. Some are deaf for congenital reasons; others, for adventitious reasons including accidents, diseases, and psychic traumas. The hard-of-hearing are those whose hearing, even though defective, remains functional either with or without the help of mechanical aids.

466 [16] John W. Jones, *The Visually Handicapped Child at Home and School,* p. 51.

Auditory impairments are of four types. The first, the *conductive* type, consists of hearing losses which result from congenital malformations in, or injuries to, the outer or middle ear. Conductive defects, as a general rule, are quite responsive to surgery or hearing devices. The second, the *neurological* type, consists of hearing losses which result from defects in the inner ear or in nerves that lead from the inner ear to the brain. Neurological defects, as a general rule, do not respond well to surgery or mechanical devices. The third is the *brain-damage* type which also is usually unresponsive to surgery or mechanical devices. And the fourth is the *psychic* type which, because emotional in origin, responds best to psychiatric treatment.

Hearing is nothing more nor less than response to both the frequency and intensity of sound waves. The fewer the number of waves, the lower the pitch; the greater the number of waves, the higher the pitch. The less intense the waves, the softer the sound; the more intense the waves, the louder the sound. A hearing apparatus that is normal, then, is one that responds in a functional way to both pitch and loudness.

The side effects of hearing deficiency accentuate the magnitude of most handicaps. The totally deaf person, unable to hear sounds, has trouble learning to enunciate and articulate language symbols. Normal people learn to speak, at least in great part, by emulating what they hear; people with defective hearing, however, are blocked to a limited extent, or completely, from this important learning source. And because their speech is adversely affected, their reading ability is too.

Because the deaf require a specialized curriculum, the more modern school systems, either individually or collectively, provide for their instruction in residential schools, in day schools, or in day classes of regular schools. These specialized approaches are more prevalent, however, in the lower than in the higher grades. The customary pattern is for schools to set the deaf apart for specialized-skill instruction in the early grades, but to inject them more and more into normal classes as they proceed up the educational ladder. Once having learned to speech-read, the deaf reap emotional and social, as well as cognitive, benefits from a more normal learning environment.

In regard to the hard-of-hearing in regular classrooms, teachers need to work closely with otologists (medical specialists in defects and diseases of the ear) to learn the nature and extent of hearing defects and to receive suggestions about remedial steps, if any to be taken. If a hearing aid is to be used for the first time by a learner, the teacher pre-

pares class members to accept it just as they would another child's glasses. Knowing who the hard of hearing are, the teacher seats them at or near the front of the room. Also, he is careful to make facial contact with them when employing oral instructional methods. And with an understanding of the hearing problems in the classroom, the teacher is alerted to the possible need for future referrals to speech correctionists and school psychologists.[17] Day in and day out, it is the classroom teacher, not the specialist, who is most active in the education of the hard-of-hearing.

THE CRIPPLED AND SPECIAL HEALTH CASES

Combined for treatment in this final section are the crippled and other learners with physical handicaps not covered to this point. The major causes of crippling disabilities are genetic inheritance, cerebral palsy, poliomyelitis, meningitis, accidents, growths, and bone diseases. A conservative estimate of the number of crippled school-age children in the United States is a half million. A small minority of these, who are too disabled to attend school at all, receive help from visiting teachers who come to their homes or to hospitals. About half of the remainder are educated in special schools or in special classrooms of regular schools; the others, in regular schools and classrooms. Diseases that seriously debilitate without necessarily crippling include, among others, rheumatic fever, asthma, hay fever, tuberculosis, growths, pneumonia, and diabetes.

The emotional and social effects of physical disorders are obstacles to educational and personality growth that are often as serious as the disorders themselves. Particularly among adolescents, in whom the desire to conform is strong, anyone noticeably different has more than his share of problems. The IQs of the physically handicapped also tend to be lower on the average—as much as 10 points lower, in fact—than those of nonhandicapped children.

What the physically handicapped need most fundamentally is warm acceptance by all associates, peers and nonpeers alike. Because of developmental immaturity, children are rarely able to meet this need in the manner required; thus, parents and teachers need to redouble their efforts in the hope of compensating for the lack. The goal, though, is

[17] I drew a number of ideas included in this section from E. W. Johnson, "Hearing Problems in Children," in Roucek, pp. 108–126.

friendly acceptance of the handicapped as important human beings; it is certainly not smothering overprotection.

In regular and special schools, the goal for the handicapped should be the same as for all pupils: optimum growth. To the greatest extent possible, the disabled child should be part of the regular program; when this outcome is not possible, realistic modifications in the program understandably constitute next steps. The disabled child needs acceptance, success, and challenge. All these it is within the power of education to give. But sensitive, insightful, dedicated individuals alone can give them.

To
Stimulate
Thought

1. When for a number of generations family members consistently measure low on intelligence tests, the conclusion may be drawn that the reason is genetic in origin. React critically to this statement.

2. Develop the thesis that the educable and trainable mentally handicapped are, or are not, as entitled as their brighter counterparts to an education commensurate with their abilities.

3. Take a stand and elaborate on it, pro or con, that the surest avenue to the emotions is the intellect.

4. Describe steps that you as a teacher might take in getting a class to relate warmly to a seriously handicapped child.

REFERENCES

Abraham, Willard, *The Slow Learner* (New York: The Center for Applied Research in Education, Inc., 1964).

American Association of Instructors of the Blind, *Information Packet for Parents of Visually Handicapped Children* (St. Louis: The Association, 1962).

American Foundation for the Blind, *Directory of Agencies Serving Blind Persons in the United States*, 13th Ed. (New York: The Foundation, 1963).

Baumgartner, Bernice B., *Helping the Trainable Mentally Retarded Child: a Handbook for Teachers, Parents, and Administrators* (New York: Bureau of Publications, Teachers College, Columbia University, 1960).

Clauzio, Harvey F., *Mental Health and the Educative Process* (Chicago: Rand McNally Company, 1969).

469

Council for Exceptional Children, *Exceptional Children;* a periodical published nine times yearly.

Dunn, Lloyd M. (ed.), *Exceptional Children in the Schools* (New York: Holt, Rinehart and Winston, Inc., 1963).

Eaton, Allen H., *Beauty for the Sighted and the Blind* (New York: St. Martin's Press, Inc., 1959).

Garrison, Karl C., and Dewey G. Force, *The Psychology of Exceptional Children*, 4th Ed. (New York: The Ronald Press Company, 1965).

Gibbons, Helen, *Education and Health of the Partially Seeing Child* (New York: Columbia University Press, 1959).

Grossman, Herbert, *Teaching the Emotionally Disturbed: A Casebook* (New York: Holt, Rinehart and Winston, Inc., 1965).

Jones, John W., *The Visually Handicapped Child at Home and School*, OE-35045, Bulletin 1963, No. 39 (Washington, D.C.: U.S. Department of Health, Education, and Welfare, 1963).

Kirk, Samuel A., *Educating Exceptional Children* (Boston: Houghton Mifflin Company, 1962).

Lowenfeld, Berthold, *Our Blind Children* (Springfield, Ill.: Charles C Thomas, Publisher, 1956).

Mackie, Romaine P., and Lloyd M. Dunn, *Teachers of Children Who Are Blind*, Bulletin 1955, No. 10, U.S. Department of Health, Education, and Welfare (Washington, D.C.: U.S. Government Printing Office, 1955).

Molloy, Julia S., *Trainable Children; Children and Procedures* (New York: The John Day Company, Inc., 1963).

Myklebust, Helmer R., *Auditory Disorders in Children* (New York: Grune & Stratton, Inc., 1954).

Rothstein, Jerome H. (ed.), *Mental Retardation: Readings and Resources* (New York: Holt, Rinehart and Winston, Inc., 1961).

Roucek, Joseph S. (ed.), *The Unusual Child* (New York: Philosophical Library, Inc., 1962).

F. Porter Sargent, *The Directory for Exceptional Children* (Boston: Porter Sargent, Publisher, lastest edition).

Segal, S. S., *No Child is Ineducable* (London: Pergamon Press, 1967).

Weber, Elmer W., *Educable and Trainable Mentally Retarded Children* (Springfield, Ill.: Charles C. Thomas, Publisher, 1962).

Witty, Paul A., *The Educationally Retarded and Disadvantaged*, The Sixty-Sixth Yearbook of the National Society for the Study of Education (Chicago: University of Chicago Press, 1967).

U.S. Department of Health, Education, and Welfare, *Design of Facilities for the Mentally Retarded*, Hospital and Medical Facilities Series No. 1181-C-1 (Washington, D.C.: U.S. Government Printing Office, 1966).

U.S. Employment Service, *Occupations in the Care and Rehabilitation of the Mentally Retarded* (Washington, D.C.: U.S. Government Printing Office, 1966).

FILMS

"Growing into Reading Through the Use of Braille," 25 minutes, 16 mm, color, silent. American Foundation for the Blind, 15 West 16th St., New York, N.Y. 10011.

"Johnny's New World," 16 minutes, 16 mm, sound, color. National Society for the Prevention of Blindness, Inc., 1790 Broadway, New York, N.Y. 10019.

Part Five

Teachers and the Profession of Teaching

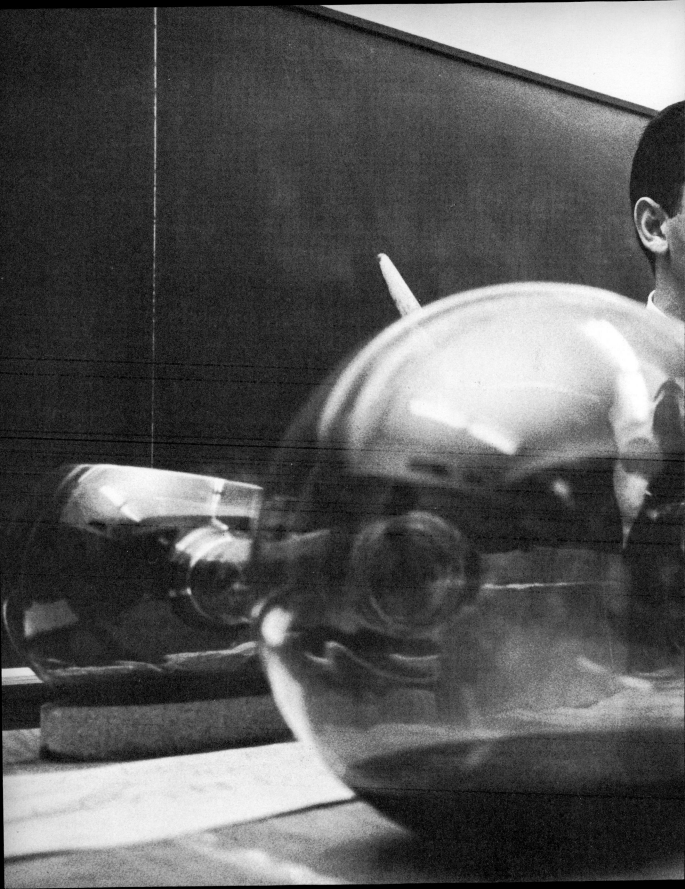

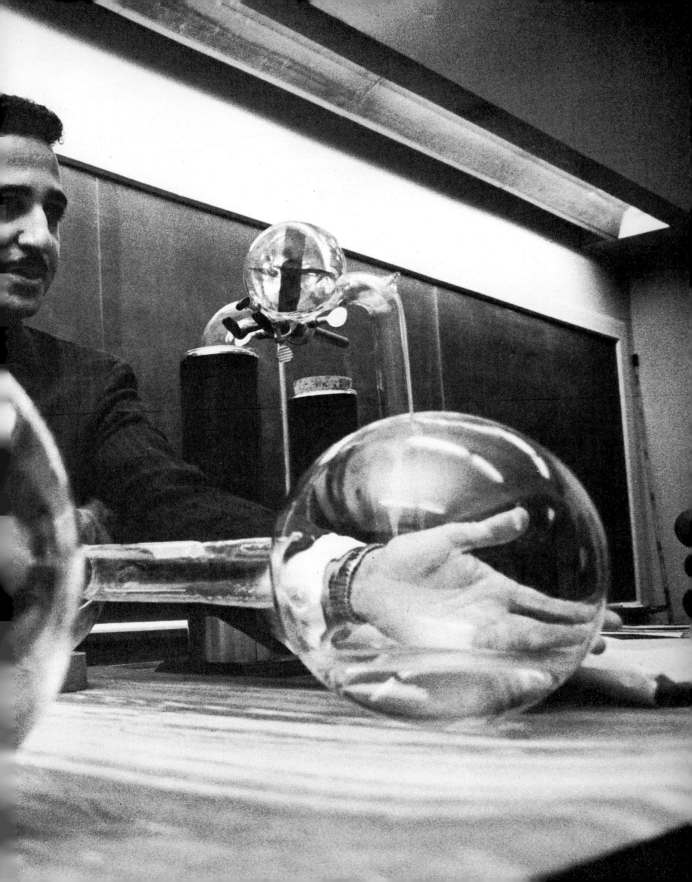

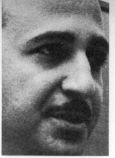

Chapter
17

Teachers in a Professional Context

The theme of the past several chapters was learners. The theme of the present one is teachers. When these two work in harmony, the probability that learning will result is tremendously enhanced. Teachers are not absolutely essential to learning, but capable ones unquestionably make the learning process more economical and efficient.

Taken collectively, teachers perform an extensive assortment of instructional duties. They impart knowledge, implant skills, build concepts, advance affective growth, espouse values, mold attitudes, and transmit cultural antecedents. They help learners to adapt to their environments, and to mature as total personalities.

In accomplishing these outcomes, they employ an extensive assortment of teaching methods. Among the more important are question-and-answer exchanges, group discussions, lectures, panel presentations, show-and-tell sessions, reading groups, demonstrations, field trips, drill, supervised study, face-to-face counseling, and visiting speakers. They use textbooks and reference books. They run the gamut from inductive methods to deductive ones, from manipulation to artistry, and from occasional dull routine to the dramatic unusual.

Selected student enrollees in any age might volunteer less complimentary descriptions of what teachers do and are. Yet for every dour teacher there are many sparkling ones. For every straw boss there are many teacher guides. For every clock watcher there are many dedicated professionals. And for every poorly informed teacher there are many well informed ones. That some teachers are incompetent is indeed regrettable. However, most measure up to acceptable standards, and many to high ones.

LEGAL STATUS OF TEACHERS

Legally, public school teachers are employees of the state in which they teach. Because public education basically is a state, not a local, responsibility, they are state, not local, employees. Thus, though teachers are functionally responsible to a local community, they are legally responsible to the state.

By legal definition, teachers are parent surrogates. Their status is

477

connoted by the legal term *in loco parentis*: that is, they stand in place of parents. For blood parenthood, biological readiness often constitutes the only requisite. For academic parenthood, the requirements fortunately are more selective and demanding.

The legal criterion of what constitutes acceptable academic parenthood resides in the standard of the reasonable man—that mythical person who inhabits every court of the land. Not a flesh and blood figure, he is a symbol, a value standard. He is a reminder to judges and juries to evaluate human behavior according to its reasonableness or unreasonableness. Thus, when in doubt about the propriety of a defendant's behavior, judge or jury renders a decision in terms of how the mythical man of reason would have acted under comparable circumstances. Guided by the implications of these two concepts, law, in effect, says to teachers: Legally, you are academic parents during the school day and your actions and human relationships must be reasonable. When they are not, you are culpable.

Because teachers are substitute parents, expected to exemplify the nobler virtues of parenthood, they are generally liable in law when acting carelessly toward children or when failing to act in situations that call for action. Tort law (law concerned with acts of individuals against other individuals), has brought teachers to legal account in a surprising number of instances. Three states—New York, Connecticut, and New Jersey, under the judicial doctrine of *respondeat superia* (the superior assumes responsibility for acts of subordinates)—assume financial responsibility when parents sue teachers for alleged civil wrongs against children. In the other states, within a wide range of variability, teachers themselves are financially responsible when found guilty of civil wrongs against children.

Teachers, administrators, or school systems are legally liable in such situations as the following.

1. Children suffer injuries or death as the result of inadequate supervision in hall corridors, on playgrounds, around dangerous stairwells, or in assemblies.
2. Teachers of science contribute to injuries by allowing students to use dangerous equipment or materials without proper instructions or adequate supervision.
3. Administrators fail to warn substitute teachers about known trouble-makers, thus contributing to preventable pupil injuries.
4. Students suffer injuries in physical-education classes, athletic practice sessions, or athletic contests as the result of improper

478

precautions being taken by instructional personnel or as a result of unqualified personnel's attending to the needs of the injured and thus aggravating injuries.

5. Teachers contribute to injuries by performing acts that the reasonable man would conclude are potentially dangerous to pupils.
6. Teachers contribute to injuries by dismissing pupils from class without taking proper precautions for the pupils' safety.
7. Teachers fail to intervene, or prevent other authorized persons from doing so, in situations that call for intervention.

To protect the society from personal and instructional incompetence in the schools, all states require teachers to meet designated certification criteria. These will undergo development in a subsequent section on teacher education.

TEACHERS AS PERSONS

Teachers who play the role of academic parenthood with distinction merit respect both as persons and as instructional figures, assuming the two to be separable. Teachers awarded such respect are as much at ease and effective in a living room as in a classroom, when performing community functions as when performing school functions, when relating to adults as when relating to children and youth. In effect, they possess the personal attributes that success in any socially oriented arrangement demands. The "good" ones, indeed, are substantial people first, then they are good teachers. Or, conceivably, they are good teachers because they are substantial people.

Education viewed not merely as a cognitive but as a total-personality concern reinforces our point that teachers need to be poised, well-rounded, mature persons as well as specialized scholars. The total-personality position, in fact, commits them to demonstrate, to symbolize, to live the outcomes that are intrinsic in the position.

The most important single need, in this connection, is for teachers to be emotionally healthy persons. I present the following personality prototype, admittedly an idealized one, to which all might well aspire. The prototype is of a person who first and foremost has a satisfactory self-image. He accepts those shortcomings over which he has no control while working to alter those that are susceptible to change. From the self, he projects outwardly into an ever-expanding world of others, reaching always toward universal truth. He is a continuing student. **479**

He projects outwardly once again, this time into an ever-expanding world of understanding, concepts, and values. To him, the status quo is merely a stepping stone to the unfolding new. He is relatively independent, flexible, consistent, composed before adversity, tolerant before frustration, and not debilitated by guilt. Nor is he defensive, escapist, or neurotic. A teacher blessed with such attributes of maturity tends to breed them in pupils. The purpose of this prototype, admittedly an ideal, is to raise the aspirations of teachers.

TEACHER OPINIONS ON SELECTED EDUCATIONAL ISSUES

Returning from the ideal to the real, we now present a summary of an opinion poll conducted serially by the National Education Association between 1960 and 1965.[1] And, although the issues of the poll re-

[1] The results of the continuing poll appear collectively in Research Division: National Education Association, *What Teachers Think: A Summary of Teacher Opinion Poll Findings, 1966–1965,* Research Report 1965–R13 (Washington, D.C.: NEA, 1965).

TEACHERS AND THE PROFESSION OF TEACHING

late exclusively to educational concerns, teacher responses to them cast some light on what teachers are like as people. The size of the sample ranged from a low of 1149 teachers to a high of 1633. The percentage of questionnaire returns was a researcher's delight throughout the five-year period, with 94.9 percent constituting the low. Page numbers after each of the items are keyed to the NEA publication cited in footnote 1.

On ability grouping in schools: 57.6 percent of elementary school teachers, and 87.3 percent of secondary school teachers were in favor (p. 7).

On class size: The majority of teachers favored a class size of 20 to 24 pupils. Only 2 percent favored a class size of 30 or more (p. 8).

On pupils' viewing commercial television: Only 23.8 percent believed that commercial television was a serious deterrent to learning (p. 10).

On sex education: A large majority, 79.3 percent, believed that sex education should constitute an important part of the curriculum of the secondary schools (p. 14).

On school work required of students: Two-thirds opined that learners in both elementary and secondary schools are learning more today than their counterparts did a generation ago, and 61 percent rejected the allegation of critics that schools are academically soft on students (pp. 15–16).

On de facto segregation: Over half the teachers were in favor of allowing pupils to transfer from crowded neighborhood schools to less crowded ones in other sections (p. 17).

On discipline: Almost 72 percent approved of corporal punishment employed judiciously (p. 18).

On television instruction: Slightly more than half the teachers believed that television instruction offered "real promise" of improving teaching; however, most were opposed to an increase in class size as a result of its employment (p. 28).

On merit pay: Almost 73 percent were opposed to merit pay in any school's program of salary administration (p. 31).

On reporting IQ scores to parents: Almost two-fifths were in favor of giving IQ scores to parents, 45.6 percent favored it only for unusual cases, 13.5 percent were opposed, and 2.6 percent were undecided (p. 35).

On shared time between public and private schools: Almost two-thirds were in favor of some kind of mutual arrangement between public and private schools whereby private schools could use the fa-

cilities of public schools on a part-time basis, 54.5 were opposed, 16.7 were undecided (p. 37).

On quality of teacher preparation: Between two-thirds and three-fourths were commendatory of the extent to which their undergraduate teacher-preparatory programs readied them in areas of their teaching specialties, of general education, of psychology of learning, of human growth, and of history and philosophy of education. Over 40 percent, however, indicated that the programs did too little in the area of teaching method; over 60 percent, that it did too little in the area of audio-visual instruction (pp. 41–42).

CONTROLS OVER TEACHER BEHAVIOR

In general, the NEA survey revealed teachers to range from mildly liberal to conservative in their attitudes on educational concerns. The extent to which controls lying outside themselves might have dictated their attitudinal postures is a matter of conjecture. However, a look at the controls might cast light on the issue.

As previously established, law is one of the more basic of these controls. It makes itself felt when evaluating teachers as parent-surrogate figures. Court cases that over the years have helped to define this role have been numerous. A rather bizarre one in 1939 shut off at least one social option to teachers. In this case, a local school board in Pennsylvania averred that a teacher "worked as a waitress, and on occasion as a bartender, in a lunchroom and beer garden operated by her husband." It further contended that she "took an occasional drink of beer, served beer to customers, shook dice with customers for drinks, and played and showed customers how to play a pin-ball machine." The court handed down this decision on the case:[2]

> It has always been the recognized duty of the teacher to conduct himself in such a way as to command the respect and good will of the community, though one result of the choice of a teacher's vocation may be to deprive him of the same freedom of action enjoyed by persons in other vocations.

All states have standards of one kind or another, which they employ to assess teacher behavior. These standards, while varying from state to state, generally require teachers to be moral, to keep the law, to avoid

[2] Newton Edwards and Lee O. Garber, *The Law Governing Teaching Personnel,* School Law Casebook Series — No. 3 (Danville, Ill.: The Interstate Printers and Publishers, 1962), p. 87.

"conduct unbecoming a teacher" (Massachusetts), and, in their academic roles, to refrain from supporting political causes. Opportunities for liberalism to express itself are unquestionably on the increase. Yet such opportunities at present are not as numerous for teachers as for nonteachers.

Through the years, various groups within the profession have conceived and promulgated statements of ethics which have acted as broad controls over teachers' attitudes and behavior. In 1896, the Georgia Education Association became the first of its kind to formulate and publish such a statement. California followed suit in 1904, and Alabama in 1908. At the present time, all but two state educational associations have codes of ethics for the profession. At the national level, the National Education Association, in 1924, brought forth a code of its own, one that has undergone revision many times since, the latest version appearing in 1968. Its major divisions consist of the following:

Commitment to the Student
Commitment to the Community
Commitment to the Profession
Commitment to Professional Employment Practices (living up to contracts, keeping confidences private, and soon)

Collectively, the ethical pronouncements are both conservative and inoffensively bland. One commits teachers to "deal justly and considerately with each student;" another, to "protect the educational program against undesirable infringement;" and a third, to "keep the trust under which confidential information is exchanged."

In the last analysis, each individual teacher works out his own code of ethics and behavior within the rather broad frame of legal, social, and professional expectations. Law, the community, and the profession understandably impose certain limits, but these limits rarely stultify or overrestrict.

NUMBER, AND SELECTED CHARACTERISTICS, OF TEACHERS

...e teachers in the nation's schools, approximately 46 percent are ...entary education, 35 percent are in secondary education, and 19 ... are in higher education. The collective total of 2,677,100 con- ..., by far, the largest group of individuals in any of the profes-

sions. This number, which has increased dramatically since the late 1940s, will continue to increase well into the 1970s.

For the fall of 1968, teacher totals were as follows.

TABLE 17.1 ESTIMATED NUMBER OF CLASSROOM TEACHERS IN ELEMENTARY AND SECONDARY SCHOOLS, AND TOTAL INSTRUCTIONAL STAFF FOR DEGREE-CREDIT COURSES IN INSTITUTIONS OF HIGHER EDUCATION: UNITED STATES, FALL, 1968.

	Public	Private	Total
Elementary school classroom teachers in regular and *other schools	1,070,100	157,000	1,227,100
Secondary school classroom teachers in regular and †other schools	856,000	90,000	946,000
Higher education teachers responsible for degree-credit courses (part time as well as full-time teachers)	299,000	205,000	504,000
Totals	2,225,100	452,000	2,677,100

Source: Kenneth A. Simon and W. Vance Grant, Digest of Educational Statistics, OE-10024-68 (Washington, D.C.: U.S. Department of Health, Education, and Welfare, 1968), p. 5.

During the past decade, the number of elementary teachers increased approximately one-third whereas the number of secondary teachers increased approximately three-fourths.

Other pertinent data about teachers pertain to their preparation, their roles outside the classroom, and the ratio of males to females in the profession. As for the professional preparation of elementary teachers, 12.9 percent (as of 1965-1966) held no college degrees, 71.4 percent held Bachelor's degrees, 14.9 percent held Master's degrees, and 0.8 percent held six-year diplomas. Comparable totals for secondary teachers were 0.6 percent (no degrees), 67.7 percent (Bachelor's), 29.6 percent (Master's), 1.9 percent (six-year diplomas), and 0.3 percent (Doctor's).[3]

In respect to teachers functioning outside the classroom, the greatest number of incumbents, in descending numerical order, are found in the three categories of (1) administrators and supervisors, (2) guidance personnel, and (3) librarians.[4]

[3] Simon and Grant, p. 41.

[4] Simon and Grant, p. 40.

TEACHERS AND THE PROFESSION OF TEACHING

As for the male-female ratio, as of 1965 women teachers exceeded men teachers in public elementary schools by 85.2 to 14.8 percent. However, men teachers exceeded women teachers in public secondary schools by a close ratio of 53.6 to 46.4 percent. During the ten-year period from 1955 to 1965, the number of men in elementary schools increased 2.1 percent; in secondary schools, 4.3 percent.[5]

TEACHER SUPPLY AND DEMAND

With the need for teachers growing yearly, how to supply that need is a continuing concern. A reasonable balance between teacher supply and demand is a continuing requirement. Colleges and universities, during the entire period since World War II, have had difficulty meeting the demand for instructional personnel. In the late 1940s and early 1950s, the supply of elementary teachers fell far short of the demand created by the growing crop of war babies. In the mid-1950s, the teacher shortage reached the junior high school; and not long afterward, the high school. At present, teachers are in short supply in elementary education and in most, although not all, fields of secondary education.

The main sources of teachers consist of the following: (1) any year's output of graduating teacher candidates, (2) teachers who return to the classroom after a protracted period away from it, (3) qualified teachers who having left teaching for other employment re-enter it later, and (4) noncertified college graduates, some of whom are temporary emergency substitutes, others of whom teach with substandard certificates while working off academic deficiencies. New teacher graduates constitute, by far, the largest source. In 1966, for instance, all colleges and universities in the country graduated 200,919 qualified teachers. Of this number, 76,304 (38 percent) were eligible for elementary school certification, 124,615 (62 percent) for secondary school certification.[6] Of the former, 81.2 percent actually entered teaching; of the latter, 66.0 percent; of both groups combined, 72.2 percent, constituting a total of 145,064 beginning teachers. Against this entering total of 145,064, the estimated need was for 232,384 new teachers. The need thus exceeded the supply of interested graduates by 87,320.[7] The deficit had to be met

[5] Research Division—NEA, Research Report 1965-R17, *Estimates of School Statistics, 1965-66* (Washington, D.C.: NEA, 1965), p. 14.

[6] Research Division—NEA, *Teacher Supply and Demand in Public Schools,* 1966, Research Report, 1966-R16 (Washington, D.C.: NEA, 1966), p. 12.

[7] NEA, p. 35.

by schools drawing on sources (2), (3), and (4), identified at the beginning of the paragraph. Unfortunately for education, noncertified college graduates constituted the major supplementary source.

In the fall of 1966, according to the National Education Association, the teacher shortage assumed the following selective dimensions:[8]

> between 37,700 and 66,500 in elementary grades; between 2,000 and 6,400 each in English, in mathematics and in the natural and physical sciences; between 3,700 and 5,300 in specialized subjects in high-school grades (including guidance, special education, remedial teaching); as many as 1,800 in commerce; and, as many as 1,000 each in home economics, in library science, in industrial arts, and in agriculture.

Major reasons for the continuing teacher shortage are competition from a healthy business economy, federal programs that compete with local school systems for teachers, unwillingness on the part of teachers to consider offers from schools undesirably located, salaries that fail to challenge, military service, graduate study, and changing certification requirements. For these and other reasons, all states report a teacher shortage. Although it is unquestionably harmful to children, it is to the advantage of teacher candidates in search of, or soon to be in search of, teaching positions.

TEACHER SALARIES

As indicated in the previous section, salary has a bearing on recruitment of teachers. More important, it has an affect on their in-service lives including their standards of living. In Table 17.2, I present the most current salary picture available at the time of publication.

486 [8] NEA, p. 5.

TABLE 17.2 ESTIMATED ANNUAL SALARIES OF PUBLIC SCHOOL INSTRUCTIONAL STAFF MEMBERS, BY STATE, 1966-1967

State	Total instructional staff*	Classroom teachers†
1	2	3
United States	$7,110	$6,820
Alabama	5,675	5,480
Alaska	9,200	8,923
Arizona	7,440	7,230
Arkansas	5,216	5,091
California	9,000	8,450
Colorado	6.855	6,625
Connecticut	7,850	7,460
Delaware	7,700	7,400
District of Columbia	8,125	7,800
Florida	6,700	6,530
Georgia	6,075	5,895
Hawaii	7,910	7,734
Idaho	6,056	5,875
Illinois	7,525	7,400
Indiana	7,650	7,377
Iowa	6,375	6,250
Kansas†	6,270	6,100
Kentucky	5,750	5,600
Louisiana	6,587	6,388
Maine	5,949	5,850
Maryland	7,710	7,308
Massachusetts	7,570	7,315
Michigan	7,650	7,300
Minnesota	7,379	7,084
Mississippi	4,782	4,650
Missouri	6,027	5,875
Montana	6,300	6,000
Nebraska	5,800	5,619
Nevada	7,763	7,390
New Hampshire	6,200	6,050
New Jersey	7,647	7,356
New Mexico	6,720	6,630
New York	8,600	7,900
North Carolina	5,763	5,604
North Dakota	5,500	5,280
Ohio	6,750	6,534
Oklahoma	6,180	6,000

TEACHERS IN A PROFESSIONAL CONTEXT

TABLE 17.2 ESTIMATED ANNUAL SALARIES OF PUBLIC SCHOOL INSTRUC-
TIONAL STAFF MEMBERS, BY STATE, 1966-1967

State	Total instruc-tional staff*	Classroom teachers†
1	2	3
Oregon	7,253	7,000
Pennsylvania	7,025	6,815
Rhode Island	6,900	6,625
South Carolina	5,486	5,300
South Dakota	5,000	4,800
Tennessee	5,775	5,650
Texas	6,190	6,025
Utah	6,750	6,490
Vermont	6,000	5,700
Virginia	6,600	6,400
Washington	7,550	7,330
West Virginia	5,900	5,445
Wisconsin†	6,860	6,700
Wyoming	6,572	6,355

Source: Kenneth A. Simon and W. Vance Grant, 1967, p. 41.
* Includes supervisors, principals, classroom teachers, and other instructional staff.
† Excludes vocational schools not operated as part of the regular public school
system.

The most significant feature of Table 17.2 is the extensive range of
salary averages among the various states. Lowest in order of rank are
Mississippi with a classroom teacher average of $4,650, South Dakota
with $4,800, and South Carolina with $5,300. Highest in order of rank
are Alaska with $8,923, California with $8,450, and New York with
$7,900. The average for the highest state is almost double that for the
lowest state. The need, in this connection, as developed in Chapters 3
and 4, is for the federal government to neutralize these gross inequities—inequities which are harmful not only to teachers and pupils but
to the total society. Salaries alone do not necessarily guarantee successful teaching, but they make it a much more probable outcome.

Teacher salaries are considerably lower than those of such other professional groups as physicians, dentists, lawyers, and engineers. And
in 1965, teacher salaries were only 15.5 percent higher than the national average of all wage-and-salary earners in industry. A time-line
comparison of the two categories appears in Table 17.3.

That teachers' salaries are less than those of most other professional
488 groups is attributable, at least in part, to the shorter period of profes-

TABLE 17.3

Year	Salary of Instructional Staffs	Salary of Wage-and-Salary Earners
1935	$1,283	$1,160
1945	1,995	2,272
1955	4,156	3,942
1965	6,700	5,800

Source: Simon and Vance, p.42. The chart is an adaptation.

sional preparation. But that their salaries are only slightly higher than those of wage-and-salary workers in industry is a definite indictment of society's values. The salary situation is gradually improving, but progress is slow.

Three controlling influences on teacher salaries are enrollment size of a school system, the length of the period of teacher preparation, and length of teaching experience. The extent of these influences may be observed in Table 17.4. In regard to size of the system, starting salaries in large systems in 1966 were approximately $300 greater annually, and maximum salaries from $700 to $1,300 greater annually, than in small systems. In regard to length of the period of teaching preparation, teachers with five years of preparation earned from $400 to $1,000 more annually than did teachers with four years; and teachers with six years earned from $425 to $1,150 more than did teachers with five years. In regard to the factor of time on the job, the considerable difference between the size of mean starting and mean maximum salaries attests to the significance of this influence.

In 1965, The National Education Association Research Division, in conjunction with the NEA Salary Consulting Service, completed an objective instrument with which schools might evaluate their teacher-salary schedules. Following are some of the criteria of salary-schedule quality contained in the instrument:

1. The *minimum* starting salaries for teachers with the bachelor's degree, or its announced equivalent, to be $6,200 or higher.
2. The *minimum* salary for teachers with the master's degree to be at least 115 percent of that for teachers with the bachelor's degree.
3. The *maximum* salary for teachers with the master's degree to be at least 200 percent of the *minimum* salary for teachers with the bachelor's degree.
4. The *maximum* salary for teachers with six years of college to be

489

220 percent of the *minimum* salary for teachers with the bachelor's degree.

5. Salary schedules to provide increases for teachers with more than six years of college preparation.

6. Salary increments between *minimum* and *maximum* salary levels to be on a consecutive annual basis and to total to not more than ten for teachers with a bachelor's degree; and to not more than twelve for those with a master's degree.

7. The average increment amount to be 8 percent or more of the *minimum* salary established for the bachelor's degree.

8. Salary increments to move from step to step in a uniform way.

9. Salaries not to be based on merit ratings, on subjects taught, or on sex of the teacher.

10. The *maximum* salary for teachers whose preparation falls just short of the doctor of philosophy degree to be $15,000.[9]

TABLE 17.4   TEACHER SALARIES: A FUNCTION OF ENROLLMENT SIZE OF SCHOOL SYSTEM AND AMOUNT OF TEACHER PREPARATION: 1966

Enrollment Size of School System	Years of College Preparation of Teachers	Minimum Mean Salary in the Nation	Maximum Mean Salary in the Nation
1,200–2,999	4	$5,075	$7,255
	5	5,487	8,126
	6	6,021	9,271
25,000–49,999	4	5,222	7,753
	5	5,681	8,754
	6	6,125	9,747
100,000 or more	4	5,362	8,575
	5	5,848	9,355
	6	6,270	9,973

Source: Table 17.4 is an adaptation from Research Division—NEA, Research Report 1966–R17, *Salary Schedules for Classroom Teachers, 1966–1967* (Washington, D.C.: NEA, 1966), p. 12. Copyright © 1966 by National Education Association. All rights reserved. Reprinted with permission. (These are the most recent totals available.)

In 1966 the National Education Association, having applied the evaluation instrument to 1101 school systems with enrollments of 6000 or more, made the following self-explanatory statement: "No perfect scores were expected, and none were found. However, the maximum

[9] Research Division—NEA, Research Report 1966–R19, *Evaluation of Salary Schedules for Classroom Teachers, 1966–1967* (Washington, D.C.: NEA, 1966), pp. 4–33. Copyright © 1966 by National Education Association. All rights reserved. Reprinted with permission.

TEACHERS AND THE PROFESSION OF TEACHING

score on each test [that is, on each of the above criteria] was reached by one or more of the schedules evaluated."[10] National averages, however, paint a far less optimistic picture. The extent of the disparity between them and the NEA recommendations are indicated in the following analysis.

Criterion 1. National averages fall short of the NEA standards by 16 to 22 percent, depending on school-system size.

Criterion 2. National averages fall short by approximately 8 percent.

Criterion 3. National averages fall short by approximately 40 percent.

Criterion 4. National averages fall short by approximately 20 percent.

Criterion 5. Reality meets the ideal primarily in certain suburban and urban school systems; falls most short in non-urban systems.

Criterion 6. The recommended ideal is rarely attained.

Criterion 7. Same as 6.

Criterion 8. Same as 6.

Criterion 9. Same as 6.

Criterion 10. The ideal is almost never attained.

Despite these disparities between the real and the recommended ideal, we close this section on a note of optimism regarding the future of teacher salaries. They appear definitely to be on the rise as do such personnel benefits as retirement plans, insurance plans, and sick-leave benefits. We eschew detail in regard to these fringe benefits, however, because to most readers of this book, who are young adults in the process of teacher preparation, such details are academic.

TEACHER TENURE

A benefit not at all academic or of a fringe nature, however, and one of interest to almost all teachers and to prospective teachers as well is job tenure. The central message of tenure is that for teachers to be professionally effective and personally secure, they need a guarantee of continuing employment—one that rises above the whims of individuals and

[10] NEA, p. 7.

the uncontrollable vagaries of circumstances. The specific aims of tenure are these:

1. To give stability to teaching by building into it lifetime career probabilities.
2. Relatedly, to encourage more people to engage in teaching as a lifetime career.
3. To advance the cause of independence of thought and expression for the teacher as private citizen and for the teacher as professional.
4. To protect teachers from petty administrative assertiveness and tyranny.
5. To encourage administrators to evaluate teachers early so as to detect the unfit as soon as possible.
6. To give cohesiveness to a school system by reducing the incidence of teacher turnover.

These aims, though convincing to educators throughout the country, have failed to convince a sizable number of people outside the teaching profession. For this reason, tenure practices vary from state to state, and occasionally from system to system in any given state. The overall status of tenure practices in the country is explicit in the following:[11]

> Legal provisions for tenure are found in thirty-seven states, either on a statewide basis or in certain designated areas only. Continuing contracts of the spring-notification type or annual or long-term contracts are found in the other thirteen states.

The primary argument of those who oppose tenure is that it leads to the retention by schools of teachers known to be incompetent. And the argument is not without validity in view of the difficulties involved in dismissing a tenured teacher. Administrators engaged in the dismissal process are, without exception, required to support all allegations made with evidence that is reasonably airtight—sufficiently airtight to hold up, if the situation warrants, in a court of law. In this connection, flagrant immorality, gross insubordination, chronic absenteeism, marked decrease in pupil population, and abolition of a curriculum area (if not for trumped-up reasons) have, when properly supported, stood up as legitimate reasons.

The thirty-seven states with tenure legislation require teachers to

[11] Leo M. Chamberlain and Leslie W. Kindred, *The Teacher and School Organization,* 4th Ed. (Englewood Cliffs, N. J.: Prentice-Hall, Inc., 1966), p. 211.

serve a probationary period, usually of two-years' duration, as a pre-requisite of tenure. In a number of these states, Illinois for one, schools may require some neophyte teachers to serve an additional third year. Teachers who are probationary customarily attain tenure status automatically unless receiving notice of planned dismissal 60 to 90 days prior to the termination of the probationary period.

Tenure unquestionably is a controversial issue in education today. That it often leads to protection of the incompetent, I cannot deny. Despite this admitted drawback, however, I am in favor of tenure because its advantages far outweigh its disadvantages.

TEACHER EDUCATION

From the single in-service topic of teacher tenure, we move abruptly now into the broad academic topic of teacher education, one that is replete with diverse and complex problems. Many readers may be living through some or many of the problems and issues that constitute the themes of the present section.

The history of teacher education is a record of change. And despite occasional critics to the contrary during any period in the historical sweep, the direction of change has consistently been toward higher standards. The record of improvement in teacher preparation is indeed a gratifying one. Historically, elementary school teachers, for instance, were often not more than elementary school graduates themselves. In contrast, today, the vast majority have the baccalaureate degree, and even those in remote rural areas generally have attended college for two years or more. Analogous progress for secondary school teachers has been from the diploma regarded as sufficient preparation for at least some, to the baccalaureate degree as a minimum essential for all. Our society has become convinced that a school's curriculum is something more than a simple compilation of factual content, that learners are not just vessels to be filled, and that instruction is more than a teacher's staying a few pages ahead of his students.

The first *normal school*, established at Lexington, Massachusetts, in 1839, constituted the maiden attempt in this country to place teacher education on an organized collegiate footing. By 1900, normal schools totaled approximately 300. Colleges and universities, however, did not welcome them into the inner circle of higher education. Furthermore, within their specialized purview of teacher education, they concen-

trated exclusively on the preparation of elementary school, rather than high school, teachers. Within this purview, the quality of their facilities and curriculum varied widely throughout the country. It ran the gamut, respectively, from run-down shacks to up-to-date plants, and from instruction restricted narrowly to the mechanics of pedagogy to instruction extending across a reasonably broad range of human development and curriculum content.

Normal schools, most of them state-controlled, but a sizable number privately controlled, continued to increase in number until the second decade of the present century; then they went into an irreversible decline. State teachers colleges, which arose as *bona fide* degree-granting institutions, became their replacements. However, these too were reasonably short-lived. By 1961, in fact, they existed in only fifteen states.[12] Most of the others by 1950 had converted to multipurpose institutions. At the time of this writing, multipurpose institutions, public and private, are the primary institutions of teacher education; colleges are second; and the few teachers colleges that remain are weak third.

The Role of States in Accreditation and Certification

Teacher education attains official status under conditions as: (1) at the institutional level, it is accredited by key public and professional groups, and (2) candidates, as individuals, are certified for teaching positions. Each of the fifty states, in one way or another, is active in both of these two functions of institutional accreditation and individual teacher certification.

Authority for accreditation at the institutional level, resided in all but a few states, as of 1964, in the chief educational agency. It resided in the state university in Alaska and Wyoming, in the State Board of Higher Education in North Dakota, and was diffused among several agencies in Massachusetts.[13]

Recent trends in state specifications for teacher-education programs

[12] Paul Woodring, "A Short History of Teacher Education in the United States," in Henry Ehlers and Gordon C. Lee (eds.), *Crucial Issues in Education* (New York: Holt, Rinehart and Winston, Inc., 1964), p. 315.

[13] W. Earl Armstrong and T. M. Stinnett, *Certification Requirements for School Personnel in the United States* (Washington, D.C.: National Commission on Education and Professional Standards, 1964), p. 19.

TEACHERS AND THE PROFESSION OF TEACHING

include the following: (1) a tendency of states (now forty in number) to approve programs in totality rather than to dictate minimum programs specifically; (2) an increase in the amount of general education required; (3) a strengthening of the academic major for secondary school teachers; and (4) the requirement of an academic major for elementary school teachers.[14] Whether number (4) above constitutes a trend or is merely a phenomenon of the recent past few years is debatable.

All fifty states are official participants in teacher education not only when they accredit institutions but when they certify teachers. And because states vary somewhat in their certification requirements, it is important that teachers try to foresee the state in which they will be teaching so as to meet the program requirements laid down in that state. Failure to do this does not necessarily lead to certification denial; however, it frequently leads to the granting of temporary certificates with the stipulation that teachers make up their deficiencies within a reasonable period following the time of their hiring. The single most authoritative and useful source of information on certification requirements in the fifty states is the publication by Armstrong and Stinnett entitled *Certification Requirements for School Personnel in the United States.*

Selected specialized information in regard to state certification includes the following.

1. As of 1968, 47 states enforced the bachelor's degree requirement for elementary school teachers. One additional state, Wisconsin, will begin to enforce it in 1972. The two nonconforming states are Nebraska and North Dakota.[15]
2. All states require at least the bachelor's degree for high school teachers.[16]
3. Nine states require the master's degree for high school teachers. However, they allow teachers to earn it (although Arizona does not specigy this in its school code), after they have started teaching under the bachedor's degree. The period of grace ranges from five to ten years. The nine states are Arizona, California, Connecticut, Indiana, Maryland, New Mexico, New York, Oregon, and Rhode Island.[17]

[14] Armstrong and Stinnett, p. 3.
[15] Armstrong and Stinnett, p. 4.
[16] Armstrong and Stinnett, p. 4.
[17] Armstrong and Stinnett, p. 5.

4. California is the only state with a fifth-year requirement (it has a few loopholes, however) for elementary school teachers.[18]
5. An oath of allegiance is required by 27 states.[19]
6. Teacher candidates need to be recommended by employing colleges or universities in 41 states.[20]
7. No qualifying examinations are required in 40 states.[21]
8. In 1945, one teacher in seven (or 13.6 percent of all teachers) was teaching under an emergency certificate; by 1962, the ratio had dropped to one in 16 (or 6.0 percent).[22]
9. Some type of regional reciprocity for certification was in vogue in 17 states in 1964.[23]

The Role of Regional Accrediting Associations in Teacher Education

In teacher education as in medicine, dentistry, or law, the profession itself plays a major role in institutional accreditation. The regional accrediting associations are one important instance of this professional involvement. Six in number, they consist of the following, by date of origin:
(1) New England Association of Colleges and Secondary Schools, 1885;
(2) Middle States Association of Colleges and Secondary Schools, 1892;
(3) North Central Association of Colleges and Secondary Schools, 1895
—the largest of the six, serving 19 states from Arizona to West Virginia, and from North Dakota to Oklahoma; (4) Southern Association of Colleges and Secondary Schools, 1895; (5) Northwest Association of Secondary and Higher Schools, 1918; and (6) Western College Association, 1948—the smallest of the six, serving California, Guam, and Hawaii.

Lacking legal authority, the associations operate from positions of professional influence. Their practice is to accredit total programs of colleges and universities, leaving specifics to other agencies. Their concern from the start has been with secondary, not elementary, education. Members of the various associations consist of college and university

---

[18] Armstrong and Stinnett, p. 4.
[19] Armstrong and Stinnett, p. 13.
[20] Armstrong and Stinnett, p. 13.
[21] Armstrong and Stinnett, p. 15.
[22] Armstrong and Stinnett, p. 23.
[23] Armstrong and Stinnett, p. 16.

teachers and high school teachers and administrators. On accrediting missions, teams are usually voluntary and unpaid except for expenses. State education department representatives almost habitually are *ex officio* members of the teams.

The Role of National Professional Groups in Teacher Education

In the first quarter of the twentieth century, as school enrollments grew and demand for teachers increased, malpractices in certification increased correspondingly. Colleges with only indifferent interest in teacher education often had a single faculty member to offer all the necessary educational theory and to supervise all the necessary practice. As recently as 1950, one college in the Midwest offered a course on Saturday mornings labeled student teaching; it was offered in a college classroom and taught via the lecture method.

The profession, convinced that college accreditation by state education departments and regional associations left much to be desired, brought into being, in 1923, the American Association of Teachers Colleges (AATC). This body assumed the function of accreditation in 1927. The next organization to take it over was the American Association of Colleges for Teacher Education (AACTE), which accredited until 1954. In this latter year, two years after its founding, the National Council for the Accrediting of Teacher Education (NCATE) became the dominant national accreditation group.

NCATE, at its founding, consisted of 21 members: six from American Association of Colleges for Teacher Education, six from the various state departments of education, six from the National Education Association, and three from local school boards. In 1957, the membership changed from 21 to 19, and its makeup broadened to include more college affiliated personnel. The 19 members consisted of seven from teacher-education institutions, six from the National Education Association, three from representative colleges, two from state educational agencies, and one from the National School Boards Association.

This broadening of committee representation was symptomatic of a growing schism that was developing in regard to accreditation between college administrators, on one hand, and professional educational personnel—at local, state, and national levels—on the other. College administrations regarded accreditation by professional educational per-

sonnel to be a threat to their autonomy. The latter, with comparable
logic, regarded unilateral administrative control over education to be
a threat to their professionalism. Conant's two books of 1963 and 1964,
respectively, *The Education of American Teachers* and *Shaping Educational Policy*, came close to kindling the long smoldering sparks into

498

a conflagration. Wrote Conant, all 16 states visited are "subject to propaganda emanating from NCATE . . . and other national organizations."[24] And again:[25]

> I was told by one faculty member that the approval of his program depended on his bowing to a state-department official on the issue of whether to give two or three credits for a particular course in physical education.

And yet a third time:[26]

> The time has not yet come when the educational sciences can play the same role in training teachers as the medical sciences do in training doctors.

And so the controversy raged, and continues to rage. Conant stopped just short of recommending unilateral institutional certification, apparently unaware of the many pitfalls inherent in any internal audit. My personal conviction is that the current debate on accreditation will culminate in a rejection of vitriolic extremism by both sides. In the meantime, the moderates of both camps will continue the debate to a point of consensus. As of the moment, debate or no debate, state departments of education, regional associations, and NCATE continue to accredit and to certify. Individual colleges and universities, however, are becoming increasingly active partners in the process. The old establishment consisting of professional educators, school administrators, and classroom teachers remains in control of professional concerns in public schools. The new establishment consisting primarily of college professors in fields other than education continues to seek control. Fortunately the two establishments are closer to a reconciliation of their views than they were in 1963 or 1964. Thus, synthesis may be not far away.

Characteristics of Teacher-Education Programs in Colleges and Universities

Synthesis, in fact, already exists generally in respect to the broad curriculum areas—namely, general education, the teaching specialty, and professional education—that teacher education should subsume.

[24] James B. Conant, *The Education of American Teachers* (New York: McGraw-Hill, Inc., 1963), p. 29.

[25] Conant, p. 59.

[26] Conant, p. 142

Indeed, only the more irrational would debate whether teachers need to be liberally educated, whether they need to be competent in the subject matter for which they are responsible, or whether they need to be knowledgeable about education as a profession and competent in the many important processes it embraces. The role of teacher education, as most would agree, is to ready teachers for the many tasks involved in helping the culture to reproduce and refine itself, and individuals to fulfill themselves. In playing this role, teacher education has many faces and patterns.

General Education

As candidates progress through programs of teacher preparation in colleges and universities, a liberal education is a foundational essential. Such an education, by common definition, is one that frees individuals from ignorance, prejudices, foolish superstitions, fears, and hypocrisy. It is one that ties people together with common cultural bonds. It is one from which balanced decisions in life emanate. It is the only stable base for a continuing education. Although no guarantor of the open mind, it may well provide the key. To facilitate the outcome of self-actualization, teacher candidates need to become steeped in the lore of the past and to be knowledgeable about affairs of the present. The more liberal and extensive the general education, the more authentic will be the self image, the more meaningful the teaching-content specialty or specialties, the keener the subsequent insights into pupil problems, and the more balanced the total personality. When general education is foundational, the greater the likelihood of teaching becoming a creative art, the less the likelihood of its assuming dimensions of a mechanical trade. Unquestionably, general education is a *sine qua non* of the maturing process. In any student's program, general education should constitute at least half, and preferably more, of the total program of academic experiences.

The Teaching Field

A second curriculum essential for teachers or teacher candidates is competency in the teaching areas for which they are, or are to become, responsible. For elementary school teachers in charge of self-contained

classrooms, this competency needs to extend across the several fields of the language arts, social studies, natural sciences, mathematics, art, music, health, and play. For teachers in departmental settings, irrespective of level, this competency customarily concentrates in one or two subjects or subject areas. The percentages of teachers who in 1966 taught single subjects only in a departmental arrangement are as indicated in the following subject listing.[27] The percentages appear parenthetically.

Music	(86.5)	Foreign languages	(55.0)
Home economics	(79.1)	Social sciences	(54.3)
Art	(79.0)	General science	(53.3)
Industrial arts	(77.7)	Physical education (m)	(48.7)
Business	(76.7)	Biology	(30.5)
Agriculture	(75.3)	Speech	(20.0)
Library science	(70.7)	Chemistry	(18.8)
Mathematics	(70.2)	Journalism	(10.3)
Physical education (f)	(70.0)	Physics	(9.2)
English	(61.9)	other	(67.0)

For secondary school teachers of departmentalized subjects, the customary requirement in most states is a teaching major and minor. The major generally ranges from 24 to 40 semester hours of course work; the minor, from 16 to 24 hours. A few states recently have eliminated the minor to allow for a stronger major. The reason generally given for the change is the recent knowledge explosion with the attendant increased demands it is placing on instructional figures. I am very much in favor of organized attempts to improve the quality of instruction in the teaching major. Yet I regard such attempts as ill advised when they harden into inflexible patterns. The high school biology teacher, for instance, is better prepared with, say, 32 semester hours of biology and 16 hours of chemistry than with 48 hours of biology per se. And the junior high school teacher of unified studies is certainly better prepared with a balanced subject-matter combination of social studies and English than with an unbalanced intensification of either. The constructive compromise is for states to approve both comprehensive and single-subject majors in deference to wholesome curriculum variability that exists in the schools.

[27] Research Division—National Education Association, *Teacher Supply and Demand in Public Schools,* Research Report 1966—R16 (Washington, D.C.: NEA, 1966), p. 39.

Curriculum Preparation in Professional Education

The teacher equipped with an adequate general-education background and qualified in a major teaching subject or combination of subjects is still not ready for the demands of teaching unless proficient in professional education. Curriculum arrangements in respect to the latter generally divide into the broad categories of educational foundations, teaching methodology, and student laboratory experiences with children and youth. The category of educational foundations customarily embraces the status and role of formal education in the social order, education's historical antecedents, philosophy of education, educational psychology, and human development. The category of teaching methodology, as the term implies, pertains to teachers engaged in the process of making learning more efficient for students. The category of laboratory experiences includes student participation in community agencies, classroom visitations, and, as a capstone, student teaching.

Teacher education needs ever to translate educational theory *about* learners and learning into practical experiences engaged in by teacher candidates *with* learners and learning. Whatever the exact teacher-education design of any given college or university, it should make teacher candidates as knowledgeable in the world of the practical as of the theoretical. Teacher education is a social as well as an academic concern. Thus it needs to develop wholesome social attitudes in students. It needs to open minds. It needs to release creativity. In essence, it needs to ready students for the many humanistic demands that teaching imposes. And it does this best when combining theory and practice into a well-knit curriculum configuration.

PROFESSIONAL EDUCATION ORGANIZATIONS

Career-minded students who have completed teacher-education programs of colleges and universities sooner or later move into roles as inservice teachers. And for them, education continues even though formal education may have temporarily stopped. While on the job, they grow in a number of ways, professional organizations serving as one avenue. In respect to functions performed, professional-education organizations advance educational thinking, promote educational research, disseminate educational information, and serve as pressure

groups to influence public opinion regarding educational issues and concerns. And they perform all these functions through periodically scheduled large conferences, through their publications, through committee activity, and through the influence of individual members.

Educational organizations are too numerous to permit even a simple listing of all of them here. However, readers interested in designated ones should consult one or both of the following publications for desired detail.

National Education Association, *NEA Handbook for Local, State, and National Associations* [latest date] (Washington, D.C.: NEA, 1201 Sixteenth St.).

U.S. Department of Health, Education, and Welfare, *Education Directory* [latest date], *Education Associations* (Washington, D.C.: U.S. Government Printing Office).

From the welter of professional organizations in existence, selected ones along with their major publications are identified forthwith. Conjectured reader appeal was the criterion of selection. Following the listing, I elaborate on two of the largest and most controversial of the many, namely, the National Education Association and the American Federation of Teachers.

Professional Education Organizations and Publications

Art
    National Art Education Association (NEA): *Art Education.*
Audiovisual
    Department of Audiovisual Instruction: *AV Communications Review, Audiovisual Instruction,* and many pamphlets and booklets.
Business Education
    National Business Education (NEA): *Business Education Forum, National Business Education Quarterly, National Business Education Yearbook,* and *Future Business Leader.*
Driver Education
    American Driver and Safety Education Association (NEA): *Safety: Journal of Administration and Instruction, Protection.*
Elementary School
Department of Elementary-Kindergarten-Nursery Education: (NEA) two bulletins and two newsletters.

English

Linguistic Society of America: *Language.*

National Council of Teachers of English: *Elementary English, English Journal,* and *College English.*

Foreign Languages

American Association of Teachers of French: *French Review.*

American Association of Teachers of German: *German Quarterly.*

American Association of Teachers of Italian: *Italica.*

American Association of Teachers of Slavic and East European Languages of the United States, Inc.: *Slavic and East European Journal.*

American Association of Teachers of Spanish and Portuguese: *Hispania.*

Classical Association of the Atlantic States: *Classical World.*

Modern Language Association: *PMLA.*

National Federation of Modern Language Teachers Associations: *The Modern Language Journal.*

Health and Physical Education

American Association for Health, Physical Education and Recreation (NEA): *Journal of Health, Physical Education Recreation* and *Research Quarterly.*

American School Health Association: *Journal of School Health.*

Higher Education

Association for Higher Education: *College and University Bulletin* and *Current Issues in Higher Education.*

Home Economics

American Home Economics Association, *Journal of Home Economics.*

Department of Home Economics (NEA): bulletins and newsletters.

Industrial Arts

American Industrial Arts Association (NEA): *The Journal of Industrial Arts Education.*

Journalism

Journalism Education Association (NEA): *Scholastic Editor,* and *Quill and Scroll.*

Mathematics

National Council of Teachers of Mathematics (NEA): *The Mathematics Teacher, The Arithmetic Teacher,* and yearbooks.

Music
Music Educators National Conference (NEA): *Music Educators Journal.*

Science
American Association of Physics Teachers, *American Journal of Physics* and *The American Physics Teacher.*
American Institute of Biological Sciences, *AIBS Bulletin* and *Quarterly Review of Biology.*
National Science Teachers Association (NEA), *The Science Teacher* and *Science and Children.*

Social Studies
National Council for Geographic Education, *Journal of Geography.*
National Council for the Social Studies (NEA): *Social Education* and *Yearbook.*
National Geographic Society, *National Geographic Magazine* and *School Bulletin.*

Speech
American Speech and Hearing Association, *Journal of Speech and Hearing Disorders* and *Journal of Speech and Hearing Research.*

Two Comprehensive Educational Organizations

National Education Association   Of the many educational organizations in existence, the National Education Association is by far the largest in terms of membership and geographical outreach and the most comprehensive in terms of professional influence.[28] Founded in 1857, its membership today totals just short of a million. In 1966, the Association had 63 state and 8511 local affiliates. Association leadership resides in a representative assembly of approximately 7000 members elected by the various affiliates, a board of directors of 92 members, an executive committee of 11 members, an executive secretary, and a number of assistant executive secretaries. The National Education Association performs its many functions through the organizational media of 33 departments, 18 divisions, and 25 commissions.

The avowed mission of NEA is to serve the educational interests of pupils, teachers, and the total society. It serves as spokesman for teachers and other professional school personnel in respect to profes-

[28] Much of the data contained in this section comes from the *NEA Handbook* of 1966–1967.

sional standards, federal educational legislation, welfare benefits, and academic freedom. It works for the profession on controversial issues. For a fee of ten dollars yearly, members receive nine issues of the *NEA Journal*, a periodical, and twelve issues of the *NEA Reporter*, a newspaper. The Association also publishes the *NEA Handbook* yearly.

The various state associations, in the words of the 1966–1967 *Handbook*,[29] "hold conferences and conventions, work for favorable legislation, issue publications, assist local education associations—all in terms of improving education and the profession within their respective states."

The various local associations, once more in the words of the *Handbook*,

> decide the type or types of organization which will best meet local needs. Some communities prefer an all-inclusive organization; others prefer departments of classroom teachers, principals, etc. within the all-inclusive organization; still others prefer separate classroom teachers organizations. Affiliation with the National Education Association is a first basic step for every active, dynamic local association.

American Federation of Teachers   A second comprehensive education association is the American Federation of Teachers, which competes with the National Education Association on many fronts. The AFT, made up exclusively of teachers (school administrators are not eligible), has a membership today in excess of 100,000. Organized in 1916, the American Federation of Teachers became an affiliate of the American Federation of Labor shortly thereafter. Its objectives are those of any union organization, namely, to raise the standards and improve the working conditions of its membership.

The specific objectives of the AFT, delineated in its Constitution "Correct as of October 1966," consist of the following:[30]

1. To bring associations of teachers into relations of mutual assistance and cooperation
2. To obtain for them all the rights to which they are entitled
3. To raise the standards of the teaching profession by securing the conditions essential to the best professional service
4. To promote such a democratization of the schools as will enable them better to equip their pupils to take their places in the industrial, social, and political life of the community

---

[29] *NEA Handbook*, p. 20.

[30] American Federation of Teachers AFL-CIO, *Constitution of the American Federation of Teachers Affiliated with the AFL-CIO* (Chicago, 716 N. Rush St.: October, 1966), p. 3.

TEACHERS AND THE PROFESSION OF TEACHING

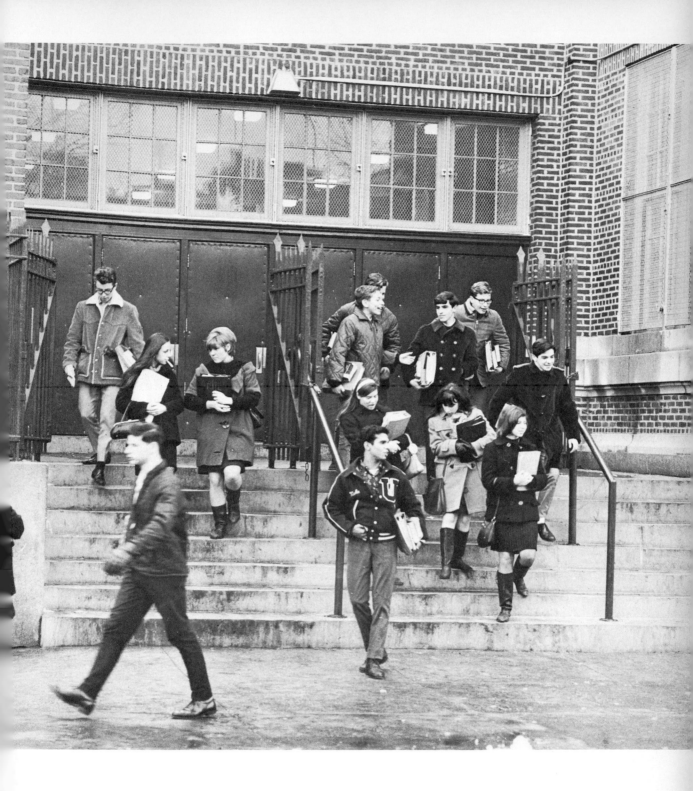

5. To promote the welfare of the childhood of the nation by providing progressively better educational opportunity for all

The topic of teachers' unions has long been, and continues to be, a controversial one in educational circles. And the AFT, because of its affiliation with the AFL-CIO, is a particularly volatile subject. This relationship frequently leads to an inappropriate transfer of biased attitudes and opinions. I hope to avoid this pitfall in my development of the topic here.

The AFT and other teachers' unions came into being in response to such conditions as these: low teachers salaries, the refusal of school administrators to include teachers in decision-making, and other acts that kept teachers less than professional. In this connection, true professionalism is a naïve expectation in organizations that are run bureaucratically. School boards and school administrators have had, and continue to have, two options: to accord teachers true professional status or to pay the price of organizational retaliation.

Whatever the attitudes of individual readers toward teachers' unions, the fact remains that they are a significant and growing force in education today. Furthermore, teacher welfare as their *raison d'être* needs no defense. The AFT specifically, however, is vulnerable in respect to the following:

1. By denying membership to school administrators, it has widened the already extensive rift between administrators and teachers.
2. By maintaining organizational ties with the AFL-CIO, it assumes responsibility for the blameworthy practices of the latter.
3. In certain instances (New York City and Gary, Indiana, as two recent examples) it illegally espouses teacher strikes.
4. Its president characteristically is not a teacher, nor usually are its sixteen vice presidents.
5. Though AFT members are in the minority in some school systems, the union attempts to speak for the majority.

Apropos of teachers' unions in general, state legislation is badly needed today to define their roles and to proceduralize their activities. Questions such as the following are awaiting legal answer in most states. Under what circumstances, if any, does a school board have the right to ignore the presence of a union or to deny it a voice in school affairs? In the process of arbitration or negotiation, what functionary or functionaries in any system have the right to represent others? Do

unions have the right, and school boards the obligation, to negotiate matters other than financial? If so, which specific ones? What is the proper role of a school superintendent in the process of negotiation: an agent of teachers? an agent of a school board? or an honest broker? Do nonunion representatives have any legal rights in a school system? Do teachers have the right to air their policy views without fear of reprisal?

My personal point of view in regard to teachers' unions is that they will continue to live and thrive as long as school-board members and school administrators are unnecessarily assertive and unreasonable in their behavior. Such behavior on their part, like unionism itself, inevitably operates at the price of teacher professionalism. The recommended compromise is for board members, superintendents, and principals to establish and maintain such sound relationships with teachers that intermediate echelons will become unnecessary. Unions, to me, are as much symptoms of malpractice in the ranks of line authority as they are instruments of change. A basic need, then, is for education and society to attack the causal forces at their source.

I conclude here by saying that whether a teacher does or does not join the AFT or a local union is strictly his own concern. The issue bears too much weight on both sides to be other than personal.

THE NATIONAL TEACHER CORPS

This chapter on teachers in education would be incomplete without some attention given to the National Teacher Corps. It is a creation of Title V-B of the Higher Education Act of 1965. The corps constitutes an attempt by the federal government to increase the number and improve the quality of teachers of disadvantaged children and youth. The ultimate purpose is the strengthening of "educational opportunities for children in areas with concentration of low-income families." A by-product is the invitation extended to "colleges and universities to broaden their teacher-education programs."[31]

The pedagogical scheme of the program is for the experienced to teach the inexperienced under a team arrangement. Each team has as its leader an experienced teacher of the culturally disadvantaged, selected because of his demonstrated competency. Under his aegis are

---

[31] U.S. Department of Health, Education and Welfare, *National Teacher Corps Guidelines*, S-20 (Washington, D.C.: U.S. Government Printing Office, 1966), p. 1.

from one to five interns with qualifications as follows: bachelor's degree, agreement to serve an internship program of two years, and announced plans to teach the culturally deprived upon completing the internship. Initially the interns complete a concentrated preservice program of from eight to 13 weeks; then, under close supervision of the teacher leader, they spend the remainder of the two-year period teaching the culturally disadvantaged. The corps embraced 1500 interns during its first year of operation.

Reactions to the corps have been mixed. Congress has never been enthusiastic about it. And a number of school administrators have opposed it on grounds that it draws team leaders from the ranks of badly needed classroom teachers. Yet in 1967 John M. Lumley, director of the NEA's Federal Relations Division, strongly defended the corps before the House Education and Labor Division, building his case on the success of the Corps.[32]

> Lumley presented a survey of superintendents and principals in the 111 school districts which now participate in the program. Seventy-five superintendents said they planned to continue the program next year (49 wanted more corpsmen than they now have) and only 12 had other views. Of the principals, 141 agreed with the 75 superintendents, while 50 had other views. President Johnson has asked that the National Teachers Corps program be extended and expanded.

With culturally deprived children almost habitually in need of more capable, dedicated teachers, The National Teachers Corps, in my opinion, should not be disbanded—not, that is, unless the team method proves ineffective. And in a very short time, the temporary shortage of older, experienced teachers created by their entrance into the Corps will be compensated for by the ever-growing number of young, enthusiastic teachers ready to replace them.

A CLOSING WORD

In this chapter, I have depicted the effectual teacher as being first and foremost an effective person: mentally healthy, knowledgeable, personable. Legally he is a parent surrogate, expected by society to play that role conscientiously and discerningly. A college graduate at the beginning of teaching, he pursues a program of formal and informal

[32] National Commission on Teacher Education and Professional Standards, *Teps NEWS letter*, Vol. 10, No. 6, April 15, 1967.

education, the latter throughout life. The material rewards of his profession are somewhat less than those of other professions; yet they hold promise of increasing both relatively and absolutely with the passing years.

The teacher-education program from which he is graduated consists of general education as a foundation, special education in one or more teaching fields, and professional-educational experiences in such areas as learning theory, teaching method, child development, and laboratory experiences with children and youth. The three agencies that accredit the program are the state board of education, a regional association, and a professional accrediting body. The teacher himself is certified and licensed by the state in which he teaches.

At the time of hiring, he is very much in demand—particularly so if he is an elementary school teacher; selectively so, depending on his teaching major, if he is a secondary school teacher. At the end of two or three years of successful teaching, he is customarily granted tenure. Tenure or no tenure, however, certain controls exert influence over him throughout his teaching life—legal expectations, professional ethics, community mores, and personal values. Predictably, he belongs to and participates in the activities of several professional organizations— minimally, the National Education Association, the association of his subject-matter specialty or the one of its elementary school counterpart, and the state education association.

As a teacher, he is a definite influence in the lives of all his pupils and may be a vital influence in the lives of a few. And, as suggested by Henry Brooks Adams, he may even affect eternity in some important way.

To Stimulate Thought

1. Develop the statement that general education may well provide the key to the open mind.
2. Take a stand, and defend it, on the merits or demerits of teacher tenure.
3. Take a stand, and defend it, on the legitimacy of teachers' unions in education.
4. Elaborate the statement: every teacher should hold membership in the National Education Association.

511

5. In the opinion survey conducted by the NEA, 72 percent of the teachers were in favor of corporal punishment employed judiciously. Do you agree or disagree with these teachers? Support your stand with reasons.

6. What important outcomes of education would be unattainable if schools (assuming no budgetary problems) organized around the pattern of one-to-one dialogue between teacher and student?

7. Critically evaluate the statement: "The primary essential of effective teaching is the emotional health of teachers. Given this quality, other essentials tend to follow."

8. Start with the legal concept that teachers stand in place of parents: *in loco parentis*. Then relate that concept to the debate on educational goals—that is, to the exclusively cognitive position versus the cognitive-affective-psychomotor position.

9. The average salary difference between teachers in the less affluent and those in the more affluent states is approximately $3500 yearly. In your opinion, is this justifiable? If not, should the federal government step in to neutralize this difference in some way?

10. Take a stand, pro or con, on the following statement made by Conant: "The time has not yet come when the educational sciences can play the same role in training teachers as the medical sciences do in training doctors."

REFERENCES

Armstrong, W. Earl, and T. M. Stinnett, *Certification Requirements for School Personnel in the United States* (Washington, D.C.: National Commission on Teacher Education and Professional Standards, 1964).

Chamberlain, Leo M., and Leslie W. Kindred, *The Teacher and School Organization*, 4th ed. (Englewood Cliffs, N.J.: Prentice-Hall, Inc., 1966).

Conant, James B., *Shaping Educational Policy* (New York: McGraw-Hill, Inc., 1964).

Conant, James B., *The Education of American Teachers* (New York: McGraw-Hill, Inc., 1963).

Gelinas, Paul J., *So You Want To Be a Teacher* (New York: Harper & Row, Publishers, 1965).

Gilroy, Thomas P., Anthony V. Sinicropi, and Franklin D. Stone, *Educator's Guide to Collective Negotiations* (Columbus, Ohio: Charles E. Merrill Publishing Company, 1969).

Hazard, William R., *Introduction to School Law* (New York: Free Press, 1970 anticipated date of publication).

Journal of Teacher Education, Vol. 15, No. 1 (March 1964). An answer to Conant.

Lieberman, Myron, and Michael H. Moskow, *Collective Negotiations for Teachers* (Skokie, Ill.: Rand McNally & Company, 1966).

National Education Association, *NEA Handbook for Local, State, and National Associations* (Washington, D.C.: NEA, latest date).

Peterson, Leroy J., Richard A. Rosmiller, and Marlin M. Volz, *The Law* and *Public School Operation* (New York: Harper and Row Publishers, 1969).

Phi Delta Kappa, *Improving Teacher Education in the United States.* (Bloomington, Ind.: Phi Delta Kappa, 1967).

Research Division, National Education Association, *Professional Negotiation with School Boards*, Research Report 1965-R3 (Washington, D.C.: U.S. Government Printing Office, March, 1965).

Robb, Felix, *Teachers:* The Need and the Task (Washington, D.C.: The American Association of Teacher Education, 1968).

Stinnett, T. M., *Professional Negotiations in Public Education* (New York: The Macmillan Company, 1967).

Stinnett, T. M., and Albert J. Huggett, *Professional Problems of Teachers*, 2nd Ed. (New York: The Macmillan Company, 1968).

U.S. Department of Health, Education, and Welfare, *Education Directory 1966-1967, Education Associations* (Washington, D.C.: U.S. Government Printing Office, 1967).

U.S. Department of Health, Education, and Welfare, *National Teachers Corps, Guidelines*, S-30 (Washington, D.C.: U.S. Government Printing Office, 1966).

U.S. Department of Health, Education, and Welfare, *Teachers Negotiate with Their School Boards*, Bulletin 1964, No. 40 OE-23036 (Washington, D.C.: U.S. Government Printing Office, 1964).

Wilson, Charles H., *A Teacher Is a Person* (New York: Holt, Rinehart and Winston, Inc., 1956).

San Fran
orphan (92)
expert (93)
stalked (93)
Juan (94)
shrivelled (95)
bloat (100)

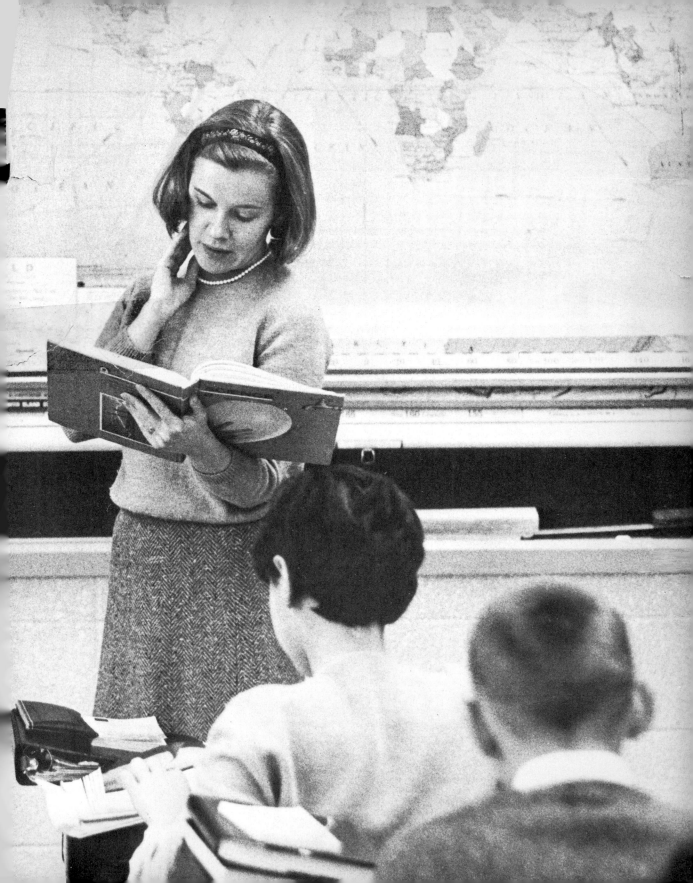

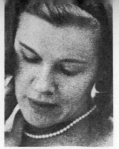

Chapter
18

Teachers
in an
Age of
Changing Values

Teachers who play their professional roles sensitively and confidently are those who remain in close touch with their times. Such teachers today look at the world and perceive an old order giving way grudgingly yet inexorably to an emerging new order. Specifically, as developed in Chapter 1, they perceive a world in which the indigent are moving toward a better life; in which heretofore downtrodden racial groups are marching toward first-class human status; in which closed political ideologies are challenging open ones, and vice versa; and in which technology poses a threat of terrifying proportions to the long-cherished humanistic values of the Western world.

OLD AND NEW VALUE SYSTEMS

Teachers like those described above perceive a world that mirrors an ethical system in transition, a system characterized historically by the labels of Protestant ethic or (less appropriately, I personally think) Judeo-Christian ethic. This ethic has long been an interesting admixture of ascetic and material values. In respect to the first, it is future-oriented, admonishing people to forego the immediate rewards of the here and now for the delayed rewards, either earthly or heavenly, of the future. The Protestant ethic, as traditionally conceived, also is oriented more to the avoidance of unapproved behavior than to the actual living of approved behavior. In this connection, many schools place more importance on students not cheating than on their measuring up to built-in potentials. Society seems to be more interested in the avoidance by individuals of sexual immorality than in their becoming truly self-actualized in marriage. And society places greater emphasis on the avoidance of law-breaking than on the building of a social order rooted firmly in human decency, which conceivably could remove many of the now existing causes of social disobedience. And the Protestant ethic, even when espousing approved behavior, tends to get lost in the acts themselves, glossing over or ignoring the importance of the personality factors that gave rise to them. Yet another of the ethic's ascetic dimensions is the worship of long hours of hard work.

With respect to the material aspects of the Protestant ethic, it em-

braces the assumption that material rewards, including eventual occupational success and prestige, will automatically redound to the hardworking and thrifty. The implication, in this connection, is that material success is attainable by all, even though only some of the many apply themselves diligently enough to attain it. That this unlimited free will point of view runs counter to biological, psychological, and sociological determinism is understatement. The assumption is particularly vulnerable in that it establishes aspirations so high as to arouse guilt feelings in the many who are incapable of measuring up to them. And when such individuals are disappointed over or outraged by their inability, they tend to rebel or retaliate against society. In the school milieu, rebellion or retaliation usually takes the form of cheating, delinquency, or apathy toward school rules and tasks. Outside the school milieu, the acts often take the form of misdemeanors or crimes against the social order that frustrated the individuals in the first place.

We note at this point that the Protestant or Judeo-Christian ethic, as a value frame, is more a home-school-church (or synagogue) phenomenon than a business-industrial one. As one point of difference, the ethic of the latter is present-oriented. Vendors, in effect, say "buy now, think later." Advertisers say "don't be rational, be impulsive." In the marketplace, things, not people, are important. And the prestige of the job, with rare exception, is a higher value than the individuality and self-esteem of the person. With the two sets of standards thus different, small wonder that teachers and parents have difficulty instilling values in children and youth. The Protestant ethic discourages with its unattainablilty; the marketplace ethics repels with its indifference to human sensitivities.

Throughout the nation's history, people have adopted one of the following postures toward the value conflict: they have been oblivious to it, they have perceived but ignored it, they have perceived but rationalized it, or they have perceived it realistically for what it is. The fourth position of realism gives every evidence of being the emerging one today. The result is a gradual shift in the social order away from the *asceticism* of the Protestant ethic toward the more attainable values, not of the marketplace ethic, but of an emerging *individual-social ethic*.

The latter, as the name implies, has the individual person as its focus, and people as its arena. The center of attention is the intrinsic self-worth of any individual. Within this frame, the question, Who am I? ideally elicits the response: I am an important person because I am a human being. Such factors as my skin color, my vocation, and my social prestige all are relatively unimportant. But the way I feel about myself

518

is very important. Thus my intrinsic worth resides, in great part, in what I assess myself to be, not primarily in what I do, except as my actions reflect what I basically am.

The ethic, despite its primary concern with the individual, is also socially oriented. It is the latter in that a world of the many is a requisite to fulfillment of individuals. And with the social factor playing this strong supporting role, the obligation of individuals to ameliorate social inequities is a built-in mandate. But so too is the obligation of an enlightened social order to assist individuals in solving their more serious personal problems. Personal fulfillment and social action in the human arena are the themes of the ethic.

Admittedly, the individual-social ethic is not, by any means, completely polar to the Protestant ethic. Yet they do differ in a number of respects. The first is more worldly; the second, more otherworldly. The first is more concerned with personality fulfillment; the second, more with individuals readying themselves for ultimate outcomes. Self-assessment is fundamental in the first; external assessment is fundamental in the second. Both are social action centered, although operating, at times, from different motives.

Irrespective of these differences, selected of which, in the opinion of many readers, may be more academic than real, the individual-social ethic commits individual man to fulfill himself and to help others to fulfill themselves. The two outcomes are reciprocally related, rising and falling together.

EDUCATION AND AN EMERGING VALUE SYSTEM

Formal education has in great part been responsible for the transitional state of social values. For this reason and also because it is a social mirror, formal education itself is in the process of undergoing change—slowly and gradually but nonetheless surely. And the direction of change is toward learners as individuals who, because human, have the right to become their potentials; who, in turn, have the obligation of helping others reach theirs.

Teachers as Central

Of all the educational contributors to this individual and social outcome, teachers are the key. They need not conform to the idealis- **519**

tic archetype sketched in the last chapter. Rather, possessed of reasonable competency in their specialized teaching fields, they need above all else to relate to the personalities of learners, to be conversant with their needs, to be sensitive to their interests and aspirations, and to be situationally flexible. This instructional position is the so-called teacher-centric one, a position that resists all stereotyping of learners or learning. It is a position that commits teachers to assess the dynamics of a learning situation before deciding on teaching postures and procedures.[1]

An Appropriate Curriculum as Essential

A second educational contributor to the individual-social outcome under discussion is a school curriculum that harmonizes with it. Such a curriculum, as developed in Chapter 2, is one that transmits cultural essentials, that helps learners adapt to their environments, and that leads learners toward their personality ultimates. Within this frame, it is a curriculum that, in the words of Fred T. Wilhelms, Secretary of the National Education Association, has a two-way stretch: from subject matter to learners, from knowledge to humanization.[2] It is made up of those educational ingredients needed to develop people as people, to make them human. In essence, it is a curriculum that culminates in a liberal education, that employs subject matter to change and fulfill people who fall within its purview.

Schools with a curriculum such as we are describing here could scarcely care less whether learners study *Macbeth* merely because tradition has long supported the practice, or even because the play, per se, meets high standards of skill and artistry. The purpose rather would be to utilize *Macbeth* as a humanizing influence; to help learners in the process to perceive and identify with the affective reactions that man has universally experienced when allowing ambition to lead him down the path of indecision, murder, guilt, regret, and finally extinction.

The two-way curriculum stretch has as its goal not just to inform but to ready learners to live. And in the process, it compels them to make value judgments about issues that schools for too long have taught as

[1] J. M. Stephens elaborates this position in *The Process of Schooling: A Psychological Examination* (New York: Holt, Rinehart, and Winston, Inc., 1867), pp. 3–15.

[2] Professor Wilhelms developed this theme in a major address delivered to the Association of Supervision and Curriculum Development at San Francisco, March 15, 1967.

TEACHERS AND THE PROFESSION OF TEACHING

mere facts. Imperialism and chauvinism, for instance, are not mere neutral realities of social existence; rather, they are disturbing social-political issues; they are instances of man's rejection of man. Also far from being neutral realities are the power syndrome in business (and education), free enterprise unbridled, racism, hunger, and disease. All these are more value issues than they are facts, and they need to be treated as such.

Learners' Need to Realize Success in School

A curriculum that humanizes is one that assures all students success as it involves them in the multidimensioned activities of learning. Such a curriculum is equally appropriate for the slow as for the gifted, for the environmentally disadvantaged as for the advantaged. Conversely, it challenges the highly creative as well as the relatively uncreative.

Convincing though the case may be for all learners realizing success in school, most institutions of formal education engage in practices antagonistic to that outcome. A case in point is comparative marking, with the symbols *D* and *F* accorded prominent places. Surely schools can deal with low achievement in a more constructive and imaginative way than this. A second case in point is honor societies. These characteristically accord distinction to students who excel others but who do not necessarily measure up to their own capabilities. In this connection, is it more "honorable" for a gifted than for a slow-learning child to perform well in school? If not, education is remiss when habitually singling out the capable for special accolades. Why should schools not, instead, stress the value of all learners, irrespective of ability levels, becoming their potentials? Under such an arrangement, more learners could know success—that all-important essential of personality growth and fulfillment.

Though formal education pays lip service to the belief that all learners are equally deserving of attention and success, it relies on person-to-person competition as a method of motivating and rewarding students. Under this method, more capable students invariably emerge winners; less capable ones, losers. The justification customarily given for competition in school is that it enhances achievement, a purpose that it may well accomplish with some, particularly with evenly matched students. However, because most students in the nation's schools are far from evenly matched, competition conceivably is harm-

521

ful both to learning and to the personalities of learners. An unfortunate by-product of person-to-person competition is its built-in invitation for learners merely to do better than others, not necessarily to do their best.

Education's ultimate goal for competition thus should be self-competition, not person-to-person, competition. It alone passes the test of sound value theory in that it does not require the many to pay for the fulfillment of the few. If this goal is too idealistic for most schools, they at least should be moving toward it.

A CLOSING POSITION STATEMENT

The book closes, as it opened, on the topic of change. The central thesis is that institutions, cultures, knowledge, values, and man himself are perpetually evolving. And the institution of formal education, at one and the same time, mirrors social change while acting as its propellent; reveals the status quo while readying learners for the evolving unforeseen. Education, possessed of no error-free blueprint for its gigantic assignment, assists learners to create their own blueprints. This it does by working with their emotions as well as their mentalities, by rejecting the closed encounter for the open, by according critical thinking high priority in its taxonomy of objectives.

The concerns of education have an immediacy without parallel in history. In the words of Norman Cousins:[3]

> Earlier generations have had the power merely to affect history; ours is the power to expunge it. . . . We have managed somehow to unhinge the permanent. Everything that has occurred in history until now has suddenly acquired interim status. . . . Our time has become a grand concourse for all the great causes and experiences of the race.

For these causes and experiences to be realized, formal education through teachers needs to be in the vanguard. The leadership requirement, however, is a subtle one, committing education to lead in the only way it can: by helping the young to become their potentials. The demands of this requirement for teachers unquestionably are far-reaching and challenging. Yet education that humanizes can scarcely make demands that are less exacting.

[3] Norman Cousins, "Think of a Man: An Editorial," 39:9, *Saturday Review of Literature* (August 1956).

To
Stimulate
Thought

1. Take a stand on the issue: Because competition characterizes life outside of formal education, it should characterize life inside it.

2. Defend the position that in a highly mature social state, competition must concede to cooperation, and extrinsic motivation to intrinsic motivation.

3. Competition that pits man against man permits the strong and/or capable always to win out over the weak and/or incapable. In what value system(s), if any, is this state of affairs comfortable? In what value system(s) is it definitely uncomfortable?

4. Identify and elaborate the value fallacies of competitive marking and the awarding of other types of honors in the schools.

5. Take a stand on and develop the statement: "The primary task of education is not to tell learners what to think but to help them learn how to think."

REFERENCES

Fromm, Erich, *The Sane Society* (New York: Holt, Rinehart and Winston, Inc., 1955).

Gezi, Kalil I., and James E. Myers, *Teaching in American Culture* (New York: Holt, Rinehart and Winston, Inc., 1968).

Gardner, John W., *Self Renewal* (New York: Harper & Row, Publishers, 1964).

Greer, Scott, *The Logic of Social Inquiry* (Chicago: Aldine Publishing Company, 1969).

Hodgkinson, Harold L., *Education Interaction and Social Change* (Englewood Cliffs, N.J.: Prentice-Hall, Inc., 1967).

Moustakas, Clark E. (ed.), *The Self* (New York: Harper & Row, Publishers, 1956).

Schachtel, Ernest G., *Metamorphosis* (New York: Basic Books, Inc., 1959).

Stephens, J. M., *The Process of Schooling: A Psychological Examination* (New York: Holt, Rinehart and Winston, Inc., 1967).

Tillich, Paul, *The Courage to Be* (New Haven: Yale University Press, 1952).

U.S. Department of Health, Education and Welfare, *Education in the Seventies* (Washington, D.C.: Government Printing Office, 1968).

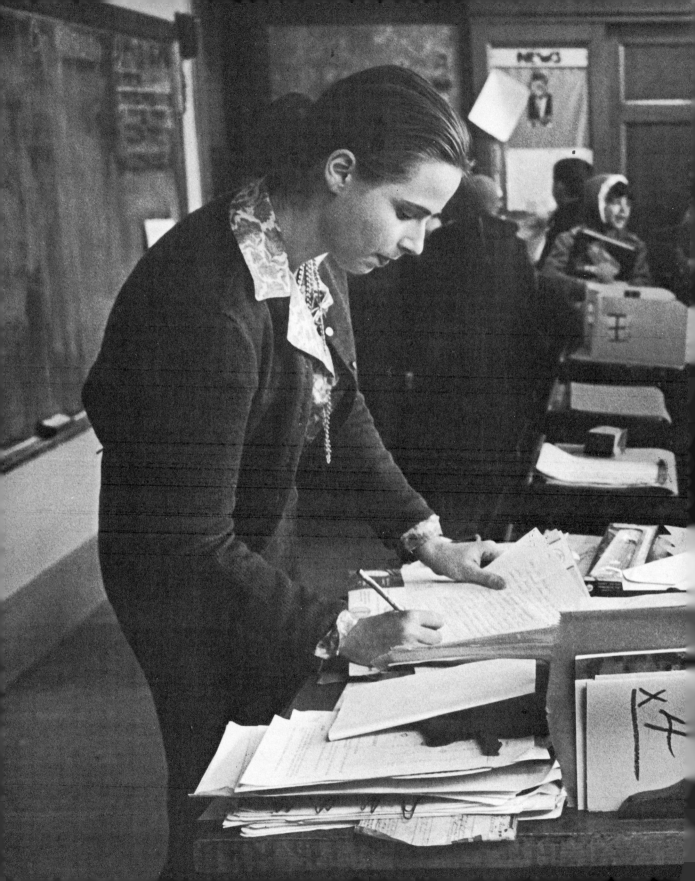

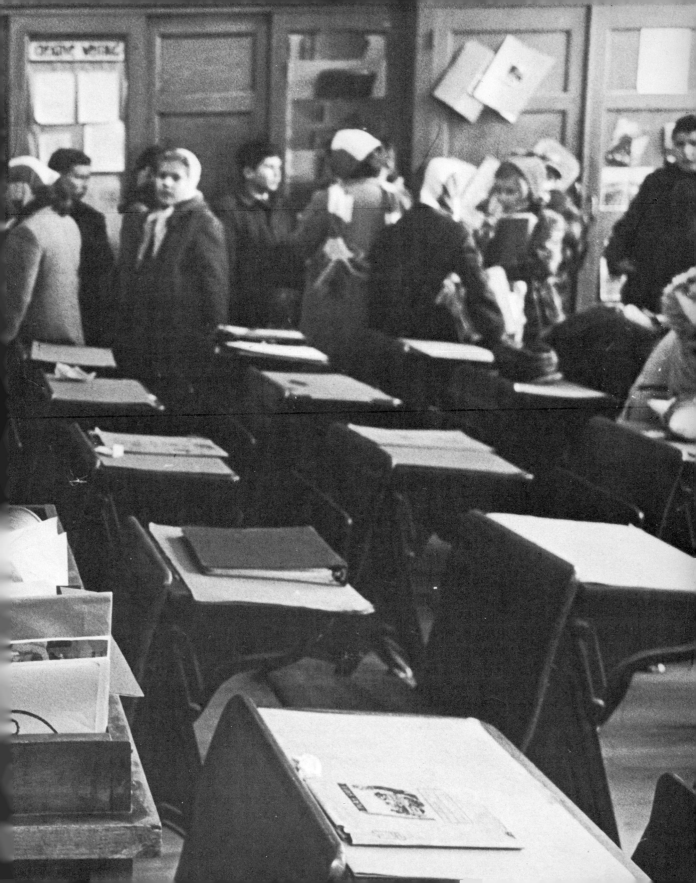

Indexes

Author Index

A

Abraham, W., 469
Abrams, I., 368
Adams, S., 325
Adler, M., 115
Aiken, W. M., 126
Alexander, W. M., 192, 259, 260, 261
Allen, D. W., 220, 221
Ames, L. B., 193
Anderson, A. W., 77
Anderson, H. A., 221
Anderson, K. E., 442
Anderson, R. H., 148, 165, 275, 286, 291
Anderson, V. E., 202, 221
Armstrong, W. E., 494, 495, 496, 512
Arnhoff, F. E., 324

B

Babbidge, H. D., Jr., 77, 388
Baer, R. M., 165
Bamman, H. A., 260
Baron, H., 400
Barzun, J., 33, 34
Baskin, S., 388
Bauer, P., 350
Baumgartner, B. B., 470
Baynham, D., 131, 284, 285, 291
Beach, F. F., 102, 342, 343, 346, 350
Bean, J. E., 102
Beauchamp, G. A., 110, 131, 152, 164
Beck, J. M., 396, 406, 418
Beers, C. W., 298
Benjamin, H. R. W., 388
Bereday, G. Z. F., 381
Berelson, B., 373, 388
Biddle, B. J., 291
Birch, J. W., 434
Bishop, W. E., 442
Blackstone, P. L., 102

Blake, P., 131
Bloom, B. S., 47, 131, 411
Bolmeier, E. C., 77, 102
Bommarito, B., 407
Bossing, N. L., 170, 173, 192
Brickman, W. W., 330
Brimm, R. P., 192
Britt, J. F., 338
Brittain, W. L., 260
Broudy, H. S., 209
Brown, B. F., 148, 291
Brown, H. S., 368, 388
Brown, J. R., 346, 347
Brownell, J. A., 131
Bruner, J. S., 115, 116, 131, 161, 221
Bunker, F. F., 170, 192
Burks, J. B., 221, 260
Burns, J. A., 350
Buros, O. K., 315, 324
Bush, R. N., 220, 221
Butts, R. F., 88, 138, 140, 359, 381

C

Cartter, A. M., 379
Cay, D. F., 109, 131
Chamberlain, E. B., 350
Chamberlain, L. M., 492, 512
Chase, F. S., 221
Chilman, C. S., 418
Clark, L. H., 221, 260
Clarke, A. M., 102
Clauzio, H. F., 470
Clift, V. A., 77
Clute, M. J., 170, 193
Collins, G. E., 252, 260
Collins, G. J., 164
Commager, H. S., 13
Conant, J. B., 33, 208, 221, 237, 305, 425, 429, 430, 499, 512
Corbin, R., 408, 411, 418

529

Havighurst, R. J., 212–213, 396, 414, 418, 442, 459
Hawkes, G. R., 25, 402, 405, 406, 409, 411, 418
Hazard, W. R., 512
Heald, J. E., 417
Heath, R. W., 266, 291
Heddens, J. W., 165
Hess, R. D., 165
Hicklin, C. R., 443
Hill, C. M., 144
Hines, V. A., 260
Hocking, E., 282, 291
Hodgkinson, H. L., 523
Hoffman, P. G., 13, 25
Hogan, U., 260
Hollis, J. W., 300, 324
Hollis, L. U., 300, 324
Hook, J. N., 260
Huggett, A. J., 513
Hullfish, H. G., 77
Hunter, J. S., 164, 252, 260
Hurd, P. D., 260
Hutchins, R. M., 33, 115, 388
Hutchinson, J. C., 291

I

Ilg, F. C., 193
Inlow, G. M., 47, 77, 110, 114, 119, 123, 147, 225, 260, 287, 291, 301, 310 320, 414, 433, 443
Irwin, R. B., 465

J

Jacks, L., 165
Jackson, P. W., 432, 433, 443
Jarolimek, J., 165
Jesse, D. L., 47
Jewett, A., 418
Johns, R. L., 86, 97
Johnson, E. W., 468
Johnson, M. C., 280
Johnson, W., 335, 350
Jones, J. W., 463, 464, 466, 470
Jones, L. B., 407

K

Kandel, I. L., 221
Kaplan, B. A., 401
Kearney, N. C., 143
Keesee, E., 158, 165
Kerber, A., 407
Kerr, C., 363, 388
Kieth, L., 131
Kimbrough, R. B., 165
Kindred, L. W., 492

King, A. R., Jr., 131
Kirk, S. A., 411, 454, 459, 470
Klein, R. L., 221, 260
Kluttz, M., 165
Kohlbrenner, B. J., 350
Koos, L. V., 193
Kornbluth, J. L., 13
Koury, R. E., 146, 165
Krathwohl, D. R., 47
Krug, E. A., 110
Kuder, C. F., 318
Kursh, H., 15, 77
Kvaraceus, W. C., 418

L

La Noue, G. R., 350
Lauwerys, J. A., 381
Lee, G. C., 424, 494
Lessinger, L. M., 428
Lieberman, M., 512
Linton, T. E., 25
Loomis, M. J., 193
Lounsbury, J. H., 193
Lovejoy, C. E., 388
Lowenfeld, B., 470
Lowenfeld, V., 260
Lynch, P. D., 102

M

Mackie, R. P., 448, 470
Mallery, D., 350
Marburger, C. A., 400
Martinson, R., 428, 443
Masia, B. B., 47
Maury, M., 25
Mayers, L., 77
Mayhew, L. B., 357, 368, 388
McGarry, D. D., 332, 338, 346, 347, 350
McGrath, E. J., 362, 372, 388
McGurk, F., 410
McLaughlin, Sister R., 350
McLendon, J. C., 261
McQuigg, R. B., 271
Mead, G. H., 142, 144
Medsker, L. L., 360, 388, 389
Meeth, L. R., 362, 372, 388
Merritt, H., 165
Mersand, J., 418
Messersmith, J. C., 388
Miller, C. H., 324
Miller, D. F., 261
Miller, F. W., 324
Miller, R. I., 131
Molloy, J. S., 470
Monroe, P., 57
Montague, A., 17, 25
Moreland, W. D., 261

531

Morphet, E. L., 47, 86, 97
Morris, V., 24, 25
Morrison, D. G., 389
Mort, P. R., 87
Moskow, M. H., 512
Moustakas, C. E., 523
Muessig, R. H., 261
Murphy, A. T., 461
Murray, R. F. III, 335
Muse, B., 418
Muskin, S. J., 389
Myers, J. E., 523
Myers, R. E., 443
Myklebust, H., 470

N

Nelson, J. L., 25
Neuwein, R. A., 350
Noar, G., 193
Noffsinger, T., 443

O

Oden, M., 427, 439, 443
Ohlsen, M. M., 324
Oinas, F. J., 282
Olds, H. F., 291
Oliver, A. I., 131
Orlans, H., 389
Otto, H., 150

P

Parker, W. R., 261
Passow, A. H., 150, 419, 443
Pegnato, C. W., 434
Peterson, L. J., 513
Pettigrew, T. F., 25, 410, 411, 419
Phenix, P. H., 115, 116, 131
Phillips, H. L., 165
Pius, XI, 337, 338
Platt, J. R., 47
Polychrones, J. Z., 150
Popper, S. H., 193
Pronovost, W., 165
Putnam, C., 410

R

Radler, D. H., 193
Ragan, W. B., 146, 165
Ramsey, L. W., 342, 350
Raph, J. B., 443
Ray, K. C., 102
Redl, F., 193
Reller, T. L., 86, 97
Remmers, H. H., 193
Remmlein, M. K., 102

Riccio, A. C., 221
Rich, W. B., 341
Riessman, F., 419
Robb, F., 513
Roberts, R., 261
Roeber, E. C., 325
Rogers, C. R., 310, 459
Rosenbloom, P. S., 260, 261, 266, 291
Rosenzweig, R. M., 77, 388
Rosmiller, R. A., 513
Rossi, P. H., 291
Rothstein, J. H., 470
Roucek, J. S., 457, 461, 465, 470
Rubin, L. J., 47
Russell, B., 12–13

S

Sands, T., 443
Sanford, N., 389
Sargent, F. P., 470
Saxe, R. W., 396, 406, 418
Saylor, J. G., 261
Schachtel, E. G., 523
Schloss, S., 102
Schreiber, D., 271
Seerley, C. C., 280
Segal, M. V., 443
Segal, S. S., 470
Selden, W. K., 389
Shakow, D., 325
Shane, H. G., 150
Shaplin, J. T., 291
Sharp, E., 165
Shaw, F., 270, 402
Shepard, S., 400
Shertzer, B., 443
Sherwood, C. C., 457
Sherwood, S., 457
Shoben, E. G., Jr., 47
Shuey, A., 410–411
Shuy, R. W., 419
Simon, K. A., 15, 23, 53, 73, 99, 100, 103,
    134, 135, 146, 236, 239, 242, 246, 261,
    332, 334, 358, 359, 449, 484, 488
Sinicropi, A. V., 512
Skinner, B. F., 278
Slipcevich, E. M., 165
Smith, B., 25
Smith, F. B., 324
Smith, F. R., 261
Smith, G. K., 389
Smith, M., 221
Snapper, J. M., 332
Snow, C. P., 76, 77
Sokolowski, C. J., 85, 86
Soule, G., 13
Spears, H., 41, 109
Spencer, L. M., 424

532

Subject Index

A

Academically talented (and gifted) learners, acceleration of, 437–441
  characteristics of, 426–427
  curriculum enrichment for, 436–437
  identification of, 425–434
  mounting interest in, 423–424
  programming for, 434–441
Academy, 137, 200–201
Ad Hoc Committee on English Language Arts in the Comprehensive Secondary School, 235
Adams, Henry Brooks, 511
Advanced Placement Program, 250, 287–288, 370, 440–441
American Association for the Advancement of Science and the Science Teaching Center, University of Maryland, 260
American Association of Colleges for Teacher Education (AACTE), 497
American Association for Health, Physical Education, and Recreation, 253
American Association of Instructors of the Blind, 469
American Association of School Administrators, 94, 102
American Association of Teachers Colleges, 497
American Council on Education, 387
American Economics Association, 245
American Federation of Teachers, AFL-CIO, 506–509
American Foundation for the Blind, 469, 471
American Political Science Association, 245
American Psychological Association, 245
American Sociology Association, 245

Andrew Hill High School (see Team teaching)
Aristotle, 33
Association for Supervision and Curriculum Development, 77, 131, 291
Aural-oral (audio-lingual) method, 240, 282

B

Bacon, Roger, 20
Banneker Project (see Culturally deprived learners)
Bay City, experiment on teacher aides, 274–276
Benezet, Anthony, 55
Bestor, Arthur, 208
Bridge Project (see Culturally deprived learners)
Brigham Young Laboratory School (see Class size)
Budd, Thomas, 137

C

Cardinal Principles of Education, 42, 47, 143, 206
Carnegie unit, 219–220, 227, 232
Change, biological evolution witnesses to, 8
  life of any individual witnesses to, 8
  a life process, 7
  phenomena that attest to, 7–12
  philosophy witnesses to, 10–12
  physical science witnesses to, 9, 10
  teleological position toward, 7
Child-benefit principle, 347, 349
Class size, 284–285
College Entrance Examination Board, 287, 401, 417, 440
Commission on Education and Labor, House of Representatives, 47

535

Commission on the English Curriculum of the National Council of Teachers of English, 235
Commission on the Experimental Study of the Utilization of the Staff in the Secondary School, 284
Commission on Reorganization of Secondary Education, 42, 47, 143, 205
Committee on Education of Exceptional Children, 442
Committee on Mathematics of the College Entrance Examination Board, 250
Committee on National Interest, National Council of Teachers of English, 260
Committee on the Objectives of a General Education in a Free Society, 44, 207
Committee on Utilization of College Teaching Resources, 369
Committee for the White House Conference on Education, 44, 47, 207
Common school, 135
Competition in school, 521–522
Computer in education, 282–283
Constitution of the United States, Article 1, 56
  and the curriculum, 340
  First Amendment, 30, 66, 68
  Fourteenth Amendment, 30, 56
  Preamble, 30, 56
  Tenth Amendment, 56, 81
  See also, Federal government
Cotton, John, 54
Council for Exceptional Children, 470
Court cases, Brown v. Board of Education, 63, 71
  Cochran et al. v. Louisiana State Board of Education, 66, 346
Cooper v. Aaron, 72
  Engel v. Vitale, 68–69
  Evans v. Buchanan, 72
  Everson v. Board of Education, 66, 347
  Goss v. Board of Education, 72
  Holytz v. City of Milwaukee, 92
  Kalamazoo case, 203–204
  Mapp v. Board of Education, 72
  Minersville School District v. Gobitis, 70
  Molitor v. Kaneland Community District, 91–92
  Murray v. Curlett, 69
  People of State of Illinois ex rel v. Board of Education of School District No. 21, Champaign County, Illinois, 67
  Pierce v. Society of the Sisters of the

Holy Name of Jesus and Mary, 63, 66, 331
  Plessy v. Ferguson, 63, 71
  Powell v. Board of Education, 63
  Schempp v. School District of Abington Township, 69
  West Virginia State Board of Education v. Barnette, 70
  Zorach v. Clausen, 67–68
  See also Federal judiciary
Creativity, 432–433
Crippled and special health cases, causes of disabilities, 468
  educational arrangements for, 469
  needs of, 468
Culturally deprived learners, Banneker Project, 399–400, 412–413
  Bridge Project, 402
  characteristics of, 402–405
  educational program for, 405–406
  an ethnic phenomenon, 18–19, 395, 397
  federal legislation for, 397–399
  Great Cities Program, 400–401, 414
  Higher Horizons Project, 270–271, 399, 414
  I.Q. issue, 410–412, 417
  language problem, 407–410
  number of, 395–396, 417
  organization for and curriculum requirements, 412–415
  preschool programs for, 405
  Project Able, 401
  Project Head Start, 164, 268–269, 398, 401, 405–406, 417
  teachers of, 415–417
  VISTA, 398
  who they are, 17–18, 395–397
Curriculum, criteria of significance, 119–124
  cultural values as a base of, 110–111
  definitions, 108–110
  educational objectives and cultural values, 111–112
  implementation, 127–128
  organizational schemes, 124–126
  participants in development, 123–124
  planning and organizational designs, 264–265
  resources and controls, 123
  sources of, 82–84, 113–119
  state requirements, 82–84
  See also Elementary school; High school curriculum
Curriculum projects, large scale, Biological Science Study Committee, 266
  Chemical Bond Approach Project, 266

537

Elementary school (*continued*)
  social studies, 159–160
  speaking, 158
  subject-matter areas, 152–163
  writing, 157
Elementary School Science Project (*see* Elementary school, natural sciences)
Eliot, Charles, 39, 170, 186, 364
Emotional maladjustment, 31, 33
Emotionally-socially handicapped learners, defense mechanisms, 458–459
  identifying characteristics of, 456–459
  organizational schemes for, 459–460
Englewood Elementary School (*see* Team teaching)
Enrollments, all levels, 52–53
  college and university, 357–358
  dual, 288–290
  elementary, 134–135
  junior high, 170–171
  nonpublic, 334
  secondary, 134–135
Evanston Township High School (*see* Team teaching; Teacher utilization)
Exceptional children (*see* Crippled and special-health cases; Deaf and hard of hearing; Emotionally and socially handicapped; Speech handicapped; Visually handicapped)
Existential (ism), 11, 29

F

Federal government (*see* Constitution of the United States; Federal statutes and education; Federal judiciary and education)
Federal judiciary and education, organization, 63–64
  and religion, 66–70
  and schools and races, 71–72
  See also Court cases
Federal statutes and education, Civil Rights Act, 60
  Economic Opportunity Act, 59–60, 268, 398
  Education Professions Development Act, 61
  Elementary and Secondary Education Act, 60, 348, 398
  Federal Impact Laws, 59
  Fulbright Act, 379
  George Barden Act, 58
  George Dean Act, 58
  Hatch Act, 58
  Higher Education Act, 60, 399
  International Education Act, 61, 379
  Land Ordinance, 56
  Lanham Act, 58
  Manpower Development and Training Act, 59, 397
  Morrill Act, 57, 362
  National Defense Education Act, 59, 62, 74, 238, 244, 280, 305, 347, 376, 398
  National Foundation on the Arts and Humanities Act, 23, 60
  National School Lunch Act, 58, 347
  National Science Foundation Act, 58–59
  Northwest Ordinance, 57
  Serviceman's Readjustment Act (G.I. Bill), 58, 347
  Smith-Hughes Act, 58, 74, 375
  Social Security Act, 397
  Statehood Enabling Acts, 57
  Vocational Education Act, 59, 255, 397
  Welfare Amendments, 397
Formal discipline, 34
Franklin, Benjamin, 10, 55, 137, 200
Franklin Elementary School (*see* Team teaching)
Fulbright Act, 379
Fund for the Republic, 350

G

Gaffney, Mathew, 321
Galileo, 20
General education, 225–227, 232, 253, 364
George Washington High School (*see* Culturally deprived learners, Higher Horizons Project)
Gerrymandering, 72
Gifted learners (*see* Academically talented learners)
Grading, 521–522
Great Cities Program (*see* Culturally deprived learners)
Grove Street Elementary School (*see* Team teaching)
Guidance and counseling, academic record, 320–321
  beginning and growth, 296–299
  case study, 321–322
  central guidance issue, 322–323
  counseling, 183–186, 295, 302
  Dictionary of Occupational Titles, 297
  educational concerns, 305–306
  emotional concerns, 300–302
  follow-up study, 322
  interview, 295, 319
  media of appraisal, 313–322
  mental health, 298–299

National Association for Mental Health, 298
organizational schemes for, 172–178, 306–309
principles, 309–313
services, 295
standardized tests, 314–317, 428–430
student personnel services, 294
vocational concerns, 296, 302–305
Vocational Guidance Association, 296
Gutenberg, Johann, 20

H

High school, basic organization, 196–197
Carnegie unit, 219–220
class length, 219–220
comprehensive versus specialized high school, 213–215
curriculum (see High school curriculum; Curriculum projects) •
departmentalization, 213, 215–216
historical beginnings, 197–204
homogeneous versus heterogeneous grouping, 149–151, 176–178, 217–219
modular scheduling, 219–220
number of, 202
objectives, 204–210
students, 210–213
High school curriculum, academic subjects, 234–250
constants, 227
definition, 224
electives, 232–233
English, 235–238
exploratory education, 227, 232
extracurriculum, 257
fine arts, 255–257
foreign languages, 238–241
general education, 225–227, 232, 253
health and physical education, 251–253
mathematics, 248–250
natural sciences, 245–248
practical arts, 253–255
Project Social Studies, 244
social studies, 241–245
special education, 228–234, 304
typical programs, 233
vocational education, 228–234, 304
Higher education, Agency for International Development, 379, 380
American Association of University Professors, 384
curriculum trends in, 366–372
degrees granted, 359
developmental trends in professional schools, 370–371
enrollments (see Enrollments)
faculties and governing boards, 381–384
and federal government, 375–381
functions of, 360, 361, 363–365, 373–374
junior college, 168, 359–360
Land Grant Colleges, 357, 362–363
liberal-arts college, 360–363
miscellaneous data, 358
multipurpose university, 363–365
National Institute for Educational and Technical Cooperation (NIETC), 380
normal school, 493–494
origins of, 355–357, 363–365
productive versus instructional function, 373–374
research and development in selected universities, 378
student power in, 384–386
teachers college, 494
See also Teacher education; Universities and colleges
Higher Horizons Project (see Culturally deprived learners)
Highland Park School District, 108
See also Guidance, media of appraisal
Homogeneous versus heterogeneous grouping, 149–151, 176–178, 217–219, 272
Honors and honor societies, 521
Hornbook, 54
Humanism, tenets of, 22–23
threats to, 29–34
values of, 28–29
See also Values and value systems

I

Independent schools (see Nonpublic schools)
Individualism (see Humanism, values; Values and value systems)
Individual-social ethic (see Values and value systems)
Industrial Revolution, 20, 169
Institute for Communication Research, 291
International Bureau of Education, 239, 454
International Education Act, 379

J

Johnson, Samuel, 55, 201
Judeo-Christian (Protestant) ethic, 9, 310
Junior high school, basic organization, 145, 168, 172–178
block-time class, 173–175

539

Junior high school (*continued*)
  class periods, 175–176
  class schedule, 181–182
  common learnings, 179
  counseling services, 183–186
  enrollments (*see* Enrollments)
  historical beginnings, 169–171
  health and physical education, 179, 186
  homeroom, 183–184
  homogeneous versus heterogeneous grouping, 176–178
  library services, 186
  number of, 170
  personal-interest offerings, 179–181
  purposes, 170–171
  student activities, 187–188
  student characteristics, 188–190
  subject-matter curriculum, 179–182
  teachers, 191
Journal of Teacher Education, 512

K

Kallikak, Martin, 449
Kierkegaard, S., 45

L

Lancastrian-Bell school, 140
Language laboratory, 240, 280–282
Latin Grammar School, 137–138, 198–199, 208
Local communities and education, boards of education, 91–94
  building principal, 97
  education a local function, 89–91
  school districts, 98–100
  school superintendent, 94–96
Lumley, John M., 510

M

Mann, Horace, 148, 285
Marie Creighton Junior High School (*see* Team teaching)
Massachusetts Bay Law (Old Deluder Satan Act), 198
Mentally handicapped learners, categories, 450
  causation, 449–450
  custodial, 456
  educable, 450–454
  number of, 450
  trainable, 454–456
Meyer, Adolph, 298
Middle school, 168
Midwest Program on Airborne Television (MPATI) (*see* Television instruction)
Modular scheduling, 219–220

N

National Association of Secondary School Principals, 261
National Center for Educational Studies, 357
National Commission on Teacher Education and Professional Standards, 510
National Commission on Technology, Automation, and Economic Progress, 304
National Council for the Accrediting of Teacher Education (NCATE), 497–498
National Council of Independent Schools, 336
National Education Association, 39, 170, 204, 205, 289, 359, 480, 505, 506, 512
National Elementary Principal, 165
National Science Foundation, 378
National Society for the Prevention of Blindness, Inc., 471
National Society for the Study of Education, 261
National Teachers Corps, 509–510
National Youth Administration, 375
New England Primer, 54, 137, 138
Newton High School (*see* Teachers, noncertified)
Newton, Isaac, 20
New Trier Township High School (*see* Guidance, media of appraisal)
Nietzsche, 45
Noncertified teaching personnel (*see* Teachers, noncertified)
Nongraded classroom, 285–287
Nonpublic (independent) schools, accreditation and certification, 341–344
  boarding schools, 333
  characteristics of private schools, 334–337
  definitions, 329
  enrollments (*see* Enrollments)
  historical overview of, 330–332
  law and nonpublic schools, 66, 339–349
  parochial non-Catholic schools, 333
  private schools, 330–331, 334–337
  public (financial) support of, 344–349
  Roman Catholic education, 333, 337–339
  sources of information about, 329–330
  statistics in respect to, 332–334
  status of, 339–341
  teachers, 336
Norwalk school system (*see* Team teaching; Teachers, noncertified)

Teachers (*continued*)
  instructional methods employed, 477
  in junior high schools, 191
  legal status of, 477–479
  noncertified, 274–276
  in nonpublic schools, 336
  number, 483–484
  opinions on selected issues, 480–482
  as persons, 301, 479–480
  salaries, 72, 486–491
  shortage, 486
  sources, 485–486
  and speech handicapped, 461
  supply and demand, 485
  tenure, 491–493
  utilization, 271–276
Teaching machines (*see* Programmed learning)
Team teaching, 216–217, 271
Technology, advantages and liabilities, 20–23
  research and development in, 23
  scope, 21
  to serve or enslave, 21–23
  and social change, 20–23
Television instruction, 276–277

U

United States Commission on Civil Rights, 419
United States Department of Health, Education, and Welfare, 47, 347, 348, 350, 351, 389, 443, 456, 471, 509, 513, 523
United States Department of the Interior, Bureau of Education, 40, 47
United States Department of Labor, 419
United States Employment Service, 471
United States Office of Education, 74–76, 347
Universities and colleges, Amherst College, 244
  University of Berlin, 355
  Brown University, 401
  University of California, 58, 244, 358, 362, 377, 384
  Cambridge University, 355
  Carnegie Institute of Technology, 244
  Central Michigan College, 275
  University of Chicago, 359, 364, 377, 384
  Colgate University, 368
  Columbia University, 355, 368, 384
  Cornell University, 368
  Dartmouth College, 355
  Dillard University, 401
  University of Georgia, 244
  Harvard University, 244, 288, 355, 368, 377, 401

Hunter College, 401
University of Illinois, 58, 244, 250, 266
Iowa State University, 362
Johns Hopkins University, 356
University of Maryland, 250, 266
Massachusetts Institute of Technology, 58, 244
Michigan State University, 58
University of Minnesota, 244, 358, 364
Missouri University, 362
Muhlenberg College, 367
Northwestern University, 244, 268, 377, 401
Ohio State University, 58, 244
Oxford University, 355
Princeton University, 355, 368
Purdue University, 362
Queens College, 401, 402
Randolph Macon College, 411
Rhode Island College, 401
Rutgers University, 355
San Francisco State College, 384
San José State College, 244
Smith College, 368
Southern University, 401
Stanford University, 250, 368
Syracuse University, 244, 266
University of Texas, 58
Whitworth College, 401
William and Mary College, 355
University of Wisconsin, 366, 384
Yale University, 250, 355
See also Higher education

V

Values and value systems, and education, 519–522
  individual-social ethic, 518–522
  individualism, 22–23, 29–34
  Judeo-Christian (Protestant) ethic, 9, 310, 517–519
  marketplace ethic, 518
  power, 32–33
  See also Humanism
Visually handicapped learners, Braille, 464
  causes of sight deficiencies, 463
  definition of, 463
  partial seeing, 464–466
  publication agencies, 466
  school-organizational arrangements for, 465–466
Vocational high school, 214

W

Wigglesworth, Michael, 54
Woodring, Paul E., 208
Writing school (*see* Elementary school, early schools)

542

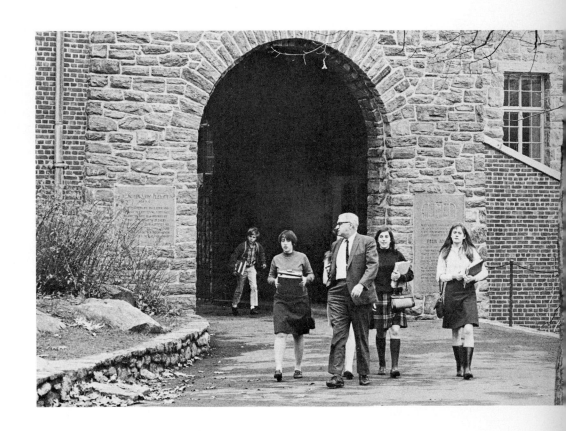